MICHAEL D. TOVEY | MARY-ANNE L. UREN | NEROLI E

Managing
Performance
Improvement

3e

PEARSON

Pearson Australia
Unit 4, Level 3
14 Aquatic Drive
Frenchs Forest NSW 2086

www.pearson.com.au

Acquisitions Editor: Elise Carney
Project Editor: Kathryn Munro
Production Administrator: Rochelle Deighton
Copy Editor: Annabel Adair
Proofreader: Emma Driver
Copyright and Pictures Editor: Emma Gaulton
Indexer: Lisa Knowles
Cover and internal design by: designBite
Cover photograph: © cisale/istockphoto.com
Typeset by Midland Typesetters, Australia

Printed and bound in Australia by The SOS Print + Media Group

1 2 3 4 5 14 13 12 11 10

National Library of Australia Cataloguing-in-Publication entry

Author:	Tovey, Michael D., 1959-2003.
Other Authors:	Mary-Anne L. Uren, Neroli Ena Sheldon.
Title:	Managing performance improvement.
Edition:	3rd ed.
ISBN:	9781442515840 (pbk).
Notes:	Includes index.
Subjects:	Performance standards. Performance — Management. Goal setting in personnel management.
Dewey Number:	658.3125

PEARSON AUSTRALIA
is a division of

CONTENTS

PREFACE

Performance management became a much-used phrase in the late 1990s as a result of the enormous pressure on all types of organisations, both private and public, to do more with less. Global competition and shrinking budgets have meant that managers have needed to find new ways of operating, and to use technology and resources to their fullest capacity. This includes a manager's human resources. This was highlighted with the global economic crisis in 2008/2009 which saw organisations looking at performance management records as part of their criteria to make reductions in their workforce. Staff need to be in top condition—maintained, updated and used to the extent of their capabilities. Human resources are the largest recurring expense for an organisation, yet management has failed to develop and maintain the resource so as to generate the best possible productivity.

Managing performance is perhaps the single most critical issue in the modern workforce. Much of the research in the area of performance management has suggested that, while it has great potential to contribute dramatically to the bottom line, it rarely works. This book suggests three main reasons for performance management systems not working: managers don't understand performance management; managers don't use a systematic approach to the management of performance; and managers don't possess the right skills to manage the performance of people.

The lack of appropriate skills has contributed greatly to a general lack of success in managing performance within organisations. These skills range from the technical skills of running a performance management system to the soft skills area, which includes listening, feedback, managing diversity and conflict management. When managers lack these skills it is doubtful whether they can effectively manage performance. Thus the process is either made or broken by managers.

This third edition continues to provide practical, specific advice for managers and students in the management of performance. It offers a range of tools to make implementation easier and to enhance understanding of why approaches may not have worked in the past. The suggestions on managing performance effectively actually work, because they are based on applied research. The design of the book is based on the conceptual framework of a large job aid. Job aids are given at the end of each chapter, and also incorporated on a CD resource, to assist people in the workplace who may not use the skills on a regular basis. Consequently, the book has been developed for students of performance management as well as for practising managers who may wish to use the book to guide their efforts on the job.

Only effective managers can bring about effective performance management. While this book offers specific guidance on how to achieve this, it also demands much practice of managers and staff to develop the breadth and depth of knowledge and skills needed. The use of this book is the start of a long journey that will offer infinite rewards through the achievement of organisational and personal goals for the rest of your career, if you invest enough time and effort in learning. Do not be disheartened by a few upsets along the way. Managing people is a complex and difficult task. Use upsets as learning experiences, turn them into advantages, and move on to the next challenge as your competency in the area grows. This book is the first step in making it easier for yourself. Good luck.

Michael D. Tovey
Gold Coast, QLD
2001

Mary-Anne L. Uren
Emerald, QLD
2006

Neroli Ena Sheldon
Murwillumbah, NSW
2010

ACKNOWLEDGMENTS

Before noting my own acknowledgments in this book, I feel it would be remiss not to mention the dedication of the first edition of this book by the late Michael Tovey to his son Andrew Tovey.

My own thanks go to:

- Mary-Anne L. Uren, who completed the revision of the first three chapters and previous edition of the book.

- Elise Carney, the Acquisitions Editor, for the opportunity to work with Pearson Australia.

- My family, Leah, Reuben and Ena, for their patience and good humour as deadlines loomed. As future employees, I hope Ena and Reuben and my nephews Isaac and Lucas have the good fortune to work with people who genuinely commit to managing performance improvement honestly and with integrity.

Neroli Ena Sheldon

HOW TO USE THIS BOOK

This book has been written to help you manage performance improvement in individuals in the workplace. Many managers will not be as good at this task as they would like to be. The skills required to manage performance effectively fall into the category of 'people skills'. They form part of the stable of skills commonly referred to as 'soft skills', which are included in the eight perceived most common weaknesses in Australian managers.[1]

It may take you a while to master the appropriate skills and to develop your knowledge of the area to be able to perform to the level you would like. You will make mistakes, you will get frustrated, it will take time, you will have to deal with people on a one-to-one basis, and you will need to negotiate and renegotiate. Soft skills take time to develop and must be supported with lots of practice. This is not always possible, especially if your organisation has only a yearly performance planning cycle with annual formal reviews. Even in this situation there is no reason why you should not practise more often and review performance with employees formally on a more frequent basis, such as once each quarter, until you all become better at managing performance. Used in this way, the process can become an action learning activity during which you and your staff practise and develop all the skills and knowledge needed to manage performance improvement skilfully.

While the book chapters are written in a logical and linear way, progressing from the first logical step to the last, you do not need to use the book in that way. Each chapter is self-contained. You do not need to have read the preceding text to use and understand a particular chapter. Feel free to pick and choose to meet your learning needs. In some chapters you will find references to other chapters because they are closely related. You can decide, at that time, whether it is useful for you to read the text to which you are directed.

Reference

1   Karpin, D. (Chair). 1995. *Enterprising Nation: Renewing Australia's Managers to Meet the Challenges of the Asia-Pacific Century*. Report of the Industry Task Force on Leadership and Management Skills. AGPS: Canberra, pp. 535–544.

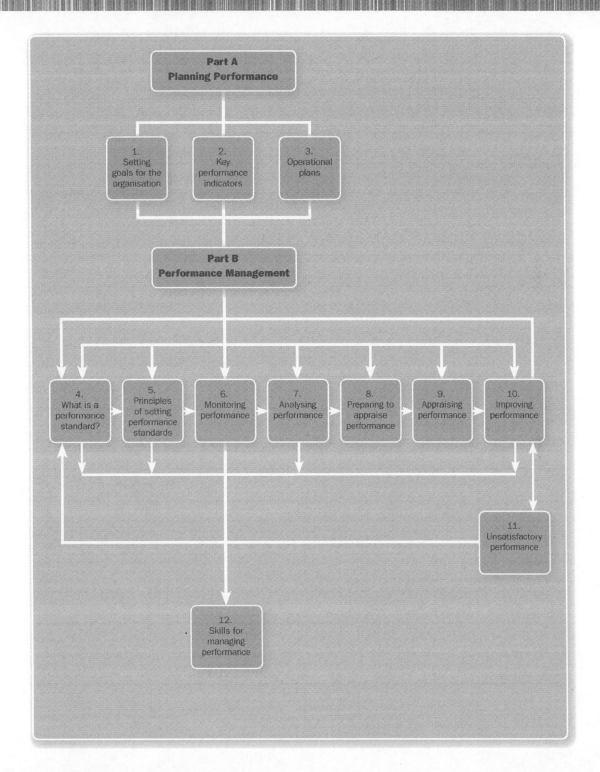

PART A

Planning Performance

This book is about how to manage individual performance so that an organisation obtains maximum productivity from its staff and minimises costs in order to facilitate quality and efficiency and greater competitiveness in the marketplace. The nature of work is changing so rapidly, dynamically and fundamentally[1] that often the knowledge and skills that managers and staff require are not available to them to deal with the new demands.[2] Continuous learning and improvement become an important factor in the performance of modern-day organisations, and are even more important for individual workers. How and when such learning occurs present a challenge for managers, trainers and workers alike. The Karpin Report in 1995[3] went so far as to say that job creation depends on better management skills, suggesting that the ability of organisations to be flexible stems directly from management and its skills in managing people within diverse and highly competitive environments that are likely to be in constant change. *The Manager of the 21st Century*, commissioned by Innovation & Business Skills Australia in 2005, built on the Karpin Report and concluded that a number of significant challenges exist for managers in the period up to 2020. These challenges include a far greater focus on the performance of people as a core organisational asset, a greater reliance on output measure to assess staff and the development of new techniques for improving performance.[4]

What is a manager?

As managers and the improvement of skills in managing performance improvement are the focus of this book, it will be useful to define what a manager is. While the literature uses a number of definitions, there is agreement on the concept that managers achieve things through others. The following definitions illustrate this point:

> *A manager is an individual who achieves enterprise goals through the work of others.*[5]

> *A supervisor is a manager who helps others achieve results by establishing and communicating goals and securing or providing the necessary resources.*[6]

Managers manage others to achieve outcomes or results through them. They use fewer technical skills and more interpersonal and conceptual skills in their job than when they were a team member or worker. Thus they become responsible for managing the performance of individuals to achieve organisational goals. This requires a different set of skills from when the manager was a non-management worker. As you move further up the management ladder, you use even fewer technical skills and more interpersonal and conceptual skills. Figure A.1 illustrates the change of skills required when moving from worker to management and the nature of the planning involved.

FIGURE A.1 Skills required at different levels of management [7]

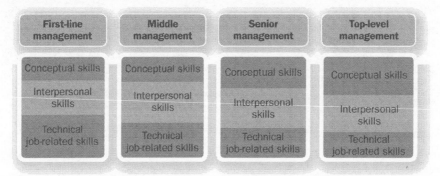

Karpin identified eight characteristics of the ideal manager,[8] which are listed in Figure A.2. The same report identified that Australian managers did not possess these skills to the level required to be competitive in world markets. Such a lack of skills has major implications for the management of human performance, as they are the platform through which performance is managed.

FIGURE A.2 Characteristics of the ideal manager

Characteristics

1. People skills
2. Strategic thinker
3. Visionary
4. Flexible and adaptable to change
5. Self-management
6. Team player
7. Ability to solve complex problems and make decisions
8. Ethical/high personal standards

There is little evidence of inroads being made into the recommendations of the Karpin Report of 1995. Cole states that in 2001, six years after the Report was produced, the training of managers and professionals had actually dropped by 0.3% to 29%.[9] This clearly evidences a lack of urgency in implementing the recommendations of the Report. With the estimate that only half of Australia's front-line managers have formal training for their roles, there is little doubt that organisations need to make management training a priority. If we keep putting managers into roles that require a great deal of ability and interpersonal skills without giving them the necessary support and understanding of how to do the job, we are setting them up to fail.

Management

For ease of understanding and to grasp the broad role of a manager, the definition of a manager was simplified in the previous section. It is not so easy to define the concept of management, as there are numerous theories and conceptual frameworks of management. Such is the nature of management that the answer to the question 'What does a manager do?' is likely to be different for nearly every manager that you ask. Gardner and Palmer suggest that management is a complex concept, diverse and multidisciplinary.[10] It is fraught with many contradictions between long-term objectives and daily operational crises, and is practised equally by those called managers and others who do not have the formal title of manager. To underpin the complexity of management, Gardner and Palmer propose an eclectic view that draws from three perspectives in the management literature.[11] These are the administrative, political and cultural perspectives, and are illustrated in Figure A.3.

These perspectives demonstrate the intricacy of management and the integrated range of skills and knowledge required to successfully manage people and their performance in the workplace.

FIGURE A.3 Three perspectives on management[12]

Administrative perspective	Relates to the efficient systems of management administration that are designed to facilitate the achievement of organisational goals through the use of classical management techniques, such as the division of labour, and formal organisational structures. Appropriate rules and controls are established to manage work and how it is performed. It is mechanistic in nature.
Political perspective	A process that endeavours to resolve conflicts between all the stakeholders in and out of an organisation. People within an organisation have different objectives, power bases and ways of acting, and they compete against each other for resources and rewards. This creates conflicts and alliances and coalitions. The political perspective takes account of how people feel and their values and the relationships that are formed within organisations.
Cultural perspective	The cultural perspective deals with the construction of meaning and values within an organisation. Culture refers to the traditional assumptions, beliefs and values that people have as members of the organisational community. It also refers to the way things are done in the organisation.

Defining performance management and performance appraisal

Performance management is a powerful tool linking an employee's responsibilities with that of the team and the overall organisation. It is done by setting and monitoring objectives on an ongoing basis, which provides an organisational snapshot of progress towards strategic plans and objectives.

The Performance Management Institute of Australia (PMIA) defines performance management as:

> *The process of setting and monitoring measures and objectives for employees, managers and executives. It is a closed loop process meaning that objectives are constantly reviewed and performance diaries are maintained by the employee and manager, which detail ongoing successes and challenge.*[13]

Performance appraisal may be defined as:

> *The process that identifies, evaluates and develops employee performance to meet employee and organisational goals.*[14]

At the time the performance appraisal is carried out, the objectives and outcomes are compared and a rating of some metric is assigned to the employee. In this, employee performance management is a continual development and improvement process. Automating this process yields reports which provide immediate visibility of performance across the entire organisation, something which is simply not possible with paper-based processes.

The global economy

In today's global economy, competitiveness is forging new links between employees and employers,[15] and these new links demand different and more flexible ways of developing people and managing performance. For example, gone are the old organisational hierarchies, replaced by flatter management structures with fewer managers. Structures that could be described as typical of current-day organisations resemble numbers of teams engaged in collaborative processes to achieve specific outcomes. Along with this process, time pressure has entered the workforce at all levels, potentially blocking development opportunities for all individuals because of the lack of opportunity to attend developmental activities off the job.[16] Nevertheless, organisations still need skilled staff, state-of-the-art technology, access to the massive information superhighway, and quick response times to customer/client requirements in order to remain competitive, profitable and efficient. Customers/clients, especially internal ones, are becoming more demanding, as they strive to meet quality and other standards as part of their performance management processes. The lack of commitment to training by Australian organisations is illustrated by world best practice for training, not just for management but for all employees, which is 20 days per employee per year. Australian managers spend an average of seven days a year, or 3% of their time, on training.[17]

Compounding this is the impact of the global financial crisis of 2008/2009, the implications of which will be felt by organisations for many years to come. Organisations have downsized by many thousands of employees at a time, leading to much uncertainty in the workplace. The need to utilise performance management information consistently to assist in the downsizing operations has never been more evident.

The challenge for organisations is to provide constant learning opportunities on an ongoing basis for all staff throughout the global financial crisis and beyond, to provide access to a range of learning resources within the organisation to facilitate learning and performance improvement, and to retain and motivate the employees that remain. To meet these challenges, and to meet the requirements of globalisation and its associated competitiveness, the Karpin Report identified six critical areas in which Australian managers needed to improve their skills:[18]

- Increase the levels of education and training undertaken.
- Use development processes, rather than short courses, to develop skills.
- In management development, focus on the future skills required.
- Handle the transition from specialist to manager more effectively.
- Specifically link management development to strategic business directions.
- Evaluate the effectiveness of management development activities.

Karpin also identified a new profile for the manager of the 21st century.[19] The manager of this century will be known more as a leader or coach, will be either male or female, will have a clear role as a leader and coach, and will be responsible for developing employees' skills. Other aspects of the profile include:

- flat organisational structures with team leaders reporting to senior management directly
- the values of the role including performance management, facilitation, participation and empowerment of other team members
- the working environment emphasising best practice, benchmarking, quality and customer service
- most managers having at least a TAFE-level qualification or a degree
- 100% of managers having had formal training for the position
- regular in-company training for further learning.

The evolving manager as identified by Cole for 2010 is one of leader/coach.[20] Much along the lines of the Karpin profile above, leaders/coaches will be either male or female and will be able to operate in a flat organisational structure, reporting direct to senior management. They will value performance management; facilitative, participative leadership; empowerment; and an environment that emphasises best practice, benchmarking, quality and customer service.

To get from where managers are now to where they need to be requires the development of what are commonly called 'soft skills'. These skills underpin the ability of managers to demonstrate the proficiencies implied by the above profile. This book is about developing the appropriate 'soft skills' to manage the performance of people. The Karpin Report identified the need to be able to manage the new structures in the workplace with increased ability in the 'soft skills' area.[21] These skills relate to communication, negotiation, counselling, listening, delegating and managing conflict. Karpin emphasised that these skills are deep and complex ones.

Training and development in 'soft skills' is vital to the success of any performance management system, because these skills underpin the major processes of performance management. Again, the Karpin Report identified 'strong evidence of the recognition of the relationship between skills development and the improved performance of the enterprise'.[22] This book provides a bridge between skills development and improved enterprise performance. For performance to be improved, however, it must be a planned activity, as with all successful endeavours. This first part of the book, Part A, concentrates on planning performance, and the activities and processes that should be used to create useful performance plans on which to base individual or team performance standards and objectives.

Training and development

Organisational training and development activities have traditionally provided core knowledge and skills for both managers and staff. This is no longer enough.[23] Employees need different knowledge and skills to cope with the 21st century.[24] They have to develop skills faster, and be more flexible, adaptable and multiskilled than ever before. The considerable change in the nature of work means that predicting the future is difficult, especially predicting the specific skills that may be required by people working in organisations. Hence, it is these very issues that employees need to manage through the acquisition of the more general skills of adaptation, change and learning.[25] They must become expert at managing change, multiple careers, the new organisation and a very different workforce—one that is currently undergoing a metamorphosis, the likes of which have not been seen since the beginning of the Industrial Revolution.

Rubenson and Schutze have identified three important factors influencing this significant change:[26]

- the introduction of new and sophisticated technologies
- new forms of work organisation
- new trends in organisational management.

These factors are operating in different forms of connectedness, which is changing the mix of skills required in the workplace and how those skills are acquired. Training is required by individuals 'on demand', as and when they need it, across a variety of situations in the workplace. In particular, new ways of organising and managing work prevent the routinisation of work and focus attention on faults, problems and unpredictable tasks in an effort to achieve quality and value. Such a situation calls for the development of expertise by workers. Problem solving is one way of learning and developing expertise.[27]

There is no doubt that we are now working in a new business environment, which requires managers to develop and manage organisational and individual performance and to ensure that all resources, including human resources, are performing to the required capacity and standards and within relevant legal frameworks.

Employment security

The essential knowledge and skills that employees must develop are those that provide them with employment security. They must learn to develop these skills and the associated knowledge themselves, as according to Baskett and Marsick, self-delegating workers with multifunctional expertise are the most desirable employees.[28] Employment security describes the state of possessing the knowledge and skills that ensure a worker is employable across a range of duties and types of jobs, rather than the single job provided by a single employer (previously known as 'job security'). This is shown in Figure A.4, which demonstrates the move from job security to employment security.

FIGURE A.4 The move from job security to employment security

Job security	Specific skills oriented towards one job in one organisation	Skill and knowledge development provided mainly by organisation, after initial qualification gained
Employment security	Many different skills oriented towards many jobs in many different organisations	Skill and knowledge development provided mainly by individual, after initial qualification gained

The Karpin Report found that many managers do not take responsibility for their own learning and development.[29] While there are many reasons for this, there is considerable pressure on individual managers to take responsibility for their own development in order to secure their ongoing employment. According to the Karpin Report, there are five areas from which this pressure stems:[30]

- Enterprises increasingly require enhanced management skills.
- Enterprises are becoming more strongly committed to helping managers improve their skills for a variety of future career possibilities.
- Enterprises are making it clear that learning and self-development is a partnership between the firm and the manager.
- Individuals are no longer guaranteed a clear career path within one organisation.
- Individuals are increasingly planning careers spanning organisations and industries.

Rubenson and Schutze cite a number of reports and competency lists that indicate the types of abilities and skills likely to be required of employees in the future.[31] They are as follows:

- the capability for analytical thinking applied to different processes of work
- a sense of quantitative appreciation of different processes
- the ability to conduct dialogue with equipment
- a sense of responsibility and a capacity for autonomous work
- the ability to link technical, economic and social considerations in the appreciation of equipment and working methods
- a planned and methodical approach to work
- the willingness to take the initiative and perform independently
- the ability to cooperate and work in groups
- competence in planning and evaluating one's own work and that of others
- understanding how to work with people from different backgrounds and cultures
- the ability to make decisions.

A quick glance over these abilities reveals that they are more generic and broader than traditional skills and competencies. This will require a major shift in emphasis for employee learning and development.

Learning and performance management

Learning is inextricably related to individual performance and the development of expertise. Learning results in new knowledge and skills so that individuals can perform their jobs in a more capable way, increasing individual competence and developing skilled vocational practice towards expertise. To facilitate learning transfer to workplaces, learning methods and activities need to link skills and knowledge development explicitly to work activities and the actual degree of competence required by organisations.[32]

This is the basic philosophy underpinning competency-based training, where training is geared towards specific, measurable outcomes for the learner that are based on particular descriptions of actual job performance.[33] Competency-based training allows for recognition of skills and prior work experience in attaining national qualifications in a variety of subject areas.

Chapters 1–3 will review the work that needs to be done to ensure that adequate goals, and strategic and operational plans, are in place within an organisation so that performance can be planned and measured.

References

1 Harvey, D. 1989. *The Condition of Postmodernity: An Enquiry into the Origins of Cultural Change*. Basil Blackwell: Oxford; Rubenson, K. & Schutze, H. 1995. 'Learning at and through the workplace: A review of participation and adult learning theory.' In D. Hirsch & D. Wagner (eds), *What Makes Workers Learn: The Role of Incentives in Workplace Education and Training*. Hampton Press: Cresskill, NJ, p. 99.

2 Karpin, D. (Chair). 1995. *Enterprising Nation: Renewing Australia's Managers to Meet the Challenges of the Asia-Pacific Century*. Report of the Industry Task Force on Leadership and Management Skills. AGPS: Canberra.

3 Karpin, op. cit., 1995, p. xiv.

4 Nicholson, J. & Nairn, A. 2006. *The Manager of the 21st Century*. Innovation & Business Skills Australia: Hawthorn, p. 3.

5 Karpin, op. cit., 1995, p. 14.

6 Cole, K. 2005, 3rd edn. *Management: Theory and Practice*. Pearson Australia: Frenchs Forest, Sydney, p. 14.

7 Source: Cole, K. 2001, 2nd edn. *Management: Theory and Practice*. Pearson Australia: Frenchs Forest, Sydney, p. 14.

8 Karpin, op. cit., 1995, p. 535.

9 Cole, op. cit., 2005, p. 6.

10 Gardner, M. & Palmer, G. 1997, 2nd edn. *Employment Relations: Industrial Relations and Human Resources Management in Australia*. Macmillan Education Australia: Melbourne, pp. 229–230.

11 Gardner & Palmer, op. cit., 1997, pp. 230–239.

12 Gardner & Palmer, op. cit., 1997, pp. 230–239. Reproduced by permission of Macmillan Education Australia.

13 Performance Management Institute of Australia 2009. <www.pmia.org.au/whatispm.html> accessed 26 June 2009.

14 Dessler, G., Griffiths, J. & Lloyd-Walker, B. 2007, 3rd edn. *Human Resource Management*. Pearson Australia: Frenchs Forest, Sydney, p. 314.

15 Murray, M. & Owen, M.A. 1991. *Beyond the Myths and Magic of Mentoring: How to Facilitate an Effective Mentoring Program*. Jossey-Bass: San Francisco, p. 9.

16 Cohen, N. & Galbraith, M. 1995. 'Mentoring in the learning society.' In M. Galbraith & N. Cohen (eds), *Mentoring: New Strategies and Challenges. New Directions for Adult and Continuing Education*, 66. Jossey-Bass: San Francisco, p. 10.

17 Cohen & Galbraith, op. cit., 1995, p. 6.

18 Karpin, op. cit., 1995, p. xi.

19 Karpin, op. cit., 1995, p. 23.

20 Cole, op. cit., 2005, p. 11.

21 Karpin, op. cit., 1995, p. 25.

22 Karpin, op. cit., 1995, p. 39.

23 Rubenson & Schutze, op. cit., 1995, pp. 99–100.

24 Karpin, op. cit., 1995, pp. 22–23, pp. 34–151.

25 Rubenson & Schutze, op. cit., 1995, p. 100.

26 Rubenson & Schutze, op. cit., 1995, p. 99.

27   Stevenson, J. 1994. 'Vocational expertise.' In J. Stevenson (ed.), *The Development of Vocational Expertise*. National Centre for Vocational Education Research: Leabrook, Adelaide, pp. 7–35.

28   Baskett, H. & Marsick, V. 1992 (eds), *Professionals' Ways of Knowing: New Findings on How to Improve Professional Education. New Directions for Adult and Continuing Education*, 55. Jossey-Bass: San Francisco.

29   Karpin, op. cit., 1995, pp. 147–148.

30   Karpin, op. cit., 1995, p. 148.

31   Rubenson & Schutze, op. cit., 1995, pp. 100–101.

32   Gott, S.P. 1989. 'Apprenticeship instruction for real-world tasks: The coordination of procedures, mental models, and strategies.' *Review of Research in Education*, 15(3), pp. 97–169.

33   Tovey, M.D. & Lawlor, D.R. 2004, 3rd edn. *Training in Australia*. Pearson Australia: Frenchs Forest, Sydney, pp. 34–35.

CHAPTER ONE

Setting goals for the organisation

Learning outcomes

After reading this chapter you should be able to:

* explain why planning is necessary
* explain why plans should be written
* explain the term 'planning'
* state why planning is a legitimate management function
* explain how better planning may reduce mistakes
* list the components of plans
* state the reasons for managers' need to plan
* explain the benefits of planning in a changing environment
* state the purpose of a vision statement
* state the purpose of a mission statement
* identify the differences between strategic and operational planning
* explain the term 'strategic planning'
* explain the term 'goal'
* outline the process of goal setting.

INTRODUCTION

While there is plenty of evidence in the research literature to suggest a connection between planning and performance, there is also a body of evidence to suggest that it may not be so directly or closely connected as is often assumed.[1] To capitalise on the connection, no matter how small or large, performance needs to be planned. The old saying 'If you don't know where you are going, how are you going to get there?' evidences the common sensibility that some planning ought to occur before you embark on a course of action, even if only to clarify what the end will be. Those organisations that are regarded as highly successful have a number of things in common, including the existence of planning processes to identify what end results are required and how they can be achieved.[2]

All managers do planning in all areas of an organisation. It occurs in all sorts of organisations, from small businesses to large bureaucracies. Planning can be formal or informal in nature and, while this chapter suggests that planning should be somewhat formal (i.e. written down and shared), planning is just as legitimate if it is not written down and is known only to senior managers. (This often occurs in small businesses.) However, research has suggested that organisations are more likely to achieve results where plans are written down and shared among staff and managers, and where staff participate in the development of them.[3] 'Planning cannot guarantee improved performance, but it should improve the probability of improved performance.'[4] Planning should be a vital part of performance management and the whole organisation if it is to achieve its goals.[5] Without a performance plan you cannot manage the performance needed to reach organisational goals. This is reasonably self-evident. A plan is an objective reference point for the employer and employee. A written plan is a clear, objective statement of how the organisational goals will be achieved to which all can refer.

In this chapter the process of planning is examined, together with the process of strategic planning that forms the basis for the setting of goals and other performance targets or measures across the organisation.

What is planning?

Planning is a difficult and intangible management function to tie down. Yet, as humans, we do it all the time. We plan holidays, career moves, buying new cars and houses, family get-togethers, and how to get to places we have never been to before. This level of planning and fine detail does not seem to be reflected in management behaviour in the workplace. Note the following definitions of planning:

> *. . . examining the future and drawing up the plan of action.*[6]

> *. . . Planning encompasses defining the organisation's objectives or goals, establishing an overall strategy for achieving these goals, and developing a comprehensive hierarchy of plans to integrate and coordinate activities.*[7]

> *. . . Plans are projected courses of action aimed at achieving future objectives.*[8]

These definitions suggest that planning is an activity that looks at the future and how you will get there. Planning requires time to think about the future, and is a legitimate and essential management function. Managers need to take the time to think and plan to ensure that goals are met. This means that a manager can, and should, legitimately block out periods of the working day on a regular basis in order to think and plan. This kind of activity is part of your management responsibilities and is essential if you are to manage successfully.

In the 1970s and 1980s, when the Western world rediscovered the quality management processes Japan was using (which they originally imported from the United States, between the 1920s and 1950s),[9] it learned that considerable time was devoted to the planning of work and much less to the actual execution of work. In fact, the ratio was approximately two-thirds of the available time set aside for planning and one-third for implementation. This underscores the perceived importance of the planning function for managers, especially in relation to managing performance. The Japanese found that more time spent in planning reduced mistakes and improved quality and productivity, thus boosting overall organisational performance. A reduction in mistakes leads to a reduction in costs incurred when organisations try to correct mistakes. The next section explores the relationship between planning and performance. Plans incorporate goals and actions, as suggested by Figure 1.1.

FIGURE 1.1 Components of plans

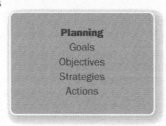

Planning
Goals
Objectives
Strategies
Actions

Why plan?

The reason that an organisation and its management must plan is simply to achieve its organisational goals, as well as the goals to which boards, shareholders and governments subscribe. Ideally, staff have some input into the process of setting the organisational objectives through the strategic planning processes. Table 1.1 provides further reasons why managers should plan.

TABLE 1.1 Why managers should plan

To:
- coordinate individual efforts
- enable action planning
- enable management of change
- facilitate decision making and reduce waste
- focus effort on results/goals
- give clear directions to others
- identify resources required
- meet deadlines
- monitor and evaluate performance
- reduce delays and disruptions
- reduce duplication
- reduce uncertainty
- set priorities
- set parameters for monitoring

In the current organisational environment the question is often asked: 'Why bother to plan?'. Things often change so quickly that plans are frequently superseded within months or weeks of their being adopted. This is especially so in the technology industry and the public service, where a change in government or ministerial priorities (sometimes driven by knee-jerk reactions to public opinion) can completely reshape the objectives and strategies of a department or branch. Other industries where rapid change is occurring are banking and finance; education; gas, electricity and water supply; and communication services. This issue goes to the very heart of the reason for planning.

Learning organisations

In order to keep up with their frequently changing environment, organisations need to aim at achieving a 'learning organisation' culture. A learning organisation is one that has developed a continuous capacity to adapt and change to achieve sustained existence. The focus is on excelling for customers, staff and owners through expanding the organisation's capacity to ensure future success.

Learning organisations do not have boundaries as part of their structure. They thrive on risk taking and growth while ensuring a total quality management (TQM) style commitment to stakeholders. The TQM philosophy has a strong customer focus, with a belief that improvement never stops and that the key to effective TQM is empowerment of employees. Learning organisations utilising the TQM framework continuously benchmark against external sources to ensure that best practice is applied. The emphasis is on how people work together, strongly highlighting honesty, two-way feedback, and personal and professional development to motivate employees. These organisations also recognise that to improve, they need to review organisational visions and objectives in response to changes that shape external influences. This is a core part of the learning organisation's philosophy.

Planning in a changing environment

A changing environment, however, is not an adequate reason for abandoning the planning process. The process itself requires a manager to think carefully about the future and to develop strategies and actions to deal with it. This takes time and effort, and as a consequence you become familiar with the myriad issues, challenges, potential problems, competitors and environmental pressures that face your organisation. Even though you may choose goals and actions that are superseded for reasons beyond your control, the process of planning is not wasted. A skilfully developed plan will always incorporate elements of uncertainty, together with appropriate contingency measures. Having planned, you will understand the nature of your business more thoroughly, which will facilitate greater flexibility in, and ensure timeliness of, your response. Remember the Karpin Report, which noted that Australian managers were inflexible and rigid.[10] A manager must accept that nothing is likely to stay the same in the new global environment. A skilled manager will be able to cope with and manage change as a matter of everyday activity, with the use of planning skills. A plan means that change is likely to reduce stress for all workers.

Planning for performance

Planning for performance starts at the very highest levels of an organisation, and a great deal of work needs to go into planning the organisation's performance. A vision must be decided on. This is a statement about the things that the organisation considers to be important. Perry et al. suggest that there are two components of an organisation's vision that are part of its culture:[11] first, there is the component of direction, which indicates where the organisation is going in the future; and second, there is the identification of values that will influence strategic decisions and behaviours within the organisation. A vision statement sets the direction. This is illustrated in Figure 1.2.

FIGURE 1.2 Components of a vision statement

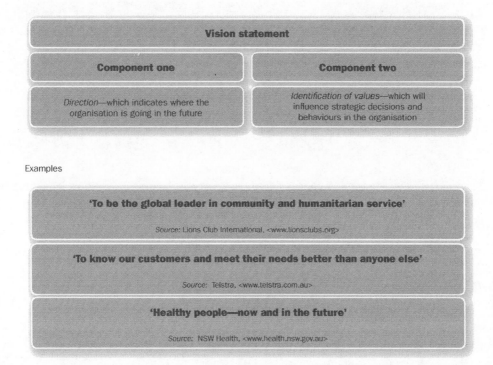

Examples

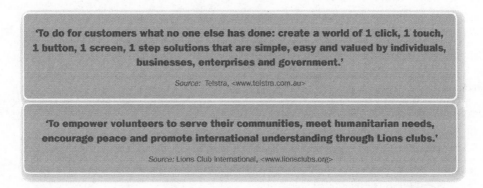

Next, the mission of the organisation needs to be developed. This involves a broad description of what the organisation is about. The mission statement defines the overall purpose of the organisation, its reason for being. Some examples of mission statements are provided in Figure 1.3.

FIGURE 1.3 Mission statement examples

'To do for customers what no one else has done: create a world of 1 click, 1 touch, 1 button, 1 screen, 1 step solutions that are simple, easy and valued by individuals, businesses, enterprises and government.'

Source: Telstra, <www.telstra.com.au>

'To empower volunteers to serve their communities, meet humanitarian needs, encourage peace and promote international understanding through Lions clubs.'

Source: Lions Club International, <www.lionsclubs.org>

Vision and mission statements may also be combined in one statement: see Figure 1.4.

FIGURE 1.4 Combined vision and mission statement

> 'The Commonwealth Bank's vision is to be Australia's finest financial services organisation through excelling in customer service.
>
> We aspire to:
> - Have people that are engaged, passionate and valued
> - Provide a service experience our customers appreciate
> - Deliver top quartile returns to our shareholders
> - Be respected and admired in our community
>
> We want to be the financial services organisation chosen by customers because of our outstanding service. Ultimately, we want to be known as a great company to bank with, work in and invest in.'
>
> *Source:* Commonwealth Bank. <www.commbank.com.au>

The vision and mission statements lead into the strategic planning process, which in turn leads to the operational or business planning processes, which form the basis for the setting of individual performance objectives. This process is illustrated in Figure 1.5.

FIGURE 1.5 The planning process

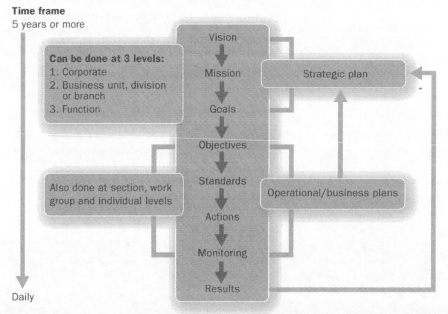

CHECK YOUR UNDERSTANDING

1 How does planning contribute to improved performance?
2 Why is planning a useful activity for managers?
3 Do you agree that managers should spend two-thirds of their time planning and the other one-third implementing? Explain.
4 Why should individual performance objectives be linked to planning activities?
5 'An organisation can survive without plans.' Comment on this statement.
6 What role do vision and mission statements play?

SKILLS PRACTICE

Plan a piece of work that you need to complete within the next few weeks. The work might be employment-related, study-related, home-related or something like a party. Use the planning process in Figure 1.5 to guide your efforts.

Strategic planning

From Figure 1.6 you will see there is a difference between strategic planning and operational planning. The difference is partly a matter of level and partly a matter of time frames. Strategic plans are focused on time frames of three to five years into the future, whereas operational plans, also known as business plans, are usually written for the next 12-month period (although they can stretch to about three years in some circumstances). Nevertheless, there are legitimate exceptions to this, with the actual time frame being determined in part by the rate of change affecting the organisation.

Differences between strategic planning and operational planning

Johnson and Scholes developed a very clear diagram that succinctly represents the major differences between strategic and operational planning (Figure 1.6).[12] Notice that operational management is more predictable, systemised and specific than strategic management. This suggests that different skills and knowledge are required to move from operational management to strategic management.[13] This was reinforced by the Karpin Report,[14] which demonstrated that the strengths of first-line managers in Australia did not correspond well with what were considered to be the ideal management characteristics. The top two perceived weaknesses of Australian management were listed as 'short-term view' and 'lack of strategic perspective'. This research was confined to first-line managers. Different characteristic sets might be reflected with higher levels of management. Karpin also identified the lack of inclusion of management development in strategic plans (only 25% of organisations surveyed included it).[15] Management development is critical if the soft skills are to be developed by managers to underpin performance management.

FIGURE 1.6 Differences between strategic and operational management[16]

Complexity of strategic management

Strategic management is demanding. Well-structured strategic plans can return the effort invested in their development through the excitement and anticipation they can generate and their capacity to energise the people within an organisation. When making strategic plans, managers make educated guesses about the future based on as much information as they can gather. This requires managers to look across the whole organisation, not just their own specialty. Generally, the literature holds very complex definitions of strategic management,[17] but they revolve around the basic concept that strategic management is about:

> *. . . aligning the organisation with the internal resources and the external environment to ensure long-term survival.*

Strategic management involves:

- identifying where the organisation is currently
- assessing how the external environment is likely to affect the organisation
- deciding what alternative actions are possible to reach the vision and mission
- choosing an action or a number of actions
- implementing the choices.

Johnson, Scholes and Whittington have identified the following characteristics of strategic decisions:[18]

- Strategy is likely to be concerned with the long-term direction of an organisation.
- Strategic decisions are about the scope of an organisation's activities.
- Strategic decisions are normally about trying to achieve some advantage for the organisation over the competition.
- Strategy matches the organisation's activities with the environment in which it operates.
- Strategy matches the organisation's activities to its resource capability.
- Strategic decisions have major resource implications for an organisation.
- An organisation's strategy will be affected not only by environmental forces but also by the values and expectations of those who have power in and around the organisation.

To develop and implement a strategic plan, Robbins and Mukerji suggest nine steps:[19]

1 Identify the organisation's mission, objectives and strategies.
2 Analyse the environment in which the organisation is operating.
3 Identify opportunities and threats to the organisation.
4 Analyse the organisation's resources.
5 Identify the strengths and weaknesses of the organisation.
6 Review the organisation's mission and objectives.
7 Formulate strategies to achieve desired goals.
8 Implement strategies.
9 Evaluate the results.

While the process of strategic planning may be complex, the activity can be easily managed with the aid of these succinct guidelines. The complexity lies in the thinking and the challenges that present themselves during the activity of planning strategically.

Strategic plans

Strategic plans are focused on the whole organisation, providing overarching objectives for the organisation, its direction and how it will interact with its environment. These provide the backdrop to the development of key performance indicators and critical success factors for the organisation (these are explained in Chapter 2) and operational plans (explained in Chapter 3). From these, the organisation can monitor its performance and individuals can develop their own performance objectives. The broad and necessary framework for a performance management system is then in place. Goals form the foundation of all plans in the organisation, and they may range from broad aims to specific targets. Figure 1.7 illustrates the relationship between goals and other planning activities in an organisation. Goals provide the direction for the future.

FIGURE 1.7 Relationship between goals and other planning activities

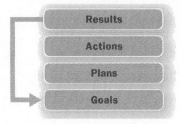

Goal setting

A definition

A goal is a direction, a point you want to head towards, a destination or a purpose. Many different words are used interchangeably with the word 'goal', such as aim, objective, target or purpose. The literature suggests that there is no great difference between these words, although there is some consensus that the words 'goal' and 'aim' refer to more general descriptions of intent, while 'objective' and 'target' are more specific in nature. Whatever word you use, the principle and the process of developing them are the same. Plans can be seen as elaborations of the path for reaching goals—the detailed steps for getting from A to Z. Plans are therefore based on goal-setting theory.

Process of setting goals

Based on the research, Robbins and Hunsaker suggest five fundamental rules for goal setting that ensure that a goal is a useful and effective tool for a manager.[20] They are:

1 Goals need to be specific.
2 Goals need to be challenging.
3 Goals must have time limits.
4 Goals must be decided on participatively.
5 Feedback must be included in the goal-setting framework.

Research suggests that goals need to be both future-based and more immediate.[21] Goals that reach too far into the future, without supporting subgoals to facilitate the achievement of the main goal, are more likely to remain unachieved. Subgoals also need to be specific and measurable. They facilitate appropriate learning and development of strategies to achieve the main goal.

Based on these five rules, goal setting becomes a disciplined, logical process to move through. The challenge in goal setting is determining the substance of the goals and deciding exactly what it is that you want to achieve. This is true for any level of goal setting—strategic plans, operational plans or individual performance objectives. The process is the same, it is just the substance that is different. Follow the eight steps below to set goals:

1 Broadly identify what it is you want to achieve (goal).

2 Narrow it down to a number of specific things (subgoals) to be achieved that will enable the main goal to be reached.

3 Identify how you will measure the achievement of the subgoal(s). At this stage, subgoals are often known as objectives because they include the measure.

4 Identify the specific level of achievement required for each subgoal.

5 Identify linkages between subgoals.

6 Set a time limit for when each subgoal must be achieved.

7 Identify and rank subgoals, from most important to least important.

8 Develop an action plan for each subgoal.

The two processes above are illustrated in Figure 1.8, which demonstrates the relationships between the main goal and subgoals and the actions to achieve them.

Having set goals, you will plan strategies and actions to achieve them. Goals, strategies and actions are the basis of plans.

FIGURE 1.8 Goals and subgoals

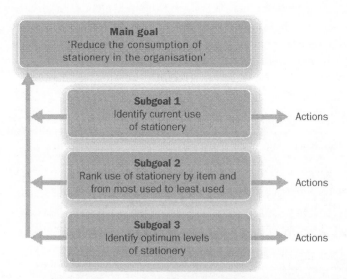

SKILL AND KNOWLEDGE APPLICATION

TASK

Take a goal that you would like to achieve. Write it down. Using the Robbins and Hunsaker rules and the steps identified above, fine-tune the goal so that it is specific and measurable, then develop a number of supporting or subgoals that will lead you to the attainment of the main goal. For example, if you wanted to buy a new car, the written goal statement and subgoals should look something like this:

Main goal

- Buy a new $30,000 red Honda car with finance from the XYZ Bank, with a $5000 deposit by March XXXX. The car has to have power steering, air conditioning, central locking, cloth seats and a four-litre engine.

Subgoals

- Achieve savings of $5000 deposit.
- Achieve maximum interest on savings.
- Find buyer for present car.

Strategies

- Reduce number of visits to the cinema.
- Reduce the price of all gifts to $15.
- Open an account at XYZ Bank.
- Decide how to advertise old car.

Actions

- Check bank interest rates and requirements for lending.
- Visit car showroom to identify the car of choice and requirements.
- Find out what delivery schedules are like and when the order must be placed.
- Test drive the required car.

CONCLUSION

Skilled goal setting has been linked to many successful individuals. While it is doubtful that the setting of goals by itself will ensure success, it does lay the foundations for success. Plans are built on goals. To be effective, goals need to be specific to and challenging for the individual, and must be part of a series that culminates in the attainment of an overall goal. Any goal will be made up of a number of smaller goals that must be achieved before the main aim can be reached. Goals that are effective and have measurable outcomes form the basis of useful plans. Strategic plans, operational plans and individual performance objectives are all based on the setting of goals. The better the goal—the more realistic, challenging, specific and measurable—the more likely it is that your plans will be useful and play a vital role in your success and that of your enterprise.

Goals and plans do change, however. Circumstances eventuate that sometimes require a complete change of goals and plans. This does not mean that the planning done to date has been wasted. The planning you have done leaves you better prepared for change and develops flexibility, enabling you to react more quickly to economic, political, consumer and other changes that affect your organisation.

Planning and performance are linked through the process of goal setting. Strategic planning is the first part of the performance planning process. This sets up the general direction of the organisation and facilitates the development of operational plans, right down to individual performance objectives. An organisation without strategic plans is like a loose cannon firing at will, with no aim or particular objective in mind. Strategic plans bring together what is important for the organisation so that lower-level plans, such as operational and individual performance plans, can be developed to contribute to the organisation's overall plans.

CASE STUDY

Annie's Nanny Service is a babysitting service located in a remote community. Annie, the owner of the business, had seen a market in this remote community for the provision of babysitting services for professionals, working mums, and parents who just needed a break. The business provides opportunities for nannies to be booked in advance, or when required on short notice for short- and long-term contracts. Initially, the service began with the employment of a couple of mums and teenagers wishing to earn extra money. However, from word of mouth, and due to the exceptional service resulting from the high standard of the nannies employed by Annie's Nanny Service, the business expanded rapidly. Annie is now finding it difficult to keep up with the demand for the service and is spending all of her time recruiting and dealing with booking requirements for new jobs.

As often happens with many small businesses that expand quickly, Annie had not had time to put in place a structure to support the growth of her business. Annie has just employed a Business Manager, Norma, to assist her with the growth of the business. Annie sees that there is a huge demand in the local community, due to its remoteness, and wants to branch out into other remote communities in the region. These communities sustain a lot of itinerant workers who do not have the support of families for babysitting services.

Annie now has 20 nannies working for her on a part-time and full-time basis within the local community and is still not filling the demand for her services. She sees the appointment of Norma as critical to the success of her expanding business.

Annie is frustrated because she can see the potential for her business but she is bogged down in the day-to-day administration of the business.

QUESTIONS

1   What steps would you expect the Business Manager to take initially to get control of Annie's Nanny Service?
2   What role should Annie now focus on as the business owner?
3   Who—Annie or Norma—should let the employees know where the company is heading?
4   What might have happened if Annie had allowed the company to continue in the way it was going?

JOB AIDS

Components of plans

Plan	A goal is:	Goals need to be:
Goals	A direction, a point	Specific
Objectives	you want to head	Challenging
Strategies	towards, a destination	Time-limited
Actions	or a purpose.	Participatively decided
		Used with feedback

The planning process

Time frame

5 years or more

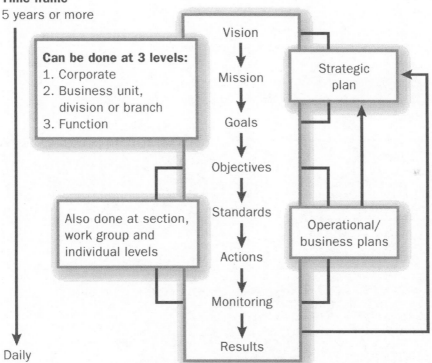

Can be done at 3 levels:
1. Corporate
2. Business unit, division or branch
3. Function

Also done at section, work group and individual levels

Vision
↓
Mission
↓
Goals
↓
Objectives
↓
Standards
↓
Actions
↓
Monitoring
↓
Results

Strategic plan

Operational/ business plans

Daily

✓ CHECKLISTS

To develop a strategic plan:

❑ Identify the organisation's mission, objectives and strategies.

❑ Analyse the environment in which the organisation is operating.

❑ Identify opportunities and threats to the organisation.

❑ Analyse the organisation's resources.

❑ Identify the strengths and weaknesses of the organisation.

❑ Review the organisation's mission and objectives.

❑ Formulate strategies to achieve desired goals.

❑ Implement strategies.

❑ Evaluate the results.

To set goals:

❑ Broadly identify what it is you want to achieve.

❑ Narrow it down to a number of specific things (goals) to be achieved that will enable the main goal to be reached.

❑ Identify how you will measure the achievement of the goal(s). At this stage, goals are often known as objectives because they include the measure.

❑ Identify the specific level of achievement required for each goal.

❑ Identify links between goals.

❑ Set a time limit for when each goal must be achieved.

❑ Identify and rank goals, from most important to least important.

❑ Develop an action plan for each goal.

References

1 Perry, C., Gibson, B. & Dudurovic, R. 1992. *Strategic Management Processes*. Longman Cheshire: Melbourne, p. 5; Robbins, S. & Mukerji, D. 1994, 2nd edn. *Managing Organisations: New Challenges and Perspectives*. Prentice Hall: Sydney, pp. 112, 114; Shrader, C., Taylor, L. & Dalton, D. 1984. 'Strategic planning and organisational performance.' *Journal of Management*, Summer, p. 152; Greenly, G. 1986. 'Does strategic planning improve company performance?' *Long Range Planning*, April, pp. 101–109.

2 Peters, T. & Waterman, R. 1994. *In Search of Excellence: Lessons from America's Best Run Companies*. Harper & Row: Sydney; Peters, T. 1989. *Thriving on Chaos*. Pan Books: London.

3 Perry et al., op. cit., 1992, p. 5.

4 Perry et al., op. cit., 1992, p. 5.

5 Cole, K. 2010, 4th edn. *Management: Theory and Practice*. Pearson Australia: Frenchs Forest, Sydney, p. 548.

6 Fayol, H. 1930. *Industrial and General Administration*, Trans. by J.A. Cougrough from the original *Administration, Industrielle et Générale* (1916). International Management Institute: Geneva.

7 Robbins & Mukerji, op. cit., 1994, p. 111.

8 Cole, op. cit., 2010, p. 548.

9 Gardner, M. & Palmer, G. 1997, 2nd edn. *Employment Relations: Industrial Relations and Human Resources Management in Australia*. Macmillan Education Australia: Melbourne, p. 70.

10 Karpin, D. (Chair). 1995. *Enterprising Nation: Renewing Australia's Managers to Meet the Challenges of the Asia-Pacific Century*. Report of the Industry Task Force on Leadership and Management Skills. AGPS: Canberra, p. 544.

11 Perry et al., op. cit., 1992, p. 16.

12 Johnson, G. & Scholes, K. 1993, 3rd edn. *Exploring Corporate Strategy*. Prentice Hall Imprint, Pearson Education UK, pp 16-17.

13 Johnson & Scholes, op. cit., 1993, pp. 31–32.

14 Karpin, op. cit., 1995, pp. 534–547.

15 Karpin, op. cit., 1995, p. 145.

16 Johnson & Scholes, op. cit., 1993, pp. 16–17. © Prentice Hall Imprint, Pearson Education UK, 1997.

17 Perry et al., op. cit., 1992, p. 1; Viljon, J. 1991. *Strategic Management*, Longman Cheshire: Melbourne, pp. 2–3.

18 Johnson, G., Scholes, K. & Whittington, R. 2005, 7th edn. *Exploring Corporate Strategy*, Pearson Education: London.

19 Robbins & Mukerji, op. cit., 1994, pp. 135–144.

20 Robbins, S. & Hunsaker, P. 2006, 4th edn. *Training in Interpersonal Skills: Tips for Managing People at Work*, Prentice Hall: New York, pp. 53–54.

21 Latham, G. & Seijts, G. 1999. 'The effects of proximal and distal goals on performance of a moderately complex task.' *Journal of Organizational Behavior*, 20(4), pp. 421–429.

CHAPTER TWO

Key performance indicators

Learning outcomes

After reading this chapter you should be able to:

* explain the basis on which organisations are judged

* explain the key performance indicators (KPI) framework used in the chapter

* describe a critical success factor (CSF)

* list four examples of a critical success factor

* state the class of managers that should be involved in setting CSFs

* explain a key performance indicator (KPI)

* explain the terms 'means' and 'ends'

* describe the relationship between CSFs and KPIs

* explain the role of performance indicators

* outline how key performance indicators might be used

* state the most common reasons for the development of key performance indicators

* use key performance indicators to monitor performance.

INTRODUCTION

An organisation is judged by the results it achieves. This is true for a company operating in the market-place to make a profit and a return on investment for shareholders. It is also true for a government agency providing services of the highest quality to taxpayers and thus providing a suitable return to them for their tax dollar. If companies don't make profits, shareholders take action and the market may react badly, which can have a negative effect on the operation of the company. In extreme cases, bad results can force the closure of a company. The poor operation of a government agency will have voters in an uproar and will sometimes force the resignation of a minister or the downfall of a government.

Performance indicators (PIs) relate to the results the organisation wants to achieve. They identify areas in which it is vital that the organisation perform well in order to achieve its strategic and operational plans for the period. However, the need for performance indicators may be more dramatic than this. There are times when organisations are in trouble for a variety of reasons—strong competition, voter dissatisfaction, poor financial results, introduction of new technologies, dollar fluctuations, and general cyclical ups and downs. At these times, key performance indicators (KPIs) are vital if the organisation is to achieve a turnaround. This chapter explores the nature and type of KPIs, together with critical success factors (CSFs), how they can be developed and how they are used in the day-to-day activities of organisational operation to define and measure business objectives.

Key performance indicators (KPI) framework

Before examining in detail what CSFs, KPIs and PIs are and how they are utilised in an organisation, it may help to visualise how these fit into the organisational structure and to give a brief explanation of their roles.

Figure 2.1 illustrates the framework in which CSFs, KPIs and PIs fit into an organisation's planning processes and shows how they are built from the strategic and operational plans of an organisation.

- **Critical success factors (CSFs)** *identify* those aspects of the organisation that are critical for its success.

- **Key performance indicators (KPIs)** are those *indicators* of performance that are seen as being of great importance to the success of the business of the organisation. A KPI is a quantifiable gauge used to measure an organisation's performance against its CSFs. KPIs can be financial or non-financial and there may be more than one KPI per CSF.

- **Performance indicators (PIs)** are *measures* of different parts of the organisation's performance.

Organisations today use different terminology to describe the various levels of the KPI framework above. For example, Key Focus Areas (KFAs) can sometimes be used in place of CSFs. Where Key Result Areas (KRAs) are referred to, these are utilised at the job level, sometimes interchangeably with Key Performance Areas (KPAs). Jones provides a useful example of this:

If OHS was a key performance area of a job, related PIs could include the number of accidents per occupational group and lost-time injuries expressed in days lost.[1]

FIGURE 2.1 KPI framework

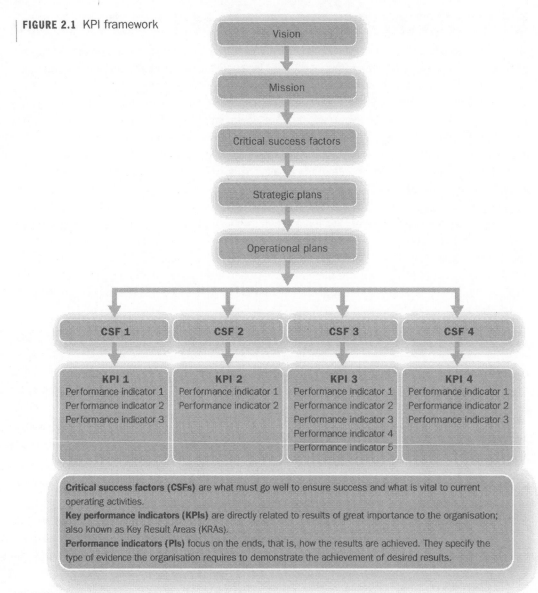

Critical success factors (CSFs)

Once the planning for a particular year or business cycle has been completed, it will be clear what the critical aspects of those plans are. You should be able to look at the plans

- see quite clearly what the critical business issues are for that planning cycle
- list the critical success factors for achieving the plans.

Critical success factors:

- identify those aspects of the organisation that are critical for its success
- are few in number
- assist the organisation in achieving its plan for the cycle.

Boynton and Zmud provide a useful definition of CSFs:[2]

Critical success factors are those few things that must go well to ensure success for a manager or an organisation, and, therefore, they represent those managerial or enterprise areas that must be given special attention to bring about high performance. CSFs include issues vital to an organisation's current operating activities and to its future success.

As you proceed through this chapter you need to bear in mind that theory and practice often differ. Because theoretical concepts are referred to by certain terms, this does not necessarily flow into the realms of practice. The key is identifying in practice what you have learned in theory. Figure 2.2 on pages 30–31 assists in demonstrating this concept. The links to these strategic plans can be found at:

<www.education.qld.gov.au/strategic/planning>

<www.health.nsw.gov.au>

KPIs assist in tackling the critical success factors in the business, government department or agency at the operational level by identifying clear measures of operational performance. In Figure 2.2 we see that operational plans can be developed with clear objectives in mind, and in the full knowledge of what the organisation considers is critical to its success and what needs to be measured.

To further illustrate how to identify CSFs, a diversified finance organisation will be considered. This sample organisation wants to integrate its services in banking and insurance to provide a more seamless service to its clients; it may want to merge certain operations and restructure the way it operates. From the vision and mission statements might flow the following critical success factors (CSFs):

1   service/sales (maintain/improve levels of customer service and sales made to customers)

2   human resources (hire the right people and retain them)

3   business culture (change the existing culture to one more focused on service delivery)

4   risk/financial management (managing the budgets will have high priority)

5   communication (both internal and external communications need to improve dramatically)

6   systems and technology (systems and technology need to be improved to compete in the marketplace and to make staff more productive)

7   infrastructure (the organisation needs an effective structure, and new assets will need to be purchased to meet the requirements of the strategic plan).

Note that all aspects of the business are identified in the abovementioned CSFs; even though the current year's planning is focused on integration and restructuring, all other CSFs, KPIs and PIs are not abandoned. For example, a mining company would become non-viable in the long term if it focused only on the production facets of its business without monitoring the financial and marketing aspects. Without profitability, return on investment for shareholders suffers; without marketing, customers for the product would be lost.

Senior management should be heavily involved with the development of CSFs because of their expertise in the business. However, more successful organisations have shown that consultation with customers, employees and suppliers as well as other stakeholders in the organisation results in more robust and better-quality CSFs.[3] Figure 2.3 illustrates sample CSFs for different industries.

FIGURE 2.2 Theory to practice[4]

Department of **Education and Training**

including the Office for **Early Childhood Education and Care**

Strategic plan 2009 – 2013

Vision: A clever, skilled and creative Queensland.

Mission: Our mission is to prepare every child and young person with the fundamentals for life success and to develop Queenslanders' skills to help drive economic prosperity and contribute to Queensland society.

Values: Excellence in endeavour; Respect for people; Integrity in service; Professionalism in performance; Environmental sustainability; Unity in purpose.

Giving children a flying start	Laying strong educational foundations
Objectives	
All Queensland children will have access to quality early childhood education and care	*Every young person will be well prepared for life success through learning and education*
Strategies	

Giving children a flying start — Strategies

- Develop and implement a Queensland early years strategy for greater integration of all early years services.
- Achieve greater integration of infrastructure and service delivery planning responsive to community needs.
- Provide the legislative basis to implement national quality standards and streamline regulatory requirements for early childhood services.
- Support the implementation of universal access to kindergarten in Queensland through:
  - centre-based service delivery models
  - unique solutions such as mobile and outreach for some small or isolated communities
  - core funding subsidies as well as additional subsidies which recognise disadvantage
  - a quality learning program and resources for teachers
  - better information management which tracks child enrolment and provides performance data.
- Continue to implement the Bound for Success and pre-prep initiatives which provide access to early education in discrete Indigenous communities.
- Work with the sector to attract and retain a diverse and highly skilled early childhood workforce, including qualified early childhood teachers.
- Establish Early Learning and Care Centres and Indigenous Children and Family Centres, in collaboration with the Australian Government.
- Support the sector to implement quality early childhood reforms.

Laying strong educational foundations — Strategies

- Provide and support high quality Prep programs to build on the foundations of increased investment in early childhood education and care.
- Improve performance of all students in literacy, numeracy and science through targeted initiatives, including implementing the government response to the *Queensland Education Performance Review*.
- Continue to ensure consistent, high quality teaching and learning across the State, through the *Queensland Curriculum, Assessment and Reporting Framework* and participation in the National Curriculum from 2011.
- Increase student attendance rates to ensure all children are engaged in learning.
- Foster strong students, strong results and strong futures for Indigenous children, designed to close the gap in educational outcomes.
- Improve educational outcomes in schools in disadvantaged communities.
- Strengthen educational outcomes for students with a disability.
- Support children's holistic well-being through health and physical activity programs; strategies that support positive behaviour; and learning environments that encourage creative thinking and actions as global citizens.
- Introduce reforms to improve the quality of teaching across all schools at all stages of teachers' career cycles.
- Encourage strong school leadership to improve outcomes for all students.
- Provide rich digital learning environments across all modes of delivery.

Performance indicators

Proportion of Queensland children enrolled in a quality kindergarten program.	Proportion of students at or above the national minimum standard in reading, writing and numeracy.
Proportion of Indigenous children and children in disadvantaged communities enrolled in a quality kindergarten program.	Queensland's relative performance against other Australian jurisdictions in literacy, numeracy and science.
	The gap between Indigenous and non-Indigenous reading, writing and numeracy achievements.

The full version of the Strategic plan can be found at: **www.education.qld.gov.au/strategic/planning**

FIGURE 2.2 (continued)

NSW Department of Health—Strategic Plan to 2010

Vision and Goals (Vision/ Mission)	'Healthy People—Now and in the Future' • To keep people healthy • To provide the health care that people need • To deliver high quality services • To manage health services well						
Strategic Direction (CSFs)	Make prevention everybody's business	Create better experiences for people using health services	Strengthen primary health and continuing care in the community	Build regional and other partnerships for health	Make smart choices about the costs and benefits of health services	Build a sustainable health workforce	Be ready for new risks and opportunities
Measuring Success (KPIs)	Improved health through reduced obesity, smoking, illicit drug use and risk drinking	Ensuring high quality care	Reduced avoidable hospital admissions through early intervention and prevention and better access to community-based services	Improved outcomes in mental health	Make the most effective use of resources for health	Build a sustainable workforce	Ensure the NSW health system is ready for new risks and opportunities
Targets (PIs)	• Continue to reduce smoking rates by 1% each year to 2010, then by 0.5% to 2016 • Reduce total risk drinking to below 25% by 2012 • Hold illicit drug use below 1.5% • Stop the growth of childhood obesity by holding it at the 2004 level of 25% by 2010. Then reduce levels to 22% by 2016 • Prevent further increases in levels of adult obesity which are currently at 50%	• Develop the means to track and reduce patient fails in hospitals • Reduce unplanned/ unexpected hospital re-admissions within 28 days • Reduce the portion of wrong patient/site/proce-dures incidents • Reduce 'sentinel' events from the current low level of one per 70,300 procedures undertaken in NSW public hospitals (Sentinel events are system failures that could potentially or actually lead to serious harm) • Work with other States and Territories to establish a robust measure of quality within the next five	• Reduce avoidable hospital admissions by 15% within five years for people who should not need to come to hospital for the following: Cellulitis, a skin inflammation caused by bacteria; deep vein thrombosis; community-acquired pneumonia; urinary tract infections; certain chronic respiratory disorders such as emphysema and chronic obstructive pulmonary disorder; bronchitis and asthmas; certain blood disorders such as anaemia; and musculotendinous disorders such as acute back pain	• Increase the percentage of people aged 15–64 years of age with a mental illness who are employed to 34% by 2016 (together with other agencies) • Increase the community participation rates of people with a mental illness by 40% by 2016 (together with other agencies)	• Increase the share of health budget allocated to prevention and early intervention • Improve access to health funding between Area Health Services by improving the equitable share of resources using a population-based Resource Distribution Formula • Increase the effectiveness of resource allocation through the continuum of care	• Reduce staff turnover in line with industry best practice • Reduce the incidence of workplace injuries • Reduce the number of paid sick leave hours taken per year by full-time employees by 5% each year until 2009 and sustain improvement • Increase the proportion and distribution of Aboriginal staff in order to meet the demand for services • Increase the proportion and distribution of clinical staff in order to meet the demand for services • Increase in job redesign changes related to different	• Progress implementation of an integrated risk management framework in each Health Service • Continually update disaster response capability of the NSW health system • Review adequacy of population health surveillance and early warning systems • Assess research outputs to ensure they are driven by health priorities and policies

FIGURE 2.3 Examples of CSFs for different industries

Industry	Possible critical success factors (CSFs)	Reasoning
Training organisation	Completion/graduation rates	Indicates success and effectiveness of the organisation's programs
	Human resources	Ensures availability and retention of qualified teaching staff
	Financial management	Provides funding for student places and teaching staff
Retail organisation	Customer service	Retaining current customers costs less than enticing new customers
	Product differentiation	Organisations such as David Jones are renowned for quality products and a one-stop shop for consumers
Mining company	Infrastructure	Ensures availability and reliability of mining equipment and transport network to customers
	Customer satisfaction	Product is supplied to contracted specification
	Human resources	The mining industry facing a shortage of front-line operators and professional staff

SKILLS PRACTICE

1 Sometimes, relating business concepts to something we understand, such as our home environment, makes them easier to understand and relate to. View your family as a business and look at its focus for the next year. List four CSFs that would help your family achieve its goals in the next year.

2 Using your current or a previous business environment, list four CSFs for that organisation.

In the example of the diversified finance organisation, the seven CSFs chosen will drive the organisation during the next planning cycle to achieve a greater market share of the business. KPIs are then developed to support the CSFs, which will help shape the operational plans of the organisation, by each division, branch, department or section. Possible KPIs and general performance indicators are illustrated for the example in Figure 2.4. From Figure 2.4 you can see how operational plans can easily be developed from a useful set of CSFs and KPIs because they clearly point the way to the next planning cycle.

Key performance indicators

KPIs are those indicators of performance that are seen as being of great importance to the success of the business of the organisation. While an organisation may use a number of performance

FIGURE 2.4 KPIs for a sample organisation

CSFs	Service sales	Human resources	Business culture	Risk/financial management	Communication	Systems and technology	Infrastructure
KPIs	• Marketing • Advertising • Service • Sales	• Skills • Training and education • Benefits and rewards systems	• Attitudes • Methodology • Relationships • Loyalty • Identity	• Strategy and tactics • Profitability • Efficiency	• Vertical • External • Horizontal • Internal	• Automated systems • Manual systems	• Technical and administrative reporting • Formal and informal interaction • Control and responsibility • Coordination
Performance indicators	• Projections made/missed • Staffing levels (FTE) • Revenue growth • Sales growth (units and value) • Profit margin • Market share • Advertising return on investment • Product and customer mix	• Average months to promotion by position • Education hours/costs per employee • Education levels of new hires • Comparative salary data for key personnel and in general • Cost of benefits × salary costs • Revenue × employee	• Premises occupancy costs × industry average • Personnel costs × industry average • General costs × industry • Employee satisfaction ratings • Public perception (image) • Market segment • Product mix • Customer mix • Vision, mission and goal statements	• Major income statement items and ratios: – operating profit/loss – return on assets – return on equity • Major balance sheet items and ratios: – return on assets/equity – leverage – long-term debt × short-term debt • Off balance sheet items × balance sheet items	• Audit results • Employee understanding of vision, mission and goals • Perceptions by level • Coordination between departments • Public image change • Advertising costs and frequency • Frequency and nature of communications • Number of channels of communication used	• Architecture adequacy • Systems costs × industry average • Average system duration • Systems cost × revenue • Systems utilisation rate • Number of sub-systems • Number of incompatible systems • Capacity × usage • Disaster recovery capability • Value-added measures	• Redundancy/overlap of functions • Mismatch of authority and responsibility • Overlap of responsibility and/or control • Change in the number of departments/units • Accuracy of charge-backs and transfer pricing • Responsiveness to environmental change • Audit results

indicators to measure its performance, there will always be certain indicators that are identified by an organisation as being of particular importance in any given operational year or cycle. For example, if the strategic and operational emphasis in a year is to boost market share in order to protect the organisation's position commercially, then key performance indicators for that year are likely to be of the type that will measure such things as sales growth, average sales costs, profitability of sales and percentage of income by source. These could be collectively captured in a KPI that might read:

Sales growth

This indicates that the focus for the whole organisation for that year would be on growing sales and increasing the profitability of sales to ensure economic viability. It also means that major decisions, projects, budgets and expenditure would be analysed in light of this KPI.

By way of a public-sector example, if an agency were to become a commercial entity, operating in the market as well as supplying services to government, it would need to identify what the most important issues were for implementing that change. For example, policies would need to be rewritten, a new enterprise bargaining agreement might need to be negotiated, a different management organisation and style might be necessary and quick decision making may need to be facilitated. A KPI that would in part determine the success of the change might be:

Change management

Any organisation will have a number of performance indicators to help it manage performance across the organisation. Each of these will relate to a specific KPI, as illustrated in Figure 2.5.

Note how the two examples of a KPI above—sales growth and change management—relate to results or ends. A KPI is usually written from the point of view of the means or actions having been completed. This method helps you to focus on the end result.

KPIs will be different for each organisation, as they will relate to what is important for a specific organisation, at a specific point in time, in a particular environment. There are no key performance indicators that are common to all organisations. KPIs are developed from the CSFs identified in the

FIGURE 2.5 Relationship of performance indicators to key performance indicators

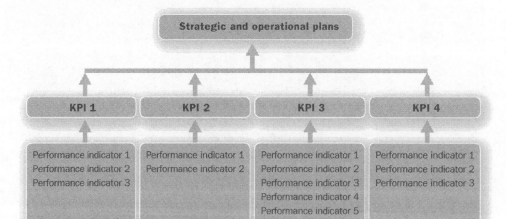

organisation's strategic and operational plans. As these plans are enterprise-specific, KPIs will be different for each organisation. An organisation develops KPIs to help it monitor and achieve the required performance. KPIs are also known as key result areas (KRAs). Use whichever term your organisation has adopted.

CHECK YOUR UNDERSTANDING

1. Identify the KPIs for your organisation for the current planning cycle.
2. Identify the performance indicators (PIs) for your immediate work area for the current planning cycle.
3. How do the KPIs for your organisation and your immediate work area tie in with your own performance objectives for the current planning period? (If you do not have any performance objectives, think about your own plans and ambitions.)

Composition of a key performance indicator

A performance indicator identifies what aspects of performance need to be measured. To be useful, KPIs must clearly relate to ends rather than means or, to put it another way, the results rather than the action of achieving the results. That is, KPIs need to be directly related to results, outputs, consequences, payoffs and performance.[5] Behaviours relating to the culture of the organisation, customer service or specific goals may also be expressed as results and thus encompassed within KPIs. Skilfully written KPIs drive the desired values and behaviours through the organisation. Actions are usually found in operational plans, not KPIs. Figure 2.6 illustrates the difference between means and ends.

Performance indicators focus on the ends, while operational plans focus on the means—that is, how the results are achieved. A KPI is focused on the result or an end point, because it provides the means by which we interpret a single result or set of results, as demonstrated in the NSW Department of Health Strategic Plan to 2010, by the KPI 'Improved health through reduced obesity, smoking, illicit drug use and risk drinking'.[6] The result in this example is the reduction in the listed items.

FIGURE 2.6 Means and ends

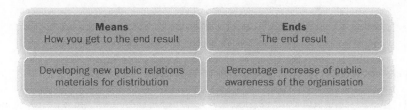

What are performance indicators?

Performance indicators are measures of different aspects, or parts, of the organisation's performance. The total performance of an organisation is the sum of its different parts, and these parts must perform adequately to ensure that the organisation achieves its overall goals. Performance indicators play an important role in focusing all staff on what significant achievements need to be accomplished in the current operating period or cycle of the organisation. Performance indicators specify the type of evidence the organisation requires to demonstrate that strategic and operational plans have achieved the desired results.

The examples in Figure 2.7 have been taken from a range of industries and the public sector to demonstrate the nature of a performance indicator. You will notice that the indicators are exactly that—indicators of what will be measured. They do not specify the actual measure but indicate what information must be collected and what the organisation will use to measure its performance. For example, the indicator 'customer complaints' declares that the issue of customer complaints is important to the organisation, for whatever reason. Exactly what will be measured may vary: the actual number of complaints, the type of complaints, the cause of the complaints, or the rise or fall in the number of complaints. What is measured and where in the organisation it is measured will depend on what specific things need to be measured to demonstrate attainment of the performance indicator. Specific measures are found in the performance standards and objectives of staff throughout the organisation. These are dealt with in Chapters 4 and 5.

FIGURE 2.7 Sample performance indicators

- Number of staff developed
- Number of accidents
- Employee costs per staff member
- Premises occupancy costs
- Public perception
- Product mix
- Customer mix
- Vacancy fill rate
- Cash flow
- Percentage income by source
- Customer complaints
- Total transactions by type
- Authority delegation levels
- Channels of communication
- Competitor advertising
- Compliance testing
- Responsiveness to change
- Number of new policies introduced

- Sales growth
- Profit margin
- Education levels of new hires
- Advertising return on investment
- Number of complaints (EEO, IR, Grievances)
- Average processing time
- Average sales costs
- Overdue balances
- Employee satisfaction level
- Error rates
- Changes in customer demographics
- Staff turnover by reason
- System failure rate
- Overlap of functions
- Legislation awareness
- System architecture adequacy
- Systems utilisation rate
- Savings from new technology

Why are key performance indicators needed?

Key performance indicators are needed to focus all the individuals in an organisation on the vital aspects of its operation in order to achieve its desired and often publicly stated results. KPIs can be used in a number of ways:

- to assess the current performance level of an organisation

- to support a framework within an organisation that will foster best practice

- to focus effort on particular areas of the organisation

- to empower employees to make decisions and take appropriate action

- to underpin performance standards and objectives for the next business cycle

- to produce consistent and reliable management information on which to base decisions

- to provide data on which to base training and development activities

- to identify areas in which interventions need to be made

- to identify and define new organisational purposes or directions

- to provide criteria for job evaluation.

Research suggests a core of fundamental reasons for the development of KPIs:[7]

- process improvement

- benchmarking

- strategic and business planning

- enterprise bargaining

- new systems such as remuneration systems, and technology advances

- supporting the introduction of self-managed teams

- increasing productivity.

If an organisation is to perform well it must manage that performance. Performance indicators provide specific targets and guidelines on which the organisation can base its decisions and actions to achieve the performance it requires.

Before looking at the steps involved in developing key performance indicators, an example may be of assistance. Consider an intensive care unit in a hospital and all the medical equipment it requires to monitor and keep its patients alive. The medical staff have, in this equipment, all they require to monitor their seriously ill patients' health. Constant monitoring of the equipment tells the medical staff whether the patient is breathing properly and whether their heart rate is normal, and notes changes in brain activity. This medical equipment gives the information necessary to assess the condition of the patients and to make decisions on whether they will recover or need further medical assistance. It has been developed to monitor the key performance indicators required to keep the patients in intensive care alive. These KPIs have been identified by skilful professionals who have the knowledge of what is imperative to monitor in a patient and what is required to keep patients alive. The equipment has been developed according to this information.

In a business context, the corporate head office of a global mining organisation requires accurate operational reporting and budgeting of its individual mining operations in order to make decisions concerning diversification or expansion of its business. The organisation will identify, through its senior management team, what it is imperative to monitor in the mining environment in order to retain the viability of the business. By means of the organisation's KPIs, the reporting and budgets have been tailored to deliver this vital information.

So choosing the KPIs that are most appropriate for your organisation may not be a life-and-death situation, as in the intensive care unit of a hospital, but poorly written and focused KPIs could spell poor performance or the eventual demise of an organisation.

Steps in developing key performance indicators

Developing KPIs for your work unit requires some care. The more you know your organisation and the industry in which it operates, the easier this process will be. Remember, KPIs need to be clear, measurable and focused.

Step 1a Gather existing data

1.1   Identify and gather copies of the organisation's vision, mission and values statements.

1.2   Review the organisation's strategic plan and the critical success factors contained in the strategic plan.

1.3   Establish the priorities and important aspects of these documents, ensuring the validity of the data being gathered.

1.4   Senior management (with input from other managers throughout the organisation) should already have put these documents, including CSFs, into place.

1.5   Where this has not been done you will need to talk to senior management about the need for these things.

Many organisations do not possess statements of vision, mission and values, strategic plans and critical success factors. Where these documents do not exist, follow from step 1.6 below.

Step 1b Develop KPIs with no strategic/planning documents

1.6   You will need to obtain as much information as possible about where you think your organisation is going and what it wants to achieve.

1.7   You may talk to senior managers and your own superiors, and gather ideas from your peers.

1.8   It is likely that you will then need to make some decisions about what is important for your work unit for the next 12 months and where your work unit can make specific contributions to the organisation.

Now go to Step 2.

   Often, the reality is that if you want your team of people to achieve, you have to take the bull by the horns and implement KPIs without the other supporting documents. The danger with developing your own KPIs is that, as the organisation does not have strategic and planning documents (statements of vision, mission and values), it may tend to change its mind and direction frequently. If you are monitoring for this, you can make appropriate changes to your KPIs as required.

Step 2 Understand the critical success factors

2.1   Understand the CSFs and what they stand for: you will base your KPIs on them.

2.2   Identify why they are important and how they fit into the strategic and operational plans of the organisation.

Step 3 Draft the key performance indicators

3.1 Draft between five and seven KPIs for your area of responsibility that can be directly linked to the CSFs. To begin with, you can just jot down ideas. The main aim is to catch the thought and record it so that you can refine it or discard it later as you work on the basic ideas.

3.2 KPIs can be more powerful if you involve staff in their development.[8] In this way you gain the benefit of each individual's experience and develop commitment in the process from everyone at an early stage.

Step 4 Check that the KPIs fit with the organisational objectives

4.1 Once you have drafted the KPIs, check that they tie in with the strategic and operational objectives of the organisation.

4.2 Check that they are sufficiently clear for staff to develop team or work group KPIs for their areas.

4.3 It must also be possible for KPIs to be used to guide the setting of standards and performance objectives (see Chapter 5).

4.4 It is an important function of management to ensure that the above matters are dealt with appropriately so that staff are able to make clear, tangible contributions to the organisation through their performance standards or objectives.

Step 5 Adopt the key performance indicators

5.1 Once the draft KPIs have been vetted and approved by your superiors, and you are sure they are the ones that will lead to the right measures being invoked, you can adopt them.

5.2 Research has shown that, to be effective, KPIs should be widely disseminated and made public so that staff are exposed to them consistently.

5.3 KPIs need to be reinforced by management through what they say and do.[9] Without this support, KPIs are ineffective.

5.4 From this step on, managers must ensure that individual and team objectives support the KPIs.

SKILLS PRACTICE

1 Develop three KPIs for your organisation in addition to those you already know of.

2 Develop four KPIs for a newly established IT organisation breaking into the market.

3 Develop two KPIs for a manufacturing organisation.

4 Develop three KPIs for a telecommunications organisation competing in a global economy.

5 Develop two KPIs for the current Prime Minister of Australia and his political party.

SKILL AND KNOWLEDGE APPLICATION

TASK

Review your organisation's CSFs and KPIs. Analyse what they tell you about your organisation. Are they adhered to in decision making and operational plans? If there are none in the organisation, what does this say about your organisation?

CONCLUSION

Key performance indicators are fundamental to a sound performance management system. They provide the focus for measurement in the organisation across all divisions, branches, departments and work groups, and form the basis of individual performance objectives. They are required to underpin the efficient operation of the organisation, and if they are developed skilfully they can, and should, contribute directly to the attainment of the strategic and operational plan of the organisation. KPIs are used in conjunction with critical success factors, which are identified by the organisation as aspects that are critical to its long-term survival. Thus, KPIs flow from operational plans and CSFs, which in turn flow from strategic plans. KPIs are made up of two components: a specific performance and some sort of indicator for the performance. Five steps have been outlined in this chapter to assist you to develop suitable CSFs and KPIs for your purposes.

CASE STUDY

The mine manager of an underground coal mine has a major problem. The mine is doing badly against one of its KPIs—meet contract specifications—and the mine manager cannot understand why. There are performance indicators that monitor and measure the performance of this KPI that are closely linked to quality procedures, none of which seemed to be contributing to the KPI that required that the coal product meet its specification requirement consistently. It appears that the customers are receiving fewer and fewer shipments of coal that meet their contracted specifications. This has led to many problems in the end use of the coal, with the iron furnaces not producing the temperatures needed for the production processes.

The mine manager has requested that you, as the marketing representative of the mine, investigate why this KPI is not being met. All departments that handle the coal product are fully trained in the quality procedures to deliver the coal to specification. Performance indicators have been set as follows:

- contract specification known and communicated
- knowledge of internal procedures
- coal preparation plant infrastructure operating at full capacity.

QUESTION

Why do you think the mine is not meeting the KPI of 'meet contract specifications'?

JOB AIDS

> Key performance indicators are generated from critical success factors as well as strategic plans. Critical success factors are broad-based areas of activity which are considered to be vital and must be performed to ensure the success of the organisation.

> Key performance indicators specify the type of evidence the organisation requires to demonstrate that strategic and operational plans have achieved the required results.

> Key performance indicators are needed to focus attention on what is important to the organisation.

> Key performance indicators are directly linked to results or outputs.

> There are five stages in the development of key performance indicators. See the checklist for this chapter.

> Performance indicators underpin key performance indicators.

Sample performance indicators from Figure 2.7

- Number of staff developed
- Number of accidents
- Employee costs per staff member
- Premises occupancy costs
- Public perception
- Product mix
- Customer mix
- Vacancy fill rate
- Cash flow
- Percentage income by source
- Customer complaints
- Total transactions by type
- Authority delegation levels
- Channels of communication
- Competitor advertising
- Compliance testing
- Responsiveness to change
- Number of new policies introduced
- Sales growth
- Profit margin
- Education levels of new hires
- Advertising return on investment
- Number of complaints (EEO, IR, Grievances)
- Average processing time
- Average sales costs
- Overdue balances
- Employee satisfaction level
- Error rates
- Changes in customer demographics
- Staff turnover by reason
- System failure rate
- Overlap of functions
- Legislation awareness
- System architecture adequacy
- Systems utilisation rate
- Savings from new technology

✓ CHECKLISTS

To prepare critical success factors you need to review:

❏ Organisational vision

❏ Organisational mission

❏ Organisational values

❏ Strategic plans

To prepare key performance indicators you need to:

❏ Gather existing data.

❏ Understand the critical success factors.

❏ Draft the key performance indicators.

❏ Check that the KPIs fit with the organisational objectives.

❏ Adopt the key performance indicators.

References

1 Jones, R. 2010, 2nd edn. *Managing Human Resource Systems*. Pearson Australia, Frenchs Forest, Sydney, p. 115.

2 Boynton, A.C. & Zmud, R.W. 1984. 'An assessment of critical success factors.' *Sloan Management Review*, 25(4), pp. 17–27.

3 Peters, T. & Waterman, R. 1984. *In Search of Excellence: Lessons from America's Best Run Companies*. Harper & Row: Sydney; Peters, T. 1989. *Thriving on Chaos*, Pan Books: London.

4 Queensland Department of Education and Training 2009. *Strategic Plan 2009–2013*, <www.education.qld.gov.au/strategic/planning> accessed 30 November 2009, copyright in this work is owned by or licensed to the State of Queensland (represented by the Department of Education and Training), PO Box 15033 City East QLD 4002 Australia and is reproduced with its permission. No part may be further reproduced in hardcopy form, electronically or by any other process without the express written permission of the Department; NSW Department of Health n.d., *Strategic Plan to 2010: A New Direction for NSW, Where We Want to Be in 2010*, <www.health.nsw.gov.au>, © NSW Department of Health.

5 Kaufman, R. 1988. 'Preparing useful performance indicators.' *Training and Development Journal*, September, pp. 80–83.

6 NSW Department of Health n.d. *A New Direction for NSW, Where We Want to Be in 2010*, <www.health.nsw.gov.au>, p. 15.

7 Kaufman, op. cit., 1988, pp. 80–83.

8 Australian Manufacturing Council 1995. *Key Performance Indicators Manual*. Pitman Publishing: Melbourne.

9 Australian Manufacturing Council, op. cit., 1995.

CHAPTER THREE

Operational plans

Learning outcomes

After reading this chapter you should be able to:

* describe an operational plan
* list those levels of management most closely involved in developing and executing operational plans
* state the items that may be found in an operational plan
* state the benefits of having an operational plan
* explain the importance of operational plans in times of change
* describe the process of achieving goals
* explain why operational plans are fluid documents
* describe the steps in writing an operational plan
* explain the relationship between operational plans and performance management.

INTRODUCTION

Operational planning is an important part of running an organisation. It is through operational plans that strategy is implemented and organisations attain their strategic objectives. Without operational plans, strategy is unlikely to be achieved, affecting program outcomes and profitability. The various operational plans for any organisation should dovetail to form a comprehensive guide as to how the organisation must work and perform to deliver the results required by the senior management group, board or government minister. There can be many operational plans in a single organisation, depending on the number of work units within it. Figure 3.1 demonstrates the number of operational plans that may be developed in any one organisation and the levels at which they are developed.

FIGURE 3.1 Dovetailing of operational plans

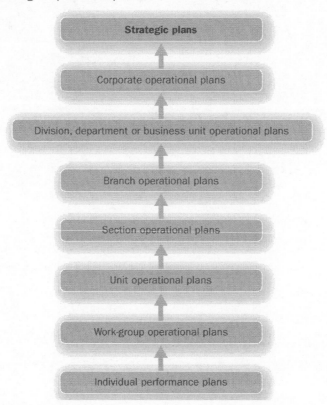

The terms 'operational plan' and 'business plan' are used interchangeably in the literature and in many organisations. In this book they are referred to as operational plans, although many private organisations call them business plans. It is more common in the public service to name them operational plans. However, there is a drift towards the use of the term 'business plan' as more and more public service agencies move towards full cost recovery of services or are completely corporatised.

It is in the operational plan that the strategies of the organisation can be actioned. It is also where the organisation finds out that the strategies decided on may not work because of local conditions or factors in the marketplace, or for a whole range of other legitimate reasons. Such information needs to be fed back to senior management so that suitable changes can be made to the strategic objectives of the organisation if the feedback warrants such a change. In Figure 1.6 in Chapter 1, you will recall that operational planning is about relatively routinised, operationally specific, small-scale change, and is resource-driven. Operational plans are usually drawn up by middle and supervisory management. Placing responsibility for this function with these two levels of management does not diminish the influence or importance of operational planning, as those who are closest to the coalface are the people who know how strategic intent can be implemented (provided they know what it is). In fact, as supervisors are the first line of management, it is they who have the greatest responsibility to develop and provide input to operational plans and implement them through working with their teams and individual workers. Figure 3.2 illustrates the relationship between strategy and operational plans.

FIGURE 3.2 The relationship between strategy and operational plans

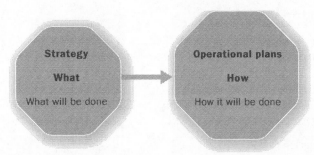

CHECK YOUR UNDERSTANDING

1 Describe the purpose of operational plans.
2 Explain the relationship between the strategic plan and operational plans.

Definition of an operational plan

Operational plans are specific types of plans that show exactly how the organisation or parts of it will achieve the goals set by the organisation. An operational plan is an action plan. It contains details about how the strategic plan will be achieved for the area in which you work. It can be written at a divisional, branch, department, section, unit or work-group level. Operational plans convert strategy into specific, detailed plans for the implementation of the organisation's strategic objectives. To be able to put an operational plan together, you must clearly understand the organisation's strategic objectives. A manager must be able to interpret the strategic plan and then convert that plan into tangible, workable operational objectives and strategies. The operational planning stage moves from the high-level, broad statements found in the strategic plan to specific things that must be done by all the members of the work team to achieve the strategic goals. This is illustrated in Figure 3.3.

FIGURE 3.3 Conversion of strategic plans to operational plans

Items covered in an operational plan may include:

1 Utilisation of resources

- money

- equipment

- plant

- time

- staff

- information

- technology

2 Delivery of product

- provision of services to customers for no fees, i.e. government agencies

- service to meet agreed standards of service levels

- operating within agreed budget

3 Allocation of agreed budget or profit margin

- varies with the type of organisation

- differs between government departments

- implements policy to a budget

- departments operating as government-owned enterprises (GOEs) that need to make a profit.[1]

Written plans should be formal and structured in a logical and sequential way to guide the daily operations of workers and management in an organisation. These plans also inform senior management of how the organisation is progressing towards the strategic objectives, and provide them with monitoring benchmarks to make sure everything is on track. The contents of these plans will vary, as mentioned above, according to the type of organisation in which you work. However, some of the areas that might be included in an operational plan are:

- marketing

- communication (internal and external)

- human resources

- purchasing

- finance
- sales
- how services will be delivered
- how policy will be implemented
- production
- potential problems
- technology upgrades
- systems
- structure
- growth
- market share or number of clients serviced
- quality
- research and development
- service delivery levels.

There is research evidence from around the world suggesting that organisations that have formal operational planning are more likely to succeed than those that do not have formal written operational plans.[2] The operational plan may be a large document or relatively small, varying from an individual's performance plan to that of a division or department. Individual performance plans usually cover three to four A4 pages, while the operational plan of a division might be a long, complex document because of the size of the work unit and the number of things it must address to ensure that strategic objectives are achieved.

As operational plans are usually quite lengthy documents, no full examples are provided here. However, the following websites allow access to full operational plans. It is recommended that you take the time to view some of these plans.

OPERATIONAL PLAN WEBSITES

ACIAR—Australian Centre for International Agricultural Research

www.aciar.gov.au

Our Publications > Annual Operational Plan

Forest & Wood Products Australia

www.fwpa.com.au

About Us > Operational Policies > Quick Find > Latest Operational Plan

ASADA—Australian Sports Anti-Doping Authority

www.asada.gov.au

Resources > Annual Reports > Current ASADA Annual Reports

Please note that at the time of publication, these websites were current. If when using the text the websites are no longer operational, use your chosen search engine on the Internet to locate other organisations' operational and strategic plans. There are many available in both the public and private sectors.

SKILLS PRACTICE

Web-based activity. Utilising the links provided above, download the Forest & Wood Products Australia operational plan. Answer the following questions about the operational plan.

1   Identify the various parts of the operational plan.
2   What has the organisation promised to deliver through its operational plan?
3   Identify the critical success factors for the organisation.
4   List the key performance indicators and their associated aims.

Why have an operational plan?

In a constantly changing world, few things are certain and few things stay the same. This argument is often put forward as the reason for not writing an operational plan, but there is a fundamental flaw in this argument. The process of developing an operational plan forces you to do some specific thinking on issues, opportunities, challenges and operational matters in general. Thus, you are more closely informed on what your work group needs to achieve and how it can be done. If you don't work through the process you are much less prepared for change when it occurs. If the goalposts are moved, or a competitor or government changes tactics, with an operational plan you will be more flexible in your approach to meet changed strategic objectives. Being more informed about potential opportunities and threats to the strategic and operational objectives you have set means you can change tack easily, without major upheaval, and still achieve the strategic objectives. The concept is similar to the movement of a sailing boat as it changes tack to catch the wind: although it may change tack a number of times, it is still heading in the right general direction. Figure 3.4 illustrates this concept.

Sometimes it will be difficult to see how the operational plan is contributing to the overall strategic objectives of the organisation or how individual performance plans contribute. If this is the case you should talk to your manager to clarify the situation. The process of achieving objectives or goals is not a linear one. You do not go straight from point A to point B. In life,

FIGURE 3.4 Changing tack

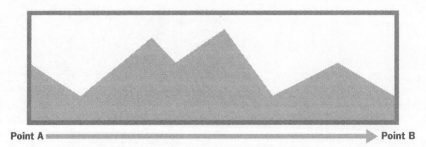

Point A ➜ Point B

before we reach our goals we must often divert our attention or swerve because of circumstances beyond our control. However, if you have clearly written goals that you understand, these will keep bringing you back on track until you achieve your goal, as Figure 3.4 illustrates.

In today's organisational environment you not only need to be flexible—you need to be able to react quickly to changes that occur in your workplace or industry, in government policy and among your competitors. Developing an operational plan enables you to use resources more efficiently, improve quality, make decisions more quickly, identify cost savings, and provide specific direction for staff so that they know where they are going. Operational plans are not just for larger organisations. Smaller organisations will benefit from writing and implementing such processes in the same way larger organisations will. Their strategic and operational plans may not be as comprehensive as those of larger organisations, but they are no less relevant.

A written operational plan clearly establishes what needs to be achieved and how it will be achieved in the next planning cycle. Individuals can refer to it at any time to see if they are on track or can use it to identify problems in reaching the objectives set down in the operational plan. The difference between strategic planning and operational planning is that strategic planning identifies *what* has to be done and the operational plan identifies *how* it has to be done. If the operational plan is written, it is easy to change if circumstances require. You will also be able to anticipate the consequences of any changes, and thus you can take appropriate action before anything becomes a problem. Operational plans need to be fluid documents. Because of the nature of organisations, the environment in which they operate and the way they are managed, these plans need to be capable of change. They must not be set in concrete. If circumstances, conditions or legislation change, you must be able to change the way you operate. How an operational plan looks at the end of a cycle can be quite different from how it looked at the beginning. For this reason it is wise to use version numbers and dates on operational plans to make sure that everyone is working off the same plan and towards the same strategic goals.

CHECK YOUR UNDERSTANDING

3   Why should organisations have operational plans?
4   Should you stick rigidly to the plan once it has been written, or should it be used merely as a guide? Give reasons for your answer.
5   State the key advantage of having a written operational plan.

Writing an operational plan

To write an operational plan you need access to your strategic plans and objectives, and you need to understand clearly what these plans and objectives say about the strategies and objectives to be reached. From there, the critical success factors and the key performance indicators will guide you as to what the priorities will be for the next planning cycle. For example, if communication was a critical success factor for the next planning cycle, some of the key performance indicators might be:

1   misunderstandings
2   clarity

3   brevity

4   time spent.

The operational plan would then need to incorporate how you will implement the CSF and the four KPIs. In planning how to achieve the objectives or targets that have been set for your work group, you need to incorporate how you will achieve the KPIs through actioning the agreed objectives. In developing an operational plan you will need to outline some measures for the KPIs as well as operational strategies that set out how you will action the KPIs in your day-to-day work. Remember to set specific performance standards for the KPIs (see Chapter 5). A sample measure for each KPI might be:

- number of misunderstandings

- clarity of written and oral communication

- brevity of written and oral communication

- time spent communicating internally.

Figure 3.5 illustrates some of the records that might be kept to monitor the KPIs.

FIGURE 3.5 Monitoring progress

Records to be kept:
- Problems with communication (internal and external)
- Number of communication problems that are handed to senior management for solving
- Number of times written communication has to be rewritten
- Number of meetings that run over time
- Length of meetings
- Length of written communications

Preliminary steps in writing an operational plan

Step 1
Review strategic plans and objectives and operational plans at the level above you.

Step 2
Understand the CSFs and the KPIs and why they were developed.

Step 3
Think about how the CSFs and KPIs affect your work group.

Step 4
Review the operation of your work group.

Step 5
Identify areas in which you can set operational objectives that will support the strategic plan.

Step 6

Identify things that you must do to maintain current performance.

Step 7

Identify the resources you will need to support steps 5 and 6.

How you put these steps together to write an operational plan is discussed in the next section.

SKILL AND KNOWLEDGE APPLICATION

Assume you are in charge of an accounting section in an organisation. Using the communication example above and the information in Figure 3.5 as a guide, outline the contents of an operational plan for your area. Use only dot points for how you will implement the communication CSF in your area. Include in your outline the following:

TASK

1   What specific resources might you use to meet the CSF and KPIs, and how would you use them?
2   How will the CSF and KPIs affect the day-to-day operations of your section?
3   Are there any other issues that you think might be pertinent from the list compiled in step 5 above?

Components of an operational plan

An operational plan is really an action plan of how you will go about achieving the strategic objectives of the organisation. The following components may form part of an operational plan:

1   an executive summary containing the highlights of the operational plan

2   a statement of the key assumptions on which the plan is based

3   recommendations regarding the contents or strategies in the operational plan

4   a statement of the strategic objectives relating to the work group for which you are creating the plan

5   an overview of what has to be achieved in the next planning cycle, incorporating the strategic requirements of the organisation

6   a statement of the operational objectives complete with the work group's performance standards (see Chapter 5)

7   a review of current operations, including present marketing, financial and workload management issues, and other appropriate issues

8   profiles of current clients/customers, products/services and suppliers

9   profiles of current staff

10   review of current management strategies

11   discussion of current competitive advantage or program results

12   identification of current problems or issues that may affect new plans

13   identification of the challenges ahead in the new planning cycle

14 a list of the operational objectives for the next planning cycle, the strategies that will be used to attain each objective, and how each objective will be evaluated. This involves detailing the specific actions that will be taken to achieve the objectives. Headings or sections that might be included in this component are as follows:

For the private sector:

- Marketing and sales
- Purchasing
- Production
- Human resources
- Organisational structure
- Systems
- Technology upgrades
- Financial information and budgets, including forecasts and profit targets
- Reporting structures.

For the public sector:

- Communication strategies
- Human resources
- Organisational structure
- Purchasing
- Financial information, including how budgets will be spent and any cost recovery details
- How services will be delivered
- How policy will be implemented
- Technology upgrades
- Systems
- Reporting structures.

There is likely to be more overlap between the private and public sectors than is suggested here, as this is a simplistic overview. It will depend on the type of function the public sector organisation performs. The above headings will provide a start to identifying what needs to be included in the operational plan. Further, you might also include:

15 discussion of any structural changes or changes to staffing required to support the new objectives

16 any supporting documentation required.

6   Why do you think there is a difference between the private and public sectors in the way they might put together an operational plan?

7   Why is it necessary to state the assumptions on which an operational plan is based?

8   What types of supporting documentation might be required for an operational plan?

The role of operational plans in performance management

If you have another look at several of the figures in this chapter, you will gain some idea of the relationship between operational plans and performance, especially the relationship between individual performance and the performance of the whole organisation. Once the operational plan has been approved, you need to begin its implementation. Implementation is harder than drawing up an operational plan because this is where you actually have to do what you have said you will do. The manager's job is to help staff establish the implementation and monitor progress towards the goals of the plan. Where things might be coming off the rails, the manager must act to bring things back on track.

Before staff can contribute to the objectives of the operational plan, and thus to the strategic direction of the organisation, they must set performance objectives for themselves (see Chapter 5). Strategic plans are implemented through operational plans. Operational plans are implemented through the individual performance objectives or standards of staff. This is an integral step in managing performance. A lack of integration at this point will render any performance management system ineffective.

To demonstrate the connection between performance and operational plans, we can use the example of a Stationery Clerk in the Corporate Services section of a large company. The job description identifies the function of the position as follows:

To ensure adequate stocks of stationery are held to meet the needs of daily requirements, to order stationery in accordance with financial delegations, and to ensure prompt delivery to users. The position also accepts requests for non-stocked stationery items and makes recommendations to the Corporate Services Manager after pricing these items.

A critical success factor for the planning period is cost reduction, and key performance indicators are:

- efficiency
- stock levels
- automation
- technology.

The operational plan for this section reads in part:

Objective 5:

Reduce levels of supplies to no more than three weeks stock based on annual usage figures and where there is a supply agreement in place with the nominated supplier.

While the Stationery Clerk would be expected to continue with routine maintenance activities such as ordering stationery, putting it away and processing stationery requests, a manager should also expect the stationery area to contribute to the cost reduction CSF of the organisation. This would require the Stationery Clerk to work out how much stock should be carried and whether there should be exceptions to the rule, whether there are any seasonal fluctuations in the demand for stationery, and whether any procedures should be changed to reduce costs. Consequently, any number of individual performance objectives could be written in consultation with the Stationery Clerk. Although clerks might not save millions of dollars, they would achieve some savings, and could be duly proud of their direct contribution to the organisation's strategy.

Managers must monitor the progress towards the operational and strategic goals of the organisation. Apart from regular reports such as financial statements, the manager needs to set individual performance standards with each employee to make sure that they are all working towards the operational and strategic goals of the organisation. Consequently, managing the individual performance of staff has a great influence on whether you achieve the operational objectives or not. Once the operational plan is complete and you are ready to implement it, unless you manage performance towards that plan there is not much point in having it! Managing performance is a complex process, however, and requires a number of skills that the Karpin Report identified were missing in Australian managers.[3] Part B of this book investigates some of these skills.

SKILLS PRACTICE

Look at your own performance plans and those of your staff. See if you can identify how these relate to the general strategic objectives of the organisation and to the operational plans of your branch, division or department.

CONCLUSION

Operational plans provide a more detailed guide to management and staff than strategic plans. They are the means by which strategy is converted into action to bring about results. It is the job of senior management to guide the development of these plans and to coordinate them. Middle management and supervisory management do most of the detailed work because they know how to apply strategy in the everyday activities of the areas they manage. An operational plan is the detailed blueprint for how the strategic objectives of an organisation will be achieved. While almost anything can be included in an operational plan to demonstrate how the strategy will be achieved, this chapter provides some of the basic broad headings that ought to appear in an operational plan.

Operational plans have two main purposes: (a) to set out how strategic objectives will be attained; and (b) to provide a starting point if the strategy alters for any reason so that the organisation can respond quickly to the various changes that affect organisations from time to time. Thus, an operational plan gives an organisation flexibility.

While an operational plan is based on the strategic plan, in developing it managers must also be guided by the critical success factors and key performance indicators that the organisation has identified. These will also help staff to identify their own performance standards when developing their performance plan for the next business cycle. Finally, the operational plan will guide staff and managers in developing individual performance plans.

CASE STUDY

Matthew and Rebekah have just started work with their organisation. During their interview and induction process, Matthew and Rebekah were informed of the performance management system in place at the organisation. During the induction they were given extensive information on how the process was administered. They were informed at induction that they would be involved in the development of their performance plans and objectives with their manager, and these would be agreed on and discussed with their manager.

Their manager has just supplied them with performance plans that she was given by the Human Resources department. Matthew and Rebekah's manager has made an appointment with them in four weeks' time to discuss the performance objectives set out for them for the next planning cycle. Matthew and Rebekah have not had previous experience of performance objectives and are confused because the information provided to them at their induction suggested that they would be involved in writing these plans with their manager. Matthew and Rebekah's careers to date have not included the use of performance management systems, so they are unsure about where to begin.

QUESTIONS

1   What documentation might it be appropriate for Matthew and Rebekah to utilise in preparation for their meeting?
2   How might Matthew and Rebekah's manager have better handled the situation?
3   What should Matthew and Rebekah do at this stage?
4   Do you think Matthew and Rebekah's manager needs further development in this area? If so, explain.

CHECKLISTS

Does your operational plan:

- [ ] have a clear connection or relationship to the strategic plan?
    - [ ] restate the strategic objectives?
    - [ ] give an overview of what has to be achieved in the next planning cycle?
    - [ ] have a clear connection to the CSFs and KPIs of the strategic plan?
    - [ ] contain a statement of how you will measure the above?
- [ ] describe how you will utilise the resources given to you?
    - [ ] contain a statement of operational objectives?
    - [ ] contain a detailed description of how each resource will be utilised?
- [ ] show how you will deliver the product or service expected of you?
- [ ] indicate how you will meet the allocated and agreed budget or profit margin?
- [ ] formally describe how you will achieve the required objectives over the next planning cycle?

References

1   Birt, I. 2010, 4th edn. *Writing your Plan for Small Business Success*. Pearson Australia: Frenchs Forest, Sydney, p. 3.
2   Birt, op. cit., 2010, pp. 3–4; Peters, T. & Waterman, R. 1984. *In Search of Excellence: Lessons from America's Best Run Companies*. Harper & Row: Sydney; Peters, T. 1989. *Thriving on Chaos*. Pan Books: London.
3   Karpin, D. (Chair). 1995. *Enterprising Nation: Renewing Australia's Managers to Meet the Challenges of the Asia-Pacific Century*. Report of the Industry Task Force on Leadership and Management Skills. AGPS: Canberra.

Strategy and operational plans are related

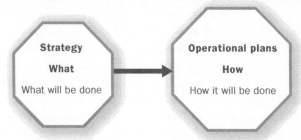

Strategic plans are converted into operational plans

Strategic plan
- High-level aims and objectives
- Covers whole organisation
- Main priorities for the organisation

Conversion
- Strategic plan broken into components:
  - department
  - division
  - branch
  - section

Operational plan
- Specific actions
- Assist in achieving strategic plan

Relationship of various operational plans to the strategic plan

Strategic plans

⬆

Corporate operational plans

⬆

Division, department or business unit operational plans

⬆

Branch operational plans

⬆

Section operational plans

⬆

Unit operational plans

⬆

Work-group operational plans

⬆

Individual performance plans

To assist you in the workplace, this Job Aid is reproduced on the accompanying CD located in the back of this book

PART B

Performance Management

In Part A there is a discussion about the changing nature of work and the workplace. One major change that has affected performance appraisals over the past five years or so is the move away from the traditional performance appraisal to a more comprehensive approach known as performance management. In this approach, people are seen as a core company asset.[1] The problem with performance appraisals is that people do not like them.[2] In research conducted by the University of Melbourne and Monash University, performance appraisals are rated as a failure due to unintended and dysfunctional outcomes and negative experiences.[3] Further, Lawson suggests that management has abused performance appraisals,[4] and that there is little agreement on the definition of the term. Other research has found that over 90% of performance appraisals are unsuccessful,[5] and that most employers are not satisfied with their performance appraisal processes.[6] Interestingly, Lawler found that performance appraisal systems do not motivate and guide individual development, effectively negating the primary reason organisations give for introducing them.[7]

Performance appraisal is one of the most misunderstood functions of human resource management. Many organisations assert that performance appraisals are necessary to give employees feedback, to identify development needs, and to decide on remuneration and, in some cases, promotions. Despite these claims, research reports that appraisals are a failure for employers as well.[8] Employees rarely receive feedback that is useful or motivating. Even more rarely do organisations actually do anything with the information collected from performance appraisals. It is commonplace for staff to receive performance appraisals without having played any role in developing their performance criteria or even being told what performance is expected of them. Performance appraisals are not working. Clearly, this is a management responsibility, as staff are unable to achieve culture change without the active participation of management. Research cited later in this chapter questions whether managers actually have the skills to implement performance appraisals. It is little wonder that the process does not work: this is because managers do not do it properly.

The problems with performance appraisal

If you take heed of the research mentioned above, you could not be blamed for deciding that performance appraisals are not worth the trouble of designing and implementing them. Despite this, the focus on improving the performance of people will remain part of the core agenda for the next generation of managers and executives. Indeed, a 2005 survey of 992 Australian HR professionals found that only 4% of respondents didn't have a formal system of appraisal (down from 7% in 2000 and 14% in 1990).[9] Performance appraisal reviews and judges the performance of individuals. On the basis of this judgment, a number of other decisions are made, including salary raises and promotions. Dessler, Griffiths and Lloyd-Walker identified the following three main steps of a performance appraisal:[10]

1 Define and understand the job: make sure you and your subordinate agree on his or her duties and job standards.

2 Appraise performance: this means comparing your subordinate's actual performance to the standards that have been set.

3 Provide feedback: here the subordinate's performance and progress are discussed and plans are made for any development that is required.

Most writers in the field would agree with this definition. Nevertheless, most managers do not do this,[11] and there is no link in this definition to the plans of the organisation that set the overall goals and objectives that the organisation must achieve.

Despite advice to the contrary, appraisals have been confined to one review each year (or never conducted at all), and there has been little involvement by staff in the process, except as passive players in the appraisal. A review of studies conducted in Australia and the United Kingdom demonstrates the significant problems associated with a performance appraisal approach. According to the Australian Workplace Industrial Relations Survey, 68% of organisations in Australia utilise performance appraisals to shift their organisational culture and align individual performance with organisational goals.[12] In the United Kingdom, research conducted by Bevan and Thompson,[13] covering 4.3 million workers, found that only 20% of organisations claimed they had a performance management program, while 60% had policies and procedures relating to managing people performance. A further study by Fletcher and Williams,[14] which complemented the research done by Bevan and Thompson, found that most of the 20% of organisations that claimed to have a performance management system in place had no basis on which to make that claim. While they may have had policies and procedures, they certainly did not have an integrated and holistic approach to managing performance in the organisation. This research underscores the problems inherent in the traditional approach to performance appraisal. It tends to be focused on the appraisal, and gives little attention to the other important factors of setting appropriate standards and providing feedback so that the appraisal process will form a continuous loop that demands continuous improvement.

There is adequate research evidence to suggest that performance appraisals have been piecemeal, unfair to employees and conducted as one-off, yearly written reviews of performance, which all parties loathe. It has been suggested that some of the reasons why performance appraisals fail is that employee performance is reviewed separately and in isolation from the strategic and operational plans of the organisation. This means that there is no connection between what employees do and what the organisation does,[15] and the process is without meaning for both manager and staff.[16] (You read about the importance of these factors in Part A of the book.) Additionally, the yearly performance appraisal interview is not seen as part of the manager's daily responsibilities.[17]

As it is most often used, neither managers nor employees see the benefits of performance appraisal, especially as a tool for training and development and performance improvement.[18]

What is performance management?

Performance management focuses on the overall achievements of an organisation by ensuring that actions and behaviours are linked to the organisation's strategic direction. Performance appraisals are one part of performance management, which is a much more integrated and holistic approach to managing continuous improved performance. The traditional method of performance management has fostered an approach that is based on identifying individuals' lack of performance, and using opinions formed on or close to the appraisal day. This is despite the fact that managers have said they do not want to 'play God' in making decisions about individuals.[19] Stand-alone appraisal schemes have lost favour simply because there has been a recognition that performance management includes more than just appraising an individual's performance on one day of the year. There has been an acceptance that performance management must be tied to the organisation's objectives and is just one part of the many components of organisational performance.[20] The principles and theory that supported performance appraisals are still used. They also underpin performance management. They have been extended and encapsulated in operational and strategic planning processes and human resource management strategies in order to integrate human performance management into the total performance management of the organisation.

Several factors have influenced the gradual shift in the concept of performance management:

- The advent of a world marketplace, the Internet, and communications that facilitate access to information far faster than ever before has created heavy competition between organisations. This has required significant improvements in productivity and cost reductions if organisations want to survive. Consequently, performance management has become a critical issue in survival.

- The public sector has not been immune from the drive to become more competitive, productive and cost-conscious. Governments are driving increased competition through deregulation, corporatisation of government departments and greater accountability for costs. Cost and efficiency therefore become the only ways that government can release more funds from a fairly stable (and sometimes shrinking) budget. Consequently, organisations contracting to government have been required to demonstrate quality assurance and meet specific service agreements so that government can be assured that it is getting value for its dollar.

- To facilitate the new global marketplace, organisations—including government—have restructured operations with the aim of streamlining and automating as many processes as possible, using the latest technology. Central to the restructuring process has been the philosophy of pushing decision making down as far as it can go so that organisations can become more responsive to customer/client needs and thus have a competitive edge. So organisations have decentralised accountability, with greater authority at more levels than ever before. The need to control this decentralisation has generated an insistence on performance management.

- To support the new structure and performance requirements of organisations, relationships with employees have been significantly altered. Primarily, this has facilitated a move away from collective bargaining approaches towards individual, or enterprise, agreements that are able to address very specific issues, something not easily tackled in collective processes.[21]

The concept of performance management is still only in its infancy, but already there are more definitions and descriptions than we can easily cope with without major analysis to determine what the important aspects are.[22] However, the following examples suggest that there are some common threads:

… performance management is about the arrangements organisations use to get the right things done successfully.[23]

… a process for establishing a shared understanding about what is to be achieved, and how it is to be achieved, and an approach to managing people that increases the probability of success.[24]

… the role of the manager is to help employees to focus their behaviour, or to translate their activity into performance.[25]

A performance management approach … emphasises the year round cycle of planning, monitoring, reviewing, rewarding and developing …[26]

Performance management is a means of getting better results from the organisation, teams and individuals by understanding and managing performance within an agreed framework of planned goals, standards and attribute/competence requirements.[27]

… the record of outcomes produced on a specified job function, activity, or behaviour during a specified time period.[28]

Each of these definitions suggests that communication is a major tool through which performance management is achieved. Also, by implication, much is invested in the soft skills discussed in Part A. Performance management looks to the future and tries to identify how things can be continuously improved.[29] It is outcomes-focused, reflecting the way that organisations are formed to perform things and to achieve certain results.[30] The above definitions of performance management also suggest that the process is a cyclical one that starts with planning by agreeing on the objectives to be reached, draws on the knowledge and skills required to achieve the objectives, and then develops plans to achieve the objectives. These may take the form of work plans or development plans or both. Finally, there is continuing and regular review through which the manager and staff member keep track of what is happening, make adjustments as required and then start all over again.

For the purposes of this book, the definition of performance management is:

… a process of managing and developing people through everyday activities, where there is a common understanding of what is to be achieved and how well it is to be achieved, based on firm agreements between managers and individuals which clearly contribute to organisational results.

Simply put, performance management has three broad stages, as illustrated in Figure B.1.

FIGURE B.1 Broad stages of performance management

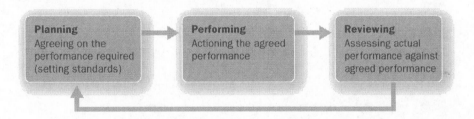

Figure B.1 is simplified for ease of understanding. There are many other components of performance management. If you look at any performance management system it is basically a three-part process: planning, performing and reviewing. These three processes form the foundation of any performance management system. Figure B.2 illustrates the multifaceted and complex process of a performance management system. You will recognise some of the processes from Part A. Others are discussed in the remaining chapters of this book.

FIGURE B.2 A performance management system

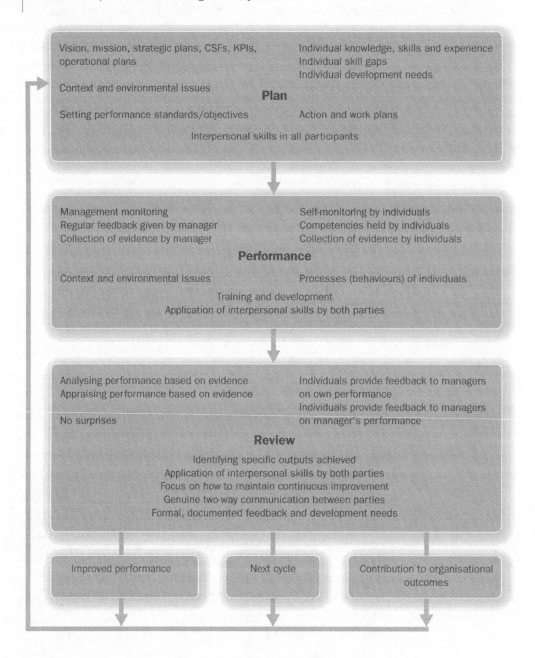

The role of human resource management in performance management

The role of Human Resources in performance management is one of policy making, providing advice, and ensuring that managers and staff have the appropriate knowledge and skills to participate in managing performance effectively. In most countries it also has a record-keeping role to ensure that appropriate records are kept in accordance with legal requirements and for the safe-keeping of evidence of both satisfactory and unsatisfactory performance. The specific involvement of Human Resources in the performance management system is likely to vary with each organisation, and will depend on the broader role that HR plays in the organisation. The importance of the HR role should not be underestimated. It can help managers do their job in the performance management system. HR's role in helping managers with skill building, appraisal tools, policy and procedural advice, and industrial matters in relation to performance is critical to the effective implementation and maintenance of any performance management system. While in consultation with stakeholders, HR often designs, prints and distributes the forms for performance objectives, appraisals and improvement plans, but it would be erroneous to regard the various forms as HR's sole contribution to the process. Managers who perpetuate this view do not understand the role of HR, nor their own responsibilities in relation to managing performance. The key to a robust performance management system is the skills of the managers in applying performance management, not the quality of the forms on which information is kept.[31]

The critical role of training and development

As with all things, appropriate skills and knowledge are required for a performance management system to work. Both managers and staff need to undertake training to get the most out of the process. Training is rarely provided to all participants of an appraisal program. One of the common difficulties reported is that managers see the annual appraisal process as something driven by the Human Resources department. It imposes on managers' time and requires the completion of many forms that go back to HR and are never used again by managers.[32] As long as the performance appraisal process is seen as an HR activity, managers will abdicate their responsibility for developing and managing people, a process that is the major responsibility of a manager. Appraisals require the use of refined interpersonal skills, which most managers need to work hard at developing and maintaining.[33] This, in part, contributes to the failure of performance appraisals. If managing performance is to be more successful, managers and staff must use a new approach.[34] When performance management is aligned with organisational objectives and is seen by all levels of management as a core business process, the chances of success are greatly improved.[35]

To enhance the effectiveness of any performance management system, the process needs to be supported by training in a number of areas:

- training in how to use the particular performance management system that the organisation has chosen to use
- training in how to minimise rater errors in making judgments about the performance of individuals
- training in the specific interpersonal skills required to manage the interaction between people, such as feedback skills, listening skills, negotiation skills and questioning skills
- training in the relevant legislation and awards that govern the conduct of performance management, such as the *Workplace Relations Act 1996* (Cth) and anti-discrimination laws.

The need for training is widely acknowledged in the literature, but the actual state of training is summed up by Nankervis, Compton and McCarthy:[36] 'A weakness of many performance appraisal programs is that managers and supervisors are not trained adequately for the appraisal task and provide little meaningful feedback'. The lack of training reported in the literature may partly explain the poor reputation performance management has with managers and staff alike.

The potential of performance management

The primary focus of managers and executives of the past decade has been the financial performance of their organisation; however, today they recognise that the value of their organisations depends heavily on the performance of their people. There is no doubt that performance management has great potential for achieving organisational outcomes,[37] where individual performance objectives are integrated with the business strategy of the organisation[38] and the objectives are focused on individual personal development, communication and teamwork.[39] This raises the question of whether the aims and objectives of the organisation and those of the individual can be in unison. There is potential conflict between the individual and the organisation if people are not managed correctly.[40] A properly managed process will allow individual career or personal objectives to be matched with organisational objectives so that effort and aims are complementary rather than in opposition to each other.[41]

To reach the potential that systematic performance management offers managers, staff and organisations, one thing is sure from the literature: great care must be taken in describing and measuring performance.[42] You will see that the second part of this book is very particular in the differences it highlights among the various processes that constitute performance management. This precision is necessary if performance management is to work effectively. Consequently, Part B has seven chapters that may at first glance seem similar. The differences may not be clear until you have read each chapter. The differences may be likened to that between competencies and performance——subtle but distinct. Some performance appraisal systems attempt to measure an individual's competency as the main sign of success or failure. There is an inherent problem with this approach. A person may hold a number of competencies and be able to demonstrate mastery of them. The attainment of competencies is not a demonstration of an individual's actual on-the-job performance. However, application of the appropriate competencies to achieve an agreed result is performance[43](dealt with in Chapter 4). This is also true of the difference between performance and work activity: the two are not the same.[44] Performance is the result of the application of competencies to the job, and results in measurable outputs. Work activity will not necessarily result in outputs, but people may be very busy.

Bernardin, Hagan, Kane and Villanova identify three prescriptions that will improve the effectiveness of performance management systems.[45] These have been distilled from their own research, practice and litigation. They are:

1 Precision in the definition and measurement of performance is a key element of effective performance management.

2 The content and measurement of performance should derive from internal and external customers.

3 The performance management system should incorporate a formal process for investigating and correcting for the effects of situational constraints on performance.

Bernardin et al. stipulate that if all these three points are not present in a performance management system, it is likely to fail. Armstrong identified 14 significant differences between the traditional performance appraisal approach and the more recent concept of performance management.[46] Performance management:

1 has greater integration with the plans of the organisation

2 is a fundamental process of management and part of the everyday activities of a manager

3 is based on all staff making contributions to the overall performance of the organisation

4 is based on agreements between managers and individuals or teams

5 is concerned with both team performance and individual performance

6 measures a variety of factors

7 is a continuous process throughout the cycle

8 looks to the future performance of staff and the organisation

9 focuses on improving performance

10 can be a basis for the development of ratings for performance-based pay

11 may not include ratings at all

12 is not based on forms or procedures

13 is based on regular, honest and timely feedback

14 is based on the cyclical process of agreements, planning, implementation and review.

Armstrong's differences between the past and the future reflect what has happened in management, organisations and the employment market over the past 15 years or so.[47]

Benefits of performance management

A performance management approach to managing the performance of an organisation requires the integration of many factors that contribute to overall performance. One of these is human performance: just like equipment, products or services, humans must produce at appropriate levels to justify their purchase and continuing use. Human performance is the most expensive resource an organisation has, and it is inconceivable that management would allow its people to wallow around in useless tasks with a lack of direction. It is absurd that such an expensive resource is not properly monitored and maintained to enable it to perform to its fullest capacity. Nevertheless, this continues to happen every day.

From the following research we know that those organisations that excel are more likely to have formal performance management systems in place. There is a connection between more specific and objective performance standards and better overall organisational performance.[48] We also know that human effort is the most important factor in determining organisational performance.[49] By linking individual performance to the performance of the organisation, individuals are able to identify clearly what is expected of them, how their performance will be measured and how they are progressing towards their performance goals.[50] It follows that they could expect to receive feedback on how they are progressing and to receive help if they find they are not on track and cannot fix the problem themselves, just as managers might do with any malfunctioning equipment, product or service. In this case, managers' efforts are focused on improving the performance of the item. Managers need to apply the same objectivity to people as to any other resource issue. Moreover, it is a process that management is faced with every day. While managers manage the performance of equipment, products and services, it is well documented that managers do not manage the performance of people.[51] It is essential for the success of their organisation that managers do manage the performance of people.

Performance management systems have the following benefits.

For the organisation:
- greater efficiency
- greater effectiveness
- greater profitability
- more programs brought in on time and on budget
- more specific training needs identified
- more specific training carried out
- more specific human resource planning undertaken
- better quality of service/product
- improved salary administration
- improved motivation of employees
- greater attraction and retention of staff
- better culture change process
- improved support for total quality management
- improved performance of the whole organisation.[52]

For the manager:
- improved relationships
- improved communication
- improved decision making
- improved problem solving
- improved performance of individuals or teams
- improved departmental, branch or work unit performance
- improved performance of the manager.[53]

For the staff member:
- improved relationships
- improved communication
- improved self-confidence
- improved job satisfaction
- improved problem solving
- improved understanding of role
- improved performance

- improved encouragement and support to perform well
- improved guidance and assistance in developing abilities and potential
- improved objectivity and fairness in assessing performance
- improved participation in the performance management process
- improved acceptance of personal responsibility.[54]

These benefits do not come without hard work. The overall framework needs to be specifically tailored to the organisation and the situation in which it finds itself.[55] It is difficult at times to link individual performance standards to organisational outcomes. It requires much thought. People also need regular feedback on what and how they are performing. This feedback needs to be specific and given in such a way as to focus on improvement where it is required. Often, considerable training needs to accompany a newly designed and developed performance management system, and people need to understand how it operates. Remember, if you are implementing a performance management system for the first time, staff are more than likely to be critical and apprehensive about the system. This is understandable, given that many staff have received raw deals under past appraisal systems that have served only to disenchant them. Hence, involvement and education of the staff is essential to minimise stress.

Theoretical perspectives on performance management

Management by objectives

The theoretical basis of this book is management by objectives. While there are a number of alternative theories on which to base a performance management system, management by objectives seems to give maximum flexibility and cohesiveness with organisational planning, while allowing individuals the freedom for creativity and empowerment. The term 'management by objectives' (MBO) was first used by Peter Drucker in 1954,[56] and has had several enhancements up to the present day. MBO is based on the process of goal setting and then reviewing performance against the goals agreed to by all parties. Part of the theory is that, because managers achieve things through others, they have to involve staff in the goal-setting process, develop employee commitment to the goals, and instil a general desire by staff to assist the organisation by contributing to its success. MBO is based on two main concepts: (a) the effort of individuals needs to be coordinated towards organisational goals; and (b) through the setting of individual goals, people are helped to grow and develop skills and knowledge.[57] Rather than hand individuals set targets or performance requirements, MBO requires the participation of individuals and their managers to identify important objectives and set suitable standards together. Thus, MBO requires:

- objectives (which are specific) to be set in a participative manner
- time frames in which objectives must be met to be set in a participative manner
- regular, specific feedback given to both parties
- both manager and staff member to be held accountable for the agreed results.

The advantages offered by MBO include:

- greater employee involvement and commitment

- higher likelihood of employees improving their performance when they know what is expected of them, receive feedback and can obtain assistance as required
- better/more realistic objectives
- more opportunity for control and self-control
- improved performance appraisal.[58]

In practice, there are many variations of MBO, from management telling staff what the objectives will be to full participation, as illustrated in Figure B.3.[59] This has been one of the criticisms of MBO. If management does not embrace the participative management component of MBO but applies only the goal-focused side of it, then it can be misused and staff will not feel motivated or gain job satisfaction. Despite this, most performance management systems are based on MBO.[60] However, having entered a new century, more than 50 years on from when Drucker developed a systematic, objective, results-focused process, it is doubtful that you will find any organisation using MBO in its purest form. Instead, organisations have adapted the process to suit their own environments, cultures and needs. Often it is used in conjunction with other theories in motivation, methods of appraisal, goal setting, and rewards and remuneration. MBO firmly established that performance appraisals are not a stand-alone function and must be integrated with the operations of the organisation. As such, MBO has had a profound effect on management since 1954.[61] Even so, there is enough evidence in the literature to suggest that most performance appraisals in organisations are still quite separate from other operations and thus not as effective as they could be.

There are genuine and acceptable reasons why organisations may find themselves at any point along the line in Figure B.3. For example, an organisation that finds itself in trouble financially, either losing market share or blowing the agency budget, may not have the time to negotiate objectives or set standards with individuals or teams, and may have to specify results in order for action to commence immediately. Ideally, the process of setting objectives and performance measures will be a participative one, but this is not always possible. Nevertheless, you should aspire to the right-hand side of the line in Figure B.3. You will see from this book just how participative MBO can be, how it can empower and motivate people, and how it can add measurable value to an organisation. To increase the likelihood of performance objectives being successfully achieved, you need to use and reinforce the principles and processes of MBO exactly. As you become familiar with them you will find that you make alterations to fit your own circumstances, but only after you have a thorough understanding of and experience in applying the principles and processes.

FIGURE B.3 Variances in the setting of objectives

MBO is not the only method of managing performance. Armstrong briefly outlines how performance management has developed from fairly subjective approaches to the present-day holistic approach of performance management.[62] These are summarised in Figure B.4.

FIGURE B.4 Development of performance management approaches

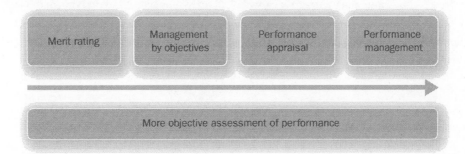

Many writers argue that each approach has tried to become less subjective and more objective, less rigid and more flexible, in the way judgments are made about how an individual might be performing. Perhaps the most important point in the journey from rating scales to performance management is the general agreement that people should be assessed on their behaviour and the results they produce, not their personalities.

A systems method

There has been an acceptance of performance as comprising more than just ratings, or the achievement of objectives in the agreed time. Performance is more complicated than that. The systems view of how organisations operate represents organisations as processing systems, which themselves comprise smaller subsystems, such as sales, purchasing, case management, human resources, stores and distribution, finance, marketing, research and development.[63] The systems view is based on the concept that inputs are fed into the organisation, then the organisation processes them in some way and produces an output of some sort. It is composed of inputs, processes, outputs and outcomes.[64] The concept is illustrated in Figure B.5.

FIGURE B.5 Input, process, output, outcome model

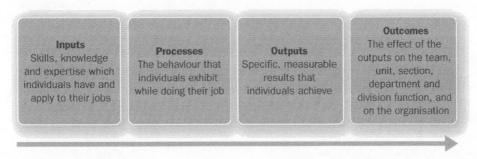

Managing performance requires that attention be paid to all four components of the model. It is based on sound theory, including motivation theory—which includes goal setting, reinforcement and expectancy theory[65]—concepts of organisational effectiveness, and beliefs about how performance is best managed by organisations.[66] These theories have all been developed through research that is still ongoing. It is when the four components are not dealt with equally that performance management becomes difficult, and staff and managers record less satisfaction. Of course, it is the manager who must ensure that the process is applied. Effective managers know this and will go to great lengths to ensure that the components of performance management outlined in Figure B.5 are participatively implemented and reviewed. Effective managers also do not use the excuse that they have no time to apply the process. Managing the performance of the organisation is the reason we have managers. Managing human performance is a large factor in determining the overall performance of the organisation. As the payroll is the major expense of any organisation, managers need to give appropriate time to the management of people to ensure that the investment in them is worthwhile.

The subsystems that exist within an organisation also take inputs, process them and produce an output. The fundamentals of the process are illustrated in Figure B.6.

FIGURE B.6 A systems view of organisations

Rummler and Brache use the term 'adaptive system' because they hold that, through the various actions of management, the organisation is continually adapting to its environment, competitor activity and demands of clients/customers.[67] In the highly competitive global marketplace, under the influence of consistent change, Rummler and Brache suggest that organisations must adapt or die. They claim that this is true of government just as much as private enterprise. The process of adaptation is a continual one, as is the rate of change. As such, it helps to put change in perspective: it is not a temporary nuisance but an ongoing requirement of management. The systems model can therefore be redrawn to demonstrate how adaptation is a continual process in the ever-present process of change. Figure B.7 illustrates the adaptive system.

FIGURE B.7 The adaptive system

Environment
Market
Political
Economic

Organisation
Processing
Subsystems

Outputs
Products
Services

Based on the systems view, Rummler and Brache have developed a methodology to improve performance in organisations. It looks at the systems within an organisation at three levels: the organisation, the processes and the job/performer. A brief description follows.

- *Level 1 The organisation*—concerned with the impact of strategies, organisational goals and measures, organisational structure and how resources are deployed.

- *Level 2 Processes*—concerned with how processes operate within the organisation in relation to customer needs, whether they work effectively, and whether organisation and customer needs propel process goals and measures.

- *Level 3 The job/performer*—concerned with how people perform. Critical to this is the recruitment and selection of staff; development of staff; job responsibilities; and standards of performance, training, feedback and remuneration.

Each level of performance must be running well if overall organisational performance is to be high. In other words, you cannot have high performance if you concentrate on only one area. Traditionally, managers have focused only on the organisational level (dealt with in Part A). However, people performance (level 3) and process performance (level 2) must also be carefully managed if organisational performance (level 1) is to be achieved.

There are many performance management evaluation methods that assist in appraising performance, which may or may not be used as part of a performance management system.

Appraisal methods

A performance appraisal is generally conducted using a predetermined and formal method. The following are some of the most common appraisal methods used in organisations to measure performance.

Graphic rating scale method (GRSM)

- This is the most popular method of appraisal, as it is less time-consuming to develop and administer than some other methods, and therefore more cost-effective.

- This is a scale that lists a number of behaviours and a range of performances for each one, from satisfactory to unsatisfactory or (1) very like this person to (5) most unlike this person.

- The performance factors used in the GRSM could include quantity and quality of work as well as several other personal traits such as knowledge, reliability, cooperation, loyalty, attendance, honesty and initiative.

- Once performance factors are selected, staff are rated by the manager for each behaviour.

- This rating would be carried out in a participative manner by discussions between the staff member and the manager.

- The overall rating of all of the performance factors would be used to allocate pay raises, bonuses etc.

Alternation ranking method

- This method ranks all staff, from the best staff performer on a specific behaviour to the worst.

- This is repeated for all behaviours until all are completed.
- A matrix is left, illustrating where staff sit in relation to each other on each behaviour.

Forced distribution method

- This method has traditionally been used in schools and universities, where predetermined percentages of rates (employees being evaluated) are placed in performance categories; for example, high achievers (15%), high-average achievers (20%), average performers (30%), low-average performers (20%) and low performers (15%).
- By using the bell curve, not all employees can fall into the top 15% percentage band and performance of an employee is rated relative to that of their colleagues.
- While popular in some Asian countries, this is not utilised greatly in Australia compared to other methods.[68]

Critical incident method

- This method evaluates behaviours key to the effective execution of a job.
- A record of specific incidents is kept by the manager or staff member, or both, which demonstrates particularly good or poor examples of work.
- Only specific behaviours should be recorded and descriptions should be clear, concise and factual.
- These incidents form the basis of discussion for performance management evaluations or performance appraisals.

Behaviourally anchored rating scales (BARS) method

- BARS is a combination of major elements of the critical incident and graphic rating scale methods.
- BARS is a scale that addresses behaviours or skills sets. The scale has critical incidents of a particular behaviour that cover both good and poor performance.
- The appraiser rates employees based on items along a continuum.
- This method specifies very definite, observable and measurable job behaviours.
- Behavioural descriptions achieved using BARS method include: can solve immediate problems, plans, anticipates, actions, orders, responds to emergency situations.
- BARS results can be useful when determining reward for good performance, considering transfers or promotions, addressing poor performance, and evaluating effectiveness of the recruitment and selection process.

360-degree review feedback

- This method gathers data from a number of perspectives on individuals being appraised.
- The data collected can be from managers, supervisors, peers, subordinates, internal clients, and suppliers.
- For example, to conduct 360-degree feedback on a clerk responsible for purchasing and supply, you might collect data from internal clients, suppliers, the clerk's manager, peer workers of the clerk and people who may report to the clerk.

- Most 360-degree feedback consists of between 5 and 10 evaluations per employee.

- This is becoming a popular tool for organisations in data collection for feedback.

- This method is used mainly to improve and develop employees, and provides a more accurate indicator of employee performance.

- Some 360-degree feedback requires the individual being appraised to complete the question-naire, and to identify gaps between actual performance and perceived performance. This allows specific structuring of performance improvement plans for the individual to address weaknesses and build on strengths.

- By collecting a range of information across a number of different levels within the organisa-tion, it is claimed that the performance appraisal is more balanced and inclusive than one based on just one or two sources.

Behavioural observation scales (BOS)

- The BOS technique involves identifying the key tasks and behaviours for a job.

- It specifies what an employee 'must do' in order to implement an organisation's vision, strategy and values.

- While it is similar to the BARS method, unlike BARS, the BOS technique evaluates an employee's performance based on the frequency with which they exhibit the required behaviours for performance.[69]

Core organisational competencies

- While they are not technically a performance evaluation method, core competencies can be used with most evaluation methods.

- Core competencies refers to activities or practices that have been identified by an organi-sation as critical to its long-term success and growth. They are typically based on skill or knowledge sets rather than products or functions; for example, technical/subject matter knowhow, culture, a reliable process and/or close relationships with customers and suppliers.

- Typically they fulfil three criteria: (1) they provide customer benefits; (2) they are not easily imitated by competitors; and (3) they can be applied to multiple products, services or markets.

- Core organisational competencies differ from the competency standards used in vocational education and competency-based training, which are approaches to education based on competency standards describing actual job performance. Competency standards may be used as the basis of performance standards and position descriptions.

Balanced scorecard method

- This method was developed in the early 1990s by Robert Kaplan and David Norton.

- This method measures a range of variables beyond financial performance associated with organisational performance and translating organisational vision and strategies into actions. Originally the balanced scorecard focused on four perspectives: financial performance, customers, business processes, and learning and growth.

- Measures of performance might also include staff retention, human resources systems and corporate social responsibility, or other external outcomes.

Narrative forms

- Narrative forms uses narrative description to evaluate and record progress and development of employees.

- While the appraiser is still asked to rate an employee's performance (for example, strong, satisfactory, needs improvement), this approach provides an opportunity to provide written detail and examples to support the final outcome of the appraisal.

- Some users may find this approach time-consuming. Depending on the appraiser's written skills, the form may become very detailed and lengthy.[70]

There are advantages and disadvantages with all the methods described above. Some of these are dealt with later in Chapter 9. Rarely does an organisation use only one method of appraisal; most companies combine several appraisal methods.[71] Indeed, the more effective performance management systems use a range of methods.

Managing performance in people is a normal and essential function of managers. Managers achieve this through the management of people, especially by setting clear expectations and work standards, gaining participation, measuring results, and giving regular and specific feedback. When this occurs, research has suggested that both staff and managers are more satisfied[72] and staff perceive they have greater empowerment. This book uses an eclectic approach to the management of performance, although it is based primarily on management by objectives. This facilitates a clearer connection to the aims and objectives of the organisation and makes the operation and success of the organisation transparent to all staff. With any of the recommendations made in the remaining chapters of the book, you can easily incorporate any of the methods described here.

The human performance system

Developed from their model of improving performance, which you will recall is based on an adaptive system model, one of the subsystems in the organisation posited by Rummler and Brache is the human performance system.[73] This system is based on the input/output model, with a number of significant additions that acknowledge the variables that influence human individual performance. The six variables are:

1. performance specifications—what the job holder is expected to do
2. task support—how the job is structured, design, work flow, logical processes
3. consequences—which support the effective completion of job goals
4. feedback—how useful the feedback is that job holders receive
5. skills and knowledge—the proficiency of the individual
6. individual capacity—the internal capabilities of the individual.

These variables constitute a diagnostic tool for managers that helps to identify problems with this subsystem and to plan performance improvement.

What do staff want from a performance management system?

Based on their research, Weiss and Hartle suggest that staff need to have the following questions answered:[74]

1 What am I expected to achieve in my job and how will success be judged?

2 How am I doing?

3 How are we doing (relative to competitors)?

4 Where do I stand?

5 Where am I going?

6 What do I need to work on?

Most of the literature in this area supports these contentions in one form or another. Honest answers to these questions, backed up by specific evidence, can be a powerful motivator and is the basis on which continuous improvement is achieved. The above six questions provide very specific guidelines for anyone developing a performance management system. They are critical in satisfying staff that performance management is a worthwhile process. There are many technically good performance management systems that are underpinned by piles of thick, good-looking documents on which you record details about appraisals, but which are useless unless the concept of performance management is endorsed and accepted by staff.[75]

A body of research conducted between 1978 and the late 1990s suggests that active employee participation in a performance management system is associated with positive staff reactions towards that system.[76] The six questions above provide a way of involving staff in the process. Further, Cawley, Keeping and Levy's research has suggested that the degree of staff satisfaction with the performance management system can affect productivity, motivation and organisational commitment.[77] They have further found that staff have a desire to voice their opinion about the performance management system, in terms of its development and their active participation in the process itself. The opportunity to voice their opinion enhances the perceived fairness of the system even if staff members do not have an effect on decisions. That is to say, staff expect to participate but do not expect to influence the outcome. Consequently, staff will have strong negative reactions from not being able to participate in the process. This is the case whether the staff member chooses to participate or not. It is the opportunity to do so that is critical in running an effective performance management system and whether it is perceived as being fair.

The manager's role in performance management

Throughout this part of the book you will gain an overview of the importance of the manager's role in the process of managing performance. In Part A the role of a manager is briefly described. In this section that definition is extended in terms of the role played in performance management. Clearly, the manager has a vital leadership role, combined with the role of facilitating outcomes and individual development that is complementary to the needs of the individual and the organisation. Additionally, the manager must accept that managing the performance of people is a significant part of the job, a factor that is illustrated in Figure A.1 in Part A. The figure shows the increasing emphasis on interpersonal skills (in managing people) as managers move up to middle management level. This is critical to how and whether results will be achieved through people.

Managers must manage critical success factors, key performance indicators and performance standards to ensure organisational success. Effective managers know how to convert strategic plans into work-group and individual plans and performance standards with their staff or teams. Interpersonal skills are required to do this successfully, and one of the major skills in this group is communication. Performance management is about managers communicating and giving feedback to staff regularly, honestly and sensitively. It is also about linking all the various parts of the organisation and the roles of individuals so that they understand clearly that they have a role to play in the wider scheme of things. To balance this process, staff also need developed interpersonal skills in order to participate effectively in the performance management process. Again, this falls to the role of the line manager. If you fail to develop appropriate skills in your staff or teams, managing performance will continue to be a difficult and laborious process for the manager and fuel job dissatisfaction in staff. The process should be welcomed and valued by both manager and staff. However, the main factor in determining the success of a performance management system is the manager. There are perfectly good performance management systems in use in organisations that do not have formal forms and that never go near Human Resource management. On the other hand, there are many examples of organisations in which information is carefully collected and recorded, filed and sent through the HR department, but where the system does not work. The point here is that managers determine the success of a system. It is clearly a line management responsibility, not the responsibility of the HR department, to manage performance.

While HR departments can provide advice, training and some tools, managing performance is the responsibility of the line manager—more important than budgets, marketing, sales, programs and daily operational issues, as without people performance nothing else can be achieved.

Potential problems

In addition to the issues documented at the beginning of Part B, there are many potential problems with both appraising performance and implementing performance management systems. Across all the research there is one single, common thread that seems to underpin all the potential problems that have been documented. Any appraisal or performance management system can be misused. Misuse tends to occur where those conducting the appraisal or performance management processes do not have adequate skills in managing people. Some of the problems that may occur are that:

- personality traits are evaluated
- staff are bullied
- prejudice and bias skew appraisals
- forms are completed but no real dialogue or feedback occurs.

Where managers do not possess the required interpersonal skills and a commitment to the process, the system will fail. Skills such as active listening, paraphrasing, questioning, giving and receiving feedback, using effective cross-cultural communication skills, handling conflict and encouraging full participation are required for a performance management system to be effective. Staff do not generally cause the problems. There is adequate evidence to demonstrate that performance management systems based on management by objectives (MBO) do work, provided that managers at all levels have a sincere commitment to the systems; to developing the appropriate skills, knowledge and leadership; and, in turn, to developing these in their staff.[78]

There is also little understanding of how long it takes to fully implement a performance management system. The first year of implementation is seen as practice, although it is expected that staff will meet their objectives. The point is that in the first year you need to be quite flexible, as people are learning to trust again and the organisation must look at eradicating institutionalised cynicism. In the second year people know what they are doing, although more skills practice may be required and there is less flexibility. By the third year the system should have begun to change the culture of the organisation, and the process of performance management should be well embedded in the day-to-day operations of the organisation. An organisation may thus not see any significant change until three or four years after the system is implemented.[79] If management does not work hard at developing its skills and the skills of its staff, as well as bedding down the processes, performance management is likely to fail and no change will be evident three or four years down the track. Sadly, many organisations abandon performance management systems because no change is observed in the first year, or managers complain that they do not have the time to do it and that it is not working. Our advice is: rather than dump the system, perhaps the managers need to be dumped. Senior management must also understand that implementing performance management is a gradual process. If it proceeds too quickly, both managers and staff are likely to miss the boat, thus sabotaging the implementation. Adequate leadtime is essential to the success of performance management.

The remainder of this book will show you how to implement much of what has been discussed here. Through your reading of Chapters 4–12, you will discover knowledge and skills derived from research that will assist you as a manager to manage performance. Remember: staff don't sabotage performance management systems—managers do!

References

1 Nicholson, J. & Nairn, A. 2006. *The Manager of the 21st Century*. Innovation & Business Skills Australia: Hawthorn, p. 3.

2 Rudman, R. 1995. *Performance Planning and Review: Making Employee Appraisals Work*. Pitman: Melbourne, p. vii; Bernardin, H., Hagan, C., Kane, J. & Villanova, P. 1998. 'Effective performance management: A focus on precision, customers, and situational constraints.' In J.W. Smither (ed.), *Performance Appraisal: State of the Art in Practice*. Jossey Bass: San Francisco, p. 3.

3 University of Melbourne 2003. 'Organisations divided? Some implications of performance appraisals.' *UniNews* 12(3), 10–24 March; Monash University, Faculty of Business and Economics. 2003. *The Dash for Cash: Performance Related Pay—An Australian Union Perspective*. Glennis Hanley & Loan Nguyen, Working Paper 4/03, March.

4 Lawson, P. 1995. 'Performance management: An overview.' In M. Walters (ed.). *The Performance Management Handbook*. HRD Press: Amherst, MA, p. 1.

5 Bernardin et al., op. cit., 1998, p. 3.

6 Smith, B., Hornsby, J. & Schirmeyer, R. 1996. 'Current trends in performance appraisal: An examination of managerial practice.' *SAM Advanced Management Journal*. Cited in J.W. Smither (ed.), *Performance Appraisal: State of the Art in Practice*. Jossey Bass: San Francisco, p. 3.

7 Lawler, E. III. 1994. 'Performance management: The next generation.' *Compensation and Benefits Review*, 26(3), pp. 16–19. Cited in J.W. Smither (ed.), *Performance Appraisal: State of the Art in Practice*. Jossey Bass: San Francisco, p. 3.

8 Bernardin et al., op. cit., 1998, p. 4.

9 CCH 2001. Human Resource Management, 'Performance appraisal and management practices', para. 85-500 (survey conducted in 1985, 1990, 1995 and 2000); Nankervis, A. & Compton, R. 2006. 'Performance management: Theory in practice?' *Asia Pacific Journal of Human Resources*, 44(1), p. 97 (survey conducted in 2005). Cited in Dessler, G., Griffiths, J. & Lloyd-Walker, B. 2007. HRM: *Theory, Skills, Application*. Pearson Australia: Frenchs Forest, Sydney, p. 314.

10 Dessler, G., Griffiths, J. & Lloyd-Walker, B. 2007, 3rd edn. *Human Resource Management*. Pearson Australia: Frenchs Forest, Sydney, p. 319.

11 Rummler, G. & Brache, A. 1995. *Improving Performance: How to Manage the White Space on the Organization Chart*. Jossey-Bass: San Francisco, p. 2.

12 Cole, K. 2005, 3rd edn. *Management: Theory and Practice*. Pearson Australia: Frenchs Forest, Sydney, p. 424.

13 Bevan, S. & Thompson, M. 1992. 'An overview of policy and practice.' In *Performance Management: An Analysis of the Issues*. Institute of Personnel Management: London. Cited in J. Storey & K. Sission, *Managing Human Resources and Industrial Relations*. Open University Press: Buckingham, UK, pp. 135–136.

14   Fletcher, C. & Williams, R. 1992. 'Organisational experience' In *Performance management: An Analysis of the Issues*. Institute of Personnel Management: London. Cited in J. Storey & K. Sission. *Managing Human Resources and Industrial Relations*. Open University Press: Buckingham, UK, p. 136.

15   Rudman, op. cit., 1995; Philp, T. 1990, 2nd edn. *Appraising Performance for Results*. McGraw-Hill: London, UK, p. 2.

16   Rudman, op. cit., 1995; Weiss, T. & Hartle, F. 1997. *Reengineering Performance Management: Breakthroughs in Achieving Strategy Through People*. St Lucie Press: Boca Raton, FL, p. 3.

17   Rudman, op. cit., 1995, p. 17.

18   Rudman, op. cit., 1995, p. viii; Lawson, op. cit., 1995, p. 1.

19   Armstrong, M. 1994. *Performance Management*. Kogan Page: London, p. 20.

20   Bernardin et al., op. cit., 1998, p. 7.

21   Storey, J. & Sission, K. 1992. *Managing Human Resources and Industrial Relations*. Open University Press: Buckingham, UK, pp. 131–153; Nankervis, A., Compton, R. & McCarthy, T. 1993. *Strategic Human Resource Management*. Thomas Nelson Australia: Melbourne, pp. 310–311.

22   Lawson, op. cit., 1995, p. 1; Armstrong, op. cit., 1994, p. 22.

23   Lawson, op. cit., 1995, p. 2.

24   Weiss & Hartle, op. cit., 1997, p. 3.

25   Rudman, op. cit., 1995, p. 2.

26   Rudman, op. cit., 1995, p. 17.

27   Armstrong, op. cit., 1994, p. 23.

28   Bernardin et al., op. cit., 1998, p. 7.

29   Armstrong, op. cit., 1994, p. 13; Lawson, op. cit., 1995, p. 2.

30   Rudman, op. cit., 1995, p. 1.

31   Nankervis, et al., op. cit., 1993, p. 310.

32   Armstrong, op. cit., 1994, pp. 20, 22; King, P. 1989. *Performance Planning and Appraisal: A How-To Book for Managers*. Kogan Page: London, p. 7; Schneier, C., Shaw, D. & Beatty, R. 1995. 'Performance measurement and management: A tool for strategy execution.' In D. Shaw, C. Schneier, R. Beatty & L. Baird (eds), *Performance Measurement, Management and Appraisal Sourcebook*. HRD Press: Amherst, MA, p. 3; Schaffer, R. 1995. 'Demand better results and get them.' In Shaw et al., op. cit., 1995, p. 24; Philp, op. cit., 1990, pp. 2–6.

33   Armstrong, op. cit., 1994, p. 22; Rudman, op. cit., 1995, pp. 7–8.

34   Weiss & Hartle, op. cit., 1997, pp. 79–99.

35   Weiss & Hartle, op. cit., 1997, p. 8.

36   Nankervis et al., op. cit., 1993, p. 317.

37   Bernardin et al., op. cit., 1998, pp. 5, 7; Rudman, op. cit., 1995, p. 1; Armstrong, op. cit., 1994, p. 13; Schaffer, op. cit., 1995, p. 22.

38   Armstrong, op. cit., 1994, p. 15; Weiss & Hartle, op. cit., 1997, pp. 4, 6; Rudman, op. cit., 1995, p. 5; Fletcher & Williams, op. cit., 1992.

39   Weiss & Hartle, op. cit., 1997, p. 3.

40   Rudman, op. cit., 1995, p. 14.

41   McMaster, M. 1994. *Performance Management: Creating the Conditions for Results*. Metamorphous Press: Portland, OR, p. 239.

42   Bernardin et al., op. cit., 1998, p. 7.

43   Bernardin et al., op. cit., 1998, p. 4.

44   Rudman, op. cit., 1995, p. 2.

45   Bernardin et al., op. cit., 1998, p. 5.

46   Armstrong, op. cit., 1994, p. 21.

47   Rudman, op. cit., 1995, p. 15.

48   Bernardin et al., op. cit., 1998, pp. 9, 17.

49   Philp, op. cit., 1990, p. 7.

50   Philp, op. cit., 1990, p. 1.

51   Philp, op. cit., 1990, pp. 2–6.

52   Philp, op. cit., 1990, p. 9; Armstrong, op. cit., 1994, p. 28.

53   Philp, op. cit., 1990, p. 9.

54   Philp, op. cit., 1990, p. 9; Armstrong, op. cit., 1994, p. 28.

55   Armstrong, op. cit., 1994, pp. 27–28.

56   Drucker, P. 1954. *The Practice of Management*. Harper & Row: New York.

57 Thomson, T. 1972. *Management by Objectives: The 1972 Annual Handbook for Group Facilitators.* University Associates: San Diego, pp. 130–132.

58 Jones, R. 2010, 2nd edn, *Managing Human Resource Systems.* Pearson Australia: Frenchs Forest, Sydney, p. 113.

59 McConkey, D. 1985, 4th edn. *How to Manage by Results.* Amacom: New York, pp. 3–5.

60 McConkey, op. cit., 1985, pp. 1–16.

61 McConkey, op. cit., 1985, p. 4.

62 Armstrong, op. cit., 1994, pp. 15–22.

63 Rummler, G. & Brache, A. 1995, 2nd edn. *Improving Performance: How to Manage the White Space on the Organization Chart.* Jossey-Bass: San Francisco, pp. 5–14.

64 Armstrong, op. cit., 1994, pp. 32–33.

65 Cole, K. 2010, 4th edn, *Management: Theory and Practice.* Pearson Australia: Frenchs Forest, Sydney, pp. 316–355.

66 Armstrong, op. cit., 1994, p. 39.

67 Rummler & Brache, op. cit., 1995, pp. 5–14.

68 Dessler, Griffiths & Lloyd-Walker, op. cit., 2007, p. 321.

69 12manage: The Executive Fast Track. <www.12manage.com/description_behavioral_observation_scales.html> accessed 23 June 2009.

70 Dessler, Griffiths & Lloyd-Walker, op. cit., 2007, p. 323.

71 Dessler, Griffiths & Lloyd-Walker, op. cit., 2007, p. 331.

72 Cawley, B., Keeping, L. & Levy, P. 1998. 'Participation in the performance appraisal process and employee reactions: A meta-analytic review of field investigations.' *Journal of Applied Psychology,* 83(4), pp. 615–633; Lam, S. & Schaubroek, J. 1999. 'Total quality management and performance appraisal: An experimental study of process versus results and group versus individual approaches.' *Journal of Organisational Behaviour,* 20(4), pp. 445–457.

73 Rummler & Brache, op. cit., 1995, pp. 69–75.

74 Weiss & Hartle, op. cit., 1997, p. 7.

75 Cawley et al., op. cit., 1998, pp. 615–633.

76 Cawley et al., op. cit., 1998.

77 Cawley et al., op. cit., 1998.

78 McConkey, op. cit., 1985, p. 2.

79 McConkey, op. cit., 1985, pp. 4, 14–15.

CHAPTER FOUR

What is a performance standard?

Learning outcomes

After reading this chapter you should be able to:

* explain the relationship between performance standards and organisational strategy
* illustrate how performance standards can motivate individuals
* explain why performance standards are required
* outline the difference between everyday standards and work standards
* explain the term 'performance'
* explain the role of communication in setting performance standards
* identify the difference between an action and a result
* describe the role of managers in setting performance standards
* illustrate the components of a performance standard
* explain the term 'performance standard'
* use multiple measures for performance standards
* link performance standards to corporate strategy.

INTRODUCTION

The setting of specific standards of individual or team performance provides a link between strategic plans and individual or team work. Standards are concerned with how well things have been done; describe the level of performance a job holder is required to achieve; and generally measure quantity, timeliness and quality.[1] Effective standards demonstrate how individuals and teams contribute to the overall performance of an organisation, as illustrated in Figure 4.1. No single individual is able to achieve the organisational outcomes and strategic direction of an organisation, but the combined efforts of a number of individuals who are focused on the critical success factors (CSFs) and key performance indicators (KPIs) of the organisation can implement strategy effectively.

To be effective, individual or team performance standards need to be specific and explicitly linked to corporate, agency, divisional, departmental, branch and section objectives. Performance standards are written against the key aspects of a job. They reflect what is important for the area in which the individual is working—that is, what is really strategically important for the organisational unit—in order to contribute to the organisation as a whole. While job specifications and duty statements can give some guidance as to what is important in a job, performance standards are written to reflect an answer to two questions:

- Why does the job exist?
- What does the organisation require of me for this next period?

Before continuing, it may help to briefly define the strategic, tactical and operational levels illustrated in Figure 4.1.

- Strategic goals and plans are set at senior management levels. *Strategic goals* relate to the organisation in its entirety, and set the scene for *what* the organisation wants to achieve. *Strategic plans* set out *how* the strategic goals will be achieved.

FIGURE 4.1 Relationship between strategy and performance standards

- Tactical goals and plans are set by middle management levels. *Tactical goals* relate to the major businesses of an organisation (e.g. a diversified resource company having several groupings, such as Minerals, Steel, Petroleum and Services) and identify *critical areas of* success, which in turn allow the organisation to achieve its overall strategic goals and plans. *Tactical plans* allow the organisation's businesses, in specific areas, to achieve the organisation's overall strategy.
- Operational goals and plans are set by front-line management levels. *Operational goals* are set for departments and individuals, and indicate the *specific and measurable results* to be achieved by both. *Operational plans* are developed from the operational and tactical goals by *stepping out the process* of how most effectively to achieve the goals. Operational-level goals and plans may be financial (expressed in dollar terms) or non-financial (expressed as quantities to be produced).

Motivation

An organisation is the sum of all its parts. Those parts are made up of many resources, one of the most important being human beings. Employees are an organisation's best asset: without them, organisations cannot function, and without motivated employees, organisations cannot achieve their overall strategies. For employees to become and remain motivated, they need to be able to see exactly how they are contributing to the organisation. Specific performance standards provide the basis on which to give constructive and helpful feedback to individuals or teams on their performance, and are the mechanism through which quality and improved performance can be achieved. Managers need to state clearly the strategic objectives of the section where staff are working, and to provide copies of appropriate corporate plans so that staff can see what the corporate directions, objectives and strategies are. It is the manager's responsibility to provide this information and to help staff develop appropriate and useful performance standards that can be agreed on and then used to monitor and evaluate individual and team performance. Together, managers and their staff set performance standards that reflect the CSFs of the organisation and enable staff to see how their own performance is progressing.

For effective performance standards to be set, employees need to possess the confidence to challenge their manager if they do not agree with the performance standards. Managers must consistently demonstrate integrity, honesty and fairness in the way they deal with their staff to create an environment in which employees feel they can give constructive input on their performance standards. Managers should bear in mind that setting performance standards is not just checking another box on the list to complete another managerial task, and that employees are likely to be passionate about the setting of their performance standards: these will relate directly to salary or wage raises and the benefits linked to them (i.e. superannuation). Well-written performance standards are key to motivating employees, but not all employees have the same motivational needs. Managers need to know what other stimuli motivate their individual employees and to manage them accordingly.

People are individuals, and the stimuli that motivate them depend on what needs they choose (consciously or subconsciously) to satisfy first. Figure 4.2 illustrates three well-publicised theories of motivation.

FIGURE 4.2 Theories of motivation

Maslow's Hierarchy of Needs Theory	ERG Theory	McClelland's 3 Needs Theory

• Abraham Maslow's five needs:
  1. Physiological
  2. Safety
  3. Social
  4. Esteem
  5. Self-actualisation
• As each need is satisfied the individual moves on to the next need
• Moves from lower order needs (1) to higher order needs (5)[2]
	• Clayton Alderfer reworked Maslow's needs hierarchy to three groups of core needs:
	  1. Existence
	  2. Relatedness
	  3. Growth
	• Existence encompasses Maslow's 1 and 2 needs, Relatedness encompasses Maslow's 3 and 4 needs, and Growth encompasses 5 on Maslow's hierarchy
	• In ERG Theory, more than one need is operative at once and if gratification of a higher need is not achievable, the lower need is heightened[3]
		• David McClelland developed this theory, comprising three main needs of:
		  1. Achievement
		  2. Power
		  3. Affiliation
		• High achievers differentiate themselves from others by a need to do things better
		• Achievement training is key[4]

Following are some examples of factors that *motivate* individuals:

- physical factors such as satisfactory pay, benefits and work conditions, including flexibility
- challenges
- recognition
- further training
- feedback on performance
- opportunities for advancement
- empowerment
- increased responsibility
- trust in and support by a supervisor or manager
- being treated with integrity, honesty, fairness and consistency
- satisfaction
- respect
- being able to measure their contribution to the organisation through performance standards.

Some factors that can cause *demotivation* of even the most motivated individuals are:

- personal problems
- poor supervision
- poor working relationships.

Managers need to be aware that the environment an employee works in provides the stimulus for motivation. Managers must ascertain the stimuli that motivate individual employees in their work environment and tailor their approach to each employee in an effort to maintain employee motivation. This can be as simple as giving feedback and providing challenges for a specific employee if the physical environment is otherwise satisfying the employee's needs.

Management and self-management tools

The tools and methodologies used to monitor performance are rapidly evolving and in the future managing the performance of people is likely to demand the same levels of rigour that financial processes do today. Standards are important tools that help to monitor the performance of individuals and organisations. To be useful they must be measurable in a way that is fair and equitable for all. Standards should be presented in a specific, stylised format for the development of measurable performance agreements between staff and management. Performance standards:

- maintain consistency
- secure improvement of service
- ensure quality
- maintain product performance
- sets personal performance levels.

Combined, all the standards of an organisation set its performance in terms of productivity, quality, efficiency and profitability. Well-written and well-implemented performance standards will reap quality performance.

While the private sector may be able to link strategy to specific outcomes like profit, sales or productivity, the public sector is also able to operationalise strategy in specific terms that relate to the outcomes required of programs run in different departments, agencies or branches. Performance standards provide the foundations for the implementation of strategy.[5]

Figure 4.3 demonstrates the links between strategy, CSFs, KPIs, and mechanisms for measuring performance and individual/team performance standards. The figure shows that performance measures or standards are relevant only when they are integrated with organisational strategy. Note how each functional area and each individual can identify how they contribute to the business strategy, the CSFs and KPIs.

CHECK YOUR UNDERSTANDING

1 What should standards demonstrate?
2 What are the two things performance standards need in order to be effective?
3 How do performance standards motivate staff?
4 How may quality performance be defined?
5 How do performance standards provide the basis for the implementation of organisational strategy?
6 How can a manager motivate an employee to give input into and achieve performance standards?

FIGURE 4.3 Links between strategy and performance standards

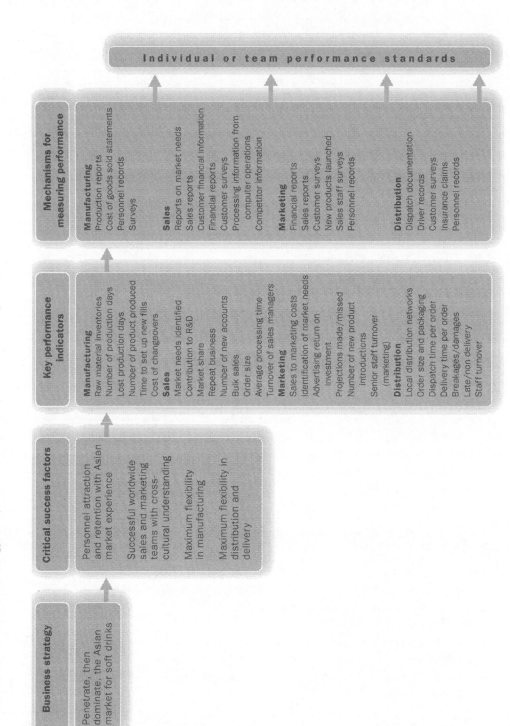

SKILL AND KNOWLEDGE APPLICATION

TASK

All employees need to feel they are making a contribution to the organisation. This contribution can be measured by the links from strategic goals and plans to the performance standards of departments and individuals. For each of the following jobs, write no more than two sentences to explain the possible link between these jobs and the overall strategic goals of an organisation (e.g. a receptionist may contribute, through her performance of politely and professionally answering telephone calls within three rings, to the strategic goal of exceptional customer service, this being one of the achievements the organisation is striving for).

- Accounts Clerk
- Cook
- Firefighter
- Plumber

- Factory Manager
- Chief Electronics Engineer
- Senior Flight Attendant
- Teacher (primary)

- Retail Salesperson
- Finance Manager
- Fitness Instructor
- Customs Investigator

The need for performance standards

Many managers and staff cringe at the concept 'performance standard', especially when used in relation to performance appraisals.[6] It tends to conjure up memories of poor appraisals and a lack of clear and constructive feedback. Yet standards are a regular part of life. Look at the following examples for which standards exist in daily life:

- driving on the road
- using a telephone
- public behaviour
- work behaviour
- electrical wiring.

Everyday standards

We are expected to maintain a large number of standards as members of our society, so the idea of having some explicitly expressed standards at work should not arouse feelings of resentment or fear. Yet it does, because in the past managers may not have used standards well or wisely, or provided useful, constructive feedback on how staff have performed against them or how they could improve.

Standards are used in society to maintain certain levels of acceptable behaviour. Standards help to keep us safe and to know exactly what is expected of us. For example, you know with some degree of certainty that when you go shopping at the local shopping centre, you will not come across a naked person cavorting down the supermarket aisles. Likewise, with some degree of certainty, you know that as you proceed through a green light at an intersection, a car will not come crashing into you from the side. This is because there is general agreement in the community that nude shopping is unacceptable, and that we will all abide by the authorised road rules for the safety of all drivers. While nothing in life is absolutely certain, standards provide us with some degree of reliability and guidance.

Work standards

Work standards are meant to achieve the same things as standards in everyday life. They are meant to be motivating for employees, and to generate confidence in doing a job, improvement in the job and satisfaction from doing a job well. In doing so, standards direct energy and effort to what is important for the organisation to achieve its strategic outcomes. Appropriate standards allow us to monitor our own performance, which contributes to job satisfaction. Without performance standards, work is likely to become misdirected and effortless because there are no guidelines as to what should be done and how well it has to be done. This leads to loss of interest by workers, uncaring attitudes, and lack of autonomy and job satisfaction that can sometimes lead to a lack of safety in the workplace. In performance management we are concerned with the quality, consistency and improvement of work performance by individuals to ensure that organisational outcomes are achieved.

Two examples of performance

If you asked an employee to put together a portfolio of sales information or to stack bricks in a designated spot, how would you know when the individual had done the job? How would you know when the individual had done the job well? On the basis of the above instructions, would it be easy to determine whether you should award a wage or salary raise? Let's have a closer look at these performances.

> **EXAMPLE ONE**
> Assume you had the following in mind when you gave the instruction: 'Put together a portfolio of sales information'.
> - Use a plastic binder with clear plastic sleeves in it.
> - Place each of the sales brochures in a separate sleeve.
> - Use only brochures that have been printed in the past 12 months.
> - Arrange the brochures so that similar products are grouped together.
> - Place the front of a corporate brochure in the front sleeve.
> - Stick a business card on the front cover.

Assume that the person you asked to put together the portfolio of sales information does the following:

- uses the cardboard company folder to hold the brochures
- places all the company sales brochures in the folder
- places the brochures in the order in which they were picked from the files
- places a business card in the appropriate slot in the cardboard cover.

The staff member carefully and proudly puts this portfolio together and hands it to you, expecting a nod of appreciation. When you are handed the portfolio you see immediately that it is not what you wanted; your face says so too, and your staff member sees as much. The incident leaves you puzzled, agitated and angry, as now you will have to do it yourself. The whole thing reinforces your concept that if you want anything done, you have to do it yourself. You prepare the portfolio as it 'should be' and ask yourself why your staff member couldn't do this.

EXAMPLE TWO

Imagine that you give an instruction to a new apprentice who has been with you for three months and is 17 years old. Assume you had the following in mind when you gave the instruction: 'Stack those bricks over there!'

- Bricks would be stacked so that they interlocked, two one way and two the other.
- Bricks would be stacked no deeper than six bricks.
- Each stack of bricks would not be longer than 10 bricks long (side to side).
- Each stack of bricks would not be higher than about one metre.
- Only enough bricks to do the job required would be stacked there.

Assume that the bricks are stacked by the apprentice in the following way:

- Eight bricks are stacked in a row side to side.
- Bricks are stacked in five piles of the above.
- Bricks are stacked to about half a metre high.

When the apprentice has dutifully complied with your request, the individual stands there expectantly, believing a good job has been done. You descend from the roof of the house where you have been inspecting some work. As you get to the bottom of the ladder you catch sight of the stacked bricks. You can see the stacking is all wrong and without thinking you let fly with, 'What the hell do you call that? There are enough bricks there to do the whole house, if they don't fall over first!'. The apprentice looks upset and confused. You walk away, muttering to yourself about why they don't teach them common sense at college. You simply can't understand why the apprentice didn't grasp a simple instruction.

The performance problem

By now you are probably aware of the problem in the examples. The performance problem is not so clear-cut. Is there a performance problem with the staff member or is there a performance problem with the manager? Clearly, there are two versions of what needs to be done in the examples. The instructor (manager) had specific results in mind when giving the instruction. The staff member also had specific results in mind when receiving the instruction. The two results were not the same because they were not discussed, nor did either party bother to check that the communication they sent or received was the one intended.[7] Two people may have completely different ideas about the same communication. What one person sees in his or her mind is not what another person sees. In Figure 4.4 it is possible to see both a white vase on a dark background and two dark faces on a white background. Two people looking at this figure may see two very different things. Unless the other perspective is pointed out to them, they may never be aware that another interpretation exists. The same is true for performance standards.

Who is wrong in the above examples—the person giving the instruction or the person receiving the instruction? Can the manager who made the requests really say the job has not been done satisfactorily? Can it be said that the two jobs were very poorly done? In each case, the portfolio was made and the bricks were stacked. That is all the individuals were asked to do. The point is that they were not being done to the standard that the person requesting the job expected. This occurred because no standards were set or communicated for each job by the instructor (manager).

FIGURE 4.4 Two views of the same communication

A further question of training also arises. For individuals to perform at required standards they need to have adequate knowledge, skills and experience. Managers should not assume that staff possess the required training or that they can do a job. This information is obtained through the negotiation stage of developing and setting performance standards. The examples above are fairly typical of the sort of stupid things that happen every day in many organisations. Unless the standards to which you want the job done are made clear to the individuals you ask to do a job, they have no idea of how well you want it done. Managers need to spend time, when giving an instruction, to include a description of the performance standard.

What is performance?

Performance, as it is referred to within the concept of performance management, relates to the carrying out of a work task, duty or objective. It is implied that it will be done to a satisfactory level. If the satisfactory level is not identified, it is impossible for the worker to reach the required standard. The definition is more complex than this, however. Performance includes:

- *inputs* (the skills, knowledge and expertise individuals have and which they apply to their jobs)
- *processes* (behaviours that individuals exhibit while doing their job)
- *outputs* (specific, measurable results that individuals achieve).

Actions are the means through which individuals perform.

People perform innumerable actions each day. Sometimes these are physical actions, such as lifting, manipulating a computer keyboard or creating a report; sometimes they are mental actions, like operational planning or developing marketing ideas or policy. Either way, because an individual is involved in action, something results as a consequence of the action and an output is created that we call performance. The process is illustrated in Figure 4.5.

FIGURE 4.5 Performance

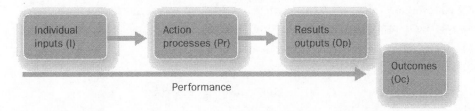

Performance and actions

You will appreciate that there is a difference between actions and results. Performance concerns itself with the achievement of specific, desired and identifiable results. A result may be defined as a change that occurs as a consequence of an action you execute. Actions lead to results or outputs. Performance is the end result of the actions an individual takes to achieve specific, desired outcomes or results, as illustrated in Figure 4.6.

FIGURE 4.6 The link between performance standards and results

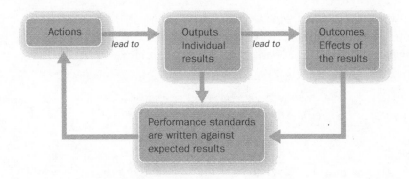

Table 4.1 illustrates the above concept with three specific examples.

TABLE 4.1 Examples of actions, outputs and outcomes

Actions	Outputs	Outcomes
Holding consultations, writing discussion or issues papers	Policy decisions made Plans drawn up	Better roads
Arranging stock on shelves, writing signs for shelves	Sales Sales targets reached	Profits Bonuses
Inspecting food preparation sites	Clean premises Appropriate procedures	Public health and safety targets met

Results are usually observable, specific and measurable. Actions tend not to be observable, specific and measurable. It is very difficult to measure actions in any precise way. When you have difficulty finding a measure, have a look at the result you are trying to measure—it might just be an action. The following examples are action statements:

- Organise report on the past six months of sales.
- Call a meeting on new equipment.
- Train the new person starting today.
- Organise a report to be word processed.

Unless actions are directed to specific results or outputs, people can be very busy in their jobs but achieve few or no results for the work they do. Actions (or activity) by themselves, therefore, do not equal performance. Performance management and the setting of performance standards is designed to focus activity or actions on agreed outputs so that specific performance can be managed to achieve organisational outcomes.

You probably understand by now that performance standards:

- are based on results or outputs
- do not include action statements
- are focused on the end result rather than how you get there.

Action statements have no place in performance standards and are a separate process from performance standards. In particular, action statements are:

- concerned with how you achieve a result, not the result itself
- concerned only with the result and whether it meets the appropriate standard(s) using the appropriate inputs and processes.

An example

Imagine you are a florist and have agreed on the following performance standard with your manager, who is also the owner of the florist shop:

In the $35.00 bowl, flower arrangements are to have seven pieces of greenery, three carnations, five roses, seven yellow pygmy and three sprays of Anaphalis nubigena, *and are to be arranged in accordance with flower-arranging principles.*

Note that the result and the standard relate to the final output expected. It is not specified how you arrange the flowers in the bowl. Each person who arranges the flowers is likely to do it differently. This is a result of the varying degrees of skill, knowledge and experience that different individuals have. It is possible to have five people making different arrangements that all meet the performance standard. This does not matter, as long as the final product meets the result required—that is, the bowl is arranged in accordance with flower-arranging principles, and using the right amount of each flower or greenery. The action of arranging is therefore irrelevant to the performance standard. However, if an individual were arranging the bowl in the shop and a customer walked in and was not attended to or was treated rudely, the behaviour would not be appropriate; this would become an issue that might need to be worked into a standard. Figure 4.7 illustrates the concept.

FIGURE 4.7 Difference between a result and an action

	Starting point	Actions How you get from the start to the finish	Result and standard
Explanation	Might be anywhere	Could be done a number of different ways; it does not matter, as long as the end result is in accordance with the performance and the measure	Agreed, firm and stable result and measure (performance standards)
Example	Raw materials: flowers, greenery, wire, base, water	Selecting flower colour Wiring flowers Cutting flowers Arranging flowers Selecting base Watering flowers	Arranged $35.00 bowl: seven pieces of greenery, three carnations, five roses, seven yellow pygmy, and three sprays of *Anaphalis nubigena* in accordance with flower-arranging principles
Stages of model	Inputs	Inputs, process	Outputs, outcomes

CHECK YOUR UNDERSTANDING

7 How do standards provide a degree of certainty in everyday life?

8 Explain how standards create confidence in people.

9 What do standards direct energy and results towards?

10 Do you think performance problems are always clear-cut?

11 How can performance become more directed?

12 Explain the term 'performance'.

13 What is the difference between an action and a result? Provide an example to illustrate your answer.

SKILLS PRACTICE

1   For the following statements, identify which are performance statements and which are action statements by placing either P for performance statement or A for action statement in the box.

   a ❑   Develop the image of the team.

   b ❑   Reduce errors in processing from 26% to 15%.

   c ❑   Eliminate backlog in filing.

   d ❑   Monitor product sales.

   e ❑   Increase internal customer business from 7% to 10% of total turnover.

   f ❑   Increase stocks of stationery from 5 days' to 10 days' usage.

   g ❑   Identify possible solutions to the distribution problem.

   h ❑   Develop a reporting system.

   i ❑   Ring phone company re problem phone.

   j ❑   Reduce the processing time for approvals from two weeks to seven days.

2   For the following results, document the actions you may need to execute in achieving the results:

   a   Reduce the processing time of all purchase orders.

   b   Increase the number of safety training sessions for employees.

   c   Reduce time lost due to accidents.

   d   Ensure sufficient staff are on hand to handle calls at average incoming call rate.

3   What might be the performances required in the following duties? List the performances in the appropriate column or on a separate sheet of paper. Remember that duties are a list of tasks to be accomplished by the job holder. You are asked to look for the performances required—that is, the end results.

Job	Duty	Performance required
Human Resources Officer	• Maintain, evaluate and revise job descriptions and performance standards. • Coordinate and conduct performance counselling sessions, as necessary.	
Sales Manager	• Develop and implement sales and marketing plans to increase market share and profitability. • Create long-term business relationships with existing and new customers.	
Warehouse Supervisor	• Establish and monitor an effective storage system to ensure that inventory is rotated and protected from deterioration and damage. • Establish and maintain appropriate inventory levels by considering ordering levels and financial resources invested.	

Job	Duty	Performance required
Accountant	• Prepare reports for taxation and management requirements. • Provide financial advice in response to proposals from other departments.	

4   Complete the following tasks using the above table.

   a   Choose two sets of duties from the table and identify possible critical success factors to which these duties might apply.

   b   Using the same two sets of duties, identify possible strategic objectives to which these duties might apply.

   c   As a manager, how might you motivate the job holders of these two sets of duties?

   d   For the two sets of duties chosen, develop two performance standards for each set.

   e   What does a manager need to do to ensure that satisfactory performance occurs in the above two sets of duties?

SKILL AND KNOWLEDGE APPLICATION

Lily has been working as a Legal Secretary for a local law firm for two years. During this time she has been studying part-time at university to become a lawyer herself. Lily has always been meticulous in her work at the law firm and with her studies. Her current boss has always given her feedback on her performance at work and her study assignments, and challenged her with new projects to develop her skills as a lawyer. There has been a new partner appointed to the firm and Lily has been assigned to him as his Legal Secretary, as she is the best the law firm has and she will be instrumental in helping the new partner settle in quickly. Lily's motivation and drive in her studies and work has been exemplary, and she has always been a high achiever. Under the new partner, however, Lily's work, attitude and demeanour have deteriorated significantly and she is no longer studying for her law degree.

TASK

➤ Explain what you believe has led to Lily's change in attitude and motivation. What suggestions could you make to rectify the situation?

Barbara runs two hairdressing salons on the north side of Brisbane. At the Chermside salon she employs Jason, Cherie and Zoe, plus Lisa, who comes in part-time over the lunch period and stays until 3 pm. On this particular afternoon, Barbara bawls Jason out because he is not cutting the hair of a client in the way she likes it to be cut. There is a huge argument, and Jason goes off into the back room while Barbara finishes the client's hair.

TASK

➤ Barbara asks you for advice on how to handle this situation and the 'overly sensitive' Jason. What advice would you give?

The role of managers

Communication

Communication is an important part of performance management, and has a crucial role in the use of performance standards. Performance management is about communication, both oral and written. Performance standards have to be negotiated, agreed on and communicated between the parties concerned. They need to be written so that they can be looked at as the need arises. Monitoring must take place and appropriate feedback be provided to individuals on how they are performing. All these tasks require communication skills in managers and staff, and leadership skills in managers. Managers must be able to use different types of communication to manage performance well. They need skills in listening, counselling, coaching, paraphrasing, reflecting, problem solving, conflict resolution, mediation and a range of interpersonal skills. Without these skills managers will be unable to set performance standards and objectives to manage performance effectively.

In communicating effectively, managers need to ensure that they do not operate on assumptions about why people are performing in the way they are. They must use their communication skills to check assumptions and to determine the actual reasons for the level of performance being demonstrated by an individual, and also the capabilities of the individual. Assumptions can be costly. On-the-job training skills are an important tool for the manager in managing performance. In helping people to develop, the manager will often need to provide developmental opportunities, and guide learning and development through coaching or mentoring. Delegation is a powerful motivator and learning mechanism available to the manager and, if done well, can be a useful process in supporting performance. These management tools are discussed in Chapter 12.

Poor managers and employees' poor performance

In many cases, poor performance is not just the fault of the staff member. Managers must share equal responsibility, especially if they have not set and agreed on performance standards with staff or ensured that adequate training is available. A lack of clear performance standards can demotivate individuals because any performance is then seen as satisfactory performance.[8] It is not possible to determine performance without a starting point against which to measure the performance. The performance standard:

- needs to be clearly communicated to the appropriate staff member
- provides a starting point as a measure by which performance will be evaluated
- creates job satisfaction and autonomy in work, which assists with motivation in the workplace.

Effective management and performance standards

Effective managers can optimise performance across whole organisations. An example of an organisation where standards effectively support the organisation's corporate plans and strategies is BHP Billiton. BHP Billiton is the world's largest diversified resource company. It applies a business model based on customer-oriented groupings which it calls customer sector groups (CSGs). BHP Billiton's nine CSGs are Petroleum, Aluminium, Base Metals, Diamonds and Specialty Products, Energy Coal, Stainless Steel Materials, Iron Ore, Manganese, and Metallurgical Coal. Its purpose is to 'create long-term value through the discovery, development and conversion of natural resources, and the provision of innovative customer and market-focused solutions'.[9]

BHP Billiton identified, in its *Strategic Framework and Performance Measures* published in February 2000, five CSFs for its business, which are:[10]

1 new business models and culture aligned with charter

2 deliver operational excellence

3 portfolio management

4 deliver significant value creating growth

5 financial management.

In order for these CSFs to drive the business to be the market leader in the diversified resource company sector, it requires a range of no-nonsense performance standards relating to all operational aspects of the business that will focus the business CSGs. Figure 4.8 shows the performance on BHP Billiton's CSFs.

These CSFs have been circulated through all levels of the organisation so that the production employee at the coalface or the receptionist in the site office is as aware of the CSFs of the organisation as the CEO. This is imperative, as their performance management programs, appraisal systems and ultimately benefits will be linked back to this strategic focus. BHP Billiton, through this approach, is allowing its employees to know exactly what is expected of them and how well

FIGURE 4.8 Performance on a diversified resource company's CSFs[11]

Diversified resource company CSFs	Achievement
New business models and culture aligned with charter	• Implementation of new business models (portfolio model, shared services) to support achievement of value objectives • Implementation of a cultural change process designed to achieve organisational alignment with shareholder value delivery objectives • Enhancement of organisational capabilities (management, commercial and leadership development)
Deliver operational excellence	• New business model based around a portfolio management concept and a large component of shared services among the business units • Margin improvements, cost reduction, project delivery on time and within budget, safety and environmental standards
Portfolio management	• Portfolio organisation involving strategic and commercial approaches to extracting maximum value through the business cycle; determination of which businesses/commodities BHP is in • Strong level of commercial discipline at the business level and broader portfolio management level
Deliver significant value creating growth	• Deliver on current projects • Expedite value from key projects • Capture and implement material growth opportunities aligned to strategic model • Manage acquisitions to capture value • BHP has an excellent portfolio of world-class production assets with significant brownfield and greenfield opportunities
Financial management	• Reduce level of corporate debt • Reduce reliance on bank debt

they must perform their job. If this approach proves successful, BHP Billiton will consistently achieve and continuously improve its business.

Managers are critical players in the performance management process. They must make a commitment to the setting of standards and do so in a way that is valid and reliable, setting an example for staff. How managers handle the process of setting standards and the whole of performance management will influence how successful it is.

CHECK YOUR UNDERSTANDING

14 What specific skills do managers need to be able to manage the setting of performance standards effectively?

15 Why must performance standards be communicated?

16 How would BHP Billiton be able to maintain consistency of performance under such a diversified structure?

17 Why are communication skills so important in the setting and using of performance standards?

18 What problems might be encountered if managers make assumptions about staff behaviours and performance?

SKILL AND KNOWLEDGE APPLICATION

You are a senior manager of a financial organisation that trades on the stock exchange. You have 15 managers who report directly to you. One of these managers is Jacinta Chalker, who starts work with you today. Your company is committed to performance management and conducts regular three-monthly formal performance reviews, providing very specific performance targets. As this is such a high priority for the organisation, you will spend about two hours this morning talking to Jacinta about the manager's role in setting standards.

TASK

➤ In point form, prepare what you will say to Jacinta.

➤ Comment on the high priority and focus this organisation places on setting standards.

The composition of performance standards

Performance standards are just one of the components of a performance objective. A performance objective guides work, and states what is to be done and how well it is to be done. Performance objectives are discussed later in this chapter. A performance standard is made up of two components: a *performance*, which is the output (or result) that is required; and a *standard* or measure of the performance, which is a statement of how well the performance has to be done. Figure 4.9 illustrates these components of a performance standard, together with two examples.

FIGURE 4.9 Components of a performance standard

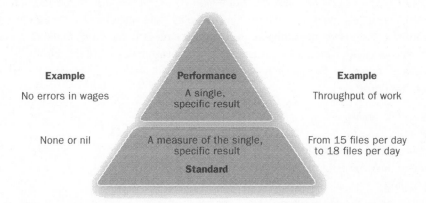

When a performance standard is written down, you should be able to see clearly its different components: the output (single, specific result) and the standards of the performance (measures of the single, specific result). A performance standard only ever has one result in it. If you place more than one result in the performance standard then it becomes very difficult to find an appropriate measure(s) for the performance of the two results. This confuses staff and management alike. For example, if the following performance standard is adopted, how do you measure it?

Decrease the number of errors in, and the number of telephone calls relating to, daily processing.

For every result you require, always write a new performance standard. In the above example, a performance standard should have been written for the number of errors in daily processing and one for the telephone calls related to daily processing. The required result would then be clear and measurable, as in Figure 4.10.

FIGURE 4.10 Clear, measurable results

Performance	Standard
1. Reduce the number of errors in daily processing	From the current level of 52 (daily average) to 20 (daily average)
2. Reduce the number of telephone calls relating to processing	From current level of 15% to 7% of total calls

Figure 4.11 illustrates a number of examples of performance standards. Notice the degree of specificity of both the result and the measure.

Precision in standards

Notice that the standards in Figure 4.11 are very precise. You could not possibly misinterpret what they mean or how they will be measured, so there can be no dispute about whether the performance has been achieved to the standard required. For example, performance standard 1 has a measure of five days. It is very clear that if the plant is down for only four days in a year, the standard has been exceeded and the individual(s) can be rewarded appropriately. Performance standard 5 is equally measurable. If word-processing is not produced within the agreed deadlines and corporate standards, the individual will not have met the required standard of performance. It is very easy to check whether performance appraisals are being conducted every three months for performance standard 10. Kris Cole identifies a useful mnemonic to assist in the writing of precise standards—SMARTT:[12]

Specific and concise
Measurable
Ambitious (achievable yet challenging)
Related to the overall department and enterprise goals
Time-framed
Trackable, or easily monitored.

FIGURE 4.11 Examples of performance standards

Result	Measure
1. Plant downtime reduced	To five working days per year
2. Orders processed more quickly	To within 24 hours of receipt of order
3. Quotes provided to customers more quickly	To within 48 hours of receipt of request
4. All telephones answered	Within three rings
5. Word processing completed	To negotiated deadlines with manager and corporate standards as per handbook
6. Written reports reduced in length	From an average of 15 pages to an average of 6–8 pages
7. Stock on the sales floor increased	Two fill-ups each day at 10.30 am and 2.30 pm
8. Trucks serviced	Every three months
9. Personal computer hard drives backed up	Once each day after 4 pm
10. Performance appraisals completed	Every three months
↑	↑
A single, specific result	A measure of the single, specific result

There are likely to be times when it is not possible to find a measure of a result that is as precise as the above examples suggest. It is then legitimate to describe carefully what the result will look like. For example, in an office environment it may be very difficult to find precise measures of the result 'Achieve a more organised approach to work'. While you could argue that this should be broken down into the specific things that need to be better organised, you might wish to describe this result, to save writing a number of smaller performance standards that could be overwhelming for an individual or team. The example is completed below:

'Achieve a more organised approach to work. This will be achieved when:

a no paperwork is lost

b filing is up-to-date

c in-tray is dealt with daily

d manager is informed of important issues on a daily basis

e tasks are completed on time 90% of the time.'

While the actual result is vague in this example, it is strengthened by the very specific standards a to e, which describe carefully and precisely what is expected when the individual or team is 'more organised'. The principles do not change—just the way you express them. It is preferable to detail specific results, but there will be times when you prefer to handle a performance standard in the way illustrated in the above example.

SKILLS PRACTICE

In the following examples, underline the result and the performance standard required.

1 Reduce downtime of machinery to five working days maximum per year by December XXXX without the use of replacement machinery.

2 Orders are processed within 24 hours of receipt by 30 June XXXX, given that all computer equipment is operating correctly.

3 Word processing is achieved to stated and negotiated deadlines and corporate standards during normal business hours by September XXXX.

4 Increase employee satisfaction levels on the XYZ instrument from 53% to 69% by 30 April XXXX with only one use of the instrument.

5 Reduce general costs to 5% less than the industry average benchmark for the per-capita staffing levels by 30 March XXXX.

Multiple measures of performance

Sometimes you will want to include a number of different standards which, when combined, will provide a very specific measure of the performance. You may include as many measures of the performance as you like, provided you have only one result. In many cases there are a number of ways to measure a result; you can agree with the individual staff member which of them you will include, or you may include them all. If you do include them all, remember that the staff member is required to meet all the measures and not just some of them. Figure 4.12 illustrates a number of performance standards that have more than one measure of performance.

Think about the actions that might be associated with each of the standards in Figure 4.12. For example, increasing productivity in the call centre requires a large number of different actions to be undertaken to achieve the result.

SKILL AND KNOWLEDGE APPLICATION

TASK

➤ Complete the following by writing down the possible actions associated with achieving the standard indicated on the left.

SKILL AND KNOWLEDGE APPLICATION CONTINUED

Performance:

Increase productivity in XYZ call centre   **Actions**

Standards:

- Cost per processing of a call
- Number of calls processed per staff hour
- Percentage of employees absent
- Number of outcomes achieved per staff hour
- Number of times a customer is called back to resolve a query

FIGURE 4.12 Examples of performance standards with more than one measure

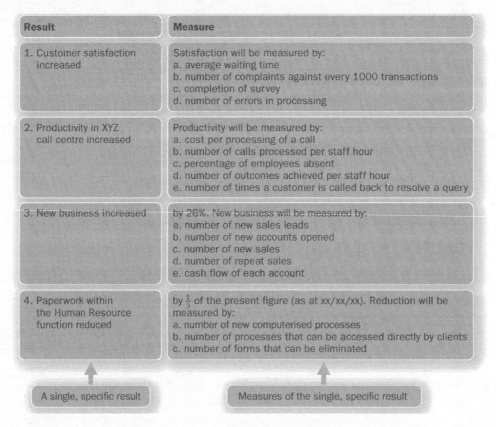

Result	Measure
1. Customer satisfaction increased	Satisfaction will be measured by: a. average waiting time b. number of complaints against every 1000 transactions c. completion of survey d. number of errors in processing
2. Productivity in XYZ call centre increased	Productivity will be measured by: a. cost per processing of a call b. number of calls processed per staff hour c. percentage of employees absent d. number of outcomes achieved per staff hour e. number of times a customer is called back to resolve a query
3. New business increased	by 26%. New business will be measured by: a. number of new sales leads b. number of new accounts opened c. number of new sales d. number of repeat sales e. cash flow of each account
4. Paperwork within the Human Resource function reduced	by $\frac{1}{3}$ of the present figure (as at xx/xx/xx). Reduction will be measured by: a. number of new computerised processes b. number of processes that can be accessed directly by clients c. number of forms that can be eliminated

A single, specific result   Measures of the single, specific result

Linking standards to strategy and operational plans

The discussion so far has concentrated on standards that might be associated with particular aspects of the duties an individual may have. However, standards are also related to the specific strategic objectives of an organisation, and should focus on the critical success factors that will deliver the required strategic outcomes for the organisation. Thus performance standards are written to support the corporate goals and objectives to ensure that they are achieved, as illustrated in Figure 4.13.

FIGURE 4.13 Hierarchy of goals for a manufacturing organisation[13]

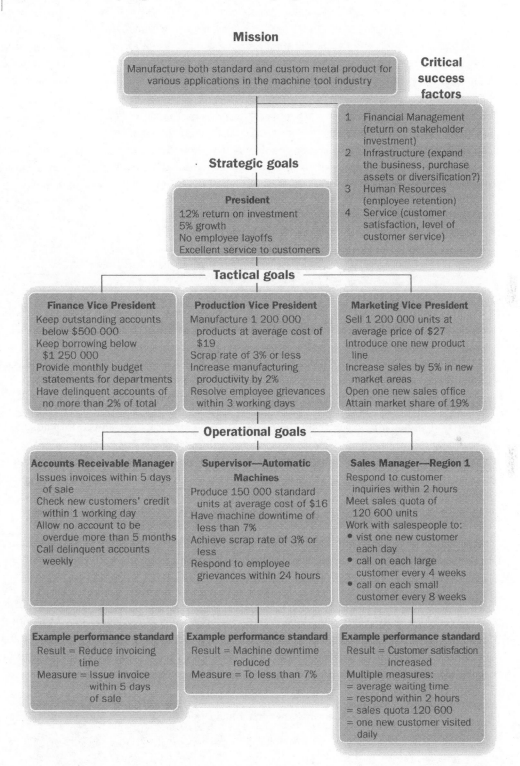

From Figure 4.13, you can see that the Accounts Receivable Manager has a goal of 'Issue invoices within 5 days of sale'. This could translate, as illustrated, into the performance standard of 'Result = Reduce invoicing time', and 'Measure = Issue invoice within 5 days of sale'. From the illustration you are able to link this performance standard back to the Finance Vice President whose goal is to 'Keep outstanding accounts below $500 000', which links back to the President's need to achieve '12% return on investment'. The levels from the performance standard link back through the various positions to the mission statement.

For performance standards to be useful they need to be linked to strategy, so the use of CSFs is a vital step in the development of performance standards. As an example, review the CSFs for BHP Billiton in Figure 4.8. If you were part of a diversified resource company management team, what standards might be appropriate to ensure the implementation of the winning strategy the organisation has developed? Figure 4.14, which looks at one of the CSFs, will give you some ideas.

FIGURE 4.14 Standards for CSFs of a diversified resource company

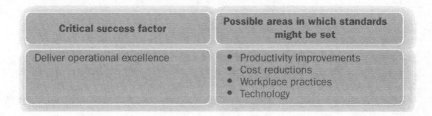

From Figure 4.14 it is possible to see that, strategically speaking, if you wish to achieve operational excellence, staff must concentrate on the things that deliver operational excellence. The four areas identified provide a specific focus for every job of every person in BHP Billiton. Further, these areas now provide opportunities to develop specific standards that everyone must maintain in their daily functioning. For example, the resource company's CSF of 'Deliver operational excellence' may trigger the following performance standards for the senior managers of each customer sector group:

1 decrease operating costs by 2% per annum

2 enhance workplace practices (manning flexibility, equipment productivity)

3 cost and productivity improvements (technological developments)

4 outsourcing options.

If these standards are implemented by all senior management in all customer sector groups of the diversified resources company then consistent, operational excellence improvements in the organisation will result. Consequently every job, no matter what it is, must be accountable for operational excellence. If you were the Production Operator on a mine site, you might not be accountable for:

• outsourcing options

• researching and implementing new technological developments in mining equipment

• delivering cost and productivity improvements.

But as a Production Operator at a mine site you would have specific duties relating to cutting coal. These duties can still be seen to be aligned to the strategic level of the organisation. Figure 4.15 illustrates this linkage.

FIGURE 4.15 Performance standards linked to strategy

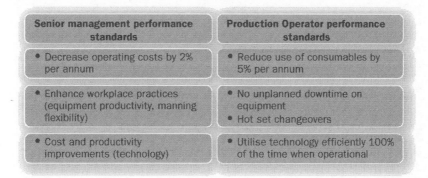

Senior management performance standards	Production Operator performance standards
• Decrease operating costs by 2% per annum	• Reduce use of consumables by 5% per annum
• Enhance workplace practices (equipment productivity, manning flexibility)	• No unplanned downtime on equipment • Hot set changeovers
• Cost and productivity improvements (technology)	• Utilise technology efficiently 100% of the time when operational

Not all the duties of the job of the Production Operator may be able to deliver operational excellence improvements. They constitute only the basics. It is all the standards, at all the levels of the organisation, which deliver operational excellence improvements. This is why performance standards are written against the things that are really important for an organisation, not specifically against a job description.

SKILLS PRACTICE

1   From your own knowledge and experience as a consumer, develop two performance standards for the following areas of 'high-quality service'.

   Performance area   **Performance standards**
   Customer service
   Product quality
   Ingredient quality

2   From your own knowledge and experience of insurance, develop two performance standards for the following areas:

   Performance area   **Performance standards**
   Customer service
   Claims processing
   Sales

3   The emphasis on productivity and improvement in the workforce is unlikely to be reduced in the future. Consequently, the area of human resources has become an important component of any organisation's strategies, and many organisations have decided that human resources is a critical success factor in their

SKILLS PRACTICE CONTINUED

overall management strategy. Below, the CSF is included together with a number of performance indicators. Develop at least two performance standards for any three of the performance indicators.

Critical success factor: Human resources

Performance indicators: Number of training programs

Turnover rates

Absenteeism rates

Employee attitudes

Average educational level of employees

Health and safety program effectiveness

Ratio of number of interviewees per vacancy

Ratio of revenue per employee

Ratio of costs per employee

Ratio of terminations to number of staff

CHECK YOUR UNDERSTANDING

19 What two components make up a performance standard?

20 What does a performance standard ever contain only one of?

21 Why must performance standards be precise?

22 What must managers allow for when setting performance standards with staff?

23 Why should a performance standard stretch an individual?

SKILL AND KNOWLEDGE APPLICATION

Hassan is the manager of all the teaching staff in a college that caters primarily for international students. He is responsible for recruitment, selection and induction of the teaching staff as well as managing the staff to help the college achieve its strategic and operational plans.

Hassan takes his management role seriously, so he puts a lot of time and effort into setting performance standards for his staff. He also ensures that the staff participate fully in the setting of the standards. Hassan has over 30 teaching staff in the various departments of the college, so he is always very busy. As he is so busy he has decided to delegate the induction of teaching staff to his assistant, who has been with the college for over 20 years. Hassan's assistant seems to be handling the additional induction responsibility well, so he decides to undertake an audit, as he is lead auditor for the college, of how the teaching staff are performing against their set standards.

As he collates his audit data, Hassan is disheartened to see that very few of his newer teaching staff are motivated towards achieving their performance standards. Hassan cannot understand it, as they have all participated in writing their performance standards.

TASK

Hassan comes to you for advice. Identify what might have led to this situation and advise Hassan on what he could do to realign his teaching staff with their performance standards.

CONCLUSION

To set performance standards, it is critical to first understand what they are and what they are intended to achieve. Performance standards create the links between an organisation's strategic plan and the work of individuals. Standards clearly establish what is important for an organisation and let individuals know exactly what is expected in terms of performance, thus motivating individuals or teams to achieve. Performance standards need to be clearly stated and use objective measures so that the performance expectations are clear and precise. Where performance standards are not clear and precise, managers will have difficulties in obtaining satisfactory performance and high productivity from staff. Further, where performance standards are missing, managing becomes extremely difficult. Managers must work hard at ensuring that staff write realistic and usable performance standards or they will set their staff up for failure. Performance standards are not about trapping people or having them fail. They are designed to obtain the greatest productivity from individuals or teams, and to help all staff develop their knowledge and skills to meet the needs of the organisation in the near and far future.

 ## CASE STUDY

Lance had been successfully breeding native birds from his home for 20 years as a hobby. He had been working for several years in the construction industry and wanted a change in career, so decided to set up a pet shop where he would specialise in native birds.

Lance had never owned a business before or managed any employees, so engaged a consultant to assist him to write a vision statement, mission and strategic plan for his business as he was eager to get it right. One of his main critical success factors (CSFs) was customer service, as he saw this as strategic to building his business.

Recruiting for an assistant for his pet shop, Lance hired Natalie, a young woman who had recently finished school and was keen to work with animals. This was Natalie's first job, so she was very unsure of how to behave and what was expected of her.

Lance was a meticulous man who knew exactly how he wanted jobs completed and to what standard. He needed to be able to communicate his standards to Natalie effectively if the business was to be a success as Natalie would be the first point of contact for all customers.

QUESTIONS

1   How could Lance ensure that Natalie shared his vision/mission for his business?
2   Identify what steps Lance needs to take next to ensure his business is a success.

JOB AIDS

Flowchart for guidelines to setting performance standards

Required by individual job and organisational objectives

To facilitate monitoring and feedback

Performance standards consistent with strategy, objectives and values of the organisation

```
┌─────────────────────┐
│ Identify individual's │
│ main result areas     │
└─────────────────────┘
          ↓
┌─────────────────────┐
│ Select result areas   │
│ linked to CSFs        │
└─────────────────────┘
          ↓
┌─────────────────────┐
│ Develop KPIs for      │
│ selected CSFs         │
└─────────────────────┘
          ↓
┌─────────────────────┐
│ Set performance       │
│ standards for each    │
│ KPI                   │
└─────────────────────┘
          ↓
┌─────────────────────┐
│ Ensure performance    │
│ standards are valid,   │
│ agreed, realistic, clear, │
│ specific, well-defined │
│ and measurable        │
└─────────────────────┘
          ↓
┌─────────────────────┐
│ Allow staff to access │
│ performance data      │
└─────────────────────┘
          ↓
┌─────────────────────┐
│ Check performance     │
│ standards are         │
│ consistent with       │
│ organisational strategy │
└─────────────────────┘
```

✓ **CHECKLISTS**

Guidelines for understanding performance standards

❏ Performance standards should be used as valuable management and self-management tools.

❏ Standards should help you to monitor the performance of individuals and organisations.

❏ Performance standards should be consistent with the strategy, objectives and values of the organisation.

❏ Result areas that are selected should support the critical success factors of the organisation.

❏ Key performance indicators should support the critical success factors of the organisation.

❏ Performance standards should be well-written so they can be used to motivate employees.

References

1   Jones, R. 2010, 2nd edn. *Managing Human Resource Systems*. Pearson Australia: Frenchs Forest, Sydney, p. 116.

2   Robbins, S.P., Millett, B. & Waters-Marsh, T. 2004, 4th edn. *Organisational Behaviour*. Prentice Hall: Sydney, p. 164, 170, 171.

3   Robbins et al., op. cit., 2004, p. 170.

4   Robbins et al., op. cit., 2004, p. 171.

5   Schneier, C., Shaw, D & Beatty, R. 1995. 'Performance measurement and management: A tool for strategy execution'. In C. Schneier, D. Shaw, R. Beatty & L. Baird (eds), *The Performance Measurement, Management, and Appraisal Sourcebook*. HRD Press: Amherst, MA, pp. 3–19.

6   Swan, W. 1991. *How to Do a Superior Performance Appraisal*. John Wiley & Sons: New York, pp. 4–10.

7   Dwyer, J. 2009, 8th edn. *The Business Communication Handbook*. Pearson Australia: Frenchs Forest, Sydney.

8   Philp, T. 1990, 2nd edn. *Appraising Performance for Results*. McGraw-Hill: London, p. 18.

9   BHP Billiton 2009. *Our Businesses*, <www.bhpbilliton.com.au/bb/ourBusinesses.jsp> accessed 14 October 2009; BHP Billiton 2009. *Charter*, < www.bhpbilliton.com.au/bb/aboutUs/charter.jsp> accessed 14 October 2009.

10 BHP Billiton, Investor Relations 2000. *BHP Strategic Framework and Performance Measures*, <www.bhpbilliton.com.au>, February, pp. 2–3.

11 BHP Billiton, Investor Relations, op. cit., 2000, pp. 2–3.

12 Cole, K. 2010, 4th edn. *Management: Theory and Practice*. Pearson Australia: Frenchs Forest, Sydney, pp. 229–230.

13 Adapted from Daft, R.L. 1997, 4th edn. *Management*. South-Western, a part of Cengage Learning, Inc. Exhibit 7.3, p. 222.

CHAPTER FIVE

Principles of setting performance standards

Learning outcomes

After reading this chapter you should be able to:

* utilise a number of principles in setting performance standards

* write valid performance standards in accordance with a formula provided

* write valid performance objectives in accordance with a formula provided.

INTRODUCTION

Writing performance standards becomes a little easier once you know the formula and a number of guidelines, but you will still have to do a lot of thinking! The formula is quite simple. It consists of a result and a measure of that result (R + M), as illustrated in Figure 5.1. If you use this formula when constructing performance standards you can't really go wrong. The difficulty lies in making sure that the measure actually measures the result. The full formula is:

PS = R + M: Performance Standard [PS] equals Result [R] plus a Measure [M] of the result.

FIGURE 5.1 The performance standard formula

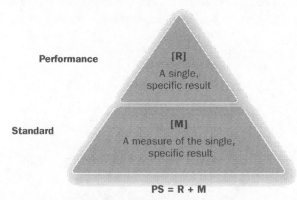

Performance

[R]
A single,
specific result

Standard

[M]
A measure of the single,
specific result

PS = R + M

In developing performance standards, it will help you to think first of the result that you want and then look for a satisfactory measure of it. In deciding on the measure, it is important to make sure it is appropriate to the result required.

Reviewing organisational objectives

Before setting performance standards you will need to review the organisational, divisional, departmental, branch and section objectives. Individual and team performance standards should support the infrastructure of the organisation, as illustrated in Figure 5.2. In Chapter 4, it is stressed that organisations only achieve their strategies and plans through people—thus, that the combined effort of all the individuals within an organisation equals its overall performance. Hence, individual performance standards and objectives that are not integrated with those of the organisation can only cause disaster, a lack of motivation, and frustration and dissatisfaction in individuals, because they cannot see what their efforts are leading towards.

FIGURE 5.2 Supporting the infrastructure

Organisational objectives

Divisional objectives

Departmental objectives

Branch objectives

Sectional objectives

Individual/team performance standards

Next, you will need to identify clearly the critical success factors (CSFs) and key performance indicators (KPIs) for your organisation, division, department, branch or agency and section. These factors drive change and improvement through organisations. You will recall that a CSF is any feature of the internal or external environment that has a major influence on an organisation achieving its goals. Originally CSFs were directed mainly at the strategic levels of an organisation; however, they are now also commonly used to help managers align strategic and operational goals to departmental and even individual goals. You need to fully understand what is important for each of the above areas before you can decide on team or individual performance standards. To add value, performance standards must support the KPIs of the organisation. In this way, when everyone in the organisation has completed their performance standards, they will contribute to the overall performance of the organisation. The significance of these issues is shown in Figure 5.3.

FIGURE 5.3 How CSFs and KPIs influence the organisation

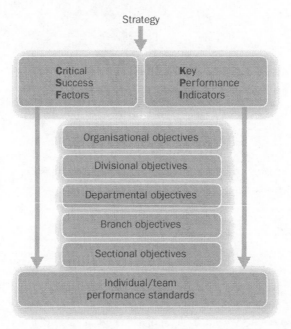

Critical outputs of the job

From the CSFs and KPIs you have identified, you now need to distinguish the critical outputs for the area in which you work and for the work a person does. Ensure that you have a good understanding of these outputs and the outcomes the organisation requires. An example of critical outputs is set out in Figure 4.13 in Chapter 4. The critical areas of output for the Production Vice President would be manufacturing 1 200 000 products at average cost of $19, scrap rate of 3% or less etc. The Production Vice President's goals then translate to the goals of the Supervisor of Automatic Machines as outputs of producing 150 000 standard units at an average cost of $16, and having machine downtime of less than 7%. It is now that you can review the job description, looking at the key accountabilities, key tasks and key activity areas of the job, and how they connect with the critical issues for the organisation. The job description is reviewed with regard to the strategic and operational plans of the organisation. This process establishes the specific areas for which you ought to write performance standards so they will contribute directly to the effectiveness of the organisation.

Principles of setting standards

There are a number of principles that should guide the development of performance standards: (1) validity; (2) agreement; (3) realism; (4) stretching; (5) clear definition; (6) measurability; (7) limitation; and (8) linkages. Each of these is discussed in detail below.

1. Validity

Validity means two things. Performance standards should be valid in terms of: (a) whether the measure is measuring the actual result required; and (b) whether the performance standard itself is valid in terms of the formula.

In ensuring that performance standards relate to the required performance, managers and supervisors must be careful not to impose their own concepts of standards on staff. For example, training programs sometimes set standards for training assessment that are higher than those required on the job. This sets up an artificial standard of performance that will not be used on the job. In other words, the assessment is not valid and is a waste of resources and the effort of the individuals being trained.

2. Agreement

It is a fundamental tenet of performance standards that they must be agreed on between the parties. If managers want commitment to performance standards, the standards must be negotiated and agreed on by both manager and staff member. The motivation aspects of this agreement are as noted in Chapter 4.

3. Realism

All performance standards must be realistic—in other words, not too high or too low. In either case, the standards will demotivate individuals rather than set up challenges for them, as illustrated in Figure 5.4. There is no point in setting a standard that requires effort and commitment that is beyond the individual. For example, on first glance the standard 'Reduce processing errors

FIGURE 5.4 Realistic performance standards[1]

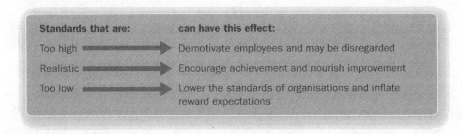

Standards that are:	can have this effect:
Too high	Demotivate employees and may be disregarded
Realistic	Encourage achievement and nourish improvement
Too low	Lower the standards of organisations and inflate reward expectations

to nil' may seem perfectly reasonable for a processing team. However, not all variables that affect the errors are controllable by the team. It is far better to agree on a standard that more reasonably reflects the capacity of the team, such as a 50%, 60% or 75% reduction in errors.

4. Stretching

Performance standards must stretch the staff member or there is a risk of demotivation. However, you must be careful where you set the standard. In particular, you need to know individuals well enough to be able to identify their skills, knowledge and abilities and to match them appropriately with what needs to be done in the job. You should also consider what developmental needs individuals or teams might have and whether it is within the capacity of your work group or budget to provide for these needs.

How much individuals can be stretched will be a matter that you will need to decide on the basis of the discussions you have with them, the regular feedback in which you engage and the particular circumstances.

5. Clear definition

When performance standards are objective and specific they are not open to interpretation. When standards are clear and defined it is easy to collect evidence about the performance because the standards are precise and particular and specify exactly what is required in observable terms.

6. Measurability

Performance standards must be measurable. The measure of the result must be observable so that you can see and verify change.

7. Limitation

If a performance standard is well written and valid in all respects, it will require a significant investment of time and energy by the staff member. If staff members are overloaded with standards, they may not achieve any of them because there will not be enough time or energy to do so. Because of this, individuals can manage no more than about five or six performance standards or objectives in any one review period.

8. Linkages

Performance standards and objectives must be linked to organisational strategies and operational plans, as illustrated in Figure 4.1 of Chapter 4. As a manager, you should be making direct connections between the performance standards and objectives of individuals and those of the organisation.

These eight principles provide a starting point for the writing of performance standards and underpin useful and workable standards. These in turn provide a basis on which to choose standards or measures of performance.

CHECK YOUR UNDERSTANDING

1 What is the purpose of reviewing organisational strategic and operational plans before setting performance standards?
2 Explain the performance standard formula PS = R + M.
3 What purpose do critical success factors and performance indicators have in developing performance standards?
4 Why is it necessary to identify the critical outputs of a job before developing performance standards?
5 Explain the term 'validity' as it is used in this chapter.
6 What does the term 'agreement' mean?
7 What is the purpose of ensuring that performance standards are realistic?
8 Why is a clear definition of performance standards necessary?
9 Why should the number of standards be limited?
10 Explain how you would go about making sure that a performance standard stretched a staff member.

SKILLS PRACTICE

1 In the following examples, identify the result [R] and the measure of performance [M] by placing a wavy line under the result and a straight line under the measure, if applicable.

a   Establish local area networks in accordance with the set-up manual.
b   Increase the number of nails used on house framing from 6000 to 7500.
c   Achieve the training of all staff in the software package ABC.
d   Reduce the number of joins in toilet installations from seven to five.
e   Open three new branches within approved budget and on time.
f   Increase sales of XYZ product from $500 000 to $650 000.
g   Respond to help calls within 24 hours of their being lodged.

2 Review the following performance standards; if they comply with the formula, place a tick in the appropriate box.

Performance standard	Correct
a Develop a work schedule to achieve better organisation.	❏
b Decrease the turnaround time for word processing.	❏
c Produce end-of-month reports by the first Monday of each month.	❏
d Stop people coming in late by the end of next month.	❏
e Implement the EEO policy by the end of the year.	❏

SKILL AND KNOWLEDGE APPLICATION

Victoria was reviewing Cameron's performance against his standards. She was frustrated because, while he was achieving the standards, she was not achieving the business plan for the branch. In fact, this seemed to be the case for all her staff. She could not find fault with their performance against their performance standards, but the branch was not achieving. She could not work out what was wrong or see how the staff could be achieving their standards while the branch was not.

TASK

- Identify the causes of non-performance of the branch.
- What steps would you take to rectify the branch's performance?

Things were getting out of hand in the half-yearly performance review. Sung Lee, an excellent computer programmer, was discussing her performance with Gary Devlin. They were both losing their patience and getting a little hot under the collar. Sung Lee felt that she had been doing a good job, based on the performance criteria she and Gary had agreed on six months earlier. The following type of exchange had been occurring for the past half-hour:

Gary	But we agreed on that point earlier in the year!
Sung Lee	No, we agreed that it was to be in XYZ language and that it had to meet the requirements of at least three client groups.
Gary	Look, I thought I made it quite clear that it should have been in ABC language and it was to be developed only for Customer Services.
Sung Lee	Well, that's not what I thought you meant. We did discuss a number of options but I am certain we decided on XYZ and three client groups.
Gary	Well, besides that, you haven't reached any of these other standards.
Sung Lee	Oh, Gary, how can you say that? On each of these, I have achieved over 85% of each standard. I know it says that it should be 100% but both you and I know that is physically impossible with the equipment we have. I assumed that we were aiming for as high a result as possible, but I had no idea you were serious about this measure. It's not on, Gary. You can't expect me to achieve the impossible.
Gary	Sung Lee, we agreed on these standards earlier this year, and now, while we are reviewing performance, you're telling me they are not satisfactory? Oh, come on!

TASK

- As senior manager for the area, you have been asked to intervene. Identify the problems in this situation. What advice would you give to Gary and Sung Lee?

Performance measures

Performance measures point to the aspects of job performance and effectiveness that need to be measured. As such, they are very helpful and assist team members and managers to achieve clarity in performance expectations and to address the question of what constitutes a 'fair day's work' or 'how good is good enough'.[2]

There are many measures (standards) from which you can choose in developing performance standards. Choosing the most appropriate one requires great care.

For example, say that a major strategy for your company for the next five years is to raise the level of repeat business because it is cheaper to retain existing customers than to find new ones. If your organisation decides to measure the sales area's performance based on sales and market share, this may work against the strategy of increasing repeat business. The salespeople may well go for quick sales with little customer service to get the number of sales as high as possible and to boost market share. They are unlikely to spend time and effort building long-term relationships with customers that will improve the chances of repeat business but possibly reduce the number of sales they can make in a given period. The specific standards of performance in this case could very well sabotage the organisation's strategy. In this example, salespeople should be measured by customer satisfaction rates, customer call rates, profit margins on sales and repeat transactions, rather than the more obvious sales targets and market share. The example is illustrated in Figure 5.5.

FIGURE 5.5 Valid standards

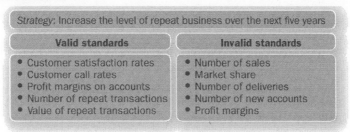

Globerson suggests five broad areas in which performance standards can be set: output, input, productivity, quality, and employee behaviour.[3]

1. Output

Standards written about output relate to quantities of finished product or services in relation to a given period such as a year, month, week, day or hour. Both relative and absolute measures may be used to quantify output. A relative measure is one that is measured in terms of a percentage or other relative quantity, such as 'Decrease bad debts by 7% each year for the next two years'. An absolute measure is one that specifically states a measure, such as 'Reduce bad debts from $19 000 to $10 000 this year'. Such standards are useful in cases where you need to manage performance associated with outputs. Examples might be the number of calls taken in a telephone call centre, number of patients seen in the emergency department of a hospital, number of products made in a manufacturing company, number of errors made in processing, or kilometres of road made in a given time—where these are seen as critical outcomes for the strategy and objectives of the organisation.

2. Input

Standards relating to input are about the resources used to create a product or service. These types of standards are often important in manufacturing organisations and in service organisations such as partnerships of solicitors and accountants, and insurance companies and government agencies. Resources are all the inputs that might go into the production process, such as human resources (knowledge, skills and expertise), money, equipment, plant, buildings and materials. These become important measures when you need to monitor closely the performance of these resources as they contribute to the costs of production or a service.

3. Productivity

In recent years, productivity has become a major factor in the workplace because it is seen as the area that will provide a competitive advantage and produce greater efficiency. Consequently, many organisations have adopted performance standards that are about managing the productivity of the workplace. Productivity is the ratio of output against a unit of input. In a banking organisation, for example, this might be the number of completed transactions per staffing hour; in manufacturing it might be the number of completed products per machine hour; in a service organisation it might be the number of completed projects per staffing hour, consumables used or word-processing time used.

4. Quality

This is perhaps the simplest of all areas in which to develop standards. This is because quality is usually carefully defined and specified to begin with, and it is only a matter of applying the quality standards to the results expected of individuals. Quality is about comparing the required specifications of the result with those of the actual result and identifying any inconsistencies. Quality performance standards can be used in almost all situations. Examples are national specifications such as electrical safety standards and regulations, and quality-endorsed standards such as standards of presentation, work and monitoring of processes.

5. Employee behaviour

This area is often referred to as human resources because it deals with the whole area of how employees operate within the organisation. Employee behaviour is a critical issue in all organisations, as it is only through the human resources that things actually get done. If the people in an organisation are not performing correctly, this directly affects all other areas of an organisation. Some examples of standards that may be used in this area are absenteeism, turnover rate, number of grievances, education hours/costs per employee, revenue per employee, industrial action, number of new hires, vacancy fill rate, skills inventories, customer interactions, conflict handling, cultural sensitivity and ethical behaviour.

Other approaches

Alternatively, you might use the balanced scorecard method (see Chapter 4) to determine performance measures suitable for your employees, based on perspectives including financial performance, customer satisfaction, growth and retention, internal operations, human resources systems, learning and development and corporate social responsibility.

Likewise, competency standards, which are often used in creating position descriptions, can be used as performance standards. Competency standards define the standards of job performance by describing in observable detail what must be done by the job holder. In other words, they are descriptions of actual job performance, usually derived from analysing people considered competent in performing a particular job. Competence is defined as the state of being competent to perform particular activities at a particular standard.[4] The competency standards are also used as training outcomes so that all the learners achieve the required standards to perform a job.[5] Competency standards are a useful tool because they have been developed in close consultation with industry, are linked to formal recognition through the Australian Qualifications Framework (AQF) and exist for almost every industry in Australia. For more information on competency standards view the National Training Information Service (NTIS) website: <www.ntis.gov.au>.

SKILL AND KNOWLEDGE APPLICATION

TASK

Classify the following list of performance indicators into one of the five areas in which performance standards can be set, using the key below.

Key:

O = Output

I = Input

P = Productivity

Q = Quality

E = Employee behaviour

Performance indicators	Classification
Staff level (full-time equivalent)	
Revenue per employee	
Employee satisfaction level	
Number of employees in study assistance scheme	
Frequency and nature of communication	
Systems utilisation rate	
Accuracy of charge-backs and transfer of pricing	
Return on investment	
Costs of benefits/salaries	
Resignation rates	
Product line profitability	
Frequency and consistency of quality assurance and quality control	
Number of/modes of communication	
Compliance testing	
Error per cent rates	
Number of training programs	
Average months to promotion by position	

You will find it helpful to think about the five areas listed above before you try to define the specific performance standards you wish to create. If the performance standard is to work, it is vital that you think about where it is that you require performance standards to be established, why they should be established and where they link into the organisation's outcomes.

Guidelines for setting performance standards

Identify the individual's main result areas required by the job and organisational outcomes.

- Select those result areas that support the key performance indicators of the organisation.
- Set performance standards against each of the organisation's KPIs.
- Make sure performance standards are valid in terms of the result that is required on the job.
- Make sure performance standards are agreed on between the job holder or team and the manager.

- Ensure that standards are realistic—neither too easy nor too difficult. The idea is to offer a challenge to the individual or team.
- Ensure that performance standards are clear, specific and well-defined.
- Ensure that staff have access to data on actual performance to facilitate monitoring and feedback.
- Make certain that performance standards are consistent with the strategy, objectives, outcomes and values of the organisation.
- Ensure that standards are measurable.

Using these guidelines and the above principles, you can now proceed to developing performance standards. Below you are taken through a step-by-step procedure to facilitate solid, successful and usable performance standards.

Process for setting standards

You now have all the knowledge you need to write valid and useful performance standards. This is the most difficult part of all—the writing of suitable standards. The following process will ensure that you stay on the right track.

1 Identify the result that is required.
2 Identify why the result is required.
3 Document how well the result must be done.
4 Review steps so far to ensure that only results—not actions—are documented.
5 Identify what will be measured and how.
6 Write the performance standard in accordance with the formula PS = R + M.
7 Check that the measures are valid, realistic and clear.
8 Agree on the standards with the individual.
9 Make adjustments as agreed.

This should be done in conjunction with individual staff members.

How to write a performance standard

You should now be ready to write a valid performance standard. The performance standard statement comprises two smaller statements: the result statement, and the standard (or measure) statement, as illustrated in Figure 5.6.

FIGURE 5.6 The performance standard statement

| Result statement | Standard statement |
| Performance standard statement |

Result statement

To focus the result part of the performance standard, use a verb to specify what the result is to be. Always go straight to the result. Do not start the result statement with the word 'to'. This suggests that the result is far off into the future and makes it more difficult to visualise. Beginning the result statement with a verb helps to focus staff on the end result. The list of verbs in Figure 5.7 is not exhaustive but will be a useful start for you in writing result statements. For easy reference, you may want to compile your own list, including the types of verbs most commonly used in your work environment. This will save you a great deal of thinking when you are trying to write result statements.

FIGURE 5.7 Useful verbs for result statements

accept	conduct	explain	plot	search
accomplish	connect	find	position	separate
account	construct	gauge	predict	service
achieve	contribute	identify	prepare	select
adapt	convert	increase	present	signal
adjust	correct	index	prevent	sketch
advise	decipher	inform	probe	solve
allocate	decrease	install	process	sort
allot	defend	institute	produce	specify
alter	define	instruct	program	stage
analyse	deliver	investigate	prove	standardise
apply	derive	isolate	raise	state
arrange	design	lengthen	recommend	supervise
assemble	detect	limit	recondition	supply
assess	determine	maintain	record	survey
balance	develop	make	recover	set
build	diagnose	manipulate	register	tabulate
calibrate	direct	maximise	regulate	tally
catalogue	dispatch	measure	render	test
classify	display	mobilise	reorganise	time
choose	distribute	mount	repair	track
collect	document	nominate	reply	transfer
combine	draft	notify	report	translate
compare	edit	operate	resolve	transpose
compile	establish	order	respond	type
comply	estimate	organise	restore	verify
compose	evaluate	overhaul	scan	watch
compute	exhibit	plan	schedule	weigh

Complete the following result statements by explaining exactly what the result is to be.

1 Respond ....
2 Implement ....
3 Reduce...
4 Increase ....
5 Achieve ....
6 Balance ....
7 Install..
8 Establish ....
9 Deliver ....
10 Notify ....

Standard statement

Once you have established the specific result, a standard must be selected. Standards must measure the verb in the result statement. For example, if you have the result statement 'Respond to customer complaints', the measure must be about how you expect the staff member to respond, not about the type of customer or complaint. When you have written a performance standard, always check that the standard actually measures the verb in the result statement. You can have as many standards as you like in a performance standard but only one result.

Write the standard statements for the following result statements.

Result statement	Standard statement
1 Respond to customer inquiries	....
2 Increase productivity of the section	....
3 Install a new telephone system	....
4 Liaise between department and client groups 1, 2 and 3	....
5 Implement a new grievance procedure	....
6 Balance cash drawer at the end of each shift	....
7 Respond to market changes	....
8 Establish a record management system	....
9 Achieve a second generator online	....
10 Reduce the number of staff on standby	....

Performance objectives

Managing is about achieving through others. As mentioned earlier, the theoretical basis of this book is management by objectives. The broad organisational goals for key performance indicators, such as sales or quality of services, are converted to team goals and then to individual goals with agreed standards of performance and time frames. It is important to remember that employees will be more motivated to improve their performance if they have been involved in identifying the objectives and setting the standards.

The focus of management is therefore on results. In planning work, results are broken down into smaller, more workable components and are expressed as objectives of a particular division, department, agency, branch, section or project. Objectives guide work and are an important component of planning. Performance objectives are objectives that state what is to be done, and how well it is to be done.

So far in this chapter, discussion has focused on two components only of performance objectives: results, and the standard of the result. Performance objectives are a more detailed statement of what has to be accomplished, and are used to direct new endeavours, projects, areas of emphasis or strategic objectives. Performance objectives consist of four components: a result [R], a measure [M], a condition [C] and a time limit [T]. *Results* and *measures* (standards) have already been discussed. A *condition* contains any specific conditions under which the performance must be performed, and might include such items as limited resources, specific specialists, normal working conditions, under periods of great stress, during a period of major change, with limited access to other staff, during an acquisition or merger of a company, amalgamation of government departments, or use of specific equipment. The *time limit* relates to when the objective must be achieved. Do not confuse the time by which the objective must be completed with standards that have time in them as a measure—for example, a 24-hour turnaround time. The latter is a measure, not a time limit for the attainment of an objective; it will still require a time frame for when the objective must be completed.

A performance objective formula is illustrated in Figure 5.8.

FIGURE 5.8 A performance objective formula

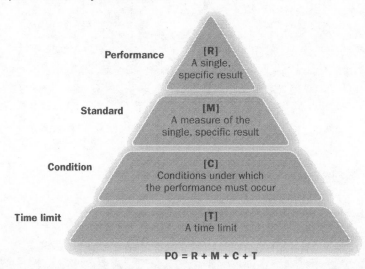

Performance   **[R]** A single, specific result

Standard   **[M]** A measure of the single, specific result

Condition   **[C]** Conditions under which the performance must occur

Time limit   **[T]** A time limit

PO = R + M + C + T

The four components make up a results-focused objective that clearly identifies what you will do, how well you will do it, under what conditions you will do it and by what time you will do it. While an effective objective must have all four components, the components may be arranged in any order the writer chooses as long as it makes sense. Sometimes it will be necessary to begin with the time limit; at other times you may begin with the result, the standard or even the condition. Figure 5.9 lists some examples of performance objectives.

Each of the performance objectives in Figure 5.9 has the four components of an effective performance objective. Where performance objectives are not written to include all four components, a number of problems can arise, as shown in Figure 5.10:

1 Where a *result* is not included in the objective, staff will become confused because they will not know what has to be accomplished. Staff will also become demotivated, as they will be trying to achieve something that is not possible.

2 Where a *standard* is not included in the objective, there will be no measure of the result; poor performance will result because there is no benchmark on which to base the result.

FIGURE 5.9 Sample performance objectives

1. Reduce downtime of machinery to five working days maximum per year by December XXXX without the use of replacement machinery.
2. Process orders within 24 hours of receipt by 30 June XXXX given that all computer equipment is operating correctly.
3. Word processing is achieved to stated and negotiated deadlines and corporate standards during normal business hours by September XXXX.
4. Increase employee satisfaction levels on the XYZ instrument from 53% to 69% by 30 April XXXX with only one use of the instrument.
5. Reduce general costs to 5% less than the industry average benchmark for the per capita staffing levels by 30 March XXXX.
6. Accurately process 95% of all patient admission forms without error for the current business cycle by 31 July XXXX using the hospital medical database.
7. Present two in-service sessions to unit staff on infection control by 31 July XXXX, including a written assessment to test understanding.
8. Complete performance management meetings with all unit staff, without the cost of hiring contract labour for coverage, by November XXXX.
9. Develop the unit policy manual by December XXXX, incorporating the organisation's strategic and operational plans and mission.
10. Identify three strategies to smoothly implement the new medication process for the inpatient department by April XXXX .

FIGURE 5.10 Effects of poorly written performance objectives[6]

Result	Standard	Condition	Time limit	Results in:
✔	✔	✔	✔	Effective performance objective
✗	✔	✔	✔	Confusion
✔	✗	✔	✔	Substandard performance
✔	✔	✗	✔	Blowouts or overruns
✔	✔	✔	✗	Never completed

3 If the *condition* of the objective is left out, budgets and targets are likely to blow out and wastage and overruns may occur.

4 If a *time limit* is not placed on the objective, there is a danger that the objective will never be completed. You cannot hold staff responsible for completion if you have not specified a date.

Performance objectives form an integral part of any performance management system and are necessary in order to focus the efforts of individuals and teams on organisational outcomes. Well-written performance objectives record for both staff and management exactly what has to be achieved in the time frames stated, and thereby help to concentrate work efforts in the appropriate direction for the organisation.

CHECK YOUR UNDERSTANDING

11 List the five areas in which performance standards can be set.

12 Provide four examples of possible performance standards in the area of employee behaviours.

13 Why must performance standards be valid in terms of the result required?

14 A performance standard statement contains two statements. What are they?

15 When writing a result statement, what should you begin with? Why?

16 List the process for setting standards.

17 What are performance objectives?

18 Explain the formula PO = R + M + C + T.

SKILLS PRACTICE

1 In Figure 5.9, identify the result, measure, condition and time limit for each of the 10 performance objectives.

2 Develop a valid performance objective for the following broad aims:

a Get better control of distribution and freight costs.

b Improve the performance of the Order Processing department.

c Obtain better productivity in the branch.

d Improve customer service in the branch.

CONCLUSION

Setting specific, measurable performance standards and communicating them effectively to staff will assist in alleviating performance problems. Performance problems often occur because of poor communication between managers and their staff. Where job requirements are not communicated to staff, they will not be able to perform well. Therefore, managers may contribute to the poor performance of staff and teams. Performance standards provide benchmarks for workers to measure themselves against and are similar to the rules and regulations we have in everyday society. These rules and regulations give us confidence, just as performance standards give workers confidence to perform as well as they can. Performance is focused on results, not actions, and performance management is about managing the outputs or results of people.

Performance standards contain a single, specific result and a measure, or a number of measures, of that result. For each specific result you will have a new performance standard. Writing to a specific formula makes the process easier and instantly recognisable. Thus all members of an organisation will be able to use and interpret performance standards. Performance standards form part of performance objectives, which set the direction and focus of an individual's work for a given period.

 ## CASE STUDY

Advantage Solutions Australia is a software company based in regional Queensland that develops client relationship management (CRM) systems. In less than five years the company has grown from a two-person show run out of a garage to an organisation with over 50 employees. One of the company's critical success factors is its commitment to customer service, including very generous after-installation support. Feedback from their clients suggests this strategy has been successful in maintaining a high level of customer loyalty and referrals. Given the strategic importance and success of this approach, the senior management team decided to raise the profile of customer support across the organisation by creating a new role of Customer Service Operations Manager. This new role will lead a team of four client relationship managers (CRMs) responsible for customer service including post-implementation support.

The Lead Programmer, Pat Dokic, is appointed to the role. Pat has worked for the company since its early days when he came in as a computer science graduate from the local university. He has shown himself to be a highly competent programmer who has expressed a keen interest in moving into a more senior role involving people management and direct involvement with clients.

However, after only three months the General Manager, Lee, is concerned about his performance. She has consistently received feedback from Pat's team that his expectations are unrealistic. Initially, Lee thought the feedback was merely related to settling-in problems, and took no action. However, after three months of escalating exasperation with Pat's performance from his team, Lee decided further investigation was warranted. She found their main concerns centred on Pat's expectations.

1   The members of Pat's team were being driven mad by their performance standards. In accordance with policy, Pat had developed standards with his team after the new structure was created. However, the number of standards had increased by almost 25% and still contained those focused on product enhancement and development. His team complained that they did not have time to concentrate on product enhancements or development because they were supporting their customers as Pat had directed. Their frustration was based on not being able to meet the standards they had agreed to.

2   The team members were also very confused about what they were really trying to achieve as a team. The senior management was clear that customer service was a core competency yet Pat was still focusing on

CASE STUDY CONTINUED

identifying product enhancements and development opportunities. In addition, Pat was still spending considerable time with his old team discussing potential enhancements and was not readily available to discuss problems or provide direction. In three months they had had only one team meeting. They complained that they were frustrated and rapidly losing motivation.

3 Lee asked for a sample of performance standards and found that the team were expected to:

a provide four potential enhancements per quarter

b conduct four formal opportunity-seeking briefings with clients per quarter

c research competitor products and provide a summary of one product per quarter

d attend monthly product development meetings with the R&D team.

Lee informally asks Pat how things are going and he enthusiastically reassures her that he loves the new role and believes the team will meet their performance objectives. Lee does not want to dampen his enthusiasm, but acknowledges that she should have monitored Pat's transition more closely and provided him with more direction. She also realises that she will need to work closely with Pat to help him align his team's goals with the broader strategic objectives, including the critical success factors and key performance indicators. He needs to ensure that the individual performance standards and objectives are integrated with those of the organisation in order to avoid lack of motivation, frustration and dissatisfaction in his team. She believes Pat is facing a problem typical to technical specialists moving into their first management role—that of continuing to be a technical expert rather than a manager. She decides that the best approach is to focus on coaching and has agreed with Pat to meet and review the team's current performance standards. Pat has also expressed interest in starting a Diploma of Management to help him better understand the role of a manager and manage the performance of his team.

QUESTIONS

Identify what needs to be included in Pat's coaching program by working through the following questions.

1 What are the specific problems that need to be tackled?

2 What needs to be done to solve these problems?

3 How would you suggest that Lee go about the coaching task?

4 Do you believe coaching is the correct way to deal with the issue? Explain.

JOB AIDS

Flowchart for writing performance standards

Performance is the result of actions

A result is the end product of an action

Performance standard formula:

PS = R + M

where:
PS = Performance standard
R = Result
M = A measure of the result.

Performance objective formula:

PO = R + M + C + T

where:
PO = Performance objective
R = Result
M = A measure of the result
C = Conditions of the performance
T = Time limit.

To assist you in the workplace, this Job Aid is reproduced on the accompanying CD located in the back of this book

CHECKLISTS

Process for setting performance standards

☐ Identify the result that is required.

☐ Identify why the result is required.

☐ Document how well the result must be done.

☐ Review steps so far to ensure that actions are not identified—only results.

☐ Identify what will be measured and how.

☐ Write the performance standard in accordance with the formula PS = R + M.

☐ Check that the measures are valid, realistic and clear.

☐ Agree on the standards with the individual.

☐ Make adjustments as agreed.

Writing performance standards

☐ Use a verb to begin the result statement.

☐ State the specific result required.

☐ Make sure that the standards measure the result.

References

1   Adapted from Schneier, C., Shaw, D., Beatty, R. & Baird, L. (eds). 1995. *The Performance Measurement, Management, and Appraisal Sourcebook*. HRD Press: Amherst, MA, p. 446.

2   Jones, R. 2009, 2nd edn. *HRM Fundamentals*. Pearson Australia: Frenchs Forest, Sydney,, p. 327.

3   Globerson, S. 1985. *Performance Criteria and Incentive Systems*. Elsevier Science: New York, pp. 23–31.

4   Tovey, M. & Lawlor, D. 2008, 3rd edn. *Training in Australia*. Pearson Australia: Frenchs Forest, Sydney, p. 36.

5   Tovey & Lawlor, op. cit. 2008, p. 35.

6   Adapted from Ainsworth, M. & Smith, N. 1993. 'What makes effective performance objectives? One view.' In *Making it Happen: Managing Performance at Work*. Prentice Hall: Sydney, p. 27.

CHAPTER SIX

Monitoring performance

Learning outcomes

After reading this chapter you should be able to:

* explain why monitoring is necessary

* identify what to monitor in the workplace

* define flexible work practices and their impact on monitoring

* explain the benefits of monitoring for staff and managers

* use a framework for monitoring performance

* explain the term 'evidence' as it applies to performance management

* collect appropriate evidence to demonstrate the performance being monitored

* provide examples of evidence.

Setting up agreed performance standards or objectives is not enough to ensure that a performance management system works.[1] Staff and managers must take up the process actively and become highly involved so that it becomes part of everyday work. Part of this process is taking note of what is happening each day and providing feedback to all parties as a result of the observations. Observation and the recording of observations of performance is known as monitoring performance. While it may sound simple, it can be a complex process to decide what and how to monitor. Too much monitoring results in managers and staff spending all their time monitoring, so that results are not achieved. Too little monitoring results in managers and staff finding out about problems only when it is too late to do anything about them, so that results are not achieved. The right balance must be found between too little and too much. Your key performance indicators (KPIs) will provide an excellent guide as to what has to be monitored, but how and when is up to managers and staff to agree on.

Just as the setting of performance standards is vital for a performance management system to operate, so is the step of monitoring, which is an information-gathering process. Without adequate information you cannot make decisions, or direct, take and execute actions aimed at achieving agreed results. Managers' ability to give specific, useful feedback is directly related to the quality of the information they gather, and thus the ability of their staff and teams to achieve agreed results is also tied to the quality of information that is gathered. This chapter provides a framework that will assist you in gathering good-quality and useful performance information. It forms the basis for analysing, appraising and improving performance, which are the subjects of the next four chapters.

Why monitor?

There are a number of reasons why you should monitor performance. Unless you monitor, there is no sense in setting performance standards or objectives. Monitoring allows you to respond quickly to new situations, new circumstances, or changes in the actual performance of individuals or teams. Monitoring also allows you and your staff to be proactive in dealing with issues and problems that might occur. Monitoring performance enables you to:

- *keep people and teams on track with what you have agreed will be achieved.* Useful monitoring systems let you know early when people or teams are going off track so that you can help them refocus quickly and without major problems. The longer you leave people off track, the harder it is for them to get back.

- *form a solid foundation on which to base feedback to individuals and teams.* Throughout the performance management process, you will need to provide feedback to staff and they will need to provide feedback to you. To be able to give specific feedback, you will need exact information on how staff are progressing towards their standards and objectives.

- *do your job as a manager.* Just as your staff will have performance standards and/or objectives, so will you. You will recall that managers get things done through others. To ensure that things get done, you will need to check or monitor progress.

- *negotiate changes to performance standards or objectives if circumstances warrant it.* As individuals or teams progress through the performance management cycle, priorities, situations or circumstances may change, rendering previously agreed standards invalid. Monitoring provides you with the evidence to make a decision to renegotiate or to agree to deleting a standard or performance objective.

- *collect information about the performance of individuals and teams.* In order to provide feedback, and to make decisions regarding performance, you will need to have evidence on which to base your decisions or views. It is through the process of monitoring that you acquire the hard evidence to support your case.

- *maintain the performance management system.* In order to gather evidence on performance, analyse the evidence, appraise the performance and set new performance standards, you will need to monitor how staff are progressing towards the attainment of their performance standards.

Monitoring provides you with vital information on which you make decisions as a manager. Staff should also be encouraged to self-monitor so they know how they are progressing and can do any fine-tuning that may be required. Without information, the rest of the performance management system will break down, as it requires information to analyse. Monitoring processes that you set up will provide the information that you need. Needs depend on the standards and objectives that have been set with staff and your own manager, which all dovetail into the corporate objectives. This process is illustrated in Figure 6.1.

FIGURE 6.1 Monitoring enables analysis of performance

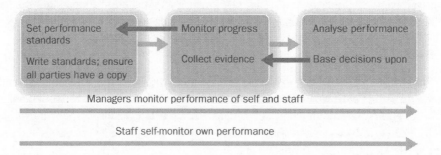

What to monitor

It is not reasonable to expect that you will be able to monitor everything that goes on around your workplace, nor is it necessary. You do need to monitor those things that contribute to the achievement of the KPIs for your organisation and those that relate to the performance standards you have set with your staff (and your own, of course). In doing so, you will monitor:

- *the progress of individuals and teams towards their performance standards.* It is vital to monitor this so that you know how individuals or teams are progressing. It will enable you to give positive feedback when appropriate and to pick up problems before they become major. If you are monitoring progress, you will be able to tackle problems as they arise or even before they arise, and deal with them with the appropriate people. It is much easier to deal with a small problem than a large one.

- *how staff are using their inputs and whether any are missing.* This relates to the knowledge, skills and experience that staff may or may not be applying to the job to achieve the standards agreed on. Where inputs are missing, you may have to intervene to provide coaching, demonstrations, training or counselling to ensure that staff acquire the appropriate inputs to achieve the standards set. Remember, the process is not to set staff up for failure, and you should be on the lookout for staff who are struggling.

- *what processes are being used by staff in their progress towards attaining their performance standards.* Processes refer to the behaviours that staff exhibit as they go about their jobs. Some processes are more important than others, depending on the job and the standards agreed on. For example, communication will be important in nearly every job but will be especially important in jobs dealing with customers, and even more so when dealing with customer complaints. Monitoring these processes will tell you a great deal about how organisational values are being accepted, whether critical success factors (CSFs) and KPIs are being attended to, and whether staff are using appropriate interpersonal skills in the job.

- *the outputs or results that staff produce.* Monitoring the results that staff produce will allow you to give positive feedback when appropriate and to redirect staff when the result does not match the standards set by agreement earlier in the cycle. Redirection may be avoided by monitoring the progress staff are making towards their performance standards and giving appropriate guidance.

- *how outputs contribute to the CSFs and KPIs.* By comparing the progress of staff towards their performance standards and the outputs they create, you can determine whether your work unit is achieving the CSFs and KPIs set by the organisation. You will also need this information to monitor your own performance standards as a manager.

- *what gaps there might be in any of the above.* Monitoring allows you to identify any weak links that may prevent the work unit's objectives being met for the period. The combined effects of the above points will allow you to identify specifically what is needed and by whom. You will then be able to arrange support and assistance, or training if necessary, to help staff reach the agreed standards. Remember, a performance management system is a process through which you help staff to do their best and to develop, a topic that is covered in Chapter 10. Therefore, it is vital to be able to identify potential or actual problems that may affect the outputs the staff produce, so that you can do something about them.

The need for time and effort

I expect that many practising managers may now be thinking that this author is crazy ('I barely have the time to do what I do now, never mind all this extra work!'). If you are one of these managers, I suggest you have a careful look at what you are actually doing in your job, as you are likely to be *doing* many tasks rather than managing them. Look back at Figure A.1, which illustrates the way jobs change as you move into management and up the management ladder. Your job as a manager is to get things done through other people. If you are not doing that, you will find it is because you are still doing much of the work yourself, which may cause you to miss objectives or targets, and to spend many extra but unnecessary hours at work. You are also likely to find that you are unable to evaluate the performance of your staff fairly. You may even find that staff have a reasonably high level of dissatisfaction with their jobs and with you as a manager. As we move through to Chapter 12, you will find that your workload appears to grow, so it is important that you review what you are doing as a manager and ask yourself the question 'Am I managing or doing?'

Monitoring depends on the situation

Exactly what you monitor in your work unit is up to you, as every situation is different. You will need different types of monitoring processes to monitor different types of performance standards, depending on the type of job and the circumstances in which work is occurring. Broadly speaking, there are two main types of monitoring—one that occurs at the end of performance, and one that occurs during performance. It is likely that you will need to use both. The type of monitoring that occurs during performance allows you to intervene if necessary to keep everything on track. Monitoring that occurs at the end of performance allows you to check the final output, but at this stage it is too late to correct problems. You will get most of your ideas about what to monitor from the KPIs of your organisation and work unit, and the specific performance standards agreed on with staff.

Flexible work practices and monitoring

There are a number of factors that have contributed to the rise in flexible work practices that enable people to combine paid work with family responsibilities. These factors include the rise in dual earner families, the increased participation of mothers with young children, and the greater involvement of fathers in child rearing. Changes to Australian demographics—including the ageing population which has seen increasing numbers of employees having to take responsibility for the care of aged parents—are also significant drivers of change. Work–family balance is thus increasingly important for long-term trends in labour supply. In addition, rapid advances in communications technology have opened up opportunities for organisations to utilise flexible work practices such as telecommuting. These practices provide mutual benefits for employers and employees by providing alternatives for work–life balance.

Flexible work practices can include part-time work, job sharing, working from home or flexible working hours. When considering monitoring employee performance and the effect flexible work practices may have on performance, working from home seems to provide the biggest challenge for managers and organisations, as job sharing, part-time work and flexible work hours are monitored in the workplace. Indeed, research conducted by the Boston Consulting Group in 2006 for the Innovation & Business Skills industry skills council identified workplace flexibility as a defining characteristic of the years to 2020. The ability to provide flexibility will be critical to motivating and retaining a demographically diverse talent pool.[2] As Human Resources professionals, we need to come to terms with monitoring the performance of employees who work under flexible arrangements, including working from home.

An employer's obligations do not change just because an employee works from home. Legislation, awards and agreements are increasingly dictating how flexible work practices are to be managed, and penalties can be high if employers act unfairly to employees in relation to these practices.

Many larger organisations have instituted guidelines or policies that encompass flexible working hours or working from home. ANZ Bank, for example, has implemented several programs to retain experience in the organisation by offering employees aged over 55 the opportunity to choose between remaining as a full-time employee, taking additional annual leave, or returning to work after an extended break to either full-time or part-time work.[3]

Other examples of flexible work policies can be found on the following websites: <www.hr. murdoch.edu.au/staff/policy/PH0016.html> and <www.hr.unsw.edu.au/employee/gen/wkhmpol.html>.

The NSW Government has published the Flexible Work Practices Policy and Guidelines, available at <www.eeo.nsw.gov.au/women/flexible_work_practices_policy_and_guidelines>.

The abovementioned policies and guidelines cover the circumstances under which home-based work may be granted to employees and the specific requirements of that work. However, it is up to the manager or supervisor of the employee to negotiate how monitoring in the home-based workplace will be undertaken. Clearly established performance objectives are required to specify the quantity of work to be completed and the quality of the work.

Both employer and employee need to bear in mind the advantages and disadvantages that flexible work practices offer both parties. Some of these advantages and disadvantages are shown in Figure 6.2:

FIGURE 6.2 Advantages and disadvantages of flexible work practices[4]

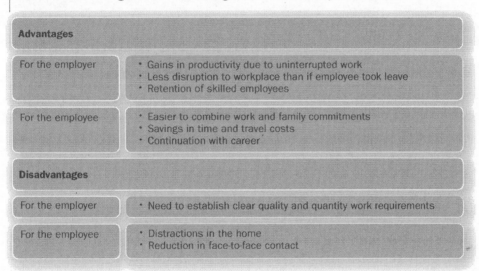

Advantages	
For the employer	• Gains in productivity due to uninterrupted work • Less disruption to workplace than if employee took leave • Retention of skilled employees
For the employee	• Easier to combine work and family commitments • Savings in time and travel costs • Continuation with career
Disadvantages	
For the employer	• Need to establish clear quality and quantity work requirements
For the employee	• Distractions in the home • Reduction in face-to-face contact

Once the employer and employee have agreed on how to monitor performance in the home-based environment, and performance standards-based outcomes and results have been established, regular communication on progress towards these outcomes is critical. When monitoring guidelines have been established, it should take no more time or effort to monitor employees in the home-based environment than it would if they were in the workplace.

Why should organisations consider flexible work practices for their employees? Organisations have the opportunity to become more effective in retaining key personnel, and they are now legally bound to do so. Figure 6.3 illustrates two cases highlighting the requirement to consider flexible work practices.

CHECK YOUR UNDERSTANDING

1 What are the benefits of monitoring for staff?
2 What are the benefits of monitoring for managers?
3 What are the potential problems in performance management that monitoring helps to overcome?
4 List three advantages of flexible work practices.
5 List three disadvantages of flexible work practices.

FIGURE 6.3 Flexible work practices[5]

Flexible work practice	Case	Facts
Job sharing	*Federated Municipal and Shire Council Employees' Union of Australia (NSW) v Nambucca Shire Council* (NSW IRC 6771 of 1997, 26/8/1998)	• Job-sharing arrangement was requested in reliance of an award provision allowing for same • Request was rejected by the employer, arguing that job sharing was inefficient • NSW Industrial Relations Commission found that women, primary caregivers to children, may need to seek flexible work practices • Employer's decision found to indirectly discriminate against the employee on basis of sex; recommendation: the employer to trial a job-sharing arrangement
Part-time work	*Bogle v Metropolitan Health Service Board* (2000) EOC 93-069	• Dental nurse requested return to work part-time after adoption leave • Employer offered either her old job back full-time or a part-time job with lesser status and responsibility • Tribunal found there was a requirement to work full-time imposed on employees undertaking supervisory positions and that this was disproportionately skewed towards women and employees with family commitments • Requirement was found to be unreasonable as the employer had failed to conduct any proper analysis or evaluation of the employee's part-time proposal

Collecting evidence

According to one dictionary, evidence is 'the available facts, circumstances, etc. supporting or otherwise a belief, proposition, etc., or indicating whether or not a thing is true or valid'.[6] Evidence provides the basis on which you will later make a judgment about how the individual or team is performing. To be valid for performance-management purposes, evidence needs to be collected over the whole period of the performance review cycle, and should relate specifically to the agreed performance standards or objectives. Evidence can be in a variety of formats, and is likely to be different for each set of individual performance standards or objectives, and for different parts of the organisation. It is also likely to differ between organisations and industries. Evidence demonstrates how an individual or team has performed or is performing. This means that you should be collecting evidence during the performance cycle and also at the end of it.

Evidence and feedback

The quality of your evidence will directly affect the quality of the feedback you can provide. Poor or invalid evidence will render your feedback invalid and may even leave you open to internal grievance procedures and/or a visit to the Australian Industrial Relations Commission (AIRC). Where you rely on invalid evidence as a basis for a decision, you may expect to be challenged. Staff are much more aware of their rights and concepts of equity and fairness than they ever were. This is probably because staff are, on the whole, better educated than ever before. Skilful monitoring provides opportunities to gather solid evidence on performance. If the appropriate monitoring is not built into the day-to-day operations of managers and staff, there is a strong likelihood that when you go to give feedback you will not have adequate evidence on which to base your statements. Remember, staff are encouraged to gather evidence also, so you will need to have robust evidence to table, especially where there is a difference in interpretation of the facts. Effective monitoring ensures that you collect evidence that is truly representative of the actual performance of an individual or team. Invalid evidence results in faulty analysis and poor appraisal of performance. It also means that you will have difficulty in helping staff and teams to develop, as you may be trying to develop areas in which they are already proficient.

What is collectable evidence?

Anything that demonstrates the performance of the individual or team is collectable evidence. By implication, this means that you need to collect evidence on satisfactory and excellent performance as well as unsatisfactory performance. At the collecting stage you will not be making judgments about the evidence. The process is merely an information-seeking step that will enable staff, teams and you to make judgments about performance. You may choose to share the collected information between staff, teams and yourself, or you may all collect your own evidence that you will present at the appropriate time. As part of your evidence collection you may speak to other people about projects in which the individual or team was involved, or any other source of reliable information. Note that your information must be reliable: unsubstantiated opinions, gossip, gut feelings and anonymous complaints or stories are not evidence of performance. You should focus on the results achieved by the individual or team and the standards of performance agreed on.

Evidence may take the form of:

- samples of written work
- information on how specific situations are handled
- work samples that demonstrate progress towards performance standards
- new skills and knowledge obtained and applied to the job
- training courses attended
- competencies applied to the job
- samples of project work
- verifiable comments from peers or subordinates
- quality of outputs
- critical stages in achieving the outputs required
- specific KPIs
- quantitative measures such as stock control, turnaround times, productivity, meeting deadlines, accuracy and budgets
- feedback from internal and external clients.

This is not an exhaustive list of examples, but it may help you to think about the monitoring you need to set up in your situation. You may not use any of these suggestions, as they may not be valid measures for the performance standards you have agreed on with staff or teams. Whatever you decide, evidence needs to be explicit and accurate.

The context of the performance

While it is necessary to collect evidence on how an individual or team performs, you also need to collect evidence on the context in which they are performing. Research has shown that the context, or circumstances, in which people perform their jobs can affect the performance of individuals or teams.[7] For example, staff or teams may achieve their performance standards despite considerable upheaval or organisational change in their work unit. People may be prevented from achieving their performance standards by situational circumstances, such as low staff morale due to redundancies in the work area or the slashing of budgets during a time of financial pressure. These factors must be taken into account during the analysis stage of the system to ensure a fair and equitable decision. Your monitoring should take note of the circumstances at the time, particularly any exceptional social, physical or systemic circumstances that may affect performance.

SKILLS PRACTICE

1 Give examples of evidence you might collect to demonstrate performance in the following:
   a Reduce the number of errors in daily processing from 15% to 7% of total calls.
   b Back up all personal computer hard drives once each day after 4 pm.
   c Increase employee satisfaction levels on the production line from 53% to 69% by 30 April XXXX.
   d Maintain stationery supplies at ±10% of fortnightly turnover by October XXXX. Stationery supplies include all items on the stationery listing as at 10 March XXXX.
2 How might you monitor the following performance examples for a home-based employee?
   a Back up all personal computer hard drives once each day after 4 pm.
   b That a part-time employee who works 15 hours a week completes the hours required.
   c Occupational health and safety issues.

How do I collect evidence?

There are many ways in which you can collect evidence. In part, the type of evidence you collect will define this. In its simplest form you may have a folder for each individual or team and place the appropriate evidence in this as you come across it. This becomes a type of portfolio, containing samples of work performance collected throughout the appraisal period. At the other end of the scale, collection may be quite complex, with predetermined stages or times at which you will collect specific items. However, be careful about creating a monitoring and collection-of-evidence process so complex that all you ever do is monitor and collect evidence. You also have to manage people and give feedback on a continuing basis!

Whether you collect evidence separately from your staff will depend on your own management style and the maturity of your staff in understanding and using the performance management process. Many managers use the folder idea, and together with staff make entries in it, on note paper, which may record a certain event or error, or general correspondence. Sometimes it may contain more substantial items, such as copies of reports or samples of work. This process helps to develop trust between manager and staff and ensures that there are no surprises in the feedback loop or at the final performance review discussion. Staff and manager have continuing access to this folder and both may make entries in it. However you choose to collect evidence, you must ensure that it is open, fair and valid.

When do I collect evidence?

You collect evidence in accordance with whatever monitoring system you have set up and also at the milestones for action of the performance standards you have agreed on with staff. Additionally, you will collect evidence when performance is exceptional or when things are off track. Remember, at this stage you are not making any decisions about the performance—you are merely collecting data about the performance. (This does not in any way preclude you from taking action when something is going wrong, as the process of collecting adequate evidence and then making a decision can be quite fast. This is dealt with in Chapter 7.) You will also collect evidence when you give feedback. This might be in the form of how the individual deals with the feedback and what action they take as a result of it. Finally, you and your staff collect evidence whenever you think it is useful to do so throughout the performance management cycle.

Discussing monitoring with staff

Staff should be actively encouraged to self-monitor their performance against the agreed standards. Research has shown that active participation in the performance management process by staff enhanced their commitment to the process and aided their understanding. Further, it met more of their needs and increased job satisfaction.[8] Where there is successful two-way communication between manager and staff resulting in a shared understanding, and a commitment to performance management, staff can self-monitor very effectively. They will know when problems arise and can take evasive action themselves in consultation with their manager. Monitoring is not about the manager being 'the big bad bully'. Staff have a need for feedback, direction, role clarity, job involvement and development that requires two-way communication.[9] It is a natural part of being human to be interested in where you are going and how you are doing. Managed well, self-monitoring can help staff to develop skills, identify problems before they become major, make their own interventions, ask for assistance and achieve their agreed performance standards.

When to discuss

At the time of setting standards, you should discuss self-monitoring with staff, guide and coach them in how to do it if necessary, and provide encouragement to come to you if they require further help or to discuss potential or actual problems. Two-way communication means that managers need to be able, and prepared, to free up time to talk with staff as and when they need to. While this process may take some time to develop if it is new to staff, once it has taken root the process of appraising performance will be less traumatic for both staff and managers. More importantly, you will find that the analysis of performance by manager and staff member will be remarkably close. Instead of being a confrontation—which is so often the case in performance appraisal—you will find that evidence from both parties is similar, the problems are already identified by staff, and there is a willingness to move forward through development to new performance standards.

Being non-judgmental

At the monitoring stage it is critical that you don't make judgments about the evidence you are collecting. Making a decision without proper analysis of the evidence may cause you to arrive at an indefensible position, which may not only be unfair and inaccurate but may also be discriminatory and irrelevant to the performance standards agreed on with staff. Being non-judgmental also protects you from your biases, personal beliefs and prejudices. If these are allowed to influence the collection of evidence you will find that the evidence is flawed, as it presents only one side or one view. Flawed evidence is likely to lead to litigation at many levels. To avoid this, your task is to collect evidence of performance on a continuing basis throughout the performance management cycle, to analyse it thoroughly, to give feedback based on analysed evidence, and to use it as a basis for overall appraisal discussions during and at the end of the cycle.

Figure 6.4 demonstrates a framework that can be used to guide this part of managing performance.

FIGURE 6.4 A framework for monitoring performance

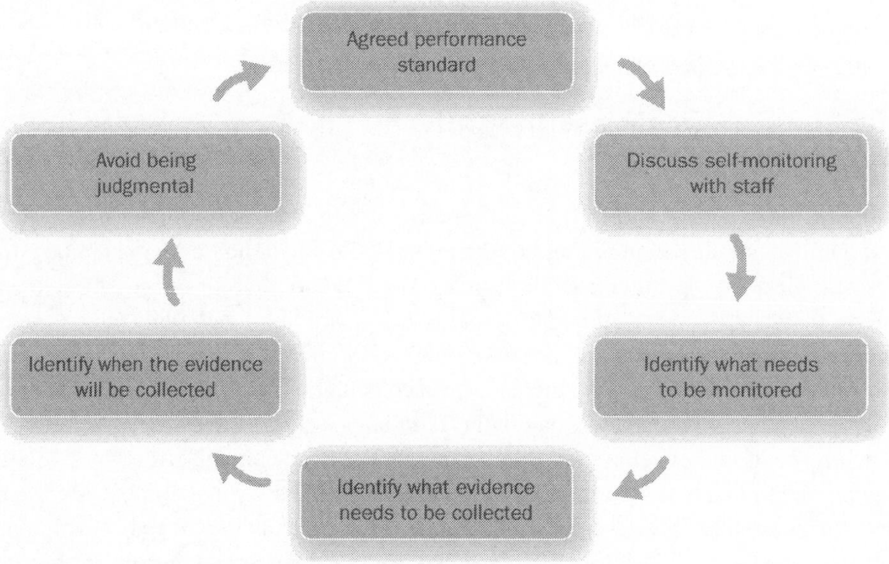

Intervention

All too often, managers see evidence and act on it without appropriate analysis. Intervention without analysis can be fatal to the staff–manager relationship, trust, the perceived fairness of the performance management system, and staff participation. Additionally, in more extreme cases you may leave yourself open to criticism, grievance procedures or even litigation under industrial relations or anti-discrimination law. This, in turn, may lead to decreases in productivity, motivation and organisational commitment by staff.[10] Before you intervene—and 'intervene' includes discussing a problem with staff or a team—ensure that you have analysed the situation. This includes the performance standards, the scope of the particular problem, the current level of performance, and the context in which performance is taking place. The process of analysis is discussed in Chapter 7.

CONCLUSION

Monitoring provides the basic information needed for analysis of performance. Information about what is to be monitored and how it is to be monitored should be shared with staff to enable them to monitor their own performance. Managers are unable to give useful feedback if they do not have evidence on which to base their feedback. Feedback that is not useful leads to behaviours or change not occurring, or not being maintained. What to monitor will depend on the standards you set with staff and teams. Monitoring requires a significant investment of time and effort by managers and staff, and is a responsibility both share. Poor monitoring will sabotage a performance management system because poor-quality evidence will be collected and staff will lose confidence in the process. The rest of the performance management system is based on collecting evidence, then analysing and appraising it. Both staff and management need to understand that jumping to conclusions about evidence that is collected but not analysed is likely to put them both in a difficult and indefensible situation, which should be avoided at all costs. The process of collecting evidence should not be influenced by judgments about performance that cannot be substantiated.

SKILL AND KNOWLEDGE APPLICATION

To ensure that the key performance indicators (KPIs) were addressed in her work units, Helen, the manager of a warehouse and distribution centre, set very specific performance objectives with her team. One member of Helen's team was a home-based employee. The KPIs for the unit were:

- distribution costs
- inventory costs
- warehousing costs.

Some of the performance objectives the team had set were as follows:

- Reduce transport costs from 8% of cost price to 5% of cost price by 30 June XXXX.
- Increase the number of orders filled in one day from an average of 890 per day to an average of 1160 per day with no increase in casual staff by 30 December XXXX.
- Increase warehousing area by 50 square metres without expansion of floor space by 30 September XXXX.

TASK

- Pick two of the above performance objectives. For each one:
  —— Develop appropriate monitors.
  —— Identify the evidence that has to be collected for the above monitors.
  —— Identify how and when you will collect the evidence.
  —— Identify potential areas where, as a manager, you may be tempted to intervene before the appropriate evidence has been collected.
- Would Helen need to set separate performance objectives for her home-based employee? Explain.
- Give two examples of either (a) performance objectives Helen could set for the home-based employee, or (b) ways in which the home-based employee would be able to contribute to the above performance objectives.

CASE STUDY

Peter has just finished writing performance goals for his administration assistant, Anne. Anne has worked for Peter in this role for five years, and each year is the same: Peter hands down his performance goals for Anne without seeking her input. Anne is becoming increasingly frustrated, as she feels that Peter does not really understand her duties, and the performance goals she is given do not reflect her day-to-day role. She also feels that the goals she is given do not relate to those of the organisation, or at least as far as she can see.

Anne has never felt she could complain about her performance goals because Peter always comments on how happy he is with her performance and has always been generous when giving her a performance-based salary raise each year. Nevertheless, Anne is beginning to feel demotivated and feels that her opinions or suggestions do not count in the organisation. She stopped collecting evidence of her good and bad performance a long time ago, because Peter has never asked for her input during her performance review anyway. Each year during her review he makes the same general comments about the great work she is doing without looking at any particular examples. The one year she did express an interest in taking on some new duties, Peter did not include it in her final performance goals.

Anne is becoming bored in her job, as a lot of her tasks have become second nature. As she no longer feels challenged or motivated in her position, Anne has started looking for a new job.

QUESTIONS

1. Identify the causes of Anne's demotivation.
2. How could Peter rectify the situation and retain Anne as an employee?
3. How could Peter evaluate what performance needs to be monitored in Anne's job?

CHECKLIST

Guidelines for monitoring performance

- ❑ Clearly identify what needs to be monitored.
- ❑ Identify what evidence has to be collected.
- ❑ Identify when evidence is to be collected.
- ❑ Identify how evidence is to be collected.
- ❑ Discuss monitoring with staff or team(s).
- ❑ Be non-judgmental about collected evidence.
- ❑ Avoid intervention without analysis.
- ❑ Ensure the individual or team has been included in the decision-making process.
- ❑ Make time for this stage of the performance management system.
- ❑ Integrate this process into the daily operations of your job and your work unit.

Evidence demonstrates how an individual or team is performing or has performed

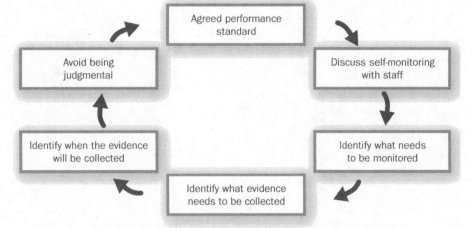

Agreed performance standard

Discuss self-monitoring with staff

Avoid being judgmental

Identify what needs to be monitored

Identify when the evidence will be collected

Identify what evidence needs to be collected

Monitor . . .

Individual and team progress towards their performance standards

How staff and teams are using their inputs

What processes (behaviours) are being used by staff and teams

Outputs that staff and teams produce

How outputs contribute to CSFs and KPIs

What gaps exist in any of the above

References

1 Longenecker, C. & Nykodym, N. 1996. 'Public sector performance appraisal effectiveness: A case study.' *Public Personnel Management*, 25(2), pp. 151–164.

2 Nicholson, J. & Nairn, A. 2006. *The Manager of the 21ˢᵗ Century*. Innovation & Business Skills Australia: Hawthorn, p. 15.

3 Griffiths, J. & Lloyd-Walker, B. 2007, 3rd edn. *Human Resource Management*. Pearson Australia: Frenchs Forest, Sydney, p. 86.

4 Office of the Director of Equal Opportunity in Public Employment. 1999. *Advanced Flexibility*. NSW Government Publication: Canberra, pp. 26–33.

5 Australian Human Rights and Equal Opportunity Commission 2001. *Pregnancy Guidelines*, <www.humanrights.gov.au/sex discrimination/publication/pregnancy/guidelines/> accessed 18 October 2009.

6 *Reader's Digest Oxford Complete Wordfinder*. 1994. Reader's Digest: London, p. 509.

7 Cawley, B., Keeping, L. & Levy, P. 1998. 'Participation in the performance appraisal process and employee reactions: A meta-analytic review of field investigations.' *Journal of Applied Psychology*, 83(4), pp. 615–633; Conway, J. 1999. 'Distinguishing contextual performance from task performance for managerial jobs.' *Journal of Applied Psychology*, 84(1), pp. 3–13.

8 Longenecker & Nykodym, op. cit., 1996; Lam, S. & Schaubroeck, J. 1999. 'Total quality management and performance appraisal: An experimental study of process versus results and group versus individual approaches.' *Journal of Organizational Behavior*, 20(4), pp. 145–457; Cawley et al., op. cit., 1998.

9 Longenecker & Nykodym, op. cit., 1996.

10 Cawley et al., op. cit., 1998.

CHAPTER SEVEN

Analysing performance

Learning outcomes

After reading this chapter you should be able to:

* define analysis as it relates to performance

* identify the potential problems in analysing performance

* use an analysis framework to analyse performance

* explain the main issues associated with each step of the analysis framework

* explain why a systematic approach should be used when analysing performance.

INTRODUCTION

Analysing performance needs to be done on a daily basis as well as on a more formal, longer term basis. Managers probably already analyse on a daily basis but do it so automatically that they are unaware of it. This chapter introduces a framework that managers can use to ensure that they are fair and equitable in the way they analyse the performance of staff and/or teams. The framework will give managers a base that will ensure they look at all the possible causes of unsatisfactory performance, including under-performance and non-performance, and provides a reminder that those who exceed performance expectations need to be rewarded for doing so.

The analysis of performance involves a comprehensive investigation of the elements or composition of performance, as it is a very complex process.[1] At this stage of the performance, management system managers need to review the actual performance of individuals or teams and look carefully at each of the components that make up the performance. As performance management is focused on developing people, managers need to discover the causes of poor performance and offer staff and teams opportunities to improve, supporting them in the process. Managers also need to discover the causes of any performance that exceeds expectations so that these methods can be applied to others and used to assist development activities.

What is analysis?

A definition

Analysis is the process of comparing actual performance with agreed performance standards and looking at the possible reasons why the actual performance is the same as, or different from, the agreed performance. This process uses the evidence collected over the period of the performance management cycle (discussed in Chapter 6). The manager's primary role at this stage of the performance management system is that of investigator. There is no evaluation of performance or passing of judgment. Managers need to discover the answer to the question 'Why is performance at the level it is?' The answer to this question will enable feedback to be stronger, more focused and supported by specific evidence, and will identify a number of options for moving forward. Given these, it is more likely that managers will achieve change in staff or teams. If a problem is discovered and intervention occurs without analysis, it is unlikely that change will be achieved.

Effective analysis

To analyse effectively, managers must understand the components of performance and the specific situations in which performance is achieved for each individual or team. The investigation that managers perform at this stage results in an understanding of all the possible influences on performance—a complex collection of many variables. To achieve maximum understanding, collected evidence needs to be systematically reviewed and organised. This can be done on a short-term or a long-term basis. It can also be done for specific incidents, thus facilitating quick intervention and the ability to keep things on track. Figure 7.1 illustrates the concept of analysing performance.

FIGURE 7.1 Analysis of performance

Agreed performance standards	Analysis of performance differences	Actual performance as demonstrated by evidence

Potential problems in analysing performance

There are many potential problems in analysing performance. These are made worse if you do not have a systematic way of reviewing the evidence you have collected on individual and team performance. The less systematic you are in your review, the more likely it is that you will fall prey to these problems. Poor analysis results in the loss, by staff, of credibility, reliability, validity and utility in the performance management system.[2]

Intervention

There are many times when, for safety reasons—to keep people on track or to reduce conflict—you will need to intervene immediately you become aware of a problem. In these cases you may issue instructions to staff or teams with little time available for analysing the situation or the performance involved. In such circumstances you should issue the necessary instructions and advise staff that you want to talk about it afterwards. Agree on a time with the individual or team and make sure the discussion occurs within 24 hours of the event. Between the event and the discussion, analyse as much evidence as you can to identify problems.

Human error

The problems inherent in performance management systems are essentially ones of human error.[3] These revolve around human frailties, such as exaggeration, seeing only what you want to see and personal prejudice. It is well documented that individuals may look at the same thing and perceive it differently.[4] For example, if a project officer takes several days to reach a decision, a manager may take that as evidence that the project officer is inefficient. Another manager may perceive the same person as being reflective and careful. In other words, our perceptions and judgments about how a person performs will be influenced strongly by the assumptions we make about the person. While such errors are difficult to eradicate because there are so many forms of them,[5] a systematic analysis framework aimed at reducing unconscious errors may reinforce the reliability and validity of the performance management system. There is evidence to suggest that evaluation of performance that is very bad or very good is more accurate than the range of options in between, primarily because the evidence is so obvious at each end of the spectrum.[6] Some of the potential problems in performance management systems can be averted if managers are aware of them, and if analysis of performance is systematic. The following are the more common problems evident in the way managers analyse performance.

Halo effect

When we form a general impression about a person based on a single positive characteristic, we are being influenced by the halo effect.[7] The halo effect refers to the way managers may focus only on the positive side of a person that they like or already think well of. The problem is well documented in the research and remains a significant issue in performance management.[8] It results in strengths being exaggerated so that they compensate for any weaknesses an individual may have. Consequently, development opportunities may be lost to that individual or team.

The halo effect may also be caused by events from the past: a person may have carried out a project extremely well, and this has coloured what a manager thinks about the present performance of the staff member. Instead of analysing current performance, assumptions are made that individuals who did such a good job in the past must be okay now. The opposite is also true.

A person or team may recently have produced very good outcomes, and this may cloud the view of the whole of the period, during which some significant weaknesses may be evident.

A particular problem of the halo effect is the existence of compatibility issues. Often, assumptions are made about people who agree with the manager or share similar interests: these people must be all right and consequently their performance is seen as satisfactory, or more than satisfactory. Finally, an individual or team may have a particular set of skills that are highly desired in the job, leading to actual performance being overlooked. Thus, the overall impression is better than would otherwise be the case.

The upward bias that the halo effect creates is illustrated in Figure 7.2.

FIGURE 7.2 The halo effect

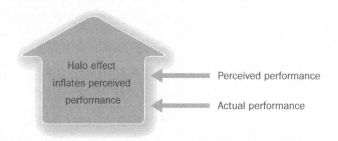

The halo effect can give rise to problems by generating attitudes in staff that suggest they are experts in what they do, and therefore do not need to engage in further learning. This very quickly makes them less effective, and possibly less flexible, as they stick to tried-and-true methods that may not be appropriate in the future. Where performance is appraised under the influence of the halo effect, it becomes difficult to deal with substandard performance or requirements to improve performance. It is almost impossible to defend a litigation where staff have consistently been given 'good' appraisals and are then suddenly given less satisfactory appraisals. As feedback should be given on the basis of honesty supported by appropriate evidence, this situation has the potential to destroy the credibility of the performance management system. Primarily, the halo effect is a problem because it causes managers to be selective in the evidence they collect (albeit unconsciously), so that it supports their personal view of the staff member or team.

Horns effect

The opposite of the halo effect, this problem is one of anticipating poor performance. A person's strengths are overlooked and weaknesses highlighted. This judgment is usually based on what is thought about a staff member or a team, resulting in a manager being blind to the strengths of an individual or team because a negative attitude is held towards them. An individual or team may be held back because the manager believes they are not capable. These people often receive negative feedback, which may not be based on fact or evidence. Feedback given without evidence makes it just about impossible for staff to do anything about the feedback. For managers, this means that a group of people may have strengths, skills or knowledge that would contribute significantly to the outcomes of the work unit but which are not being utilised.

The horns effect can be created in a number of ways. Information may be used that is based on a manager's personal experience of an individual or team but is not related to the performance standards. For example, a manager might know that an individual had been forced to resign as treasurer of the local cricket club because, allegedly, the job was done so badly. A manager may also be negative towards staff because they do not do things the way the manager would. Some staff become known as 'problem people' in an organisation. A problem person or team may be so branded for things such as agreeing with unions, pushing for change, complaining about particular things, or simply not performing. Consequently, a manager may think that problem people cannot achieve performance standards because they are always wanting change, or complaining! People may also be branded by being associated with a particularly poor manager or project, or job that went wrong. Subsequently, the performance of these people is not fully and objectively analysed, and they are viewed negatively because of their association with a particular problem or mistake.

Sometimes the horns effect develops as a result of differences in values, gender, or cultural or ethnic origins. Finally, managers who expect a perfect job every time will have a negative view of staff or teams who do not do a perfect job all the time. This is an unreal expectation and is demotivating to individuals and teams. The downward pressure on perceived performance created by the horns effect is represented in Figure 7.3.

FIGURE 7.3 The horns effect

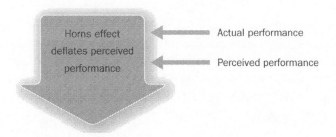

The horns effect can have serious consequences for self-esteem, job satisfaction and future performance. Staff and teams subjected to this effect are likely to be annoyed, frustrated and angry, to the point where they will eventually leave the organisation. These feelings are driven by a helplessness that is usually fuelled by vague feedback with little evidence. The type of feedback given will not enable the staff to identify specific needed improvements. Managers should be aware that negative feedback is much easier to give and receive if specific evidence is presented and plans are made to improve performance. Additionally, the feelings of frustration and anger could well support litigation that might not be easy to defend if decisions have been made on the basis of a manager's negative 'gut' feelings.

Both halo and horns effects are created by the personal prejudice or bias of managers. They result in very little objective analysis of the job people are performing. Managers need to be diligent to recognise these biases and to ensure that they analyse only the evidence collected on the performance of an individual or team. A systematic framework is the best way to minimise the bias in any analysis.

CHECK YOUR UNDERSTANDING

1 Why does the analysis of performance need to be done systematically?
2 What is the primary task of managers in analysing performance?
3 Describe in your own words the term 'analysis' as it is used in this chapter.
4 Why is it important to know the potential problems in analysing performance?
5 Explain the halo effect.
6 Explain the horns effect.
7 Explain the possible consequences of poor analysis of performance by a manager.

Categorical statements

If you have ever caught yourself saying that a person or team *never* does this or *always* does that, you have made a categorical statement. But is there evidence to support your statement? While categorical statements may be based on some fact or evidence, it is clear that the behaviour of people is not as specific as these statements suggest. It is unlikely that managers will find sufficient evidence to support such a contention. Avoid using the terms 'never' or 'always' when analysing performance or in performance discussions, because it is unlikely that these two extremes will be true.

Simplification

Managers sometimes simplify the appraisal of people. If things look very complex, it is often much easier to confine analysis to an overall result. This is a vague and unsubstantiated basis on which to give a person feedback and to conduct a performance discussion. For performance management to work, managers must invest considerable time and energy.[9] This is particularly so for the analysis phase. You must base your analysis on evidence of actual performance over the entire performance management cycle.

Stereotypes

When we judge someone on the basis of our perception of a group of which they are a member, we are engaging in stereotyping. Stereotypes are representations of what is considered typical of a certain group of people. For example, you may often hear the saying that accountants do not have any personality, or used-car salespeople can't be trusted, or people who play extreme sports need their heads read. This has led to stereotypes in the workplace that are not only discriminatory but erroneous in nature, and clearly are not relevant to determining job performance. The characteristics or attributes of one individual, or the experience of one single interaction with a member of the group, leads you to conclude that all people in this group are the same. Stereotypes have no place in the analysis of performance of individuals or teams. They rarely have anything to do with the performance of the job.

Inflexibility

Inflexibility relates to the opinions that managers may have of individuals or teams (however these are formed) regardless of the actual evidence before them. The opinions may stem from personality conflicts, a general lack of compatibility, or differences in values or beliefs. The result is that some managers are absolutely inflexible about individuals or teams and consistently stick to their opinions, even to the extent of collecting only evidence that supports their view. Inflexibility can relate to both negative and positive aspects of performance, but is equally destructive for both. It is doubtful that the whole body of evidence available can support such opinions, and managers who are so inflexible are likely to find themselves in litigation.

Leniency

Leniency is the preparedness of some managers to be tolerant of performances that do not reach the required standard. There can be enormous pressure on managers to be lenient, especially when the results of the performance management system cycle determine the pay levels of staff. Where managers and organisations do not develop in their staff an understanding of performance management as a process that is based in development and improvement, staff see it merely as a means of obtaining a raise. Research has demonstrated that managers tend to be more lenient in these circumstances.[10] Such behaviour by management destroys the credibility of the performance management system.

Central tendency

The concept of central tendency is that managers will move to the centre rather than adopt an extreme position. Rather than see evidence of poor performance, or particularly good performance, managers will tend to see evidence that places the staff member or team in the 'average' category. Staff are seen as satisfactory so that managers do not have to 'stick their necks out' and explain or defend an 'extreme' position. This approach is likely to lead to litigation, especially where there is evidence to the contrary.

Discrimination

The Australian workplace is characterised by diversity, with employees coming from a wide range of ethnic and cultural backgrounds. As we have seen, managers will often favour employees with whom they feel compatible. However, it is illegal and discriminatory to collect and interpret evidence on the basis of an employee's membership of a specific group. Australia has anti-discrimination legislation designed to prohibit discrimination based on, for example, race, gender, religion, nationality, social origin, age, sexual preferences, disability, marital status or family commitments. These attributes have nothing to do with job performance. Analysis that relies on these factors is invalid and will most certainly be subject to litigation.

Lack of organisational commitment

This problem can sabotage an organisation's performance management system even before it is implemented. Where there is no organisational commitment, staff cannot be expected to embrace the process. In this situation, managers, too, cannot be expected to pay much attention to the process or bother to take it seriously. Without organisational commitment it is unlikely that managers will invest the necessary time and effort to make a performance management system work. Little analysis will be done and it is likely that staff will be given a satisfactory rating in the system, rather than one that reflects actual performance. Organisational commitment is evidenced by senior management participating in significant training, being part of the system, holding more junior managers accountable for developing standards with their staff and team, and implementing the system fully.[11]

Figure 7.4 demonstrates the balancing effect of a systematic analysis of performance.

FIGURE 7.4 Balancing effect of a systematic approach

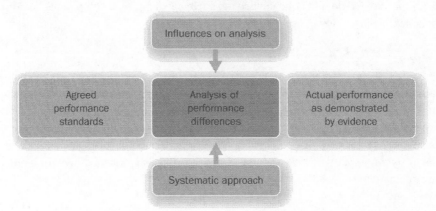

The problems discussed above all have the ability to reduce your analysis of performance to subjective and/or irrelevant opinions. In order to avoid this, Chapter 6 emphasises the need to collect evidence throughout the performance management cycle. This chapter emphasises the need to compare the evidence collected with the required level of performance (performance standards) and to see what the difference is without making judgments about performance. To further avoid subjectivity, it is suggested that a systematic approach to analysis is useful. A systematic approach allows managers to work through the evidence methodically, thus avoiding jumping to conclusions or strengthening personal bias. It also ensures that managers will analyse all options and variables that might have affected the performance of the individual or team.

SKILL AND KNOWLEDGE APPLICATION

You are Helen, the Human Resources Manager for a national pharmaceutical company. Yesterday, Mervyn from the production team rang to make an appointment with you to talk about some problems his team had with their supervisor and manager. Mervyn had been elected the spokesperson. He tells you the following story.

'For some time we have been complaining to our manager, George, that we are unhappy with our team leader, Linda. Essentially we seem to see two different sides of the one problem. Every time one of us discusses our problems with George, he finds reasons to explain Linda's actions. We constantly get told that Linda is an excellent employee who is doing a fabulous job, and that George is sure Linda can deal with the matter. For example, you know the performance appraisals we are supposed to have regularly each quarter? Well, we are lucky if we get more than 10 minutes with her. That is not enough time to review performance. Yet at the end of the year our salaries depend on this. Linda also seems to favour some of the team over others with the type of work she gives us. Carol is very good at organising the supplies, which she did at her last job, but Linda always seems to give those sorts of jobs to Kevin. While he doesn't mind them, he is snowed under with work and Carol does not have enough to do. All of us have a number of similar complaints. The problem is, George doesn't seem to see it.'

After Mervyn leaves, you do some preliminary investigation and discover that George and Linda did the same degree at the University of Queensland. You also note that George has been in the position for only four months. Talking with their peers, you also discover that George and Linda are members of the same photography club.

SKILL AND KNOWLEDGE APPLICATION CONTINUED

TASK

- What are the problems you will need to bring to the attention of George and Linda?
- What would be the best forum in which to tackle these problems?

The remaining part of this chapter introduces a framework for analysis and discusses how to use it. The analysis framework is presented in Figure 7.5.

FIGURE 7.5 An analysis framework

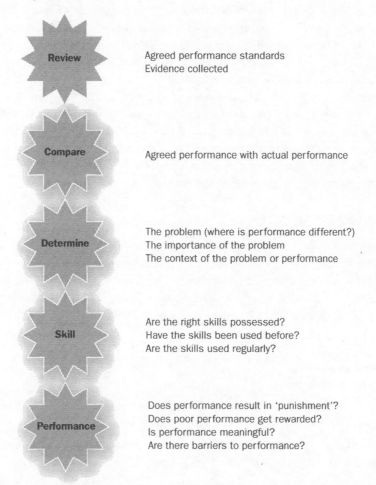

Review	Agreed performance standards Evidence collected
Compare	Agreed performance with actual performance
Determine	The problem (where is performance different?) The importance of the problem The context of the problem or performance
Skill	Are the right skills possessed? Have the skills been used before? Are the skills used regularly?
Performance	Does performance result in 'punishment'? Does poor performance get rewarded? Is performance meaningful? Are there barriers to performance?

Analysing performance

The beginning of this chapter provided a definition of analysis as a comprehensive investigation of the elements or composition of performance. It is critical to objectivity, reliability and validity that the investigation be comprehensive. Figure 7.5 demonstrates the level of comprehensiveness needed to ensure objectivity, and illustrates the five main issues around which analysis should be based:

- reviewing information
- comparing information
- determining problems
- identifying skills
- identifying negative influences on performance.

The term 'problems' as it is used in this framework has a specific meaning. Problems are created when the comparison between agreed performance and actual performance reveals there is a difference. The difference can be above the agreed performance or below the agreed performance. Recall that no judgments are being made at this time, so the framework represents a difference as being a problem that needs further investigation.

The framework in Figure 7.5 can be used for long-term analysis of performance, such as formal performance reviews, and it can also be used with short-term or daily issues of performance. For longer term use you will spend a good deal of time working through the steps, but with daily use you will move quickly through the framework as you will be dealing with only one issue of performance at a time. Analysis for the longer term requires more time because there will be much evidence to review against a number of performance standards.

The analysis framework

The framework has been developed from the literature in the field, and is based on the original work of Mager and Pipe.[12] Their book, *Analysing Performance Problems*, is a useful source of further information on analysing performance. The framework will be built on in the remaining part of this chapter and developed further in Chapters 8 and 9. Figure 7.6 illustrates the framework as a flowchart. Each step in the flowchart will now be further defined.

Review

Performance standards

Before analysing performance:

- Appropriate performance standards should be reviewed to ensure that you know exactly what was expected of the individual staff member or team.
- Have a copy of the standards with you while you are analysing performance. This will be the baseline to which you will keep coming back.
- Identify conditions of performance agreed to, such as time, special equipment or access to information.
- Managers should also review what they promised to do as part of the staff or team's performance agreement.

FIGURE 7.6 An analysis flowchart[13]

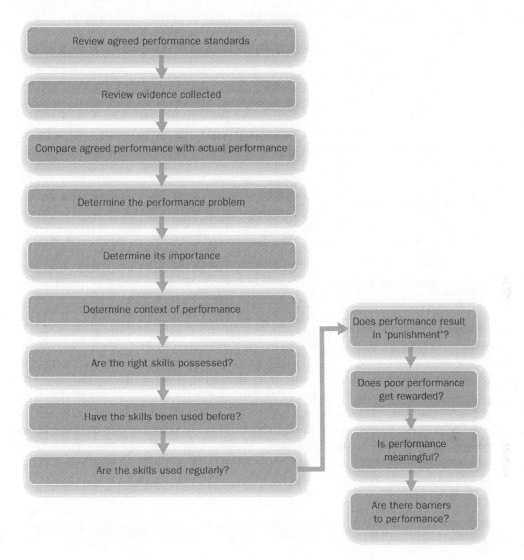

Evidence collection

- The manager should review and become familiar with the collected evidence.
- Is the evidence collected skewed to one view or does it represents a good cross-section of the work performed by the individual or team?
- You should retrieve appropriate examples of performance when you compare actual with agreed performance. Sometimes, a cursory glance at the evidence will identify holes in the collected evidence.
- The manager should be satisfied that sufficient evidence has been collected. If more evidence is needed, it should be collected before moving to the next step.

Compare

Agreed performance with actual performance

In this step:

- Compare evidence collected with the agreed performance standards.

- Sort the evidence around the agreed performance standards. Some evidence will reflect a number of agreed performance standards (e.g. where the evidence is a report in which a number of performance standards are addressed).

- If there is not sufficient evidence to demonstrate the performance standard, stop working through the framework and collect further evidence of performance.

Determine

The performance problem

- From the evidence, you should be able to describe the nature of the problems discovered in the previous step. (Remember, the term 'problem' means that there is a difference between the agreed and the actual performance.)

- It is important to determine exactly what the performance problem is, in your opinion, based on the evidence you have.

- Unless you are very precise about what it is, you will arrive at solutions that will not work because you have not identified the real problem.

For example, when staff are not performing, many managers immediately think of training as the problem. Lack of training is a cause only where a person does not have the knowledge or the skills required. Even then, the problem is still one of the job not being performed properly. This can have many causes, only one of which may be lack of training. If you incorrectly identify the problem as being a need for training when really it is a problem of lack of suitable resources, no amount of training will fix the problem and you will waste valuable and often expensive resources training people to do what they already know how to do!

SKILLS PRACTICE

On comparing the agreed performance with the actual performance of one of your staff, Timothy, you identify a problem. Timothy is an administrative officer, level 5, and is responsible for policy in your program unit of the Department of Family Services. He agreed to develop policy to draft stage in four areas for the past 12 months. You find that only two sets of draft policy have been completed.

The two completed sets of policy conform to the department's requirements for draft policy in every way. You notice that they have skilfully addressed some difficult issues. While the other two sets are incomplete, you still have a great deal of evidence about them; there are copies of meeting dates with stakeholders, notes of decisions made, dates of phone calls, and copies of memos asking for input to the process. Numerous sections of policy have been drafted but some of them are obviously incomplete.

What do you think the problem is in this case?

Managers should try to identify the problem as precisely as they can. The remaining steps of the analysis will help you do this. Be alert! Do not be tempted to say, 'Overall, things look all right'. Performance is not something that can be 'averaged'. If evidence is suggesting that one standard was not achieved, two were satisfactory and one was in excess of expectations, the three 'good' ones do not cancel out the 'bad' one so that the overall perception is that no 'problem' exists. This is unfair to the individual or team, the manager, the work unit and the organisation, and will reduce productivity.

The importance of the problem

In this step:

- Establish how important the problem is. Would fixing the problem involve more effort, time and expense than the problem creates? If nothing was done about it, what would be the impact?

- Determine that the problem is important enough to solve, then continue through the framework. In the majority of cases this is likely to be the outcome.

- If you decide that the problem is not important enough to solve, it is likely that you have agreed on a poor, or invalid, performance standard with the staff member or team. The outcome of this is that you need to set a new performance standard.

The context of performance

This is a vital step in understanding the reasons for performance. Research has shown that the context in which performance occurs can have significant effects on the performance of individuals and teams.[14] The effects can be positive, which facilitates performance, or negative, so that they constrain performance.[15] There are two aspects to the concept of 'context'. First, there is the physical and mental environment in which performance takes place—it may be during periods of great change or upheaval in the organisation, with outdated equipment, when understaffed, with equipment failure and poor training, or with interesting décor, continual training and development opportunities, team dynamics that facilitate performance, and mentoring. Second, there is the idea that context relates to the work people do that adds value to the organisation.[16] This means work that people do, beyond the usual boundaries of their job or performance standards, through which they enhance the performance of the organisation—for example, where people use their initiative to solve a problem, identify how work processes or procedures can be improved, build networks across the organisation, and share skills and knowledge to help develop other workers.

The context of performance is not tackled in most performance management systems.[17] Yet context is a powerful determinant of outcomes. Research demonstrates that contextual factors consistently influence supervisors' impressions of subordinate performance.[18] Further, supervisors tend not to see issues of context as a problem, whereas those being appraised do.[19] Where this is the case, there is great danger that the performance management system will be seen by staff as biased and unhelpful. Thus it will lose credibility and become dysfunctional. A dysfunctional performance management system will lead to grievances and possibly litigation. It will also affect staff and work units, resulting in reduced performance for the organisation.[20] Analysing performance requires the analysis not only of how individuals or teams perform against performance standards but also of what contextual factors influenced the performance and to what extent these were out of the control of the individual or team. This must be taken into account when analysing the reasons for performance, and managers should aim to discourage those contextual factors that constrain performance and develop those that support performance.

CHECK YOUR UNDERSTANDING

8 How might contextual issues in the workplace shape the performance problem?

9 Why would staff perceive the performance management system to be biased if a manager did not take contextual issues into account?

10 Might there be cases where the context blocks achievement of the performance standards? Explain your answer.

Skill

Are the right skills possessed?

The framework so far has dealt with external influences on individual or team performance. In this step, managers look at the internal influences on performance—that is, the skills that staff or teams possess, and use to bring about performance. If a problem has been identified, it is doubtful that only external influences will be affecting performance. The manager will need to:

- understand what skills are needed to perform at the required standard
- use competencies and job descriptions as useful aids in pinpointing exactly what is necessary
- further review the evidence arranged around each performance standard to help managers determine whether appropriate skills are being used
- identify where evidence suggests that skills are not being used and document these for discussion and appraisal during the performance discussion (see Chapter 9).

Have the skills been used before?

Where a perceived lack of skill is documented, it is important to determine whether the skills have ever been used before. This could be found in the personnel file of the staff or team or, if it is not recorded, it must be an item for attention in the performance discussion dealt with in Chapter 9. If the skills have been used before, clearly they have been learned. There is no point in thinking that training is a solution here, as it will not help. There are probably other reasons for not using the skills. Where the skills have not been used before, training is likely to be the most common and appropriate tool to use. Training can be delivered in a variety of formats, and does not include just classroom training. Training may be done on the job or off the job and may take a variety of formats—self-paced, one-on-one (e.g. coaching), and group training.[21]

Are the skills used regularly?

If the skills have been used before in either this or another job but there is no evidence of them being used now, it could be the case that the individual or team has the skills but is not performing them on a regular basis. People do forget procedures or skills that are not used regularly. What is needed here is for the skills to be refreshed in the mind of the individual or team. There are a number of ways this can be achieved:

- Job aids, such as those used in this book, are helpful when specific skills or procedures are used infrequently.

- Giving individuals practice in the use of the skills helps, especially when you can schedule this on a regular basis to avoid the skills being forgotten by the individuals or team.

- Demonstrations, coaching and observation are other useful ways of keeping skills current.

- It may also be possible to redesign the job so that the individual has more opportunities to use the skills. (Remember, if you don't use it you lose it!)

If the skills are used regularly yet there is little to suggest that they have been applied in the performance being analysed, there may be other reasons why the skills are not being used. There are factors that can cause non-performance but which are out of the control of individuals or teams; these barriers are explored in the next step.

Performance

Does performance result in 'punishment'?

Punishment for doing a good job comes in all sorts of ways. For example:

- Individuals or teams that have agreed to cut expenses by 3% and achieved the goal are often expected to cut expenses again in the next cycle.

- If staff achieve an objective relating to resolving and reducing customer complaints, they often find they are given all the customer complaints.

- If a team works back for a week or two to achieve a specific goal this often creates the expectation that they are happy to work extra hours all the time, and they are given more than their fair share of work.

Consequently, individuals and teams soon learn that achieving the performance standard results in being punished in ways that management may not see, realise or anticipate. This dilemma is known as 'moving the goalposts'. As long as the goalposts keep moving, people will not be motivated to try to reach them. Search the evidence for any sign of punishment. If you find any, this may be an item for the next performance discussion.

Does poor performance get rewarded?

Managers, staff and teams can accidentally reward unsatisfactory performance in a variety of ways. In particular, underperformers may enjoy the extra attention they get because they have not met the performance requirements. For example, there may be some status attached to being in the boss's office on a regular basis, or having the boss visit the individual. In some cases, staff who are non-performers have been promoted to get them out of the way because they are a nuisance and difficult to work with. Look at why the individual or team may be underperforming:

- Does underperforming have some sort of status attached to it?

- Is it easier not to perform than it is to perform?

- What are the consequences of not performing?

- Is work taken off the individual/team when not performing, thus making their workload lighter?

- Do individuals/teams get more attention for not performing than they do when they perform?

- What other 'rewards' might individuals/teams get for not performing?

If you find there are rewards for non-performance, these should be noted for further action by the manager as an issue separate from the analysis of performance. You may need to invest effort and time identifying the rewards and then working out how to remove them. However, as long as the reward for non-performance remains in place, you are not likely to force any change in the individual or team. The reason may even come down to your personal management style, which you may need to change, or you could be guilty of not monitoring closely enough, or not taking appropriate action when things go off the rails.

If you find that non-performance is not rewarded, and that staff and teams are held accountable for non-performance, other reasons will be influencing the problem.

Is performance meaningful?

This question is fundamental to job satisfaction and esteem for individuals and teams. There needs to be some purpose and meaning in performing to the required standard. If staff cannot see a rationale for achieving the performance, it is unlikely to be achieved. This is one of the basic reasons that staff and teams need to be involved in setting standards, and to participate fully in the performance management system, as you will recall from Chapters 4 and 5 and the overview of Part B. It is also why Part A exists—so that performance standards can be tied to organisational objectives and key performance indicators, thus providing some purpose for the individual and team standards no matter how removed the organisational objectives might be.

You know yourself that you are unlikely to feel motivated and excited about doing a job for which you can see no outcome or purpose. If you discover that there is little meaning in the performance standard, you need to link it explicitly to outcomes. If you are satisfied that the required performance is meaningful for the individual, then there is another possibility to explore.

Are there barriers to performance?

Barriers to performance are anything that may prevent an individual or team from achieving the agreed performance standard. A barrier might be physical, environmental, perceived, emotional or psychological. It may or may not be within the control of staff. Some barriers are:

- lack of appropriate authority
- conflicting priorities imposed by other, more senior staff
- insufficient time in which to complete work
- policies or procedures which make it difficult or impossible to obtain the appropriate information or to act in a way that facilitates the required performance
- outdated equipment
- outdated software
- informal ways of going about things in your organisation, which restrict the ability of staff to perform
- an organisational culture that restricts the ability of staff to perform
- environmental barriers, such as noise, décor, constant interruptions or lack of appropriate desk space
- lack of access to necessary information
- difficulty with interpersonal skills
- fear of particular individuals.

Where such barriers exist, they need to be removed. If it is not possible to remove them, the performance standard will need to be renegotiated. You may not be in a position to understand what barriers there are and may need to discuss them with the job holder in the performance discussion.

SKILL AND KNOWLEDGE APPLICATION

Beryl is really annoyed at her assistant, Clare, as she is consistently late in preparing the monthly statistics. It was agreed eight months ago between them both that the stats were to be completed by the third working day of every month and given to Beryl by the close of business on that day. When asked about the stats, Clare always claims there were other more important things to be done. Clare always leaves them to the last minute, and because of that she is rushed and the figures do not add up.

Over the past four months the statistics have arrived later and later. Last month Beryl lost her temper with Clare, shouting at her. The stats were not ready until the sixth working day of the new month. Beryl is very uneasy about the statistical report; for the past two months she has received negative feedback from her boss because she has not been able to present the report at the committee meeting held on the fifth working day of each month. Without statistical information, the committee cannot recommend the appropriate strategy for the next month. If such a situation were to occur regularly, the organisation would have to cut back the three projects that are run through this committee. This would result in a number of retrenchments. Beryl is getting ready to give a warning to Clare over the issue.

TASK
- Analyse the situation above and determine what the problem might be.
- Make a list of the steps you would take in rectifying the situation.
- Should Beryl have handled this situation in a different, more timely, manner?

Once the framework has been used to analyse the collected performance evidence, you should be clear about the level of performance achieved by an individual or team. You should have identified what performance problems exist and how they were created. You might also have questions you cannot answer, and these will need discussion with the job holder to clarify certain performance issues. You have determined how the context of performance may have influenced the performance and can identify whether this was an enabling influence or a constraining influence. You have also reviewed the skills demonstrated by the individual or team, looked at barriers to performance, and decided whether performance is meaningful/rewarded or punished.

You have now learned how to apply a framework to reduce the influence of errors on the final evaluation of an individual or team performance. The framework has helped you to not jump to conclusions, to be more aware of your personal values, perceptions and opinions and to curb them where they cannot be supported by evidence. By working through the various steps you have taken an analytical or problem-solving approach to reviewing the performance evidence before you make a decision about the level of performance. While it is true to say that you are probably forming an opinion as you work through the evidence, that opinion will be based on evidence and facts, rather than on feelings and specific events that may stick in your mind. The result of using a framework is a more equitable review that is as objective as possible. Nevertheless, you do not make a determination about performance until the next stage in the performance management system—appraising performance. This is dealt with in Chapters 8 and 9.

CONCLUSION

The need to analyse collected performance evidence is clearly demonstrated in this chapter. Evidence provides the basis for the fair and equitable treatment of all employees. However, in order to deliver an unbiased review of performance, systematic analysis of the evidence with particular attention to the potential problem areas created by human error is required. Poor analysis leaves the way open to bias of all types, which manifests itself in skewed performance reviews: that is, a performance record is made that does not reflect the actual performance but is an expression of a manager's opinions, based on feelings and faulty recollection of events. Judgments about performance that are not based on collected evidence and analysed in such a way as to minimise human error will destroy the credibility of the whole performance management system. The system then becomes dysfunctional, reducing the performance of the organisation. Performance reviews that are flawed may also result in litigation by staff.

Skilful analysis of performance is achieved through the systematic investigation of the performance evidence collected, to minimise the degree of human error. A series of questions provide a guide to sorting through the performance evidence. The analysis framework is designed to force objectivity into the review process. While it may appear clumsy and pedantic at first, after using it a few times you will see the value of it, especially where there are indications of unsatisfactory performance.

The process used in the framework helps you develop necessary interpersonal skills, such as managing conflict, negotiating, and giving feedback. It also forces you to look widely for causes of performance. You need to know the causes of satisfactory, unsatisfactory and excellent performance so that you can take appropriate action to reduce unsatisfactory performance and recreate the conditions for satisfactory and excellent performance for other staff or teams. This takes time. For a performance management system to operate effectively, managers must be prepared to invest time and effort in the process. Without that investment, managers will sabotage the performance management system.

 CASE STUDY

Ali Jaffrey is the academic manager for a large national registered training organisation (RTO) that develops and delivers competency-based, accredited training in hospitality for large hotels across Australia. He has recently been asked by his manager to provide the six-monthly performance management reports for his staff members, Sandy and Phil. He is expecting that the performance appraisal for Sandy, his assessment officer, will be straightforward. They have worked together for two years and have developed a close working relationship. In fact, over time they have found many common interests: they often go out to lunch together and are both members of a bird-watching group outside work.

However, Ali is worried about Phil, who assists Sandy as a student support assistant. Phil was employed 12 months ago, through the company's diversity program which promotes the employment of people with mild intellectual disabilities. His main duties are to update student records, process assessments and to answer simple student enquiries relating to the processing of their assessments. While Ali will perform Phil's performance review it is Sandy who supervises Phil on a daily basis. Ali is dependent on Sandy's feedback on Phil's performance as he is too busy to monitor Phil's day-to-day activities.

The following performance objectives were written into Phil's position description.

1 Enter correctly all details into the student administration system to the following standards:
- Enter correct personal details as provided by student or client relationship managers.
- Enter correct course and competency codes as indicated in the Course Directory.
- All data entry to be entered by close of business of day received.
- Prepare monthly reports for the client relationship managers.

2 Answer student enquiries to the following standards:

- ➥ Provide correct course names and codes and related competency information as outlined in the Course Directory.
- ➥ Provide correct information regarding the process of submitting completed assessments and requesting extensions as outlined in the Student Handbook.
- ➥ All enquiries are to be answered by email or phone within 24 hours.

For the first six months both Ali and Sandy were happy with Phil's progress and he was able to cope with the volume of work and meet his performance standards. He was enthusiastic, polite and willingly under-took training in the student administration system and in course structures in order to perform his duties. In addition, he often took the Course Directory and Student Handbook home with him to study. He has twice been nominated for an employee award in customer service by the sales staff for his telephone manner and attention to detail when compiling reports for the corporate clients, who in the past had complained about the accuracy of reports. His first performance review was successful and Phil acknowledged Sandy's patience in helping him learn his role and being available to answer questions.

However, over the past six months a number of events have occurred that have impacted on Phil's role. First, the volume of work has increased significantly due to the sales team bringing in two new major accounts. Second, there have been changes to a number of the hospitality courses which means the Course Directory he has been using for six months is out of date. The company has decided not to update the directory for cost reasons and information about the changes are relayed to staff through meetings. Third, the student administration system has been upgraded with new functionalities. In addition, Sandy (unbeknown to Ali) has started to offload some of his tasks, including answering specific questions about assessment tasks and preparing non-standard reports, arguing that it is time that Phil took on additional responsibility.

While no one has complained about Phil's work, he is having to work back regularly to ensure that all the data is entered and student enquiries are answered within the 24-hour time frame. Phil is losing confidence and is uncomfortable asking Sandy for assistance as he senses Sandy's impatience. Phil has tried to discuss his concerns with Ali and asked for additional training and assistance to take on the new tasks assigned by Sandy as well as learn the new course requirements and database functionalities. Ali, who has recently been assigned a new project, simply refers him back to Sandy.

At lunch on the day of Phil's performance review, Sandy complains that he has overheard Phil giving incorrect information to students about their assessment tasks and that his non-standard reports have been incomplete. Sandy says he would like to be able to assist Phil but is already tied up with his own workload. Ali realises he knows little about Phil and because he values Sandy's opinion he makes a note to himself to formally caution Phil in his appraisal that 'disability or not' he will have to lift his game. He will also make sure that Phil understands that if he is unable to meet the performance standards his job may be at risk. Secretly he wishes he'd never agreed to have Phil work in his team as he has always believed the role was too complex for someone with even a mild disability.

QUESTIONS

1 Do you think that Phil will receive a fair and equitable performance evaluation from Ali? In your answer identify the main problems with the way in which Ali has handled the preparation for the analysis of Phil's performance.

2 Describe what Ali should do to provide a fair and equitable performance review for Phil.

3 Consider Sandy's position. What suggestions or advice might Ali provide to Sandy?

JOB AIDS

An analysis flowchart

```
┌─────────────────────────────────────────────┐
│      Review agreed performance standards      │
└─────────────────────────────────────────────┘
                      ↓
┌─────────────────────────────────────────────┐
│            Review evidence collected          │
└─────────────────────────────────────────────┘
                      ↓
┌─────────────────────────────────────────────┐
│  Compare agreed performance with actual performance  │
└─────────────────────────────────────────────┘
                      ↓
┌─────────────────────────────────────────────┐
│       Determine the performance problem       │
└─────────────────────────────────────────────┘
                      ↓
┌─────────────────────────────────────────────┐
│            Determine its importance           │
└─────────────────────────────────────────────┘
                      ↓
┌─────────────────────────────────────────────┐
│        Determine context of performance       │
└─────────────────────────────────────────────┘
                      ↓                        ┌──────────────────────────┐
┌─────────────────────────────────────────────┐│   Does performance result │
│         Are the right skills possessed?       ││       in 'punishment'?    │
└─────────────────────────────────────────────┘└──────────────────────────┘
                      ↓                                      ↓
┌─────────────────────────────────────────────┐┌──────────────────────────┐
│         Have the skills been used before?     ││   Does poor performance   │
└─────────────────────────────────────────────┘│       get rewarded?       │
                      ↓                         └──────────────────────────┘
┌─────────────────────────────────────────────┐             ↓
│           Are the skills used regularly?      ├─────┐┌──────────────────────────┐
└─────────────────────────────────────────────┘     ││      Is performance      │
                                                     └┤       meaningful?        │
                                                      └──────────────────────────┘
                                                                  ↓
                                                      ┌──────────────────────────┐
                                                      │     Are there barriers    │
                                                      │       to performance?     │
                                                      └──────────────────────────┘
```

Source: Adapted from R. Mager & P. Pipe 1990, 2nd edn, *Analysing Performance Problems*; Kogan Page: London, p. 1.

CHECKLISTS

Potential problems in performance analysis
- [ ] Halo effect
- [ ] Horns effect
- [ ] Categorical statements
- [ ] Simplification
- [ ] Stereotypes
- [ ] Inflexibility
- [ ] Leniency
- [ ] Central tendency
- [ ] Discrimination
- [ ] Lack of organisational commitment

Analysing performance
- [ ] Review
  - [ ] Agreed performance standards
  - [ ] Evidence collected
- [ ] Compare
  - [ ] Agreed performance with actual performance
- [ ] Determine
  - [ ] The performance problem
  - [ ] The importance of the performance problem
  - [ ] The context of performance
- [ ] Skills
  - [ ] Are the right skills possessed?
  - [ ] Have the skills been used before?
  - [ ] Are the skills used regularly?
- [ ] Performance
  - [ ] Does performance result in 'punishment'?
  - [ ] Does poor performance get rewarded?
  - [ ] Is performance meaningful?
  - [ ] Are there barriers to performance?

References

1   Roberts, G. 1998. 'Perspectives on enduring and emerging issues in performance appraisal.' *Public Personnel Management*, 27(3), pp. 301–320.

2   Roberts, op. cit., 1998.

3   Longenecker, C. & Nykodym, N. 1996. 'Public sector performance appraisal effectiveness: A case study.' *Public Personnel Management*, 25(2), pp. 151–164; Roberts, op. cit., 1998.

4   Robbins, S., Bergman, R., Stagg, I. & Coulter, M. 2009, 5th edn. *Management*. Pearson Australia: Frenchs Forest, Sydney, p. 532.

5   Roberts, op. cit., 1998.

6   Roberts, op. cit., 1998.

7   Robbins et al., op. cit., 2009.

8   Fried, Y., Levi, A., Ben-David, H. & Briggs, R. 1999. 'Inflation of subordinates' performance ratings: Main and interactive effects of rater negative affectivity, documentation of work behavior, and appraisal visibility.' *Journal of Organizational Behavior*, 20(4), pp. 431–444.

9   Roberts, op. cit., 1998.

10   Roberts, op. cit., 1998.

11   Longenecker & Nykodym, op. cit., 1996.

12   Mager, R. & Pipe, P. 1990, 2nd edn. *Analysing Performance Problems*. Kogan Page: London.

13   Adapted from: *Analysing Performance Problems*, by Robert F. Mager and Peter Pipe, © 1997, The Center for Effective Performance, Inc., www.ccpworldwide.com

14   Cawley, B., Keeping, L. & Levy, P. 1998. 'Participation in the performance appraisal process and employee reactions: A meta-analytic review of field investigations.' *Journal of Applied Psychology*, 83(4), pp. 615–633; Conway, J. 1999. 'Distinguishing contextual performance from task performance for managerial jobs.' *Journal of Applied Psychology*, 84(1), pp. 3–13; Bernardin, H., Hagan, C., Kane, J. & Villanova, P. 1998. 'Effective performance management: A focus on precision, customers, and situational constraints.' In J.W. Smither (ed.), *Performance Appraisal: State of the Art in Practice*. Jossey Bass: San Francisco, pp. 28–32.

15   Bernardin et al., op. cit., 1998, pp. 28–33.

16   Bernardin et al., op. cit., 1998, pp. 28–29.

17   Borman, W., White, L. & Dorsey, D. 1995. 'Effects of ratee task performance and interpersonal factors on supervisor and peer performance ratings.' *Journal of Applied Psychology*, 80(1), pp. 168–177.

18   Van Scotter, J.R. & Motowidlo, S.J. 1996. 'Interpersonal facilitation and job dedication as separate facets of contextual performance.' *Journal of Applied Psychology*, 81(5), pp. 525–531. Cited in Bernardin et al., op. cit., 1998, pp. 28–32.

19   Bernardin et al., op. cit., 1998, p. 32.

20   Villanova, P. 1996. 'Predictive validity of situational constraints in general versus specific performance domains.' *Journal of Applied Psychology*, 81(5), pp. 532–574.

21   Tovey, M. & Lawlor, D. 2008, 3rd edn. *Training in Australia*. Pearson Australia: Frenchs Forest, Sydney.

CHAPTER EIGHT

Preparing to appraise performance

Learning outcomes

After reading this chapter you should be able to:

* define the management role and responsibilities in the performance appraisal process
* describe the culturally diverse nature of Australian workplaces and its effect on performance management
* explain the role of self-appraisal in performance appraisals
* describe the role of values in performance appraisal
* explain the role of communication in the performance appraisal process
* explain how staff can be motivated through the skilful application of performance appraisals
* define the term 'performance appraisal'
* explain the purpose of performance appraisals
* explain the review, planning and development cycle of performance appraisals
* define the terms 'performance gap' and 'anticipated performance gap'
* identify the benefits of performance appraisal for the organisation, the manager and the staff member
* explain how often appraisals should be conducted.

INTRODUCTION

Preparing to appraise performance is critical to the overall effectiveness of the performance appraisal. Appraising performance is not something managers can decide to do because they find they have an hour or two to fill in and are aware that performance review time is just around the corner. Both managers and employees need to be prepared for and committed to the performance appraisal process. To achieve the best results possible and to make it a positive experience, both manager and employee require time to be allocated for this preparation and need to be aware of the overall appraisal process. This chapter covers the manager's role in appraising performance, definitions of performance, and the purpose and benefits of performance appraisal. Chapter 9 will comprehensively cover the steps in a performance appraisal discussion, the conduct of the appraisal and the responsibilities of those involved.

Key concepts in performance appraisals

The management role

Australia exists in a complex, interconnected, hypercompetitive world economy. This complexity is reflected in the workplace in many ways—frequently changing business models, new labour markets, demands for flexible working arrangements, cultural and generational diversity, new retirement requirements and other demographic issues, and community and social pressures including increased corporate social responsibility.

While the main focus for executives and managers over the past 10 years has been the financial performance of companies, research conducted by Boston Consulting Group, and Innovation and Business Skills, suggests that workplaces will increasingly focus on the performance of people as a core company asset.[1] In particular, managers will need to manage cultural diversity and employees who come with a varied range of personal and work values that will determine their expectations and motivators for work and the way in which performance management is viewed.

In other words, the role of the manager continues to evolve. In addition to the five traditional roles of management[2]—planning, organising, staffing, leading and monitoring—today's managers are required to have considerable business acumen to contribute to organisational objectives.

The performance appraisal process tends to be classified in the staffing area as a Human Resources function, rather than across all the management functions as a strategic imperative. Thus, appraisals are often seen to be separate from the management function. Appraising performance and providing feedback is a means by which managers can execute the functions of management and motivate staff. Figure 8.1 demonstrates how performance appraisal and feedback are part of all the management functions.

In Figure 8.1 a manager's role and responsibilities are grouped around the functions of planning, organising, staffing, leading and monitoring. There are significant aspects of managing performance and improvement in each functional area, and some of these are shown in the figure. In part, how a manager manages will determine how successfully individuals perform and meet the individual requirements and objectives that, combined, form the vehicle through which the organisation achieves its plans and objectives. Managers therefore have an important and involved part to play in appraising performance, both informally, through day-to-day management activities, and formally, in performance appraisals.

According to the literature, performance appraisal has been handled badly by management for many years.[3] It tends to have negative connotations because of the lack of skills management has used in implementing schemes or systems and the negative attitude some managers have towards the concept of performance management. Appraisees have not been provided with the appropriate skills to get the most out of an appraisal. Appraisals have tended to concentrate on the completion of forms and compliance with the rules set down by Human Resources rather than the performance and potential of appraisees and the specific needs of work groups.

FIGURE 8.1 The management role and performance appraisals[4]

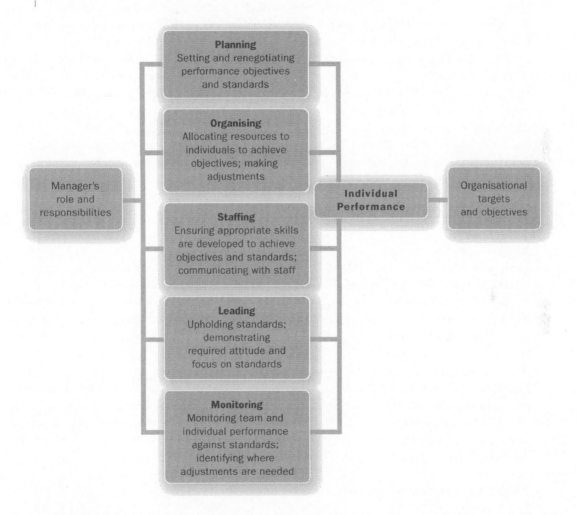

Self-appraisal

People appraise their performance all the time. Look around any car park and you will see drivers turn in and then back out, straighten up and reposition the car. To do that, drivers have made an appraisal of their performance in parking the car. Then they have taken some corrective action to improve the performance, tried again, and succeeded in achieving a preset standard of parking the car that they had in mind.

There are always consequences for others when people do not self-appraise. These consequences are likely to be more significant at work because of the team-based nature of organisations and the interdependence of workers.

Appraisal is a naturally occurring process in humans. We give ourselves continual feedback on how we are doing against a set of personal standards and objectives, whether in playing sport, working, bringing up children, cooking or doing jobs around the house. Some of us have very high expectations of ourselves, such as an urge to climb mountains, while others have more modest objectives and standards by which they live. Whatever your personal standards or objectives may be, you appraise yourself against them daily. This self-feedback provides guidance, motivation and reinforcement in your life, precipitating rethinks and new directions, or feelings of elation when objectives are attained. Thus, feedback is an important and fundamental component of performance appraisal in the workplace.

While individuals tend to provide self-feedback, it is not sufficient in the workplace to leave them to their own devices. Outside work, people are responsible to themselves, so it is up to them to take an objective view of how they are going and to make adjustments. If they fail to do so they suffer the consequences, whatever these may be. In the workplace, however, people are responsible to others. While we continue to give ourselves feedback, this must be supplemented with feedback from superiors and major stakeholders in the work that we do, because their perspectives are likely to be different from ours. What we do not see ourselves is documented in the literature as blind spots—things that others know about us but we do not know ourselves.[5] In order to improve our performance we need to know what these things are. The only way we are going to find out is if people provide us with feedback.

Motivation

Just as self-appraisal can be motivating for the individual, when a workplace performance appraisal is conducted with skill, both parties should be motivated. An appraisal where both parties have had an opportunity to discuss openly their fears and concerns, and then focused on how their hopes and aspirations can be attained, creates a more productive work environment. Relationships will strengthen, and personal pride and performance will be enhanced. Appraisees will feel empowered and motivated to achieve their best; they will feel more comfortable alerting management to problems because they know that the important thing will be to solve the problem rather than look for a person to blame. Managers will also feel more motivated after conducting a skilled performance appraisal, as they will be able to get on with the job of managing and will see individuals achieving results. Figure 8.2 illustrates the principle that a skilled performance appraisal discussion can motivate the parties involved and then underpin future performance, and thus the cycle continues.

FIGURE 8.2 Appraisals can motivate future performance

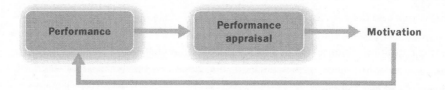

Managers are not only concerned with motivating an employee at the time of appraisal—the manager also needs to sustain that motivation for future performance. Some employees will enter the performance appraisal interview equating it to a pay raise and not much else. There have been many motivational theories put forward over time in an attempt to prove what motivates people, as shown in Figure 4.2 in Chapter 4. But motivation is not tied to money alone, and in most organisations pay raises are not always a good indication of performance, as they can be dictated by company profits, industry pay standards or experience. As mentioned earlier, individual motivations are strongly influenced by one's personal values. This is particularly relevant to Australian managers who generally work in environments characterised by cultural diversity. Therefore, skilful managers, when preparing for, conducting and assessing performance appraisals for their employees, will consider all factors that can be tapped into to motivate an employee, including their cultural background and identity. The performance appraisal process allows the manager to identify the career aspirations of an employee, assess the abilities of the employee to achieve his or her aspirations and, if in line with the organisation's objectives, initiate a training and development plan for the employee. Such a training and development plan could motivate employees by making them feel valued and setting a clear path for career achievement and self-actualisation, the peak of Maslow's motivational theory (see Chapter 4).

The management challenge

Managers will need to develop and embrace new approaches to performance management to accommodate the new business environment. Different measurements, processes and approaches, including output-based remuneration, will need to be considered as organisations treat people management as a core operational process as opposed to a support function.[6]

The other important challenge for managers in performance appraisals is to ensure that trust and honesty are developed with staff. This can be achieved only through effective communication and interactions during day-to-day workplace activities and feedback during the appraisal period. The manager has most direct influence on staff through daily workplace activities.[7]

An appraisal discussion provides the foundation on which to base new learning, in order to exploit more of one's potential. The feedback you give and the discussions about performance that you have with staff will set the tone for your relationship with individual staff members. How the manager coaches, guides, directs, delegates, communicates, and provides learning and developmental opportunities for staff will also influence the degree of trust and honesty that is developed. The yearly formal performance appraisal should simply be a review of matters that you have both previously dealt with. During the discussion, you formally record what has happened and concentrate on the period ahead, facilitating new knowledge and skills, new standards of performance, and greater realisation of organisational, appraiser and appraisee needs. When this is done skilfully, it has a great influence on the motivation, attitude and achievement of individuals. This chapter concentrates on how managers can conduct a performance discussion skilfully.

CHECK YOUR UNDERSTANDING

1 How can managers motivate staff through performance appraisals?
2 What have been the major problems with performance appraisals in the past?
3 How does the management role incorporate performance appraisal?
4 Why is appraising performance part of the management role?

SKILLS PRACTICE

1 Think about the last time you appraised your own actions. This is likely to have been in the past 24 hours. Answer the following questions.

- On what did you self-appraise?
- What was your performance like?
- What learning occurred?
- What did you resolve to do differently?
- Why is it important to self-appraise?

2 Form groups of two for the following exercise. Follow these instructions.

- Individually, write down one thing that you are really good at.
- Describe what it is you like to do.
- Describe the levels of performance you like to attain.

Ask each other the following questions:

- How do you feel when you attain the levels of performance you set yourself?
- How do you feel when you do not attain the levels of performance you set yourself?
- Why do you set these levels of performance?
- Does the setting of the performance levels help you or hinder you? How?

Discuss the answers you each give. How are they different, how are they the same? Do you share similar feelings about the performance? How does the level of performance you set yourself motivate you to do better?

SKILL AND KNOWLEDGE APPLICATION

Tina is the Project Manager for a large multinational construction company and has been in the role for around 12 months. On taking up the position, she encountered several major financial issues that needed immediate attention. However, of even more importance to Tina was the low morale and lack of motivation of the employees with whom she works.

Under the previous manager, feedback was not provided to the employees, and performance appraisals, although a requirement of the organisation, were not conducted. Tina quickly rectified the situation by conducting formal sessions with each of her employees, setting clear goals and objectives for each of them, linking them to the organisation's overall objectives to show how they contributed to the company's success. Tina also, with the employees' input, put in place personal development plans for each of the employees.

Within six months all of Tina's employees were motivated and more productive in their roles. Tina delegated challenging work to her employees and provided continuous feedback on their performance, something they had never experienced before.

Due to Tina's accomplishments, she has now been appointed the first female General Manager for the organisation, and will be making the move to head office. There is likely to be a few months before a new Project Manager is appointed to take over her current position. Tina's employees are happy for her but can see their environment returning to the unhappier days experienced before her arrival, and their motivation is beginning to deteriorate.

TASK

- Make some suggestions about how Tina might be able to maintain the employees' motivation at the project site before her departure.
- What could Tina do to make sure her good work is carried on in the absence of a manager, and when the new manager is appointed?

What is performance appraisal?

A definition

Before proceeding to more practical matters of how to appraise performance, it is important to establish how this book defines the term 'performance appraisal'. Any definition of a performance appraisal must acknowledge that it is a process of communication. It must also acknowledge that the manager, or appraiser, has a strong influence over the effectiveness of the appraisal. Within that framework, a manager and an employee review the employee's performance for a defined period, and then plan the performance of the employee for the future. The definition used in this book appears in Figure 8.3.

FIGURE 8.3 Definition of performance appraisal

> A specific communication, facilitated by the appraiser, about the existing work performance and the planning of the future performance of an individual.

Values

Appraisal is a real and vital part of our existence. Without appraising the value of certain actions, effort, materials, equipment and people, our decision making would be impaired because we would be unable to determine priorities, or the worth of doing one thing over another. For example, people may have different values and attitudes about mowing the lawn. Depending on how they value the activity of mowing the lawn, or what it can bring them, they will mow or not mow the lawn or find other ways of achieving the same outcome. Figure 8.4 demonstrates the different perspectives people may have of mowing the lawn.

Appraisal is essentially a very subjective activity and is tied closely to an individual's values and ideas of what is worthwhile. It is vital to get agreement on standards of performance to bring some objectivity into the process. There must be a shared understanding of what has to be done and how well it must be done so that all parties value similar things about the performance and the result.

FIGURE 8.4 Activity values

Value	Activity	Possible actions
1. Lawn should look good and reflects upon the individual		1. Mows lawn regularly and spends a lot of time looking after it
2. Not a good use of my time (want to be doing other things)		2. Pays someone to do the lawn
3. Activity for children to earn some pocket money	Mowing the lawn	3. Children mow lawn, subject to whims of children and desire to earn money
4. Not an important activity, hate doing it		4. Leaves lawn, only mows infrequently or pays someone else to do it
5. Usual weekend activity around house		5. Schedules into other household chores on weekends, mows regularly
6. Want good-looking lawn but don't want to spend the time or effort		6. Pays someone to do the lawn, may check work

In the workplace, people make decisions based on their appraisal of situations, people and performance. Similarly, exact records are kept of the financial performance of organisations. Such records have been highly valued by the business world and governments, and legislation has been enacted to enforce the preparation and release of records such as annual reports. Organisations also have strategic, marketing and business plans for which a large number of records need to be kept to facilitate the monitoring and achievement of the plans. Until quite recently, there has been little emphasis on the monitoring of the performance of individuals within the organisation.[8] It has been difficult to determine the contribution that people make to the organisation. The return on investment in people was in many cases unknown, and few records were kept to monitor performance and achievement.

The modern age has brought with it a focus on productivity and global competition that has made it necessary to monitor the worth or value of the performance of individuals. Staff represents one of an organisation's largest expenditures. Today, when the productivity and competitiveness of an organisation determines whether it will survive,[9] it is vital to ensure that all the organisation's resources are operating at maximum capacity. This includes the human resources through which the activities of the organisation are achieved. The appraisal of human performance is vital to the success of the organisation.

Workplace appraisal

Appraising an individual's performance at work is similar to the process we use outside work as individuals living in society. However, there is at least one significant contextual difference. In the workplace, the appraisal is done in conjunction with another person. At work, the appraisal involves your superior and—if 360-degree methods of appraisal are used—your peers, your subordinates, your customers and your suppliers. Outside work, appraisal tends to be an informal and sometimes unconscious process. This may partly explain why many people do not like formal workplace performance appraisals: they are seen as threatening because you have to share the process with someone else. So that it can be a useful and motivating activity for all concerned, it is vital that both parties involved in the appraisal use appropriate skills.

A communication process

The performance appraisal is primarily a communication process between two people who share information about the performance of one party, with the aim of coming to a shared understanding of that performance.[10] It is the time when the manager and staff member evaluate the performance of the staff member against the standards and objectives agreed on earlier in the appraisal period. Note the joint approach: both parties will have perspectives that should be shared, and any differences should be investigated and talked through to arrive at a better understanding of the performance of the staff member.

It is possible to come to a shared understanding only by communicating effectively. As a specialised communication process, performance appraisal demands high-level communication skills in both appraiser and appraisee. This includes highly developed cross-cultural communication skills. The lack of sufficient high-level communication skills will destroy a performance appraisal within the best performance management system. Even systems that provide lots of guidelines, formulas and paperwork in an attempt to manage performance effectively will fail if appraiser and appraisee do not have the appropriate communication skills.

Instead of motivating and inspiring individuals to perform, a lack of communication skills will create defensive strategies and responses, misunderstanding, distrust, lack of honesty and an unwillingness to talk. In such cases the appraisal becomes an unpleasant experience for all involved and reinforces the general opinion that appraisals do not work. This serves to build further resistance to performance management systems.

It is the lack of appropriate skills and attitudes in managers that has prevented the successful implementation of performance management schemes and appraisals in the past,[11] and that will undermine future endeavours if appropriate communication skills are not developed. Unfortunately, too many managers see performance appraisals as unconnected with the running of the business,[12] conflict-ridden,[13] merely administrative and ineffective,[14] thus providing further evidence that the design of a performance management system—the forms and measures that are used—are not enough for the process to be effective.

Wayne Cascio found that employees often act negatively towards performance appraisals: they are often less certain about where they stand after being appraised; they tend to evaluate their supervisors less favourably after an appraisal; they often report that few actions or improvements result from appraisals; and they feel that the traditional 'tell and sell' approach to appraisals is entirely inappropriate.[15] Managers are in the driver's seat here. The manager controls the appraisal process. Managers should show leadership and demonstrate the appropriate skills. Where managers feel they do not have the skills to conduct appraisals skilfully they should undertake development activities. Cascio implies that it is the manager who most strongly influences the outcome and therefore the success of the appraisal process. Thus, part of the success of a performance appraisal will be a function of the manager's skills in conducting it and of the manager's ability to develop appropriate skills in appraisees.

In many organisations it is assumed that managers have the appropriate skills to conduct effective appraisals.[16] The Karpin Report demonstrated that many managers in Australia did not have these skills.[17] Managers need, deliberately and methodically, to develop key skills in interpersonal communication to be effective managers of performance. Figure 8.5 demonstrates the building blocks of an effective performance appraisal. This model illustrates that it becomes very difficult to conduct an appraisal if the interpersonal communication skills are not in place.

FIGURE 8.5 Building blocks of an effective performance appraisal

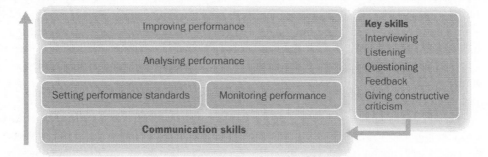

The model assumes that communication skills are at an adequate level to facilitate the development of performance standards, the monitoring of performance, an analysis of performance and its improvement where desirable. As these skills underpin the knowledge and skills required for the other activities, no amount of training in the other building blocks will produce results if the communication skills are not at a competent level, through which the skills and knowledge of the other building blocks can be articulated. This chapter and Chapter 9 will help you develop some of the key skills required for conducting performance appraisals.

CHECK YOUR UNDERSTANDING

5 Why are values so important in performance appraisals?
6 Why has appraising performance become so important in modern society?
7 How is workplace appraisal different from self-appraisal?
8 Why is communication such a vital part of the appraisal process?
9 What are the key communication skills required in a performance appraisal?
10 In your own words, what is a performance appraisal?

SKILLS PRACTICE

In groups of two, try to have a conversation with each other without asking any questions. Try this for about three minutes, then answer the following questions.

1   What was the effect of not asking any questions?
2   Did it interfere with the communication process?
3   If yes, in what way did it interfere? If no, why not?

SKILLS PRACTICE   CONTINUED

In groups of three, each of you selects a letter, A, B or C. A will hold a conversation with B, but B will have his/her own agenda to talk about and will steer the conversation towards things he/she wants to talk about regardless of what A says or asks. C will observe the discussion and comment on the following:

- Did a discussion occur?
- What happened during the interaction?
- Did listening happen between the two individuals?
- Were questions used and were they helpful in the conversation?
- Was A managing the conversation?

Discuss C's observations in light of what you have learned about communication and appraisals in this section of the chapter. What are the lessons learned from this activity?

SKILL AND KNOWLEDGE APPLICATION

TASK

Write down the values you have about study.

- From the above values, what behaviours can you expect from yourself in relation to study?
- What might you need to do to change any of these behaviours?

Scott is usually a happy individual who takes great pride in his work and has set realistic performance objectives with his boss, Marcus Steinberg. Over the past few months Marcus has had to discuss Scott's performance with him a great deal, because he seems to be slacking off and his performance is now bordering on the unsatisfactory. No matter what Marcus does, he can't seem to get Scott out of what seems like some sort of depression. His happy disposition has gone, he seems to be distracted all the time and he doesn't want to talk.

TASK

- What might have happened?

Purpose of performance appraisals

Learning and development are essential aspects of the appraisal process, and it would not be complete without the inclusion of this focus. The appraisal process is not just one of looking at past performance and identifying good and bad performance. It includes the more general and wider-ranging focus on how you as a manager can help an individual staff member achieve, learn and develop, thereby assisting the organisation and yourself to grow, develop and achieve the organisational plans and objectives. Figure 8.6 illustrates the concept of performance appraisals as being focused on a review and development planning basis that emphasises the future as well as the past or current performance.

FIGURE 8.6 Review and development planning

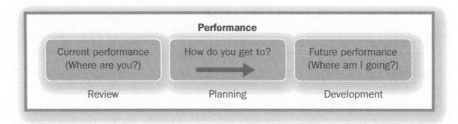

Note that the weight of the appraisal process is on planning and development for the future. That is, two-thirds of the process is focused on the planning and development of future performance, with one-third focused on past or current performance. Analysing current or past performance provides a basis and starting point for the planning and development process but is not the sole reason for the performance appraisal. A performance appraisal is therefore a process through which we move into the future.

There are many views on the purposes of a performance appraisal.[18] Organisations use them for widely different purposes, all of which may be legitimate. Some of the more common purposes for performance appraisals are to:

- discuss past performance
- plan for the future
- identify training needs
- identify developmental needs
- document current skills held by employees
- agree on performance standards and objectives for the future
- identify career aspirations of employees
- identify promotional potential
- decide on pay raises
- develop succession plans
- motivate individuals
- evaluate how the organisation is performing across multiple indicators
- validate organisational strategy and objectives.

Organisations may choose to concentrate on some or all of these purposes. To be truly effective, however, managers need to utilise all the purposes above to build strong teams and establish solid planning processes. Randell has developed a taxonomy that captures all these purposes and groups them into more focused management activities, which should form part of a manager's day-to-day functions:[19]

1 *Evaluation*—to enable the organisation to share out the money and promotions fairly.
2 *Auditing*—to discover the work potential, present and future, of individuals and departments.

3 *Succession planning*—to construct plans for staffing, departmental and corporate planning.

4 *Controlling*—to ensure that employees reach organisational standards and objectives.

5 *Training*—to discover learning needs.

6 *Development*—to develop individuals through advice and information and by shaping their behaviour through praise or punishment.

7 *Motivation*—to add to employees' job satisfaction by understanding their needs.

8 *Validation*—to check the effectiveness of personnel procedures and practices.

Figure 8.7 illustrates the connection of Randell's taxonomy of performance appraisal purposes to the operations and management of the organisation. Without the loop that connects performance appraisal with strategic and operational plans, through management, there can be no effective organisational performance. Effective organisational performance is defined as the ability of an organisation to meet its strategic and operational goals.

Randell's taxonomy is helpful in putting into perspective the many uses of the performance appraisal. However, it can be folly to place too much emphasis on any one of these purposes, because they are too specific. For example, organisations do not implement performance management systems solely to identify training needs; there are other ways of doing this. Performance appraisals are conducted to gather data on the performance of an individual and to plan the future. These data are part of the plethora of data collected to measure the performance of an

FIGURE 8.7 Relationship of appraisal purposes to the operations and management of the organisation

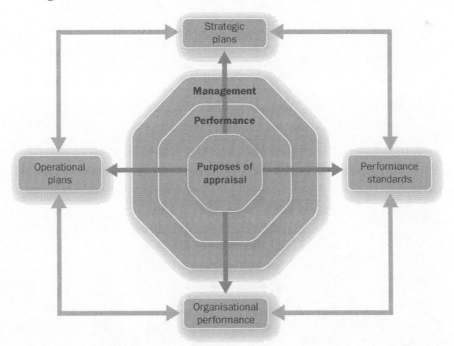

organisation. Personal performance data, correctly and appropriately fed into the management system of an organisation, will enhance the decision-making processes and thus the overall performance of an organisation.

To illustrate the point further, the various purposes of a performance appraisal can be inserted into the model in Figure 8.6 to highlight the focus on planning and development in a performance appraisal. Remember that performance appraisals are conducted to check how things are going and, specifically, to identify the current level of performance and plan for future required levels of performance. Figure 8.8 demonstrates some of the activities that might be involved in the three phases of the performance appraisal model. It also attempts to include Randell's taxonomy in the model to show how it fits with the performance appraisal model.

In Figure 8.8 you can clearly see the one-third/two-thirds division discussed above. Performance appraisals that concentrate only on reviewing past or current performance don't do the whole job, just a small part of it. Where only part of the appraisal is performed, negative results such as those observed by Cascio will permeate the staff within the organisation, thus effectively disengaging the performance management process as a viable management and motivational tool.

The purpose of performance appraisals is to review an individual's performance to date and to plan performance and development for the future. To achieve the purpose of the appraisal, both parties must have the evidence to support their views and the communication skills to be able to articulate and discuss them in both a formal and an informal way. Put very simply, performance appraisals allow managers to measure actual performance against required performance, as illustrated in Figure 8.9. This figure deals with current performance against current performance

FIGURE 8.8 Appraisal purposes and performance

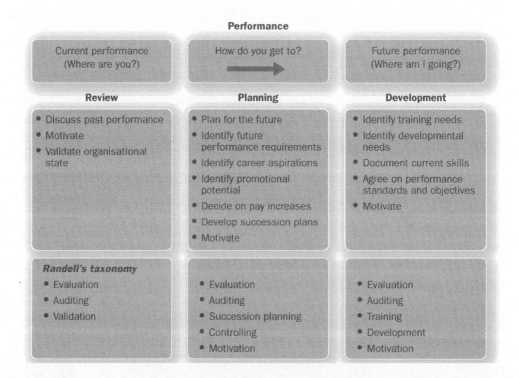

Performance

Current performance (Where are you?)	How do you get to?	Future performance (Where am I going?)
Review	**Planning**	**Development**
• Discuss past performance • Motivate • Validate organisational state	• Plan for the future • Identify future performance requirements • Identify career aspirations • Identify promotional potential • Decide on pay increases • Develop succession plans • Motivate	• Identify training needs • Identify developmental needs • Document current skills • Agree on performance standards and objectives • Motivate
Randell's taxonomy • Evaluation • Auditing • Validation	• Evaluation • Auditing • Succession planning • Controlling • Motivation	• Evaluation • Auditing • Training • Development • Motivation

requirements, even where actual performance exceeds performance requirements, but does not tackle the issue of how performance may change in the future. Appraisals that use only current performance as the basis for an analysis of performance will not cover future requirements, and thus the process becomes ineffective. Life in organisations today is not static; it is in a state of constant change, flexibility and adaptation in response to the demands of a large number of stake-holders (from customers to shareholders). No organisation, no individual, will be able to meet these needs without looking at the requirements of the future, and this includes the performance required of all workers in a workplace as well as the organisation as a whole.

FIGURE 8.9 A performance gap

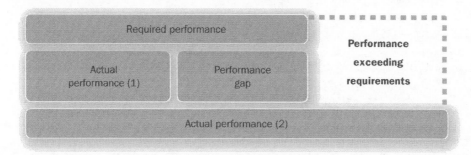

Figure 8.10 incorporates the concept of future performance requirements that will be tied to strategic plans and objectives, and developmental requirements that will be tied to both the current level of performance against standards and anticipated performance gaps for future performance requirements.

FIGURE 8.10 Anticipated performance gap

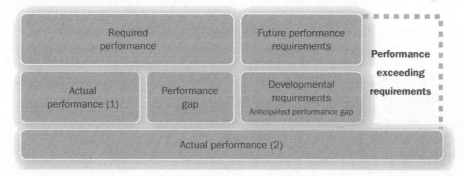

CHECK YOUR UNDERSTANDING

11 On what is two-thirds of the performance appraisal process focused?
12 Why does the above emphasis exist?
13 List the eight activities in Randell's taxonomy of performance appraisal purposes.
14 What is a performance gap?
15 What is an anticipated performance gap?

SKILLS PRACTICE

Place the following actions in one or more of the three concepts of performance described in Figure 8.8: review [R], planning [P] or development [D], by placing R, P and/or D before the action.

- Discuss past performance.
- Plan for the future.
- Identify training needs.
- Identify developmental needs other than training.
- Document current skills held by employees.
- Agree on performance standards and objectives for the future.
- Identify career aspirations by employees.
- Identify promotional potential.
- Decide on pay raises.
- Develop succession plans.
- Motivate individuals.
- Evaluate how the organisation is performing.
- Validate organisational strategy and objectives.
- Ensure the quality of products and services.
- Check whether policies and procedures are working.
- Identify people who could be fast-tracked into more senior positions in the organisation.

SKILL AND KNOWLEDGE APPLICATION

Thomas was really pleased with the feedback he received about his performance from manager Caitlin Buckmill. They spent an hour discussing his performance and, while there were about five things that she said he needed improvement in, she spent a great deal of the discussion saying how good it was that he was doing everything else so well. Finally, Caitlin said, 'Well, the hour is up, Thomas. Keep up the good work'.

TASK

- How could this appraisal be improved? What dangers are inherent in the way Caitlin conducted the appraisal?

Bridget was preparing to conduct Mari's yearly performance appraisal. While she was quite sure that she had a good idea of the performance gaps in Mari's performance and what things she might suggest for improvement, she was not sure how to determine the future requirements of the job, the department or the organisation.

TASK

- Where might Bridget find the information she is looking for? What documents might be helpful for this purpose?

Benefits of performance appraisals

By now you will have realised that there are numerous benefits in conducting performance appraisals. However, you will also understand that these benefits are predicated on the assumption that both parties conduct the appraisal with skill and competence. The benefits of conducting a performance appraisal will be directly related to the skills of the individuals who participate in it. When an appraisal is conducted effectively, there are real and tangible benefits for the appraisee, the appraiser and the organisation. Conducting an appraisal should be hard work for all concerned, not because it is difficult to do but because it requires skill, time, effort, knowledge and the appropriate attitudes. There is the same requirement whether the appraisal is formal, such as a yearly performance review, or informal, such as the day-to-day feedback that you provide as a manager. Figure 8.11 identifies some of the specific benefits of performance appraisals for the appraisee, the appraiser and the organisation.

One of the difficulties in developing the appropriate skills for conducting performance appraisals is that they are not conducted often enough for participants to be able to practise the skills regularly and therefore become more expert at the process. If you feel this is the case with your own development, then you should schedule performance appraisals more often so that you

FIGURE 8.11 Benefits of performance appraisals[21]

Appraisee	Appraiser	Organisation
• Increased motivation	• Improved relationships with staff	• Improved performance due to:
• Increased job satisfaction	• Improved decision making	– more effective communication of the organisation's objectives and values
• Increased sense of personal worth	• Increased job satisfaction	– increased sense of cohesiveness and commitment
• Increased self-confidence	• Increased sense of personal worth	– improved relationships between managers and staff
• Improved working relationships with the manager	• Improved departmental or branch performance	– managers who are better equipped to use their leadership skills and to motivate and develop their staff
• Improved communication	• Opportunity to develop an understanding of individual jobs and complete work teams	• Improved overview of the tasks performed by each member of staff
• A clear understanding of what is expected in the job	• Identification of areas for improvement	• Identification of ideas for improvement
• A clear understanding of the performance standards required	• Opportunity to link team and individual objectives and targets with departmental and organisational objectives	• Development of expectations and long-term views
• Opportunity to discuss work problems and develop solutions	• Opportunity to clarify the contribution the manager expects from teams and individuals	• Training and development needs identified more clearly
• Opportunity to discuss career aspirations and any guidance, support or training needed to fulfil these aspirations	• The opportunity to re-prioritise targets	• Creation and maintenance of a culture of continuous improvement and success
• Identification of training and development needs		• Conveying the message that people are valued
• Individual talents recognised		

and your staff get better at participating in them. Of course, this should be discussed with staff, and a sincere effort should be made to explain the reasons and benefits of the action, so as not to threaten staff. Gaining their cooperation and agreement in this way will establish further trust between you and the staff and consolidate the performance appraisal process.

Consider the opposite argument for a moment. The skills used in performance appraisals are no different from those a skilful manager uses in everyday practice. Hence, if performance appraisals are not being conducted effectively, there is the possibility that the manager lacks some of the skills required for effective management. Of course, it may not be solely because of the manager's lack of skill—the appraisee may lack the skills to handle the performance appraisal effectively. Yet this is still a management problem: staff do not possess the appropriate skills. Such situations provide a rich source of information for the appraisal discussion, however. Further, if you are in the early stages of implementing performance management processes within your organisation and you believe that your staff do not have the appropriate skills to handle the process, train them. Do not try to implement formal performance appraisals without the proper training. Doing so will only threaten staff and consolidate opposition to the process.

The benefits of performance appraisals are not guaranteed, nor will they happen overnight, but a well-run performance management system will develop these benefits over time and influence the culture of an organisation.

Frequency

Linked to the issue of how beneficial performance appraisals can be is the issue of how often they should be scheduled. The first point that should be made about frequency is that performance appraisals are an ongoing process[22] and part of the daily management responsibilities of a manager. So, in a sense, the question of 'How often?' does not arise, as appraisal should be continuous. The question is more 'How often should formal appraisals be conducted?' There are two issues associated with this: the administrative support required for a formal appraisal,[23] and the system of appraisal your organisation uses.

Formal appraisals require a lot of paperwork and time, and so tend to be scheduled only once each year.[24] It is unrealistic to expect that formal appraisals can be conducted on a monthly basis, given the documentation and consequent filing that goes hand in hand with formal appraisals. However, it is not unreasonable to have quarterly formal appraisals, especially if the documentation can be converted to allow for quarterly comments on performance standards and objectives.

The performance management system that your organisation uses will also influence the frequency of your formal appraisals. Most systems provide for a formal review only once a year, the reason for which is probably reflected above. These yearly systems tend to reinforce the likelihood of invalid appraisals, because it is difficult to remember performance for a whole year unless all parties involved write regular notes. Managers and staff alike tend to become bound by the rules and regulations set by their organisations, regardless of whether the system works for them. The concept of a yearly performance appraisal should not limit the activities of individual managers in working with their staff and formally appraising their performance.

Despite the apparent barriers discussed above, appraising performance needs to be done on a regular basis so that individuals are receiving feedback in time to do something about the issues raised. It is not sufficient to limit this process to a once-yearly activity. How often you schedule formal appraisals outside the daily informal appraisals that take place will depend on the dynamics of your organisation, the internal and external environments, and the individuals you are working with. For example, if you are in an organisation that is changing rapidly in response to market forces, it is likely that you will need to conduct a formal review of performance much more often than once a year. If you are in a government agency that is undergoing restructuring or merging with other departments, then appraisals will need to be more frequent. If you are working with highly adaptive and flexible individuals you may not have to appraise performance so often. The minimum frequency you should aim for is once a quarter. A lapse of only three months between appraisals makes it easier to review the period—it is more easily recalled—and easier to correct unsatisfactory performance. Figure 8.12 illustrates this point.

FIGURE 8.12 Correcting unsatisfactory performance

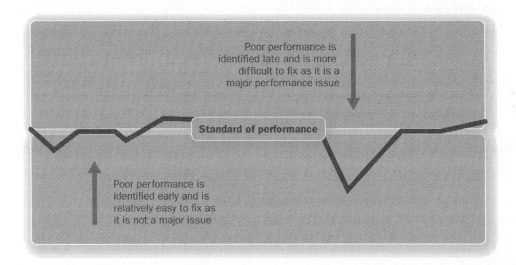

The yearly formal performance review can be counterproductive to a successful performance management system. For example, most organisations insist on conducting performance appraisals at a given time of the year. Managers are expected to get around to all their staff and complete a useful and competent appraisal of each staff member. This is satisfactory if you have only one or two staff reporting to you, but managers who have many people reporting to them will have difficulty finding the time to conduct effective appraisals in the given period allocated by the organisation. The result is poorly conducted appraisals that satisfy no one.

Several options could be utilised to overcome this problem. The yearly performance appraisal could be conducted on the nearest date possible to the birthday of the staff member, or on the anniversary date of when the employee joined the company.[24] This would smooth out the number of appraisals to be done at any given time, thus ensuring that adequate time, effort and preparation will be invested in the activity.

Whenever the yearly performance appraisal is scheduled, it must be integrated with the formal planning processes of the organisation. If performance appraisals are isolated from the planning process they become meaningless, the standards become hollow, and they do not contribute to the objectives of the work area and the organisation. Managers need to be assertive and insist that the timing of performance appraisals meets operational and planning needs.

In summary, performance appraisals need to be regular, and should have some degree of formality so that both parties take notice of the activity. Meeting quarterly to go over the past three months adds immediacy to the process, allows for adjustments to be made to standards, and permits the rewriting of standards and objectives if necessary. Appraisals should be scheduled to fit into the operational and strategic needs of the organisation.

CHECK YOUR UNDERSTANDING

16 Explain one way in which managers and staff could develop their skills in conducting performance appraisals.

17 What are the benefits to the appraisee, the appraiser and the organisation of conducting performance appraisals?

18 What are the problems associated with yearly performance appraisals?

19 How does regular feedback help you manage poor performance?

20 Is the frequency of performance appraisals important?

21 What are some of the options managers have for scheduling performance appraisals?

SKILL AND KNOWLEDGE APPLICATION

TASK

➤ If you wanted to establish a new focus on performance in your team and you were in a rapidly changing environment, how often might you schedule performance appraisals? Why?

Julio and Ding Yao are two branch managers in the Department of Transport. They are having coffee with you one morning and complaining that it is appraisal time again. They both talk about it being such a bother and how, with all the staff they have reporting to them (Julio has 15 and Ding Yao has 9), it is just not realistic for the department's Human Resource section to expect that all the appraisals will be completed within one month. Just finding the time to do one in the month will be difficult enough for Julio and Ding Yao. Both of them say they are committed to the concept of performance appraisals and try to give regular verbal feedback to their staff. However, they complain that they do not get time to plan and conduct the appraisal properly and feel very guilty for being responsible for what they see as a poor appraisal. They ask if you have any suggestions for how they might be able to manage them better.

TASK

➤ What would you advise?

➤ How would you ensure that Julio and Ding Yao understood the importance of the performance appraisal to their role as managers, to the employees and to the organisation?

The company you work for has just decided to introduce performance appraisals and line managers have been given the responsibility for implementing the process. You must call the staff of your department together and 'sell' them the concept.

TASK

➤ What would you say to them? Identify three strategies and, in a paragraph for each one, describe how each strategy will assist the managers.

CONCLUSION

Even though the role of manager is becoming more complex and multifaceted, appraising performance remains an integral part of day-to-day managing. Managers play a key role in providing feedback to employees about their performance, both formally and informally. Appraisal is a natural part of being human and we self-appraise every day in order to correct our own behaviour and learn new things. It is only through knowing where we are at the present moment that we can plan for the future. Just as self-appraisal can be uplifting and open new doors to personal development and change, so can work-based performance appraisals. A skilfully conducted performance appraisal should be motivating for both appraiser and appraisee.

Performance appraisals are essentially a communication process about current work performance in an effort to plan performance for the future. Together, appraiser and appraisee review current performance, plan future performance, and then identify what development has to occur to enable the future performance. Appraisals are used for many purposes by organisations, and are inextricably linked to the organisation's strategic and operational plans. The ability of a manager to use effective cross-cultural communication skills will better ensure valuable performance appraisals. The sum total of the performance of all individuals in an organisation equals the total organisational performance. Thus it is vital for organisational performance that individual performance be monitored and kept on track. By determining the performance gap and the anticipated performance gap of individuals, appropriate development plans can be made to ensure that appraisees have the appropriate skills and knowledge to reach the required performance levels. There are benefits in performance appraisals for the appraisee, the appraiser and the organisation. Careful and considered preparation for the performance discussion will assist in achieving those benefits.

CASE STUDY

Rodney is the General Manager at a golf club. He worked his way up to the position after 20 years with the club. Rodney had no formal educational training in business or management, but had years of front-line experience at the club.

Rodney was keen to make a good impression in his new role so began preparing for the appraisal of his staff well in advance. Rodney had been on the receiving end of performance appraisals which were conducting annually for the past 10 years; they did not exist prior to this. Rodney had never come away from a performance appraisal feeling happy with the outcome, nor with how it was conducted. He was determined not to make his employees feel the same way.

Jenny, who has been with the club for 10 years, is the first employee's file he looks at. Rodney has never conducted a formal performance appraisal before or worked with a performance management system from the management perspective, and is at a loss where to start.

QUESTIONS

You are a consultant HR specialist whom Rodney has hired to assist him in the process of preparation for performance appraising his staff.

Advise Rodney as follows:

1 what his roles and responsibilities are as a manager in the performance appraisal process
2 how the performance appraisal interview should be conducted
3 how to incorporate the review, planning and development cycle into his performance management system
4 how he should handle his preparation for and first performance appraisal with Jenny.

JOB AIDS

Building blocks of an effective performance appraisal

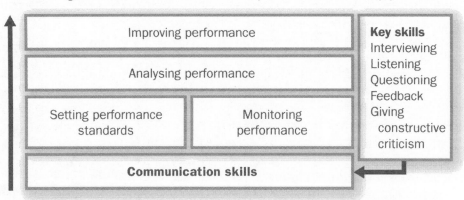

Improving performance	**Key skills**
Analysing performance	Interviewing
	Listening
Setting performance standards	Monitoring performance	Questioning
	Feedback
	Giving
Communication skills	constructive criticism

Definition of performance appraisal

A specific communication, facilitated by the appraiser, about the existing work performance and the planning of the future performance of an individual.

References

1 Nicholson, J. & Nairn, A. 2006. *The Manager of the 21st Century*. Innovation & Business Skills Australia: Hawthorn, p. 14.

2 Cole, K. 2005, 3rd edn. *Management: Theory and Practice*. Pearson Australia: Frenchs Forest, Sydney, pp. 21–22.

3 Fisher, M. 1996. *Performance Appraisals*. Kogan Page: London, pp. 11–17; Philp, T. 1990, 2nd edn. *Appraising Performance for Results*. McGraw-Hill: London, pp. 1–7.

4 Adapted from Robbins, S. & Mukerji, D. 1994, 2nd edn. *Managing Organisations: New Challenges and Perspectives*. Prentice Hall: Sydney, p. 7.

5 Hanson, P.G. 1973. 'The Johari Window: A model for soliciting and giving feedback.' In *The 1973 Annual Handbook for Group Facilitators*. University Associates: San Diego, pp. 114–119.

6 Nicholson & Nairn, op. cit., 2006, p. 165.

7 Billett, S.R. 1994. 'Authenticity in workplace learning settings.' In J. Stevenson (ed.), *Cognition at Work: The Development of Expertise*. National Centre for Vocational Education Research: Adelaide, pp. 36–75.

8 Fitz-enz, J. 1990. *Human Value Management*. Jossey-Bass: San Francisco.

9 Screwvalla, Z.S. 1988. 'Performance appraisals: A framework for effective implementation.' *Management Update*, October.

10 Screwvalla, op. cit., 1988.

11 Fisher, op. cit., 1996; Philp, op. cit., 1990; Rudman, R. 1995. *Performance Planning and Review*. Pitman: Melbourne, p. 65.

12 Redman, T., Snape, E. & McElwee, G. 1993. 'Appraising employee performance: A vital organisational activity?' *Education and Training*, 35(2), pp. 3–10.

13 Barlow, G. 1989. 'Deficiencies and the perpetuation of power: Latent functions in management appraisal.' *Journal of Management Studies*, 26(5), pp. 499–517; Bush, G. & Stinson, J. 1980. 'A different use of performance appraisal: Evaluating the boss.' *Management Review*, November, pp. 14–17.

14 Teel, K. 1978. 'Self-appraisal revisited.' *Personnel Journal*, July, pp. 364–367.

15 Cascio, W.F. 1996. 'Managing for maximum performance.' *HRMonthly*, September, pp. 10–13.

16 Philp, op. cit., 1990.

17 Karpin, D. (Chair). 1995. *Enterprising Nation: Renewing Australia's Managers to Meet the Challenges of the Asia-Pacific Century*. Report of the Industry Task Force on Leadership and Management Skills. AGPS: Canberra.

18 Cole, op. cit., 2005, p. 426; Fisher, op. cit., 1996, p. 11; Randell, G. 1989. 'Employee appraisal'. In K. Sisson (ed.), *Personnel Management in Britain*. Basil Blackwell: Oxford.

19 Randell, op. cit., 1989.

20 Fisher, op. cit., 1996, pp. 15–17.

21 Adapted from Fisher, M., *Performance Appraisals*, 1996, Kogan Page: London, pp. 15–17.

22 Randell, op. cit., 1989.

23 Robbins, S. & Hunsaker, P. 2006, 4th edn. *Training in Interpersonal Skills: Tips for Managing People at Work*. Prentice Hall: New York.

24 Cascio, op. cit., 1996.

25 Armstrong, M. 1994. *Performance Management*, Kogan Page: London, pp. 95–96.

CHAPTER NINE

Appraising performance

Learning outcomes

After reading this chapter you should be able to:

* select a preferred method and documentation for reviewing performance
* describe advantages and disadvantages of different appraisal methods and documentation
* describe the characteristics of an effective discussion
* describe the four stages of the performance discussion model
* describe the main responsibilities of the appraiser and the appraisee in a performance appraisal
* identify strategies for managing the performance appraisal
* explain how to develop a performance improvement plan
* identify the main problems associated with performance appraisals.

INTRODUCTION

Appraising performance is not simply a matter of filling in the form that Human Resource management sends you once a year.[1] Nor is appraising performance an impost on the time of a manager. It is part of a manager's duties and the process of managing. Managers who do not regularly appraise performance and provide feedback will find their job very difficult. Managers achieve their work through others. They are evaluated on the results others produce. To be able to achieve through others, managers need to monitor and appraise performance and make appropriate adjustments to performance where necessary while providing support, as required, to individuals.

Appraisal and analysis

In Chapter 7 you were introduced to a framework for analysing evidence of performance. That framework can be extended to include the functions involved in appraising performance by changing it into a decision flowchart. When you appraise performance you are making a decision about whether performance is satisfactory or not. Your initial judgment should be tentative until you have the performance discussion with the individual or team. Figure 9.1 extends the analysis framework used in Chapter 7 to include decisions that you make about the analysis that lead to an appraisal about performance.

You will notice that the framework now identifies the decisions you need to make about the analysed evidence, and in some cases there are suggested actions. Decision boxes have been added to the framework.

Preparing specific feedback

At this stage you need to establish what specific feedback you will give to the individual or team about the actual performance, to point out what the agreed performance standard was and, from your evidence, indicate what the actual performance demonstrates. You will also need to identify what has to be done to get performance back on track and, as a result, you may want to suggest new performance standards or objectives. Alternatively, having determined that the individual or team has the skills, that these skills have been used in the past and that they are used often, there may be other reasons for non-performance. If you feel this is the case, you will need to work through the steps on the right-hand side of the analysis framework.

An employee's potential

Having worked through the rest of the analysis framework, you have enough evidence to suggest that the individual or team can do the job and there is nothing preventing the agreed standard from being achieved. It is at this point that you need to question whether the staff member has the commitment to achieve, is capable of achieving, or simply does not care. The evidence on which you have been making your decisions as you work through the framework will help you identify whether the person has potential. If the evidence suggests that there is potential, you move back to the feedback step and prepare specific examples of where performance is not satisfactory and how you will approach the issue. To do this, you will need to be convinced that there is potential. It is likely to take a serious investment of time and energy on your behalf to get the individual or team back on track and to sustain the investment long enough, with close monitoring, to ensure that standards are reached.

FIGURE 9.1 An analysis-appraisal flowchart[2]

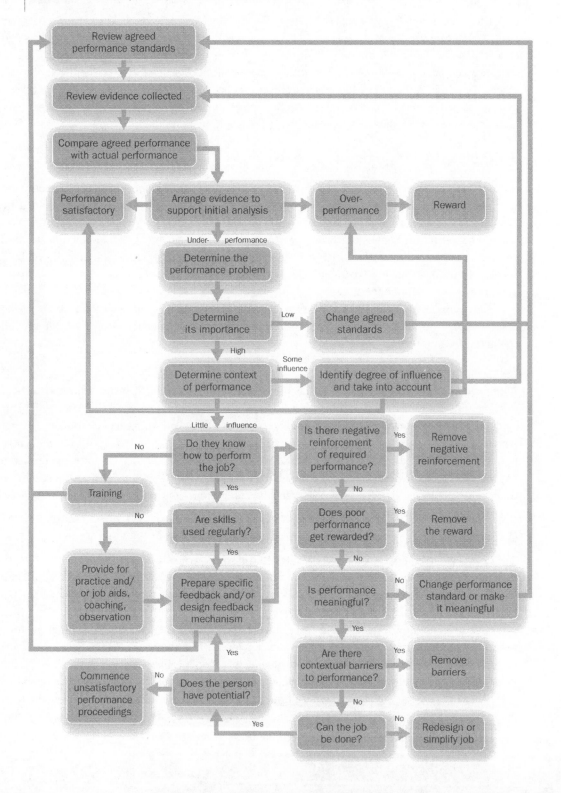

Where you do not consider the person to be a good investment of your time and energy, you have reached the stage of preparing to terminate their employment or seeking to relocate them to another part of the organisation where they may be better suited. It is at this time that you will use your organisation's unsatisfactory performance procedures to begin termination proceedings. It is feasible that, through this process, the individual or team may be prepared to commit to achieving outcomes, or through your intervention develop appropriate skill(s) to meet required standards. In this case you would not continue with termination proceedings. Chapter 11 contains further information on this point.

The framework now guides you in preparing for the performance discussion so that evidence is arranged appropriately and can be used in the discussion to support your position.

Selecting a method and documentation for reviewing performance

Most organisations that engage actively in performance management systems will have a preferred method and documentation for appraising or reviewing performance. The method may focus on the mutual identification of goals as in the management by objectives (MBO) method, or may be the simple technique of graphic rating scales. Regardless of the method chosen, you need to assess people on their behaviours and the results they produce rather than their personalities. Generally speaking, managers today prefer to take a collaborative approach to performance appraisals.

In making your decision you first need to ensure that you have completed a thorough job analysis, and possess detailed and accurate position descriptions to determine what needs to be measured and how. Ask yourself what your objectives are and which approach will best meet your needs. It is very possible you will combine methods. Although performance appraisal refers to a set of procedures, the system often revolves around the documentation provided by the HR department or that which you might develop yourself. Questions to ask when deciding which method and documentation to use might include: Is it useful? Will it motivate improvement in employees? Will it enable comparisons between employees? Is it reliable and valid? Is it practical and cost-effective to develop and use? Figure 9.2 briefly describes the advantages and disadvantages of common appraisal methods.

The performance discussion

While methods of appraisal are many and varied, nearly all use a discussion format in which to provide feedback to the individual or team and to extract feedback about the manager. The discussion has generally been known as the performance appraisal interview. The word 'interview' is suggestive of one individual asking another questions—that is, one person being in control and the other reacting. As that is not the purpose of the performance appraisal, this book uses the term 'performance discussion', which suggests a more equal footing of participants (the appraiser and the appraisee) and a process in which two-way communication occurs. The difference is illustrated in Figure 9.3.

FIGURE 9.2 Advantages and disadvantages of appraisal methods and documentation[3]

Appraisal method	Advantages	Disadvantages
Management by objectives (MBO)	Able to tie organisational goals to individual goals. Jointly agreed so team members are held directly accountable.	Time-consuming. Process depends on appraiser and appraisee having a clear picture of what they are trying to achieve, the ability to set objectives, and very good communication and negotiation skills.
Graphic rating scale method (GRSM)	Relatively simple to use and less time-consuming to develop and administer than some other methods, and therefore more cost-effective. Provides a quantitative rating for each employee. Feedback can be aggregated and compared, which enables management to identify trends.	Human error, such as the halo effect, stereotyping or bias; standards may be unclear.
Alternative ranking method	Simple to use because it is based on a single criterion of overall performance.	Difficult to evaluate performance if employees perform identically in a job. Because not anchored to behaviours, results can be influenced by appraiser bias, therefore unreliable and not valid.
Forced distribution method	Ends up with a predetermined number of people in each group.	Appraisal results depend on the restriction of the original choice of cut-off points.
Critical incident method	Helps specify what is 'right' and 'wrong' about an employee's performance; forces manager to evaluate team members on an ongoing basis.	Difficult to rate or rank employees relative to one another.
Behaviourally anchored rating scale (BARS)	Is very accurate and has clear standards. Use of critical incidents provides good feedback. Independent performance dimensions. Consistency and reliability of different rater appraisals.	Complex and time-consuming tool to develop and implement, therefore expensive. Is dependent on appraiser's ability to choose accurate behavioural descriptions.
360-degree review feedback	Provides an accurate indicator of employee performance. More balanced and inclusive than one based on just one or two sources.	Bias in raters.
Behaviour observation scale	Clearly specifies what an employee must do to implement an organisation's goals and how frequently they exhibit the behaviour. Based on a systematic job analysis. Performance improvement goals observable and specific. Measures of behaviour can be weighted to reflect importance of the measure to the role.	Can be costly and time-consuming to develop. Focus on behaviours may ignore the importance of outputs to many roles where behaviour may not be an important consideration.
Balanced scorecard method	Strategically links employee goals to organisational goals; considers a broad range of variables which affect organisational performance.	A relatively new system so may take time to implement into organisational culture; may be complex.
Narrative forms	Provide plenty of written detail and examples to support the final outcome of the appraisal.	Some users may find this approach time-consuming. Depending on the appraiser's written skills, the form may become very detailed and lengthy.

FIGURE 9.3 Difference between an appraisal interview and a discussion

	Appraiser	Appraisee
Interview	Asks questions Controls Takes an active role Is judgmental Plans future actions	Answers questions Reacts Takes a passive role Is judged Complies with actions
Discussion	Asks questions Answers questions Takes an active role Considers evidence Draws conclusions Suggests future actions Agrees on future actions	Asks questions Answers questions Takes an active role Considers evidence Draws conclusions Suggests future actions Agrees on future actions

The performance discussion is the central tenet around which the appraisal is built, and needs to be handled skilfully if it is to be a useful activity for all parties involved. The broad aim of the discussion is to pool information about performance and how it can be improved. In the course of the discussion, both parties present examples and evidence of performance to support opinions and conclusions. From this, an understanding of performance is gained and can be analysed to determine how further improvements can be made. Finally, agreement can be reached on how to proceed in the future.

The performance discussion is reviewed below in depth and a model is introduced to help you manage the discussion.

Characteristics of an effective discussion

While it might be stretching the concept to say that the two people involved in a performance discussion constitute a group, it is useful to look at group theory to determine the qualities of effective discussion. In any case, the issue is relevant when working with teams. Johnson and Johnson suggest that for group discussion to be effective there must first be evidence of the development of an effective group.[4] From their identification of 12 elements of an effective group, the guidelines shown in Figure 9.4 have been developed and must exist if the performance discussion is to be effective.

These guidelines reinforce the main points already made in the preceding two chapters but they also make it very clear that, prior to the actual performance discussion, much work has to be done for the discussion to be successful. For example, communication and interpersonal skills need to be developed by both appraiser and appraisee. It is unreasonable to expect that staff will attend a performance appraisal discussion and be able to contribute in a useful way if they are not adequately prepared and have developed appropriate skills and an understanding of the process.

Similarly, the manager or appraiser must be adequately equipped to handle this specialised form of communication, particularly if there are any cultural issues that need to be considered. The appraiser needs to be aware of any cultural issues that may discourage the appraisee from active participation. For example, in collectivist societies it is common for the manager to make major decisions and the team members to readily comply. The appraiser may find employees reluctant to provide feedback if it appears to criticise the manager. Likewise, in cultures where people believe they have little or no control over their destiny, participation in performance appraisals may appear meaningless. Given Australia's workplace diversity it is likely that managers will conduct appraisals with staff who come from cultures in which formal workplace appraisals may not be conducted.

This work is not onerous but merely part of being a skilful manager. However, the chances of completing an effective performance discussion are considerably reduced if any of these skills or adequate preparation is missing—a point made by Dove and Brown,[5] who claim 'appraisal training needs to be more ambitious and sophisticated so as to fulfil the great latent potential of the process'. They suggest that appraisal training ought to take in the factors contained in the 12 guidelines to strengthen the appraisal process. It can be self-destructive to conduct performance discussions if guidelines have not been established, because the lack of an appropriate climate and skills by both parties will sabotage the discussion. A sabotaged process, resulting in the outcomes described by Cascio earlier in Chapter 8, is worse than not appraising performance at all.

FIGURE 9.4 Elements of effective group functioning required for successful performance discussions

1. A clear set of performance standards for the work area and for individuals

2. Accurate two-way communication between staff members and manager

3. Widespread distribution, participation and leadership among staff members

4. The use of consensus to arrive at answers, solutions and decisions

5. Power and influence based on expertise, access to information and social skills, not on the authority of the manager

6. The frequent occurrence of controversy within the section managed by the manager

7. The open confrontation and negotiation of conflicts of interest among staff members and between staff members and the manager

8. High cohesiveness between manager and staff members

9. High trust between manager and staff members

10. A climate of acceptance and support between manager and staff members

11. A climate of individual responsibility and accountability, helping and sharing, and achievement between manager and staff

12. A high level of interpersonal skills in both parties

A model of the discussion is presented below to help appraisers and appraisees make the most of the appraisal opportunity. Before discussing the model in depth, Figure 9.5 provides an overview. You will see that there are four stages in the model, with a number of parts within each stage.

FIGURE 9.5 The performance discussion model

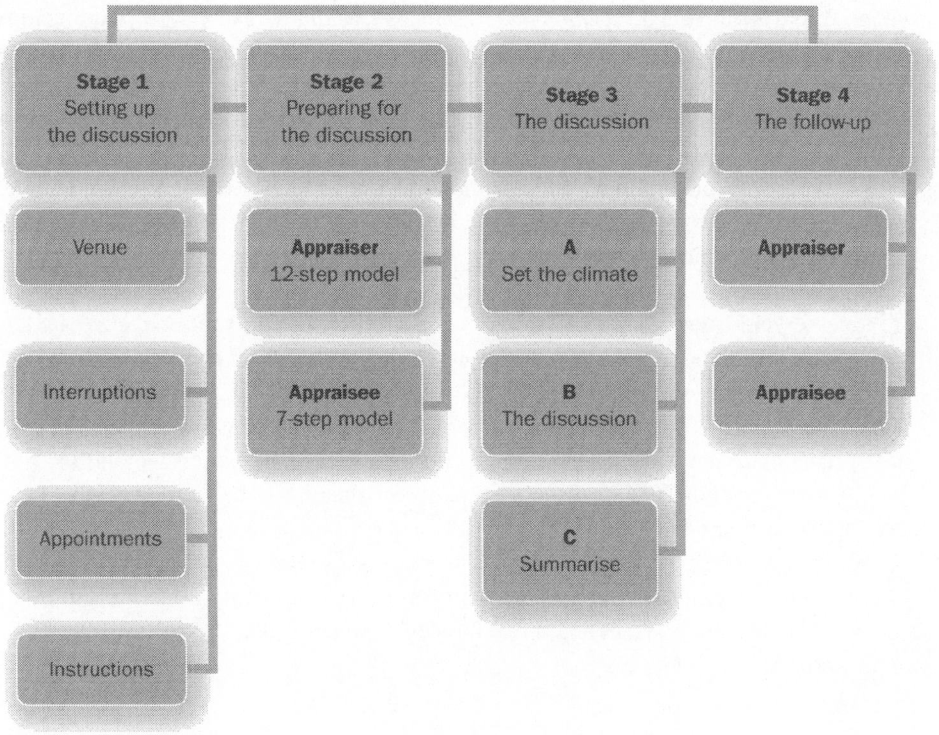

Stage 1—Setting up the discussion

Adequate preparation is needed for the performance discussion to be beneficial. Unless enough time is given to preparation by both appraiser and appraisee, the discussion cannot be full, open and honest. On average, it should take each party about one hour to prepare for the appraisal discussion. The appraiser must also put in further time preparing for the whole process—how much is likely to depend on how many staff you have to appraise. The responsibilities of the appraiser are discussed next.

Appraiser responsibilities

The appraiser is the facilitator of the appraisal discussion, and as such you need to focus on the process and outcomes of the discussion. Before scheduling appointment times for the discussions, you need to give considerable thought to how you will prepare the appraisees for the discussion. There are four important areas that need your attention in setting up the discussion: the venue, interruptions, appointments, and information or instructions for appraisees.

1 *Deciding on the venue*
   Finding a suitable venue can be difficult. In choosing a venue, consider privacy, freedom from interruptions and ease of accessibility to appraisees.

   While your office may satisfy these criteria, it is always a good idea if you can hold the discussion in a room other than your office so as to be on neutral ground. Holding the interview in your office may add to the anxiety of appraisees. However, you may not have any options other than to hold the discussion in your office. If this is the case, you must attend to the following matters.

☞ Avoid having the discussion across the desk, as this sets up power relationships that you want to avoid in a performance discussion. If you do not have a table in your office that you can use, arrange the chairs near each other and as far away from the desk as you can practically manage. This is a legitimate attempt to ensure equality in the discussion and will facilitate a better quality of discussion.

☞ Ensure absolutely that your telephone will not ring. A ringing phone can be off-putting when you are in a delicate stage of discussion. This single item has the potential to wreck your performance discussion.

☞ Ensure that you will not be interrupted in any other way—for example, by people barging into your office wanting to talk to you. This sort of interruption can create havoc when you are in the middle of a discussion and cause a great deal of embarrassment for all concerned.

☞ Move all distracting papers and work from the immediate vicinity. Files and papers can sometimes attract the attention of yourself or the appraisee and trigger lapses in concentration, causing discussion to falter, thoughts to be confused, misunderstandings to occur, and false assumptions to be made.

☞ If your organisation has open-plan workstations you may not have an office, so you will need to locate an appropriate room for the performance discussion. In this case, you could meet appraisees at a venue outside the organisation, provided it satisfies the above criteria.

2   *Containing interruptions*

Ensure that you will not be interrupted for anything except emergencies. Clarify your definition of 'emergency' so that there is no misunderstanding. Allowing the performance discussion to be interrupted sends signals to appraisees that they are not important enough to have your undivided attention for a specific period of time.

☞ Turn off all mobile phones and pagers and redirect other phones if necessary; ask the appraisee to do the same, if applicable.

3   *Scheduling appointments*

Give appraisees as much time as possible to prepare for their performance discussion. One month is adequate. This gives them enough time to go over the documentation and to think about how they are doing.

When scheduling appointments, avoid making too many appointments on the same day. For example, if you have five people to appraise, holding one interview each day over five days is preferable to holding them all on the one day. The reason for this is that you should spend about one hour getting yourself ready for the discussion, about one hour (or more, depending on the job) in the discussion, and at least half an hour after the discussion thinking about it. This means that the average performance discussion should take about two and a half hours to complete if it is done effectively. Thus it is possible to manage only two effective performance discussions in the one day. More than two in a day creates the possibility of confusing the discussions, and that could have significant consequences for decision making.

Whatever basis you decide on for scheduling the appointments, when you do make an appointment with an appraisee, that appointment must be fixed. That is, only under the most urgent circumstances should you alter the appointment. This must be so for appraiser and appraisee. Failure to adhere to the schedule shows disrespect for the other as well as undermining the appraisal process and its importance.

4   *Information/instructions to be given to appraisees*

Appraisees will need some guidance and support in preparing for the discussion, especially if this is a new process and they have not been through it before. The more information you can give them the less anxious they will be, although you will not be able to eradicate all anxiety until you have been through the process with them a couple of times.

The information needed by appraisees fits into three categories:

- process
- housekeeping
- instructions.

It is useful to provide this information in both written and spoken format to ensure that you achieve a shared understanding in your communication. Thus, a memo and a discussion when giving out the memo will go a long way to allaying fears about the appraisal discussion.

The more that appraisees know about what is going on, the less threatened they will feel and the more cooperative they will be. This approach reinforces that it is a serious matter and that all concerned must invest appropriate time and effort in the process.

The memo should first deal with the process to be used, then the housekeeping and, finally, the specific instructions for preparation. Once you have written a memo you will probably find that it will suffice for each subsequent appraisal discussion with a few minor changes. The items you should deal with under each of the three categories are shown in Figure 9.6.

Finally, attach any appropriate forms to the memo and discuss them when you hand it to each appraisee.

When you get to this stage you have set up the performance discussion, but you now have a great deal of work to do yourself in preparation for each appraisal discussion.

FIGURE 9.6 Memo of information to appraisee

Memo

Process
- Review the organisation's performance management system
- Introduce the performance discussion phase
- Explain the purpose of having a performance discussion
- Explain what happens after the performance discussion
- Explain how the discussion will run

Housekeeping
- Identify the date and time of the discussion with the appraisee
- Clearly state the venue for the discussion and provide an address such as building number and room number
- Provide an estimation of the time required for the discussion

Instructions
- How the appraisee should prepare for the discussion
- Responsibilities of the appraisee
- Instructions specific to the forms that may need to be completed

Appraisee responsibilities

Appraisees also have responsibilities in setting up the discussion. These are not as exhaustive as those of the appraiser but they are still required for an effective performance discussion. In the lead-up to the formal performance appraisal period in your organisation you should be letting your staff know what their responsibilities are in relation to the discussion. Appraisees should:

- note the date, day and time of the appointment and take steps to ensure they will be able to attend
- ensure that others know of the appointment
- make arrangements for phones or desks to be covered as necessary during the appointment time
- follow any instructions provided by the appraiser
- schedule personal preparation.

The next section of the chapter works through what each party has to do in order to achieve an effective and purposeful performance discussion. The preparation for the discussion can make or break the appraisal in terms of the evidence and examples—and thus the quality of discussion—that the preparation will generate. It is therefore an important stage in the whole appraisal process.

CHECK YOUR UNDERSTANDING

1. What common feature is there between nearly all methods of appraisal?
2. What is the difference between an interview and a discussion?
3. What are the 12 characteristics of a good discussion?
4. What are the four stages of a performance discussion?
5. List the responsibilities of the appraiser in stage 1 of the model.
6. What should be contained in the advice to appraisees of the performance discussion?
7. What responsibilities do appraisees have in the first stage of the model?

SKILLS PRACTICE

1. Prepare a memo to an appraisee informing them of their performance discussion.
2. Draw up a 12-month plan to develop interpersonal communication skills in your staff.
3. Document how you might model appropriate interpersonal communication skills as a manager.

SKILL AND KNOWLEDGE APPLICATION

Sinead Murphy is a busy and successful Production Manager for a company specialising in solar technology who manages a team of 24 employees. Her team has been runner-up several times in the yearly production competition for the best safety performance. Every year the top safety performance team wins an overseas trip for two weeks. Sinead has been trying for the past five years to win this award. It is appraisal time once again, and Sinead knows she must schedule the appraisals. She usually tries to do them while the employees are between production runs because it saves time and does not detract from production. In preparation for the appraisal Sinead normally has a think about how she feels the appraisee has done through the appraisal period, and then has discussions with as many employees as she can between production runs. Invariably, no one is happy with their appraisals due to the rushed approach Sinead takes to the process. Everyone knows she just wants to win the trip.

TASK

- Advise Sinead on how she might be able to win that award through better performance appraisal preparation and the benefits that might flow from it.

Emily is the Team Leader of the customer call centre in a large financial institution. This is her first supervisory role, and she has just been told that she must complete the annual performance appraisals within the next four weeks. She has always been disappointed with the way in which her supervisors have conducted her performance appraisals and is keen to use 'best practice' with her staff. Her 'office' is a desk in the middle of the customer call centre. While Emily is aware that she cannot conduct the appraisals at her desk, she does not quite know what to do and approaches you for advice.

TASK

- What would you suggest that Emily do?

Stage 2—Preparing for the discussion

The appraiser

Solid preparation and firm evidence will result in greater cooperation from the appraisee, more open and honest communication, fewer defensive strategies being used and a greater willingness to problem-solve. Figure 9.7 provides a model of the appraiser preparation process. You may use this to start with, but feel free to add steps to it and change elements of it once you have developed your own way of doing things. The model will lead you systematically through the evidence that you have available on the performance of the appraisee. This will ensure that you can conduct an in-depth discussion with the appraisee as objectively as possible. The more specific answers you have to the questions in the model, the more prepared you will be for the discussion. The more prepared the appraiser is, the greater the benefit for both appraiser and appraisee. Your preparations will be greatly aided by the in-depth analysis you have already completed (see Chapters 7 and 8).

Each step in the model is now discussed in detail. In answering the questions in the model you may create new questions that you cannot answer. This is a positive outcome of the process and you should note these questions to be asked during the discussion with the appraisee. Some of the questions in the model may not be applicable. If this is the case, ignore them.

| **FIGURE 9.7** A model of the appraiser preparation process

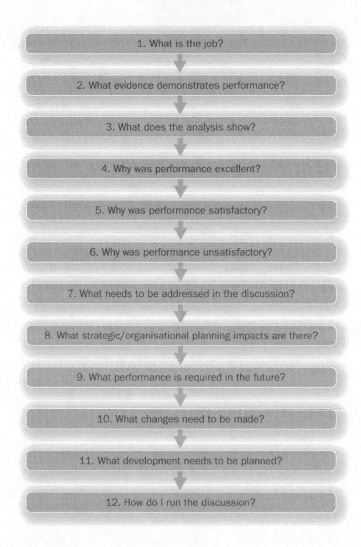

Step 1 What is the job?

Review the job specification for the appraisee. From the analysis you completed in Chapter 7, note any area in which the job has changed and where the description needs to be rewritten, as this will need to be discussed with the appraisee. In particular, look at the level and classification of the position. If the work has changed fundamentally, you may need to reclassify the position and arrange for a different salary scale, if this is appropriate. It is fundamental to the performance discussion that, as the appraiser, you understand the job and how it operates prior to the discussion. It is particularly important that you know exactly what is expected of the position in terms of outputs.

Step 2 What evidence demonstrates performance?

Arrange the analysed evidence around each of the performance standards to develop a solid picture of performance for the whole appraisal period. It is likely that you will have evidence of satisfactory performance, unsatisfactory performance and even performance that is beyond expectations—or any combination of these—for each performance standard.

Step 3 What does the analysis show?

Look for examples of where performance standards have been exceeded, where they are satisfactory and where they are unsatisfactory. Here you are making your decisions about the performance of the individual. Ensure that you have enough evidence to support your position and you are confident that you can maintain a case for the decision you have made. This applies just as much to excellent or good performance as it does to unsatisfactory performance. One or two examples are not enough to develop a case. You will recall that there should be no surprises in the formal performance discussion, so there will be no 'new' evidence that has not already been discussed with the appraisee.

Step 4 Why was performance excellent?

In the case of excellent performance, consider why the performance was excellent. Ask yourself the following questions. If you are unable to answer them they will form the basis of questions to ask during the appraisal discussion.

- Did the appraisee:
  — bring any special skills to bear on the standard that need to be recognised?
  — put in an extra special effort that needs to be recognised?
  — come up with an innovative idea that needs to be recognised?
  — deal with a particularly difficult issue well?
  — change any procedures or processes?
  — use any different materials or equipment?
  — use any new software?
- Did the excellent result in one area negatively affect results in other areas?
- How was the excellent result achieved?
- Who else was involved in achieving the result?
- Can the result be achieved on an ongoing basis?
- What factors that were out of the appraisee's control influenced the result?

These questions allow you to probe for the way the excellent performance was achieved, and for the appraisee to bask in the glory of having achieved excellent performance. The questioning allows you to document how things were done so that different approaches may be incorporated in practice within the workplace. It further allows you to determine whether this individual, and other staff members, can maintain the level of performance.

Remember, excellent performance needs to be dealt with and recognised just as much as unsatisfactory performance.

Step 5 Why was performance satisfactory?

In the case of satisfactory performance, consider why the performance was satisfactory. Ask yourself the following questions. If you are unable to answer them they will form the basis of questions to ask during the appraisal discussion.

- How was the performance achieved?
- Was anything different about the materials, equipment or software used?
- Can the performance be maintained?
- Could the performance be moved to excellent? How?
- Were there any performance impediments?
- How did these impediments affect the result?
- How were impediments overcome?

These questions allow you to recognise performance that is satisfactory and demonstrate your interest in how it was achieved. (The appraiser gets to share the pride in achieving the standard.) They also enable you to document practices, procedures and methods applied by the successful individual so they can be utilised elsewhere.

Step 6 Why was performance unsatisfactory?

In the case of unsatisfactory performance, consider why the performance was unsatisfactory. Ask yourself the following questions. If you are unable to answer them they will form the basis of questions to ask during the appraisal discussion.

- How big is the gap between satisfactory performance and the unsatisfactory performance?
- What, exactly, was not achieved?
- Was the standard of performance understood by the appraisee?
- Was adequate support given to the appraisee?
- Was adequate training and development given to the appraisee?
- Was the appraisee properly monitored through the appraisal period?
- Did the appraisee receive appropriate feedback during the appraisal period?
- Was there anything in the environment that might have prevented the appraisee from achieving the performance standard?
- Were there any extenuating circumstances that should be taken into account?
- Why did performance not meet the standard?
- What problems were encountered during the appraisal period?
- Might there be any personal problems affecting performance?
- How might performance be improved?
- How can it be done better?

The full range of these questions is important because they can highlight the complex array of reasons for lack of performance. Many of these you will not be able to answer, and you will need the guidance and cooperation of the appraisee during the discussion. It is important not to jump to conclusions or to form firm opinions of the performance until you have fully explored the reasons for the non-performance during the discussion; otherwise, you may judge an appraisee unfairly.

Step 7 What needs to be addressed in the discussion?

From the evidence you have collected, and from the tentative inferences you have drawn about the individual's performance, you now need to identify the following:

- specific questions you wish to ask in the discussion
- specific areas that need clarification or elaboration during the discussion
- specific examples of performance where you might be unsure of the level of performance
- specific areas that need joint problem solving during the discussion
- specific developmental areas that need to be addressed in the discussion.

Step 8 What strategic/organisational planning impacts are there?

You need to note any strategic planning impacts on your work group and any operational planning impacts for the group. Determine how these will affect individual jobs and what impacts there are for new performance objectives and standards.

Step 9 What performance is required in the future?

Identify carefully the specific performance that will be required during the next performance appraisal period. Again, seek guidance from the strategic and operational plans of the organisation, department, branch or work group. You must also consider the specific abilities and skills of appraisees. Will the next period stretch them? Will it provide enough of a challenge? Are they ready to move on to other jobs within the organisation? Are they ready to take more responsibility, and how might this be reflected in the performance standards and objectives? You will need to have some ideas on this subject so that you can facilitate thinking about the issue during the discussion.

Step 10 What changes need to be made?

What new performance objectives need to be set? Also, identify those that must change, and those performance standards that may need renegotiating as a result of this performance discussion. You will need to review carefully strategic and operational plans to be clear on what the important issues are for the next appraisal period. If the job description or duties are to change, this is the time to discuss it with the appraisee. It is vital to have their considered and committed involvement and support for the changes. If you expect that the appraisee will not fully support the necessary changes, you will have to develop strategies for how the issues are to be introduced and handled in the discussion.

Step 11 What development needs to be planned?

Think about what developmental planning (including training) is required for the appraisee. Develop a number of options with specific outcomes that you could discuss. Tie these into increased performance. For developmental opportunities to be taken up with enthusiasm, they must be jointly agreed with the appraisee. While you should prepare some options, you should not provide answers for the appraisee but instead introduce your options during discussion or add to those suggested by the appraisee. This area of the appraisal will need careful consideration. As the appraiser, you should be very clear in your own mind how much you can afford to spend on the individual for training and development purposes. You should also have some ideas about what activities, projects and options are available for internal development for the appraisee. This process is developed further in Chapter 10.

Step 12 How do I run the discussion?

Based on the discussion stage (stage 3 below), determine how you will conduct the discussion. What things should be looked at first and how will you group issues that go together?

You are now ready to go to the performance discussion. Before this area is reviewed, we look at what the appraisee ought to be doing in preparation for the discussion.

CHECK YOUR UNDERSTANDING

8 Why does the appraiser need to review the job of the appraisee in preparation for the appraisal?

9 Why is it necessary to specify and document where you think the level of performance sits?

10 How does the nature of the questions asked about unsatisfactory performance differ from those asked about satisfactory and excellent performance? Is this important?

11 Why is it necessary to determine the performance that is required in the future?

12 What is the usefulness of having a model to guide preparation for the appraisal discussion?

SKILLS PRACTICE

- Identify ways of using the appraiser preparation model. Discuss how it might be applied.

Appraisee responsibilities

For a performance appraisal discussion to go well, each party must put rigorous effort into the preparation. The appraisee has a responsibility to be equally prepared and not leave it all up to the appraiser. If, early in the discussion, you find the appraisee is unprepared, you should probably terminate the discussion, make very clear the precise reasons for doing so, and set a new appointment time with the individual in a few days' time. Do not give appraisees too much time, as they should feel a little pressure because of their lack of original effort.

The following guidelines will help appraisees prepare for their performance discussion. You may also like to use them as instructions in your memo about the performance discussion. Figure 9.8 presents a model for the preparation of the appraisee.

The model parts are useful for instilling the responsibility of appraisees for preparing for the performance discussion. You will be able to determine very quickly if the appraisee has put the required effort into preparation for the discussion. Each part of the model is explained below.

FIGURE 9.8 A model for the preparation of the appraisee for the performance discussion

Review	Job description Performance standards Feedback on performance Actual performance
Collect	Evidence of performance
Document	Reasons for performance Suggestions for improvement Training and development Reasons for renegotiation
Identify	Problems encountered
Develop	Suggestions for new objectives
Participate	Open, honest communication Voice opinion, suggestions
Appraise	Give feedback to the appraiser

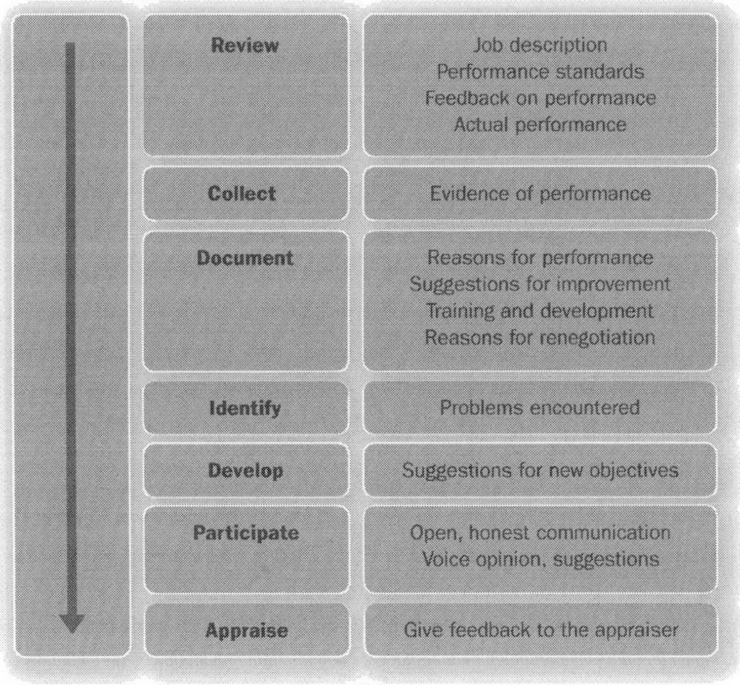

Appraisees need to:

1 **Review**
   - *job description to check that nothing has changed.* If things have changed, an agreement to rewrite the job description should be gained at the performance discussion. Appraisees should note anything in the job that has changed since the last appraisal in relation to responsibilities or duties. Appraisees should be encouraged to provide specific evidence of these changes to develop a case for the rewrite of the job description.
   - *performance standards and performance objectives.* It is important that appraisees have these clearly in their minds when they enter the discussion, so that the discussion can be specific. They should base their collected evidence around each of the performance standards.
   - *feedback on performance received throughout the appraisal period.* Feedback received during the appraisal period is valuable evidence when considering how performance has changed from the previous appraisal period. Appraisees should note the examples of feedback, and be able to report on what changes have occurred and how these have affected performance. Areas in which feedback was not received and would have been appreciated should also be noted for discussion in the formal performance discussion.
   - *actual performance against the above.* If adequate performance feedback has been provided throughout the appraisal period, appraisees should have a good understanding of their own performance levels and should be able to clearly support their position with evidence—which will be similar to that which the appraiser has collected. Appraisees

should be made aware that they need to collect sufficient evidence against each of the performance standards to substantiate their opinion of their level of performance.

2 **Collect**

- *evidence of their performance for the appraisal period*, including performance that is excellent, performance that is satisfactory and performance that is unsatisfactory. Evidence should be factual and as comprehensive as possible, and must represent numerous examples of the type of performance the appraisee wants to present. Appraisees must understand that appraising performance is based on performance for the whole period, not just one or two incidents.

3 **Document**

- *why they think their performance was excellent, satisfactory or unsatisfactory.* Appraisees should sort through the data they have collected on their performance and group them into categories—excellent, satisfactory, or unsatisfactory performance. Reasons for why they think the performance was at a particular level should also be documented so that a case can be made during their discussion with the appraiser. Document particular circumstances that influenced the result for discussion.

- *suggestions for improvement of performance.* Where appraisees think performance can be improved, they should document these ideas so they can be discussed. The documentation need not be confined to things that only the appraisee can do. Suggestions for improvement in equipment, procedures or methods can be included here.

- *training and development done during the appraisal period.* These activities need not be just formal training courses. Appraisees should think about the things they have learned from others, either on the job or by being a member of a project team. It is likely that more learning will have been achieved through processes other than formal training courses. Appraisees may be surprised at the degree of new learning that has been achieved, when they think about it. It is important to capture these data for personal reinforcement and motivation, and so that appraisees can discuss their development and progress during the appraisal discussion.

- *why performance objectives and standards may need to be renegotiated.* For many reasons, performance objectives and standards may need to be renegotiated. Situations change all the time, and it may be necessary to discuss major alterations to performance standards and objectives that occur as a result of changes in the workplace. Appraisees should ensure that they develop sound arguments for changing objectives and standards, and that the proposed new objectives can be evidenced in the data they have collected.

4 **Identify**

- *problems that were encountered during the performance appraisal period* and how they were overcome or how they affected performance.

5 **Develop**

- *suggestions for performance objectives* for the next period.

6 **Participate**

- *actively in the discussion.* Appraisees should come to the discussion prepared to have a full, open and honest talk about the future. They should be ready to voice their opinion and discuss all aspects of their performance.

7 Appraise

➤ *the performance of the appraiser over the appraisal period.*

— Are there things the appraiser does that make things difficult for the appraisee?

— Are there things the appraiser does not do that would make things easier for the appraisee?

— What does the appraisee like about the way the appraiser works, manages, leads?

— What does the appraisee not like about the way the appraiser works, manages, leads?

— What things does the appraisee want the appraiser to continue doing?

— What things does the appraisee want the appraiser to stop doing?

CHECK YOUR UNDERSTANDING

13 How might appraisees use the appraisee preparation model?

14 Why is it necessary to review feedback received during the appraisal period?

15 How does documenting performance improvement, training and development activities, and renegotiation of standards/objectives help prepare the appraisee for the performance discussion?

16 What is the benefit of reviewing the performance of the appraiser?

SKILL AND KNOWLEDGE APPLICATION

William has been preparing for his performance appraisal discussion, which is coming up in 10 days' time. He is a little worried because he has realised that, while he has done well, he has not attained any of his performance objectives. He would not mind so very much if it had been his own fault, but he feels quite strongly that matters were beyond his control. Time and time again his boss, David, has redirected William's activities onto his own priorities so that William has found it very difficult to get on with what he has been charged to do. David also has the habit of wanting to discuss things whenever they arise, so he calls William and asks him to come to his office immediately. William has found that many hours each week have been wasted in these ad-hoc meetings, and it was no wonder that he hasn't been able to meet his performance objectives; he has hardly had time to attend all the discussions with David.

TASK

➤ Advise William how to prepare for his discussion.

Stage 3—The discussion

The performance discussion should not contain any surprises for the appraisee or appraiser. Most books on performance appraisal say this, but what does it mean? It means that anything dealt with in this formal discussion should already have been dealt with outside the discussion in the day-to-day management of performance and workplace activities.

A. Set the climate

There are three dimensions to setting the climate of the discussion: the physical, the psychological, and the process. They are interdependent—that is, they affect each other—which is why it is necessary to address all three when setting the climate of the interview. Both physical and process factors will affect the psychological state of the appraisee, so by addressing these two factors first you will be helping the appraisee to cope better with the appraisal discussion. Figure 9.9 illustrates the relationship between the dimensions of setting the climate.

FIGURE 9.9 Dimensions of setting the climate

Physical dimension

To facilitate quality discussion, a number of components within the physical dimension need to be addressed. For example, people will not have honest, open discussions if the environment they are in is not private. You should ensure that the room temperature is comfortable, that seating is arranged in a non-threatening way and is comfortable, and that there is a table to put things on. Preferably, seating will be arranged in a way that allows you to be close, although not next to each other. Likewise, you should not be directly facing each other, because this sets up feelings of confrontation and will not be conducive to discussion. Try placing the seating on an angle, forming a V-shape. This gives each party their own space but allows proximity, which is necessary for such specific discussions. Seating and the positioning of a coffee table is indicated in Figure 9.10.

FIGURE 9.10 Seating arrangements for the discussion

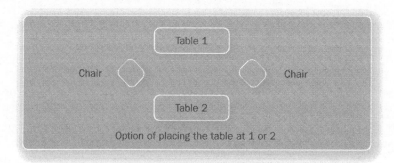

When people are nervous they sometimes develop a dry mouth, so having water available in the room is necessary to ensure comfort. If you anticipate conflict in the discussion, and maybe tears, it's wise to have tissues at hand on the table so that appraisees can help themselves or you can offer them at an appropriate time. Appraisees may forget to bring writing materials with them, so have pens and paper on the table close by in case these are needed. From your own preparation you will know what references and files might be needed in the discussion. Place these on the table within easy reach.

What is important here is that the appraisee's requirements and need for comfort do not interfere with the running of the discussion. Once you have entered and begun the performance appraisal discussion you should not have to leave the room. If you do, it will destroy the dynamics that have been created up to that stage. You will also lose control of the discussion so that it is handed to the appraisee, who can then interrupt or sidetrack the discussion with diversions.

Process dimension

'Process' means a course of action. It is important to share with appraisees the course of action you intend to take with the discussion so that they know where things are going and what to expect. This will alleviate some of their nervousness about the discussion, especially if this is the first time they have been a part of the process. It is equally important to reinforce that the process is negotiable by asking appraisees if the framework also meets their requirements. If it does not, renegotiate so you have something that satisfies everyone's needs.

Psychological dimension

This dimension deals with appraisees as individuals and with their specific thoughts and feelings. It will be different for each of the appraisees you see. Some will be more nervous than others, some will be more forthright; some will require support, while others will be confident. Consider these issues carefully when choosing the communication strategies you will use. Be sincere in the way you greet each appraisee, in line with the way you would normally communicate. Invite them to take a seat and make them as comfortable as possible. Try to ensure that you are doing all the right things in terms of positive body language.

It is not appropriate to launch straight into the reason for being together. Some preliminary talk is desirable, to relax the appraisee and start a communication process that will flow smoothly. Broad questions about the appraisal may be useful for this purpose: 'How did the preparation process go?', 'Were the instructions I gave you useful?', 'How are you fixed time-wise?' You might also say how much you appreciate the appraisee's effort and investment in the process of perform-ance management within the organisation and your work unit.

Topics such as football, organisational politics and the weather are not really appropriate unless these are things you normally discuss with the appraisee. Only you will know the most appropriate questions to ask to help put the appraisee at ease and get the conversation going. When you are sure the appraisee is at ease and the communication process is open, discuss the role of perform-ance appraisal in the performance management system of your organisation. This will set up the purpose of your discussion clearly. Once this is complete, you can discuss the process dimension as detailed above. At this stage you will be ready to launch into the main part of the discussion, 'the central discussion'. Figure 9.11 summarises the components of each dimension of setting the climate.

FIGURE 9.11 Components of each dimension of setting the climate

Physical dimension	Process dimension	Psychological dimension
• Privacy • Room temperature • Furniture arrangement • Water available • Tissues available • Writing materials available • Appropriate references/files handy	• Discuss framework you will be using • Outline how you will move through the framework • Ask if framework also meets the needs of the appraisee	• Put the appraisee at ease • Address body language • Choose communication strategies carefully • Ensure sincerity

CHECK YOUR UNDERSTANDING

17 Why are the seating arrangements in the discussion room important?
18 How does each dimension of setting the climate influence the others?
19 What purpose does the process dimension serve for the appraisee?
20 Why is there a need to set the climate at all?

B. The central discussion

This part of the appraisal process requires the appraiser to use communication and interpersonal skills skilfully to guarantee a useful discussion for both parties. These skills are at the micro level of operation. Initially, in this part of the chapter, we explore the macro picture, which is the broad framework on which you can map out your appraisal discussion with the appraisee.

The framework presented here is not the only one and as you become more experienced in conducting performance appraisals, you might make adjustments or adopt other frameworks. However, for the purposes of this book, we will use the framework represented in Figure 9.12 as a starting point and basis for your discussion.

A problem-solving approach

Facilitating useful and purposeful discussion is not an easy task. It is not just a matter of sitting down and talking. The facilitator must be able to guide and manage the discussion so that it is productive for both appraiser and appraisee. This means being able to manage success, conflict, lack of cooperation, overenthusiasm, overconfidence and underperformance, as well as all the emotions that go with these.

FIGURE 9.12 The discussion model

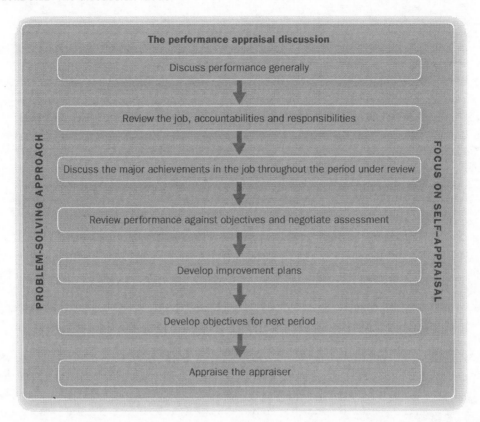

Within the framework in Figure 9.12, a problem-solving approach is adopted. A problem-solving approach supports the 'equalness' of the two individuals participating in the performance appraisal discussion and reinforces the consultative nature of the process. It also extends the process you began in the analysis stage in Chapter 7. It should not be an approach where the appraiser constantly asks questions and the appraisee answers, as this would turn the discussion into an interview, or even an interrogation. While skilful questioning by the appraiser can open up the discussion and facilitate elaboration and the presentation of evidence, questioning is not the only strategy to employ in the appraisal discussion.

A problem-solving approach means that you are both involved as equal partners in the discussion and that you explore all the issues together, providing input and discussing the material before you. Finally, you arrive at a decision together, rather than the appraiser making the decision and imposing it on the appraisee. This does not mean to say that you will always agree on the decision. However, this approach ensures that both parties are involved in the decision-making process, and that matters are dealt with as fully and comprehensively as possible. Cole provides a useful seven-step problem-solving and decision-making process:[6]

Step 1.   Identify the problem clearly.

Step 2.   Establish desired outcomes.

Step 3.   Analyse the problem.

Step 4.   Generate alternative solutions.

Step 5.   Evaluate alternatives and select the most suitable.

Step 6.   Implement the decision.

Step 7.   Follow up and evaluate results.

You will notice many similarities to the process advocated in this book, because in a sense the performance appraisal process is one large problem-solving activity. You will also notice that each of the seven steps can be accommodated within the performance discussion framework. The point of this is that problem solving is a process that is methodical in nature and can be applied to facilitate better quality decisions. Hence, using a problem-solving approach in performance discussions helps to generate the best possible solutions to managing performance for the appraisee, the appraiser and the organisation.

Focus on self-appraisal

As much as possible, the focus of the performance discussion should be on self-appraisal by the appraisee. Appraisees should be encouraged to reflect and comment on their own performance and be willing to express their own concerns and successes. Again, be mindful that some employees may find this difficult and you may need to show patience until the appraisee becomes comfortable disclosing information. The discussion should flow from what the appraisee says; appraisers should manage the discussion on the basis of the reflections and comments provided by the appraisee. This is not a difficult thing to achieve: most people have a very good idea of how they are performing, especially if managers have been doing their job during the appraisal period. Potential for difficulty lies in cases of unsatisfactory performance, and strategies to manage this aspect are dealt with later in this chapter and in other chapters.

It is against this background that we now explore the performance discussion model presented in Figure 9.12.

CHECK YOUR UNDERSTANDING

21 Explain the features of a problem-solving approach to performance discussions.
22 What are the benefits of a problem-solving approach to performance discussions?

Discuss performance generally

To introduce the performance discussion, it is useful to talk about how appraisees see their performance in a general sense or as an overview of how they have done over the review period. This approach helps appraisees to focus on self-appraisal and sets the tone for the discussion in this direction. It is also the least threatening way to begin the discussion and allows the appraisee to talk freely. When you know that appraisees are not likely to be forthcoming, you will need to prepare some questions to ask to nudge them along a bit. During this process, be alert to whether appraisees have a realistic understanding of their performance over the review period. This will give you some indication of how tough the assessment part of the discussion will be and will give you time to plan further strategies if necessary.

The idea of the performance discussion is to have appraisees do most of the talking. The appraiser needs to be able to frame questions that will keep the appraisee talking, and to elicit responses that will cause the appraisee to think carefully. Under normal circumstances, however, appraisees will have a realistic understanding of their performance level, especially if appraisers have been providing regular, quality feedback to staff on their performance. Here are some questions to help you get this early part of the discussion started.

Sample questions on general performance

- How have things been over this review period?
- How would you summarise your performance over this period?
- Are there any particular things that stand out during this period?
- What are the major organisational issues that have influenced you during this review period?
- What effect do you think these issues have had?
- How do you feel about the job?

Review the job, accountabilities and responsibilities

From a general discussion of performance, it is logical to move on to talk about the job the appraisee holds. Here, you discuss the job and the job specification to see whether there have been any changes. You are unlikely to agree to changes being made to the job specification at this stage of the discussion—you will probably want to deal with performance issues before making any decisions. It is important for you to discuss with the appraisee any perceived changes in the job, and its accountabilities and responsibilities, to see if they align with your perceptions. Where they do not, you will need to seek clarification so that you understand how appraisees feel and why they feel the way they do. This is important if changes in accountabilities or responsibilities are likely to affect the appraisee's ability to achieve performance objectives and standards.

Sample questions on job review

- What may have changed about the job during this period?
- What has been the specific impact of strategic and operational plans on the job during this period?
- What new duties or accountabilities are you expected to perform?
- What, if any, responsibilities have changed during this period?
- How have the responsibilities changed?
- What would you like to change about the job?
- What are your current priorities?
- What do you like best about the job?

Discuss major achievements in the job during the review period

At this stage of the discussion, discuss the highlights and major achievements for the appraisee during the review period. Using the evidence and data you collected during the monitoring and analysis stages of the system, base the discussion on facts and provide specific examples to support your statements. You should also expect appraisees to base comments on facts and provide specific examples. If they do not, ask for examples and other evidence to support their statements.

This section of the discussion is to acknowledge the accomplishments of appraisees, and offers the appraiser a specific opportunity to give positive feedback for achievements and strengths. It is appropriate to discuss and acknowledge those accomplishments that were particularly difficult to achieve because of the activity or the context in which performance occurred. Here you should also recognise performance that has exceeded expectations, standards or objectives.

Remember that any praise, recognition or acknowledgment must be based in fact and be supported by evidence; otherwise, it is too general to be of use to the appraisee and may sound insincere. For example, 'Great job' is not very useful feedback; nor are 'Wonderful!', 'Excellent' and 'Well done'. After a few of these phrases, appraisees begin to switch off. Feedback such as:

> '. . . the processes you used to keep that project on track despite the dysfunctional operation of the group allowed you to bring the project in on time and within budget . . .'

lets appraisees know exactly what they did well so that they can continue to do it. Finally, ensure that you cover all the appraisee's accomplishments for the whole period of the review, not just one or two recent ones that have occurred.

Sample questions to identify achievements

- What achievements have you accomplished during this review period?
- What were you most pleased with during this review period?
- What were you most proud of during this review period?
- What were the highlights of the period for you?
- What made these things so special or pleasing for you?

Review performance against objectives and negotiate assessment

In this section of the discussion, you will need to examine every agreed standard of performance and performance objective against how the appraisee performed during the review period. This is different from the step above, which seeks more to develop confidence and ensure appropriate recognition of accomplishments. In this step, appraiser and appraisee are reviewing the specific measures of the performance standards and objectives and how the appraisee performed against them, regardless of whether the performance was unsatisfactory, satisfactory or beyond agreed standards.

Remember that not all problems can be solved. Sometimes there needs to be compromise on both sides, and sometimes one party will not be happy with the solution. At other times, it will take all your skills and patience to draw out appraisees and to get them to problem-solve. There are also times when the appraiser, by virtue of the position held, has to impose a solution on an individual or team. Although this should be a rare occurrence, it should not be discounted. For many reasons, the discussion may go off the rails at this point, especially where the performance being dealt with is unsatisfactory. The strategies listed in Figure 9.13 will help you manage the discussion and guide it to productive ends.

FIGURE 9.13 Strategies for reviewing standards

For each standard or objective, guide the discussion around the following items:
1. Review the objective/standard
2. Ask the appraisee to comment on the actual performance
3. Ask the appraisee for evidence to support the claim if it has not been provided in the comments above (this applies equally to satisfactory and unsatisfactory performance)
4. As appraiser, comment on the performance and supply evidence to support your claims (this applies equally to satisfactory and unsatisfactory performance)
5. Discuss the different views, if they are different, and explore what the differences are, why they exist, and the difference in the evidence presented, if there is a difference
6. Together decide on what the assessment of the performance will be. If you cannot obtain an agreement on the assessment, you, as the appraiser, will have the final say in the matter
7. Record the decision.

Strategies for managing the discussion

1 *Where an appraisee will not admit there is a difference in perspectives of the level of performance*

This strategy applies equally where there is a difference in perspective in relation to satisfactory or unsatisfactory performance.

- Review for a second time the evidence that both parties have presented.
- Clearly link the evidence to measuring the standard. (If this cannot be done the evidence is invalid.) This is a task you would first ask appraisees to do; only if they are unable to would you link the evidence yourself.
- Clearly state the differences between the collected evidence. Again, ask the appraisee to do it first.
- If you are still unable to reach agreement about your different perspectives, you will need to restate the standard of performance required and explain the implications of the weight of evidence presented.
- If an agreement is still not forthcoming, you must make a decision on the basis of the evidence presented.

2 *Where the appraisee does not agree that performance is unsatisfactory*

- Restate the standard of performance required.
- Review the evidence presented by both parties.
- Draw conclusions on what the evidence says about the performance against the standard required. Ask appraisees to do this first; only if they are unable to would you draw the conclusions yourself.
- Clearly and specifically explain where the performance is unsatisfactory.
- If the appraisee is unable to agree, repeat the first four steps.
- If the appraisee still does not agree with the unsatisfactory rating, make it clear that the final decision is yours and that the performance is unsatisfactory for the specific reasons stated.
- Record the decision.

3 *Where an appraisee becomes emotional*
- You are unlikely to know whether the tears are genuine or 'put on' for effect. Either way, if you react to the tears you will hand over the management of the discussion to the appraisee, and you want to avoid that at all costs.
- Do not react to the tears except to halt the discussion temporarily.
- Pass the waiting box of tissues to the appraisee.
- Wait until the appraisee is composed again and continue the discussion as if nothing has happened.

This strategy works because if the tears are genuine, appraisees will appreciate the pause to compose themselves and wipe their tears, and will be grateful for your consideration; nothing is lost except a small amount of time. On the other hand, if the tears are for effect, appraisees will feel rather silly after a while as you wait patiently for them to compose themselves. They will soon stop and continue the discussion; again, only a small amount of time is lost, and not the management of the discussion. Either way, do not be afraid of silence. In such circumstances two minutes can seem like an eternity, but wait out the process patiently until they are ready to continue.

If the waiting lasts longer than five minutes, say that you should now be getting on with the discussion and that you will give them a few seconds to prepare to go on. You must make it perfectly clear that the discussion will continue. Your actions up to this time will demonstrate this.

4 *Where an appraisee keeps trying to deflect an issue or change the focus of the discussion to avoid an item*
- Summarise where you had reached before the deflection or refocusing by the appraisee.
- Ask a direct question regarding the issue and keep focusing on the topic you wish to discuss.
- If the avoidance continues, point out that the discussion is getting off track and that you need to come back to it.
- If it continues further, use some reflection on the appraisee, such as 'I gather that you are reluctant to discuss this issue, because you keep changing the subject or deflecting the discussion. I would like us to explore and understand this issue. Will you agree to discuss it?' Except in very extreme cases this should regain the attention and focus of the appraisee.
- If the appraisee still does not cooperate or declines to give you the commitment you asked for, consider the issue and decide whether it is critical to the appraisal. If it is, make this clear to the appraisee and state that you will form an opinion based on the discussion. If appraisee does not wish to engage in the discussion then they will not have an opportunity to put their point of view, or to elaborate the issue with examples. Make it clear that the issue affects the performance review of the appraisee and ask for their cooperation one last time.
- If cooperation is not forthcoming, make your decision and record it.

5 *Where the discussion seems to be going round in circles, has become stuck on an issue and appears unlikely to move forward*
- Summarise the discussion on this point or topic so far.

- Link the point to the framework and the performance issue.
- Invite the appraisee to make any final comment.
- Suggest that you move on to the next point.

Sample questions on assessing performance

- How practical was this standard/objective?
- How do you feel you performed against this standard/objective?
- Why do you hold that view?
- What examples of that performance can you cite?
- What was difficult or unusual about achieving this standard/objective?
- How did you manage to overcome the difficulties?
- What prevented you from achieving the standard/objective?
- What could you have done differently?

In this section of the discussion, be careful not to pass judgment through either the words you use or the intonation of your voice until after the appraisee has explained all facets of the performance to you. Where you feel there is a difference of opinion, first ask for more evidence or examples, rather than say you have a different view. When you are sure you have allowed the appraisee enough time and opportunity to explain all aspects of the performance, you can begin your own comments based on the evidence you have.

When you have shared your views and discussed them you will need to arrive at an assessment of the performance. Note that if a standard has been set or an objective is written, an appraisee either attains it or does not. There can be no halfway measure. If appraisees do not meet agreed performance standards, record it as such. Where there were extenuating circumstances that prevented attainment of the standard/objective, and these were agreed on during the discussion, comment should be made to that effect in the official documentation. Nevertheless, the standard/objective was not attained. Likewise, where there has been performance far beyond the standard/objective, it has been met. Again, there should be some formal comment about performance requirements being exceeded so that the appraisee receives recognition for the more than satisfactory performance.

Once the assessment of performance has been made, you will need your discussion notes and previously collected data to develop improvement plans with the appraisee.

Develop improvement plans

The development of improvement plans is the rationale for conducting the performance appraisal. The idea is to find out how performance can be improved, both generally and specifically. Performance improvement relates to the areas where the appraisee has not performed to the required standard and where performance must be improved across the organisation in support of strategic and operational plans for the next review period. It also relates to areas where performance may be satisfactory but could be improved. At this stage discussion should focus on these two areas. First, it is logical to work on the areas in which appraisees did not perform to the required standards/objectives and to develop improvement plans, as you have just been discussing this with them. Second, it is important to review organisational, divisional, branch and sectional operational plans for the next review period and to incorporate any new skill and knowledge requirements in the improvement plan to assist individual performance.

The philosophy behind this approach is that organisations and the individuals who work within them should be continuously improving performance if they are to be competitive in the current economic climate. The focus on performance improvement is not a negative focus but one of constantly trying to improve the overall standard of individual performance and hence that of the organisation.

You don't need reams of official-looking forms in order to develop and record improvement plans. They can be written up as action plans, formal development objectives or a series of answers to the questions below. The important point is that the development is documented in some way so that both appraisee and appraiser can review progress and check exactly what was agreed on. For a discussion of a specific framework for a performance plan, see Chapter 10.

It is important that the appraiser does not lead the discussion at this point in the performance discussion. The danger in this is that the appraiser will offer solutions to improving performance. Offering a solution provides appraisees with a very simple way out if they want to move on—all they need do is say 'yes'. In such cases, appraisees may not be committed to the outcomes or the solution to improving their performance. Clearly, it is more desirable for appraisees to come up with possible solutions to the problem of improving performance. You may guide and counsel them, but providing the answers does not help appraisee development.

The questions below will help you develop specific, measurable and practical development plans. You may have questions of your own to add to the list.

Sample questions to guide the creation of a development plan

- What needs to be improved?
- What *can* be improved?
- Why does it need to be improved?
- What can be done to improve performance?
- What skills and knowledge need to be developed to enable performance improvement?
- What resources are required for development?
- What does the appraisee have to do?
- What does the appraiser have to do?
- How might you go about achieving that?
- How realistic is that given the current or future anticipated constraints?
- How would you know when you have achieved it?
- How might you measure that improvement?
- When does it need to be achieved?

Once the development plan has been agreed, it becomes part of the next stage—the objectives and performance standards for the next review period. Performance improvement is discussed in more depth in Chapter 10.

Develop objectives for next period

To develop objectives for the next review period, you will need to take into account the following points:

- organisational strategic and operational plans
- divisional strategic and operational plans

- branch strategic and operational plans
- section strategic and operational plans
- local work group issues
- the appraisee's development plan
- the key job accountabilities and responsibilities.

The new objectives for the next appraisal period should flow naturally from the discussion to this point. You and the appraisee may prefer to identify the areas in which standards/objectives need to be written; then the appraisee works on them and comes back a few days later to discuss the new objectives. Remember, good objectives take time to develop, and it may be a better option to allow time for considerable thought and input to the process. Alternatively, you and the appraisee may wish to develop the new standards/objectives at this stage in the discussion. For guidance on this process, see Chapters 4 and 5.

Appraise the appraiser

When all the issues have been dealt with, so that appraisees do not feel threatened in talking about how you perform, you can ask them to comment on your performance as their manager. You should already have some idea of possible problem areas from what your appraisee said or didn't say. Don't make an issue out of the question, as this may unnerve the appraisee. In a quiet and matter-of-fact way ask appraisees if they have any comments for you that will help you to manage better and work with them more productively. If you have picked up on a problem in the discussion, you may like to say:

> *'For example, when you were talking about XYZ objective, we agreed that I was partly responsible for you not achieving that because I didn't give you all the information. In future, I will be more aware of my actions and how they affect other people. That was very useful feedback for me, for my own growth and development.'*

Gently coax comments from the appraisee. It will probably take a number of performance discussions to develop enough trust and credibility in the process for appraisees to comment freely on your performance. Do not be discouraged if you don't get quality comments the first few times. Stick at it, because it will reap results eventually.

CHECK YOUR UNDERSTANDING

23 What is the purpose of discussing performance generally at the beginning of the performance discussion?

24 Why might job accountabilities and responsibilities shift between appraisals?

25 Why is it necessary to be specific with feedback?

26 What might you do if appraisees cannot back up their performance claims with evidence?

27 Why is it desirable for there to be an agreed assessment of the performance between appraiser and appraisee?

28 Explain the strategy you would use if the appraisee kept avoiding an issue you wanted to discuss.

29 How would you use the appraisee's development plan during the next review period?

SKILLS PRACTICE

1   In groups of two, practise listening and summarising, with one person telling a personal story while the other one listens. When the first person has finished telling the story, the second person summarises the story and asks the first person for confirmation. You may not take notes during this activity. The activity should take about three minutes each time. Discuss how it went and what improvements could be made. How did each participant feel during the activity?

2   In groups of two, practise giving feedback to each other. The first person will talk about some of the highlights and accomplishments in their life while the other listens. The second person will give positive feedback to the first person during the discussion. This activity should take about five minutes. Discuss how it went and what improvements could be made. How did each participant feel during the activity?

3   In groups of three, perform the role play set out below. Elect one person as the observer; the remaining two play the appraiser and the appraisee. You will role-play only that part of the discussion that deals with the review of performance against objectives and negotiates assessment. Spend about 20 minutes preparing the role play and about 15 minutes conducting it.

Both Anita and Reba work for a large accounting firm. Anita is a middle-level manager in the firm and Reba is Anita's secretary. The performance objectives to be dealt with are:

a   Reduce the number of daily interruptions to the appraiser from 10 per day to 4 per day by 30 June XXXX.

b   Increase the number of graphics used in overhead presentations from none to at least one every two slides, using Microsoft PowerPoint, by 30 September XXXX.

c   Increase the number of draft replies to inward correspondence from 15% to 50% of total inwards correspondence by 31 May XXXX.

d   Maintain filing at the level of all items filed within three days of receipt or creation by 30 December XXXX.

Anita

Select one objective that you think Reba has not performed satisfactorily. Identify several possible causes for the unsatisfactory performance. Develop evidence to support your contention and evidence to support satisfactory performance on the other three objectives. During the role play you are to press your point firmly, as you believe there is adequate evidence to support your beliefs.

Reba

Select one objective that you think you have not performed satisfactorily. Identify some possible causes for the unsatisfactory performance. Develop evidence to support your contention and evidence to support satisfactory performance on the other three objectives. During the role play you are to defend yourself firmly, as you believe there is adequate evidence to support your beliefs. At some stage during the discussion you should burst into tears.

The observer should use the following checklist to assist in providing feedback to the role players.

❑ Anita and Reba review the objective/standard together.

❑ Reba is asked to comment on the actual performance.

❑ Reba is asked for evidence to support the claim if it has not been provided in the comments above (this applies equally to satisfactory and unsatisfactory performance).

SKILLS PRACTICE CONTINUED

❑ Anita provides comments on the performance and supplies the evidence to support the claim (this applies equally to satisfactory and unsatisfactory performance).

❑ They discuss their different views (if they are different) and explore what the differences are, why they exist, and the difference in the evidence presented (if there is a difference).

❑ Together they decide on what the assessment of the performance will be. If they cannot agree on the assessment, Anita will have the final say in the matter.

❑ The decision is recorded.

At the end of the role play discuss the observer's comments and how both Anita and Reba felt about the discussion. What went well in the role play? What went wrong? Were appropriate strategies used? How could it be improved?

Change roles and repeat the role play until all three members of the group have taken a turn in each role.

SKILL AND KNOWLEDGE APPLICATION

TASK

➤ Research and develop a list of possible development activities and tasks other than training for use as a general resource.

➤ Using the performance appraisal discussion framework, develop a 'Code of Appraisal' for use in your organisation that sets out the principles of best-practice appraisal discussions.

➤ Create a development plan for yourself for the next 12 months. This can relate to personal, work or social goals.

C. Summarise

Finally, you approach the end of the discussion. Both parties should be feeling comfortable with the discussion by this time and be ready to wind up the process. It is not appropriate to say 'Okay, that's done. Thanks very much' and end the discussion. If the performance discussion has been conducted skilfully, a great deal of talking and soul searching will have been done. Ending the discussion abruptly may undo all the motivation and goodwill you have created. Wind up the discussion with care and ensure there is a full understanding of what has happened and what is expected of both parties in the future.

Summarising is a six-stage process that you should work through at a steady pace. The stages are set out below, together with the actions associated with each stage.

1. Verify understanding

Both appraiser and appraisee should have a joint understanding of the discussion, and a good way to check understanding is to review the discussion. This does not mean that you start it all over again, or argue points already decided. You simply summarise what has been agreed on each of these five points.

1 Review the accomplishments.

2 Review the performance against standards/objectives.

3   Review the development plan.

4   Review specific actions agreed to by both parties.

5   Review the new standards/objectives.

If you find there is any confusion as you work through the summary of points, clear it up immediately so that you both know exactly what has been decided. There may have been times when your appraisee did not agree with you and you had to impose a decision. This summary process does not suggest that you reopen these items for discussion. The review is to check that you both have a similar understanding of what has taken place so that there will be no misunderstandings about what actions and level of performance are expected during the next review period.

2. Complete any necessary documentation

Fill in any necessary forms. You will often be required to give an overall rating of the appraisee's performance for the review period. This should be done in the presence of appraisees so that they can see what you have written. Where required, you both sign the appropriate areas of the appraisal form and you ensure that appraisees have a copy to take away with them.

3. Agree on follow-up actions and dates

Agree on and ensure that the follow-up actions and dates for completion of actions are clearly understood. Carefully document who is to do what and make sure that meetings and other important dates and times are entered in diaries before you leave the discussion room.

4. Congratulate appraisees on their successes

Use the final moments of the discussion to reinforce the accomplishments of appraisees. This should motivate them to achieve their agreed standards/objectives for the next period and make them feel good about themselves.

5. Encourage appraisees in their development plans

No appraisees are perfect. So, while reinforcing their accomplishments, you must remind them about their development plans. This, too, is meant to motivate them. You need to promise support and assistance to help them achieve their objectives, reinforce the need for continuous improvement and emphasise the satisfaction that comes from seeing the improvement. You do not remind them of their failures or unsatisfactory performance, but reinforce development so that the mood is uplifting and gives appraisees a sense of purpose.

6. Thank appraisees for the effort they put into the process

Finally, thank appraisees for attending the discussion and for putting the required effort into the preparation and the discussion itself. Let them know that you look forward to working with them through the next review period and reinforce the point that you are willing to help whenever they need assistance.

CHECK YOUR UNDERSTANDING

30 Why is it necessary to verify understanding of the performance discussion?

31 How might you document the follow-up actions and dates?

32 What form might your encouragement take when encouraging appraisees with their development plans?

33 How does summarising the performance discussion motivate appraisees?

34 What is the purpose of formally thanking appraisees for the effort they put into the process?

SKILLS PRACTICE

In groups of two, practise thanking an appraisee for his/her active participation in the appraisal discussion. Remember, it must sound sincere or it will feel uncomfortable and destroy the trust built up in the discussion.

SKILL AND KNOWLEDGE APPLICATION

TASK

- In groups of four or five, brainstorm the possible consequences—for the appraisee, the appraiser and the organisation—of not verifying understanding at the end of the performance discussion.
- In groups of four or five, look back over the framework for the discussion and explain why appraisees should be motivated if the appraiser has conducted a performance discussion skilfully.
- If you have been appraised in your current job or a previous job, identify what process was used and compare it with the process in this chapter. What was different about the two processes used? If this framework had been used, do you think you would have learned more about yourself and the job? Why, or why not?
- From your own experience, say why performance appraisals may not be effective.

Stage 4—Following up the discussion

This is the final stage of the discussion model and one that is often forgotten by both appraisees and appraisers. Without follow-up there might as well not be a performance discussion, because nothing will change. In this stage, as with many of the other stages, both appraisee and appraiser have responsibilities. The appraiser needs to manage this process just as effectively as the other stages in ensuring that the performance management system works effectively. To facilitate this you may also need to make appraisees aware of their responsibilities in the follow-up stage.

Appraiser

1 Do what you said you were going to do. Make sure that you provide access to resources or time to achieve goals, targets and training if you have promised to do so.

2   Schedule regular follow-ups to see how appraisees are going with their development plans. These do not have to be formal affairs but they do need to be entered in your diary so they are not forgotten. You should aim to have a semi-formal review midway through the review period. This helps keep everything on track.

3   Provide adequate and regular feedback on performance so that appraisees know how they are doing. This can be formal or informal.

4   Provide opportunities for appraisees to discuss how they are going if they feel the need to.

Appraisee

1   Do what you said you were going to do.

2   Take responsibility for your own development and pursue every developmental opportunity you can. You need to organise your developmental activities in line with your development plan.

3   Ask for regular feedback from your manager. Communicate regularly with your manager about your performance and your standards/objectives.

4   Review your own performance regularly against your standards/objectives.

Problems in performance appraisal

Performance appraisals are full of potential problems. The processes discussed in this chapter may help to reduce some of the problems but you must still be aware of many others that could sabotage your performance discussion and make things difficult for you and the appraisee. Problems associated with the analysis of performance are discussed in Chapter 7 and they are also relevant to the performance discussion. Other problems that you need to watch out for in the performance discussion are listed below.

1   *Generalisations.* Avoid generalising: use specific evidence and concrete examples of the kind of performance you are talking about. Generalising will create a lack of trust in the appraisee.

2   *Defensive behaviour by appraisees.* Using the strategies discussed in this chapter should preclude this behaviour. If it does happen, pause and rethink the strategy you are using. You may have to deal directly with the defensive behaviour rather than use strategies to work around it. Only you will know the particular circumstances of the discussion and the best way to proceed.

3   *Changing criteria for evaluating performance.* Problems occur where the performance standards/objectives have not been set or agreed on before the performance appraisal takes place. Each time performance is discussed, the standards seem to change because they are not agreed on or recorded. This makes it difficult for the appraisee to perform at the required standard, because it is constantly changing. To avoid this problem, always set performance standards/objectives with appraisees and record them.

4   *Personal bias.* When appraising someone's performance there is no place for personal bias, whether it's in the form of how you would like to see the job done, the type of clothes you would prefer to see the appraisee wear, the attitude of the appraisee, or his/her personal

career background. The best way to reduce personal bias in performance appraisals is to prepare well, to have specific examples of the performance you wish to discuss, and to evaluate the *performance of the job*, not the individual person holding the job.

5   *Loss of credibility.* If you do not conduct the discussion professionally and skilfully, you may lose credibility and trust in the eyes of the appraisee. Your best protection against this is to prepare well and practise the skills required as outlined in this chapter.

6   *No preparation for the future.* As discussed earlier, a performance appraisal is based·on using the past as a starting point to plan the future. Many appraisals are not successful because they fail to plan for the future and thus to motivate the appraisee. Following the steps and the strategies in this chapter will help avoid this pitfall.

7   *Managing conflict.* You must be able to manage conflict if it arises in the course of the appraisal discussion; otherwise, the discussion will not be helpful to appraiser or appraisee. If you feel you are not in control of the discussion, suggest to the appraisee that you both have a break and resume later. If necessary, allow a couple of days to elapse while you plan a strategy, then resume in a few days. Alternatively, you may have to put that particular issue to one side and deal with it later at another meeting, outside the appraisal discussion.

Adopting a systematic approach to the preparation, conduct and follow-up of a performance discussion is the best way to avoid problems.

CONCLUSION

To maximise the benefits of performance appraisals, the appraiser and appraisee need interpersonal and communication skills that enable them to participate fully and manage the performance discussion. A lack of the appropriate skills in either party—but especially in the appraiser, who must facilitate the process—can sabotage the appraisal and render it ineffective. Feedback is required by appraisees on a regular basis, not just at the once-a-year formal review. If appraisees are not receiving quality feedback throughout the review period, performance is not being monitored adequately by the manager.

The performance appraisal is a four-stage process: setting up the discussion, then preparation (both covered in Chapter 8), the appraisal discussion itself, and, finally, the follow-up (covered in this chapter). This framework helps to ensure that nothing falls through the cracks and that the appraisal is as comprehensive and professional as possible. Both appraisers and appraisees have responsibilities at each stage of the appraisal and must carry out these responsibilities in full if the appraisal is to be a useful and effective process. Adequate time and effort must be invested by both parties for the process to work effectively. Managers can anticipate and prepare for many of the problems that arise in performance appraisals. Appropriate preparation, and well-developed interpersonal and cross-cultural communication skills, are the keys to successful performance appraisals.

'REAL LIFE' CASE STUDY

The following case study describes how a large company integrates the use of values into its performance management system. The case study also describes how the performance management system is successfully used to identify and develop potential leaders in preparation for succession planning.

Boral Limited is Australia's largest building and construction materials supplier. They operate in Australia, the USA and Asia, and have over 14 700 employees working across 717 operating sites. Boral comprises seven key operating divisions, aligned along three business segments. Its strategic intent is to be a values-driven and market-driven building and construction materials supplier operating in Australia and increasingly offshore; its overriding objective is to 'achieve superior returns in a sustainable way' in a financial, social and environmental sense.

The performance management system has essentially three steps: first, setting objectives; second, identifying values and career development; and third, managing performance. Values are used to guide both corporate and personal behaviour across all levels of the organisation. The values of leadership, respect, focus, performance and persistence are underpinned and supported by a comprehensive performance management system which ensures employees have work and behavioural objectives based on the corporate values. These values are referred to in the company's strategic intent to reinforce their ongoing importance in Boral, and are incorporated into each employee's annual performance review to assess behaviour or workplace style and effectiveness. Examples of expected behaviour are provided for managers to ensure a common understanding of Boral's values across the organisation. The values being demonstrated by employees are questioned twice annually via the performance management system, and, along with meeting objectives, can affect employee pay increases.

These values are also promulgated through Boral's leadership programs including the Executive Development Program (EDP) designed for senior managers, the Emerging Leader Program designed for high performing emerging leaders, the Management Development program and the Frontline Leadership Development Program. All development programs are designed to identify, grow and retain potential first, middle and senior managers. Boral has developed innovative approaches to leadership development, such as Outward Bound experiences and using learning and development program to tackle important business issues.

Boral has positioned the EDP as a prestigious program targeting candidates earmarked as high-potential performers. Other strategies that reinforce this reputation include a rigorous selection process, proactive efforts to obtain organisational buy-in, and the proven track record of the program to deliver tangible improvements to the business.

Candidates for the program are selected through 'calls for nominations', completion of an 'employee estimate of potential' and personal invitation. The feedback of managers, an assessment of the potential of the candidate and their most senior likely position in the organisation, and their personal commitment are also taken into account. Acceptance into the program is a positive reflection of both the candidate's contributions to date and the confidence of others in their ability to deliver in the future. For many employees, this is an opportunity to showcase what they are capable of and what they are able to achieve when given the opportunity.

All the EDP development outcomes are intended to transform the learning experience into demonstrated leadership behaviours and competencies that reflect the core values and strategic intent. There are two major processes incorporated into the EDP that ensure participants apply what they learn to real-life situations. These are the action learning projects and the inclusion of a Boral-specific case study.

Boral uses succession planning to identify talent and future leaders. The process involves assessing employees' estimated potential and helping them to manage their career development across the organisation. Boral conducts a formal succession planning process focused on managerial and leadership positions on a regular basis. Identifying potential at more senior levels takes place every two years. This enables Boral to identify talent and future leaders and develop their leaders through aligning individual development plans with participation in Boral's Leadership Development programs and providing opportunities for internal promotion.

The careful and methodical approaches Boral takes to succession planning enables managers and leaders to support Boral's strategic direction and any related change management strategies.

References

Benchmarking Partnerships 2009. *Leadership Development Framework*, <www.benchmarkingpartnerships. com.au/w_LDF8Sept.htm>

Boral Limited 2002. *Boral's Key Programs*, <www.boral.com.au/HR/borals_key_programs.asp>

Boral Limited 2002. *Organisational Structure*, <www.boral.com.au/corporate/organisational_structure.asp>

Boral Limited 2008. *Boral Limited Sustainability Report 2008*, <www.boral.com.au/Images/common/ pdfs/2008_Report_Sust.pdf>

Boral Limited 2009. *Boral Limited 2009 EOWA Employer of Choice for Women*, <www.eowa.gov.au/ EOWA_Employer_of_Choice_for_Women/2009/Documents%20for%20media%20page/BORAL.pdf>

Human Resources Leader 2004. *Balancing Executive Development: the Boral Approach*, <www.hrleader. net.au/articles/14/0c01f114.asp>, 2 April.

Telephone interview with Michael Craner, General Manager, Learning and Organisational Development, Boral Limited, 14 August 2009.

QUESTIONS

1 Explain how the use of corporate values can contribute to effective performance management.
2 Identify three potential challenges for an organisation in establishing core values.

References

1 Redman, T., Snape, E. & McElwee, G. 1993. 'Appraising employee performance: A vital organisational activity.' *Education and Training*, 35(2), pp. 3–10; Screwvalla, Z.S. 1988. 'Performance appraisals: A framework for effective implementation.' *Management Update*, October, pp. 6–7, 17–18.

2 Adapted from Mayer, R. & Pipe, P. 1990, 2nd edn. *Analysing Performance Problems*. Kogan Page: London p. 1; Laird, D. 1985, 2nd edn. *Approaches to Training and Development*. Addison-Wesley: Reading, MA, p. 99.

3 Adapted from Dessler, G., Griffiths, J. & Lloyd-Walker, B. 2007, 3rd edn. *Human Resource Management*. Pearson Australia: Frenchs Forest, Sydney, p. 336; Jones, R. 2009, 2nd edn. *HRM Fundamentals*, Pearson Australia: Frenchs Forest, Sydney, pp. 377–381.

4 Johnson, D. & Johnson, F. 1991. *Joining Together: Group Theory and Group Skill*. Prentice Hall: Englewood Cliffs, NJ, p. 394.

5 Dove, P. & Brown, S. 1993. 'Issues for appraisal.' *Education and Training*, 35(2), pp. 16–19.

6 Cole, K. 2010, 4th edn. *Management: Theory and Practice*. Pearson Australia: Frenchs Forest, Sydney, p. 582.

JOB AIDS

The performance discussion model

Stage 1 Starting up the discussion	Stage 2 Preparing for the discussion	Stage 3 The discussion	Stage 4 The follow-up
Venue	**Appraiser** 12-step model	**Part A** Set the climate	**Appraiser**
Interruptions	**Appraisee** 7-step model	**Part B** The discussion	**Appraisee**
Appointments		**Part C** Summarise	
Instructions			

Performance appraisal

Company logo

Employee name:	
Employee title:	
Supervisor:	
Period of appraisal:	From: To:

Before you begin

To make the most of this performance appraisal process, you need to:

- be aware of the company's objectives and what you have to do to help achieve them
- set clear, concise and meaningful goals with your supervisor
- set goals that are measurable and challenging
- identify and discuss with your supervisor any training and development you need to be effective in your role, and for your future development and career aspirations.

To assist you in the workplace, this Job Aid is reproduced on the accompanying CD located in the back of this book

Steps in the performance appraisal process

1. Your supervisor will make an appointment with you to discuss your performance for the period of the appraisal (this could be 3, 6 or 12 months), monitor how you are going against the goals set from the previous period, and set new goals for the next appraisal period.
2. Your supervisor will have reviewed your stated performance against your actual performance for the appraisal period and will have considered future goals for you.
3. At your performance appraisal, your supervisor will discuss with you your performance and then rate and comment on your performance.
4. You will be required to comment on your own performance for each of the criteria discussed by your supervisor.
5. Discuss and understand the company's goals for the next appraisal period, your supervisor's goals, and how these goals will assist the company to meet its objectives.
6. Discuss, set, agree on and document goals for your next appraisal period—both you and your supervisor should keep a copy of these goals.
7. Discuss the training and development that will help you to achieve these goals. In addition, set out your future training and development needs in a development plan that will help you achieve your career aspirations.
8. Both you and your supervisor should sign off on the performance appraisal and agreed development plan.

Evaluation of performance goals for the review period

Record the agreed goals for last year in the Goals column and review performance jointly with your supervisor. Your supervisor will record his/her comments and rating for each goal. Goals should be linked to the overall company mission, vision and, more specifically, the critical success factors (CSFs).

Goals	Evaluation comments	Rating

 **JOB AIDS** CONTINUED

Performance goals for the next review period

After discussion between you and your supervisor, set and agree on your goals for the next review period. Goals should be linked to the overall company mission, vision and, more specifically, the critical success factors (CSFs).

Goal	Measure

Performance appraisal rating

Place an X in the Overall Rating column which corresponds with the most relevant rating.		Overall rating
Outstanding results	Exceptional performance against job criteria. Exceptional contribution.	
Exceeds expectations	Exceeded job standards for all goals. Contributed to team success.	
Meets expectations	Met the required performance for all or most goals. Guidance may have been required for complex goals.	
New in role	Less than 6 months in role. Successful completion of some job goals.	
Improvement required	Several goals not completed to required standard. Ongoing coaching of performance required. Performance improvement required to retain current role.	
Performance issues	Few or no goals completed leading to major shortfall in performance. Performance improvement plan needs to be initiated immediately.	

Employee comments:	
Signed:	**Dated:**

Supervisor comments:	
Signed:	**Dated:**

Development plan

Employee name:	Employee Title:
Supervisor name:	Supervisor Title:

Development need	Action required	Date
e.g. Tertiary studies to support role	Complete university degree	December XXXX

Employee signature:	Dated:
Supervisor signature:	Dated:

✔ CHECKLISTS

Characteristics of an effective discussion

- ❑ A clear set of performance standards for the work area and for individuals
- ❑ Accurate two-way communication between staff members and manager
- ❑ Widespread distribution, participation and leadership among staff members
- ❑ The use of consensus to arrive at answers, solutions and decisions
- ❑ Power and influence based on expertise, access to information and social skills, not on the authority of the manager
- ❑ The frequent occurrence of controversy within the section managed by the manager
- ❑ The open confrontation and negotiation of conflicts of interest among staff members and between staff members and the manager
- ❑ High cohesiveness between manager and staff members
- ❑ High trust between manager and staff members
- ❑ A climate of acceptance and support between manager and staff members
- ❑ A climate of individual responsibility and accountability, helping and sharing, and achievement between manager and staff
- ❑ A high level of interpersonal skills in both parties

Discussion model

- ❑ Stage 1—Setting up the discussion
  - ❑ Venue
    - ❑ Seating
    - ❑ Papers
    - ❑ Office
    - ❑ Book
  - ❑ Interruptions
    - ❑ Mobiles and pagers
    - ❑ Telephone on message
  - ❑ Appointments
    - ❑ One month's notice
    - ❑ Fixed in diary
    - ❑ Maximum two per day
  - ❑ Instructions
    - ❑ Process
    - ❑ Instructions
    - ❑ Housekeeping
- ❑ Stage 2—Preparing for the discussion
  - ❑ What is the job?
  - ❑ What evidence demonstrates performance?
  - ❑ What does the analysis show?
  - ❑ Why was performance excellent?
  - ❑ Why was performance satisfactory?
  - ❑ Why was performance unsatisfactory?
  - ❑ What needs to be addressed in the discussion?
  - ❑ What strategic/organisational planning impacts are there?
  - ❑ What performance is required in the future?
  - ❑ What changes need to be made?
  - ❑ What development needs to be planned?
  - ❑ How do I run the discussion?

CHECKLISTS CONTINUED

❑ **Stage 3—The discussion**
  ❑ A. Set the climate
    ❑ Physical dimension
    ❑ Process dimension
    ❑ Psychological dimension
  ❑ B. The central discussion
    ❑ Discuss performance generally
    ❑ Review the job, accountabilities and responsibilities
    ❑ Discuss major achievements in the job during the period under review
    ❑ Review performance against objectives and negotiate assessment
    ❑ Develop improvement plans
    ❑ Appraise the appraiser
  ❑ C. Summarise
    ❑ Verify understanding
    ❑ Complete documentation
    ❑ Agree on follow-up plans and actions
    ❑ Congratulate appraisees on their successes
    ❑ Encourage appraisees in their development plans
    ❑ Thank appraisees
❑ **Stage 4—The follow-up**
  ❑ Appraiser
  ❑ Appraisee

CHAPTER TEN

Improving performance

Learning outcomes

After reading this chapter you should be able to:

* describe the role of improving performance in the performance management system
* explain why planning and development are the most important features of a performance management system
* state where the greatest opportunity for performance improvement lies
* explain why pinpointing the causes of a performance problem is necessary in relation to a performance improvement plan
* explain how Chapters 1–9 relate to this chapter
* draw a performance improvement model
* explain the difference between development and non-development needs
* explain the reasons why strategies for improvement need to be selected carefully
* describe the role of resources in an improvement plan
* construct a performance improvement plan in accordance with the model provided.

This chapter explores the process of planning and implementing improved performance. To a large extent, all the other chapters in the book have led to this chapter. The work you have done in Part A, and in setting standards, monitoring performance, analysing and appraising it, lead to this outcome: how to improve performance. Performance improvement is the goal of managing performance. The reason for conducting performance appraisals is to plan individual future performance and identify areas for improvement. Performance does not need to be unsatisfactory to enable performance improvement to be planned. To survive, organisations must be continuously improving their performance.

This chapter could have been included in Chapter 9 as part of the performance discussion model. However, this model is so important that only an introduction to the process of improving performance was included there. The initial questions to be answered were posed in Chapter 9, but this chapter goes into more detail on how you go about improving performance, and walks you through the establishment and implementation of a performance improvement plan.

Performance and performance improvement

Despite the importance of improving performance, research and practitioner evidence suggests that this area of performance management is rarely managed.[1] While all performance appraisal forms include a section for development, there is very little action on this section of the form: it appears to be ignored once the appraisal is over. This is alarming. You will recall Figure 8.6 in Chapter 8, which demonstrated that planning and development activities accounted for two-thirds of the total appraisal process. Development itself accounted for one-third of the process. Planning and development are the most important features of the performance management system. Without them, future performance is in doubt and little if any improvement will be generated. Performance improvement in human behaviour needs to be as well planned, for example, when organisations choose to boost market share, move to a new IT operating system or reduce costs. Figure 10.1 extends the concept in Figure 8.6 to demonstrate the relationship between planning and development and future performance.

FIGURE 10.1 Relationship of performance improvement to future performance

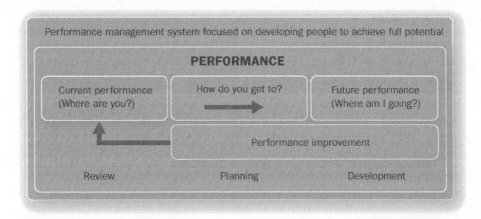

Where performance improvement is not planned and implemented, thus assisting staff and teams to reach more of their potential, the performance management system is again sabotaged. The credibility, validity and reliability of the system falter because the system is marketed to staff as one that focuses on developing people to their full potential. If managers fail to implement development activities, people do not grow and, from the staff point of view, nothing changes as a result of participating in the performance management system. Consequently, the system may have the effect of reducing performance. While the responsibility for the implementation of development activities should be a joint one between the manager and staff or teams, it is management's responsibility to ensure that it actually happens. It is an integral part of managing.

The key

The key question to be answered at this stage of the performance management system is 'How can performance be improved?' All the previous stages of the system, dealt with in previous chapters, have prepared the way to answer this question. The degree of evidence collection, analysis and appraisal has been intense and thorough to meet the immediate needs of those processes, and also to provide enough in-depth understanding of the performance and its associated problems to facilitate the planning of development activities. The depth of the investigations conducted in previous chapters has ensured that you have a solid understanding of performance and, more importantly, of what has caused the specific performance. It is only by understanding what caused the performance you have recorded that you can plan effective performance improvement strategies. You may recall that assuming the wrong cause for a particular performance will have significant consequences on the overall performance of the organisation. This is because if you are trying to push performance further where performance has been satisfactory, you may falsely assume that certain variables have influenced the performance. In this case you will expend resources to bring about a specific level of performance in others but it will have no effect, and valuable resources will have been wasted for no return.

The same is true where there has been unsatisfactory performance. If you wrongly conclude that certain variables influenced the performance and you address these, the performance will not change because you are manipulating variables that have no bearing on the performance. You cannot plan improvement unless you know exactly what the current situation is and what caused it. In many ways the key question 'How can performance be improved?' unlocks future performance and the potential of individuals and teams. Where future performance is not unlocked there is no development in individuals. Locks are usually not within individuals; they are external influences operating on the individual.

No quick fixes

There is as much effort required for planning and implementing development as there is for other stages of the performance management system. You will have gathered by now that there are no quick fixes. Yet researchers and practitioners in the field are finding that the most common responses to people problems exposed by the analysis of performance are focused on quick fixes. For example, Rummler and Brache suggest six common responses that clearly assume the performance problem lies with the individual or team.[2] These are:

1   Train them.
2   Transfer them.

3 Coach and counsel them.

4 Threaten them.

5 Discipline them.

6 Replace them.

It is unlikely that any of these will solve a performance problem for the organisation unless the problem is actually one that is attributable to a lack of skills or knowledge in an individual or team. In fact, Rummler and Brache suggest that 80% of performance improvement opportunities lie in the environment (referred to in this book as 'context') rather than with individuals.[3] Studies have found that only 15% of performance problems were attributable to individuals, with 85% being management problems.[4] (For a discussion on the role of context, see Chapters 6 and 7.)

Protecting the integrity of the performance management system

If improved performance were related to punishment or the amount of training an individual received, there would be no need for this book because very few performance problems would exist. From the management literature we know that managers often exhibit the reaction documented by Rummler and Brache—that is, they look for the quick fix. This may, in part, explain why so many performance management systems fail. The literature also shows that managers have little under-standing or training in identifying the true causes of performance and thus the appropriate strategy to select to improve performance. Clearly, if staff are being identified as the performance problem while real and quantifiable problems that constrain individual performance exist in the context of performance, there will be no change in performance. Further, staff will be aware of the context problems and become cynical about the true value of managing performance, and about manage-ment's commitment to the ideals espoused when introducing a performance management system.

There is some cause for hope, however. Literature suggests that change is beginning to occur. Organisations in the public and private sectors are embracing the benefits of systematic appraisal and diagnoses in the development of staff.[5] It is unlikely that great change will be achieved unless managers receive appropriate training and development in order to build the necessary skills and knowledge and to practise them in managing performance improvement. This process is illustrated in Figure 10.2.

FIGURE 10.2 Contextual constraints on performance

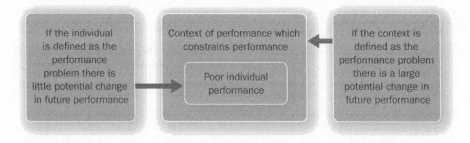

CHECK YOUR UNDERSTANDING

1 Why is improving performance an important part of the performance management system?
2 What is the relationship between monitoring, analysing and appraising performance, and improving performance?
3 According to research, where do most of the performance improvement opportunities lie?
4 What do managers need in order to facilitate performance improvement?
5 What may be one of the reasons for the failure of performance management systems?
6 What may be the possible consequences of misdiagnosing a performance problem?

All organisations are faced with the question of how to improve performance to remain competitive in the global market in which we now operate. Human performance contributes to the wider issue of organisational performance. You have seen the many influences that act on individual performance, including the planning and management of the organisation, the context in which performance occurs, and the resources with which individuals must work. You will reap improved performance only in line with the effort expended in tracking the cause of performance and then selecting appropriate strategies on which to base improvement plans.

Monitoring, analysing and appraising performance

Performance monitoring, analysing and appraising form the basis on which you develop and implement performance improvement plans. Without the evidence of current performance you cannot analyse the performance and the causes of it. Without appropriately detailed analysis you are unable to make appraisals of performance that identify where performance improvement is needed. Figure 10.3 demonstrates how Chapters 1–10 are interrelated.

Chapters 6, 7, 8 and 9 provide the base data, analysis and appraisal of performance which, in turn, pave the way for you to make a decision on the level of performance after consultation with the job performer. The analysis and appraisal of the evidence also provide a starting point for the performance development plan, together with the future requirements of the organisation, which are distilled from the plans and strategies that are the subject of Chapters 1, 2 and 3. Finally, appropriate development objectives are written (Chapters 4 and 5) and the process is monitored again. If the work you have done so far is faulty in some way, your performance improvement plans are unlikely to result in better performance. This has consequences in litigation: if you hold someone accountable for performance and do not provide them with the appropriate resources or development activities after having identified them, it will be very difficult to defend your position if you endeavour to take action against the individual for non-performance. To preclude this possibility, a model for performance improvement is presented below.

FIGURE 10.3 Relationship of Chapters 1–10

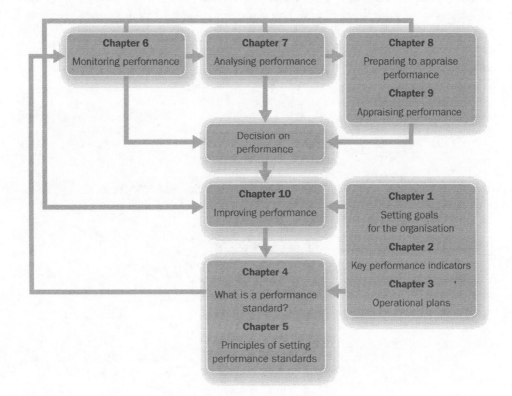

A performance improvement model

The performance improvement model reorganises the data you have already collected and analysed to focus on what and how development needs to be planned. The model is designed so that it can be used as a stand-alone process (Figure 10.4). That is, if you need to identify development requirements during an appraisal cycle in which you have not analysed and appraised data, the model will guide you through the process. Where you have already analysed and appraised, all you need to do is locate the information. The first steps of the model return you to previous chapters if you have not already analysed and appraised performance.

Step 1 Identify gaps and needs

If you use this model after appraising a staff member or team, you have probably already identified the performance gaps. You may not have looked at what the job performer needs to be able to do to meet the organisation's objectives for the next performance cycle. Here you should identify what development the individual or team needs in order to be able to achieve the work unit objectives for the next cycle. For example, if new technology will be introduced, you need to identify the training that will be required so it can be scheduled and budgeted for. If jobs are likely to change through a restructure, you need to identify how individual jobs might change and to begin preparation for this. If there is to be a change of focus from customer service to cost reduction, what new knowledge do staff need? Will new manuals or job aids be necessary to help them focus on cost reduction? Do you need to give a presentation to all staff in your work unit? These are just a few of the questions you need to ask to ensure that you have identified all new requirements of staff and teams for the next cycle period.

FIGURE 10.4 A performance improvement model

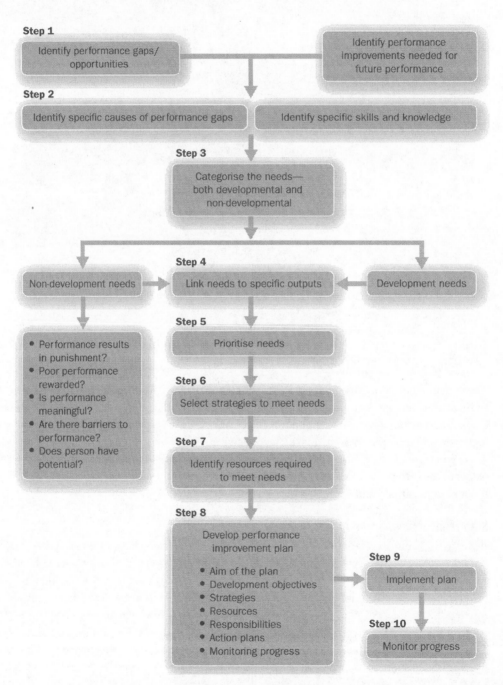

Where an individual or team is not performing for some reason, and you identify this through monitoring during the cycle, it will be necessary to begin this process from scratch. Analyse the performance using the strategies discussed in Chapter 7. Appraise performance with the strategies given in Chapters 8 and 9. After making a decision about the current level of performance, you will have a clear indication of the performance problem and where the performance gaps are. You may recall from Chapters 8 and 9 that it is necessary to have a clearly defined statement of the problem to enable you to understand the cause. The following questions may help you identify where performance needs to be improved:

- What are the performance gaps?
- Where might performance be improved?
- Why should performance be improved?
- What are the benefits of the improved performance?
- What might be the specific outcomes of improved performance?
- Will the outcomes contribute to the overall performance of the organisation? How?
- What improvements are needed to meet future performance requirements?
- What changes will occur in the next performance management cycle that may demand improved performance or changes to performance?
- What new challenges is the work unit likely to face in the next cycle?
- How will the challenges affect the performance requirements of the individuals or teams in the work unit?

The answers to these questions will provide a high-level view of the need for performance improvement. There may be other industry-specific or occupation-specific questions that you could add to this list. When intervening in situations of poor performance during a cycle, the answers will also point to what needs to be looked at in developing a performance improvement plan. Even though you might think you know exactly what is wrong, work through a systematic approach to ensure that you include all possible evidence and the consequences. Jumping into the problem as you see it may enable you to begin remedial action, but this is not useful to you at the end of the day if it does not improve performance. It is equally useless if you end up in litigation because you are trying to hold people accountable for something that is out of their control.

Once you are satisfied that you have a good understanding of what the performance improvement challenge is, proceed to the next step.

CHECK YOUR UNDERSTANDING

7 How does step 1—identifying gaps and needs—differ from the work you were encouraged to do in the chapters on analysing and appraising performance?

8 Explain how the performance improvement model can be of help to you in improving performance.

Step 2 Record the specific causes of performance gaps and the specific skills/knowledge required for future performance

Step 1 provides an overview of the challenge of improving performance. Step 2 moves on to identify the specific causes of the challenge so that you can decide on possible solutions. It is not sufficient to simply identify the challenges. To bring about performance improvement you must identify the specific causes of the non-performance. In the case of performance gaps, you will need to review the evidence, analysis and appraisal stages in which you identified the causes of non-performance. You will need to do the same for areas in which you identify performance that could be improved. You may also have to review the results of other staff to determine what they are doing that has taken performance to a new level. Where you have identified future performance needs, you will also need to specify the skills and knowledge required by each individual; any new resources they might need, such as an upgrade in computer software; and contextual issues to which attention must be paid.

This step frames the 'problem space' you will need to solve in developing a performance improvement plan. You will notice that a problem-based approach is being used again here, because it has been demonstrated that a problem-based approach facilitates better outcomes and reduces human error. If the development of a performance improvement plan is presented as a problem, a systematic and logical approach to solving the problem can be developed, as shown in Figure 10.4. This contributes to superior, valid outcomes—improved performance.

The breadth of this task is illustrated in Figure 10.5, which depicts the contribution of the work you may already have completed, and how the future plans of the organisation need to be taken into account.

FIGURE 10.5 Breadth of Step 2

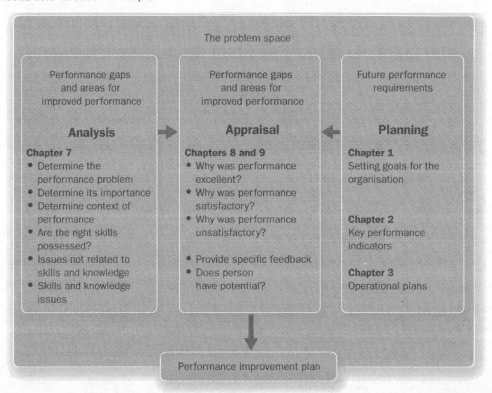

Specificity is the aim in this step. The more specific you can be, the better the performance improvement plan, because it will cover all the requirements for improved performance. This analysis is person-specific or team-specific, so you need to conduct it with all staff and teams reporting to you. Again the cry is heard, 'Where will I get the time to do all this?' If you haven't realised it yet, this is what managers are paid to do. If you are not doing this you are not managing. You may have the title 'manager', but you are not one. It is absurd for managers to claim that they do not have the time to identify performance improvement opportunities, as it is exactly this process that will deliver more time to them. Better performance means increased efficiency and more time for managers to devote to planning and managing people. The following questions will guide you in being specific about improvement opportunities.

- What are the causes of each performance gap?
- What specific improvement opportunities are there?
- What contextual influences are operating on performance?
- What contextual influences are likely to influence performance in the future?
- What new skills are required?
- What new knowledge is required?
- What changes to the workplace are imminent?
- What are the consequences of doing work?
- Do the systems in use support the completion of tasks?
- Are processes as efficient as they might be?
- What customer aids or education might reduce the need for contact between staff and customer?
- Do procedures support the performance levels required?
- Do staff behaviours support the attainment of performance requirements?
- What are the consequences of performing?
- Is feedback to the staff member/team adequate?

Add further questions to this list as you discover a need for them. What you want from this step is a very precise list of things you could do to improve performance. It is not necessary to make decisions about the affordability, practicability or importance of the items on the list in this step.

SKILLS PRACTICE

1   Greg had the performance objective of developing a greenfields mine site in a remote area of Australia in accordance with company guidelines, to be delivered on budget and operational by 30 June XXXX. Greg is a qualified engineer and has had several years in senior management roles, where he has completed several performance objectives similar to this one, on time and on budget. Greg is a competent person, diligent and reliable. It is 3 June and Greg comes to see you to say that it will not be possible to achieve the objective because of obstacles encountered in the remote area of the mining site.

List several questions you would ask Greg to ascertain the extent and cause of the issues blocking completion of the performance objective on time. How will you go about responding to Greg?

2   Taryn is a very experienced traffic controller employed by a large road construction company. She is given the job of controlling traffic at a busy intersection that receives traffic from a major motorway and three other major roads. Each of the three major roads has traffic lights within 200 metres of the intersection Taryn must manage. Her performance standard is to ensure that traffic leaving the motorway does not bank and cause an accident. She is also required to give priority to construction vehicles, ensuring that all traffic stops to allow freedom of movement of all construction traffic. Lastly, she must not allow traffic to bank up past each of the three sets of traffic lights on the three major roads. You are the project supervisor.

You are in an unmarked car and are furious that you have been stuck in traffic just behind a set of lights on one of the three major roads. As you finally approach the intersection that Taryn is managing, you can see that traffic is banked back onto the motorway. You park in a safe place and talk to Taryn.

How should you handle this interaction? What possible causes might be responsible for this performance problem? What solutions might there be?

Step 3 Categorise the needs

Your list from Step 2 will contain development needs for the individual and non-development needs. *Development needs* are defined as those things the individual or team needs to develop as individuals. They are most likely to be knowledge or skills. Knowledge may be needed of a system, procedure, product, software, use of a resource, the operations of the organisation, a section, other jobs, client profiles, customers or the market. Skills are what staff need to perform well in their job. Skills might be required in writing, using software packages, presenting, occupational-specific skills such as marketing or coordinating an area, driving a train, operating plant or machinery, applying complex mathematical calculations, or photography. The exact knowledge and skills required by any individual or team will depend on what they do.

Non-development needs are defined as those things that are not in the control of staff members, or which they cannot act on by themselves. They are external to the individual. Such items may be redesigning jobs, changing work flows, removing barriers to performance, re-engineering systems and procedures, developing or curbing the influence of context where appropriate, making resources available, upgrading equipment and developing feedback systems. These are items in which management must be involved, and they usually affect other job holders as well as having resourcing implications. They are just as important as development needs, but they probably need discussion at management level and will need more time to arrange. This does not mean that non-development needs are placed in a basket and left there. They must form part of the performance improvement plan, and the responsibility is clearly tied to the manager. It should also be noted that where performance is hindered by a failure to tackle non-development needs, the manager must accept responsibility; thus, the individuals' performance may be satisfactory even though they might not have achieved their performance standards or objectives.

Step 4 Link needs to specific outputs

Looking at the lists of development and non-development needs, you must explicitly link the needs to the particular outputs expected when the needs have been addressed. This process acts as a check to verify that the output generated by the individual or team will be an improvement in performance. Where you cannot link an outcome to the need, it is doubtful that any improved performance will occur as a result of meeting the need. Alternatively, the performance improvement may be so slight that it is of negligible impact. Instead, your energy should be directed towards those needs that will provide a discernible impact on performance. In this step you can eradicate those needs that will not contribute significantly to improved performance.

SKILL AND KNOWLEDGE APPLICATION

One of your programmers, Salesh, writes programs for one division of the organisation. Customer service agreements have been negotiated with all internal clients of Information Technology. One of Salesh's performance objectives is 100% of programs to be written within the agreed time frame negotiated with the client, and approved by the systems manager, by 31 December XXXX. It looks as if only 89% of Salesh's programs will meet the performance standards. In identifying the performance gaps and the causes, you discover that the reason that 11% of programs are not meeting the criteria is as a result of clients' inability to reach agreement among their staff. This is something Salesh has no control over. In every case, you have noticed that it is very clear and easy to prove that the delay was caused by the client. In fact, there are memos on file from clients specifically requesting more time to make a decision.

You consider writing into the customer service agreement that clients must finalise the approvals by the agreed date, otherwise the performance agreement is void. While this approach would protect the IT department from criticism, it does not support the organisational goal of providing technology solutions on a just-in-time basis to facilitate external customer service. The need is to increase the number of programs completed on time. However, when linking to the output, you find that demanding that the client meet supplier-driven deadlines is likely to inflame clients and encourage a blame mentality. Additionally, forcing decisions before the client is ready may result in programs that do not meet the client's requirements, and this would have an adverse effect on customer relationships for the organisation. Given the amount of work involved in trying to enforce the proposed action, it does not seem worthwhile. That is, the resulting benefit for the investment means that the solution to the problem is likely to be worse than leaving it alone. Linking the need to increase the number of programs completed from 89% to 100% to the output—100% satisfaction by the client—it is obvious that forcing completion is out of Salesh's control and is likely to result in greater dissatisfaction by the client.

TASK

➤ Analyse the situation and describe how you would manage this performance issue to improve performance.

The example in the following skill and knowledge application demonstrates the steps in the performance improvement model so far.

The Cool-a-Cola bottling company is focused on boosting market share this year. In the manufacturing section this translates to increased production using existing equipment more economically. Look at the following:

SKILL AND KNOWLEDGE APPLICATION   CONTINUED

- *CSF for the organisation:* Boost market share.
- *KPI for manufacturing:* Number of production days lost.
- *Performance objective:* Reduce downtime of bottling plant from 3 working days per month to 2 working days per month by 30 September XXXX.
- *Actual performance:* Downtime has been reduced by half a day to 2.5 days.
- *Performance gap:* One half-day.

Causes of performance

Routine maintenance has been scheduled between shifts. No human error stoppages have occurred, but Cool-a-Cola cannot reduce downtime any further. The remaining half-day of lost production costs results in $39 000 of lost sales and a greater chance of a retailer running out of stock, which would affect market share. Apart from stoppages due to unforeseen breakdown, there are some statistics that demonstrate that the automatic labeller is not performing correctly. An investigation shows that the labels are not peeling off the waxed tape properly, creating automatic shut-offs because the labels get jammed in the roller that applies the labels. A comparison of the label tape with a sample of old label tape reveals that they are different. The manufacturer has changed the label tape without informing Cool-a-Cola. This is contrary to the quality assurance process. Further investigation reveals that fixing this problem could reduce the downtime of the number 3 bottling machine to just 2.2 working days per month, generating another 43 820 Cool-a-Cola packs.

Needs category

This is a non-development need because it does not require the learning of new skills or knowledge by a staff member(s). The analysis of the causes of the performance problem confirms this. All staff are trained in routine maintenance procedures, they are familiar with the quirks of the particular plant they are operating, and no stoppages have been recorded that are due to human error.

Linking of needs to outputs

Reduced downtime in manufacturing leads to a more economical use of plant and greater numbers of product leaving the warehouse and being shipped to customers. Fixing the label tape problem will reduce downtime and have a significant effect on product availability, providing the means by which manufacturing can meet the extra number of orders. There is an explicit link to an outcome—more products with customers—which directly supports the strategy of the organisation.

Review the above example. Assume that, in addition to the label problem, the electrician discovered that the number 3 bottling plant was consistently shorting out and reverting to the automatic cut-in of the emergency generator. He discovered this accidentally. It appeared to be related to the label problem: each time there was a label problem the electrician observed that the bottling plant shorted out. The short would not have been discovered except that the electrician happened to be next to the generator when it started up.

As a manager, you need to analyse the information provided and make a decision on how to improve the performance of the plant. Timing of the decision and rectification of the problem is critical to performance.

TASK

1   Write a list, in order of priority, of what needs to be done to rectify the problem.
2   Given that there is a significant opportunity for improvement in relation to the shorting problem, how would you determine the best course of action to take?
3   Would you deal with the labelling problem and shorting problem separately, or investigate both simultaneously? Explain. (Remember, timing of the solution is critical.)
4   Comment on how the solutions reached in your answers above will assist in achieving the performance objectives set for the KPI of manufacturing and CSF for the organisation.

Step 5 Prioritise needs

Based on the linking of needs to outputs, where does the greatest opportunity for performance improvement lie? To put it another way, which need is most likely to affect performance and which is the least likely? It is doubtful that you will have unlimited resources to meet all needs, and so you must trade off the needs for which there is least likelihood of improved performance against those with the greatest likelihood of success. The needs that have the closest link to outputs ought to be attended to first. This step may not be as simple as it sounds. There will be times when meeting the needs seems to have the same minimal effect on output, and you may require assistance in trying to measure the final output of meeting each need. Remember, you must be aware of the effort and resources invested in attending to needs, and the output must at least match the investment—if not surpass it. There will be times when, legitimately, you decide to leave the need unattended. Costing the development need and the solution is a useful way of deciding on priorities. The cost of the solution should always be at or below that of the problem.

Step 6 Select strategies

Where you are convinced that the effort and investment of resources to meet the identified need will be productive, you need to select the best strategy/strategies to solve the performance problem at hand. Don't worry about what resources are available to fund the exercise, as this consideration comes later. This applies to development needs and non-development needs.

Development needs

Strategies for development needs will be individually focused and will relate to the building of knowledge and/or skills. It is quite likely they will involve training or learning of some type. One of the first decisions to be made is whether the learning should take place on the job or off the job. This will depend on what the need is and whether there are other staff who need to develop the same knowledge and/or skills. When a number of people need the same learning, it may be feasible to deliver off-the-job training in classroom format. However, most learning takes place on the job, and there is research evidence to suggest that this method facilitates greater transfer of knowledge and/or skills.[6] If you are able to arrange learning on the job, the skill is likely to be learned faster and to have specific meaning for the individual, who will be able to see an immediate use for it. It is likely that a number of strategies will be required to provide the depth and breadth of learning required, over a period of time.

On-the-job strategies include:[7]

- coaching
- mentoring
- questioning
- modelling
- demonstration
- practice
- scaffolding and fading
- job aids
- self-paced materials
- study guides
- observation
- special projects
- special short assignments
- delegation.

There are valid reasons for choosing off-the-job training, especially where new technology is being introduced. It makes sense to train as many people as possible at once, so they all learn together and costs are minimised. Even when there is only one individual involved, it may prove too expensive to deal with the issue on the job, or resources may not be available, so sending the individual or team to a training course may be the most appropriate way of providing the knowledge and skills needed. Training courses may be run internally, or there are external courses run by the Australian Institute of Management, TAFE colleges, universities and private providers.

Off-the-job strategies include:[8]

- computer-managed learning
- internal training course
- external training course
- residential training course
- interest groups
- tertiary study
- reading
- discussions
- problem-solving groups
- critical incident analysis
- self-paced materials
- conference.

Non-development needs

Strategies for non-development needs will be as many and varied as the problem that presents itself. They are likely to take up a large slice of your time and effort, as only managers can implement them, and you will often need to discuss the matter with other staff and managers. This is especially the case when work flows need to be changed, equipment updated, barriers removed, punishments for not performing satisfactorily reduced, work made meaningful or software rewritten. While staff members or teams can help out with the process, it is likely to be beyond their authority and so they will require your close support and assistance. Some needs may be met easily and require little of your time, while others could take weeks or months to resolve. You need to factor this into the management of performance of the individual or team concerned so that these people are not treated unfairly as a result of the delay in being able to meet the identified need.

You might also find that you have to develop feedback loops because the need is a lack of useful feedback. Jobs may have to be redesigned to take account of changes in the workplace, new technology, job responsibilities or work flow. You may even want to expand the responsibility of the individuals or teams and their authority level so they can do the job required of them; naturally, this will be accompanied by an increase in accountability. More challenging work may also be assigned to individuals or teams.

As with development needs, do not worry about the resources to meet the need, as this is dealt with in the next step. The most important process in this step is to identify the best solutions to the need that exists.

Step 7 Identify resources required to meet needs

Once you have determined how best to meet the needs identified, you can tackle the question of what resources are required to meet the needs. Resources refer to a whole host of matters that will have an effect on the cost of providing the solution to meet the need. Resources will tend to centre around four areas:

1 *money*—budgets to buy other resources such as people and their time
2 *time*—time to meet the identified need or time for the met need to be consolidated
    —time to practise new skills or new knowledge before an individual or team can apply them

3 *people*—involves identifying the people within your organisation who are in a position to
- coach or mentor others
- provide demonstrations
- agree to new work flows and job redesigns

4 *materials or physical resources*—such as
- updated telephones
- computer equipment or other office equipment
- new desks
- more raw materials
- references
- access to databases, reports, discussion papers, files and training.

All these examples might relate to either development or non-development needs.

When you have identified the resources that need to be harnessed to implement the selected strategies, you should evaluate these against the resources over which you have control. Before proceeding to the next step, you will need to decide whether the chosen strategies can be implemented. It may not be possible to decide this during the performance discussion, or discussion of a particular incident, so you might suggest that you break the discussion and resume in two days' time. By then you will have investigated all the strategies selected and decided whether they can be used. Where a lack of finance, people or other resources prohibits you from implementing that strategy, go to the next best one. It is possible that as a line manager you do not have a complete understanding of the strategies, and it would be a legitimate use of the training and development staff in your organisation to ask them to help. Once you know what can be done and have agreed on it with the staff member or team, proceed to the performance improvement plan.

Step 8 Develop performance improvement plan

The performance improvement plan captures all the information in Steps 1 to 7 and presents the information as a formal written record. The suggested content of a plan is included in this section, but sample forms are not. You will recall from earlier chapters that forms do not make a better performance appraisal or improvement plan. The plan can be written on a piece of A4 paper without the need for any printed forms at all, provided the appropriate elements are included. Suggested content of the plan is included in Figure 10.4.

Aim of the plan

You already know the purpose of a performance improvement plan, and the title is self-explanatory. However, the purpose of each individual or team plan will vary because you are dealing with unique problems. In the aim of the plan, state clearly what problem you are trying to fix. Describe it in detail so that there can be no misunderstanding about what problem the plan is addressing.

You will also need a plan when the problem is one of unsatisfactory performance. Industrial laws require that staff members be offered opportunities to improve before they are dismissed for non-performance. This topic is discussed in Chapter 11. Sample aims might be:

- to reduce the number of processing errors when orders are entered into the system
- to erect a sound barrier between Bernadette and the photocopier

- to improve the reliability of the monthly report
- to maintain the milling of sugar at four tonnes an hour
- to reduce wastage of beer cartons for ZYZ product
- to use five Microsoft applications at an advanced level.

The aim extends naturally from the problem, and you should be able to infer the problem when reading the aim of the performance improvement plan.

Development objectives

In the aim, you record what it is that you and the staff member or team want to achieve. Converting an aim into a performance development objective, using the formula discussed in Chapter 5— **Performance Objective = Result + Measure + Conditions + Time limit**—makes it specific and measurable. It is just as important to have development objectives as it is to have performance objectives. This format is especially useful in cases of unsatisfactory performance, where you want to be very precise about what it is the staff member or team must achieve so you can measure performance improvement. You will want to keep a close eye on the progress of the performance improvement plan to ensure people remain on the right track. A development objective may have a negative effect on attaining performance standards or objectives if staff put more effort into achieving a development objective than a performance objective.

Write only one objective on each A4 page. If you have more than one development objective for an aim, place each objective on a new sheet of paper with the aim repeated at the top of the page. There is a great deal of documentation to record on the sheet, and it will be impossible to fit it all on if you have more than one objective.

Strategies

To maximise learning in individuals and teams in development activities, a number of learning strategies should be selected to develop knowledge and skills. Preferably, they will be on-the-job strategies to legitimise the learning experience. They should be the most suitable for the problem you are trying to rectify. Likewise, a number of strategies should be used for non-development activities. Where possible, don't rely on one person or one solution to solve the problem. The difficulty lies in depending on other people to keep their word and, where the problem is not related to one of their own staff, managers may have to give priority to their own personnel. It is better to identify a number of solutions to non-development problems even though they may not all be perfect answers. At least, if you attempt solutions and keep your staff members or teams informed, you will maintain credibility with your staff and preserve the performance management system. On the performance improvement plan, note the strategies you propose to use and describe them in as much detail as you can (see Step 6).

Resources

Record the resources that will be made available to the staff member or team. Points to follow when recording resources are:

- Ensure that you record the specific time commitment you discussed with your staff or team so that the team do not 'outstay their welcome'.

- Record the budget that the individuals have to spend, and the time frame allowed.

- Time frames will also dovetail into the time frames set for achieving the development objective. For example, time must be allowed to develop necessary skills or knowledge, and this must be reflected in the time frame allowed for achieving the associated performance objective.

- Identify specifically the materials and/or physical resources available to the person to achieve their development objective.

- To ensure that there are no misunderstandings about what the staff member or team has access to or can reasonably request, it is important to list all agreed resources.

- You do not want a staff member to forget about a resource and, as a consequence, not achieve the objective; that will move you into the unsatisfactory performance process discussed in Chapter 11. Development objectives are just as important as performance objectives—in fact, they *enable* performance objectives.

- It is therefore important to monitor progress carefully and not set people up for failure.

Responsibilities

In any performance improvement plan there will be responsibilities that the staff or team must fulfil, and ones that you as the manager must fulfil. The literature is full of examples of managers who failed to meet their agreed responsibilities and thus sabotaged staff attempts to achieve development objectives. Not only is this unforgivable after making a specific agreement, but you cannot then commence unsatisfactory performance proceedings with the staff member. It is now the manager who should be held accountable for unsatisfactory performance. Points essential to managers' responsibilities are:

- Ensure that you do what you say you will.

- If a legitimate reason prevents you from fulfilling your agreed responsibilities, renegotiate them with the staff member.

- Should you be the cause of a staff member not achieving a development objective (and thus performance objectives), you may find you have a litigation to deal with. This will be indefensible if you have ignored your 'contract' with a staff member or team.

- Record the agreed responsibilities for both staff member or team, and manager, on the performance improvement plan.

Action plans

The literature indicates that people tend to write action plans rather well. Action plans should reflect each step that needs to be taken to achieve the development objectives. There will be many steps, using different strategies and different resources. The following points will make monitoring easier for manager and staff member:

- Identify all the actions needed to achieve each performance development objective and record them on the improvement plan.

- You may well need more than one sheet of A4 paper for each objective.

- This process may need to be worked through by the staff member or team; if more time is required, allow them to go away and work on the action plan.

- This is a useful activity because it provides staff with a good overview of what has to be achieved.

- Each action should have a 'completed by' time frame to help staff manage time well in achieving the objective.

- Before staff go to work on the actions, schedule a time to look these over and agree to them. With your wider experience you may be able to pick up potential problems with the action plan, and you may have to guide staff in rewriting sections.

- Once you are satisfied with the action plans and are sure that they do not set staff up for failure, agree to them.

- Ensure that formal monitoring stages are built into the plans and note these in your diary for follow-up, informally and formally.

Monitoring progress

Monitoring the progress of a performance improvement plan is a similar process to that for performance standards or objectives (see Chapter 6). You may need to check on progress more often with development objectives and their action plans, as it is easy to come off the rails with development objectives. Things to look for when monitoring progress are:

- Staff often erroneously believe that they can put off development objectives and action plans if they are busy. A typical problem occurs when using a training course as a strategy: the date arrives but staff believe they are too busy to attend, and do not go. This is not acceptable. Attending the training course is just as important as the day-to-day work.

- If staff have failed to achieve previous performance objectives or standards, the course is absolutely necessary to enable them to do their job and thus becomes more important than day-to-day activities.

Step 9 Implement the plan

Implementation of the performance improvement plan will be guided by what the plan contains and by prevailing workplace circumstances. There will be things that staff or teams must do and things that the manager must do. The plan should be completed before you finish the performance discussion process (see Chapter 9). Remember, you may need time to check the availability of resources, so it might be necessary to break the performance discussion to do this. You will come together again to complete the plan and the performance discussion.

Things to include in the performance improvement plan:

- Make sure there are specific milestones that can be used to monitor progress.

- Expected completion dates for action items will help the staff or team to monitor their own progress and you will be able to diarise informal discussions to check on progress.

- Both manager and staff or team should keep a copy of the improvement plan for ease of reference. The Human Resources department may require a copy for files, but the literature suggests that it is rare for HR departments to do anything with this information so this is not an important function. However, where you have developed a performance improvement plan as a result of unsatisfactory performance, it would be wise to ensure that HR has a copy, as they are the people who will assist you in any formal unsatisfactory performance proceedings. This point is discussed in more depth in Chapter 11.

Make it clear to staff that you expect work on the improvement plan to begin immediately. It is worth scheduling in your diary some follow-up in the first few weeks of the improvement plan to demonstrate support and to check that implementation has begun.

Step 10 Monitor progress

Monitoring is dealt with in detail in Chapter 6. The same principles apply for performance improvement plans. You will need to collect evidence of progress. The most efficient way to do this is to incorporate the development objectives in the performance objective monitoring that you will have to do once the performance discussion is over.

A well-structured performance improvement plan designed to help staff reach their full potential is a necessary tool in managing performance in the workplace. It also facilitates monitoring by making it easier for the manager to check progress at appropriate milestones and to note evidence of how development is progressing, how it is applied, and how improvement is affecting performance on the job. Appraisal without a performance improvement plan is likely to lead to no improvement at all. It is a critical tool in managing unsatisfactory performance and in upholding the validity of any performance management system.

CONCLUSION

A performance improvement plan completes the appraisal process. It applies equally to performance that has been found to be satisfactory, unsatisfactory or exceeding expectations. It is the means by which performance is improved on after each review period. Improvement does not happen by itself, however. The whole of the performance management system requires considerable effort by managers and staff or teams alike, or it will not work. The quality of the monitoring, analysis and appraisal processes will be reflected in the quality of the perfomance improvement plan. The plan will be made easier if the input is precise and supported by specific evidence on which decisions about types of need, priority, strategies and resources can be made. While the plan will require some work to make it useful and to facilitate improved performance, without the preceding processes of monitoring, analysis and appraisal the plan becomes an exercise in futility because the appropriate opportunities to improve performance will not be sufficiently or precisely identified.

Improving performance is a joint responsibility between staff and managers, and each will have their own tasks to complete based on the actions of the improvement plan. However, managers must monitor the progress of improvement, just as they do for performance standards or objectives, to ensure that improvement occurs. Where progress is not in accordance with plans, appropriate interventions should be made to get staff back on track. Finally, there is no excuse for managers not to deliver on the promises they have made in the performance improvement plan. A failure to deliver may result in achievement of neither improvement objectives nor performance objectives. Litigation is a real threat in cases where managers try to hold staff or teams accountable for results when managers have intentionally or unintentionally sabotaged their efforts. Litigation stemming from performance issues are investigated in Chapter 11.

'REAL LIFE' CASE STUDY

The following case study describes how a large retail employer manages a holistic approach to performance improvement, linking it to corporate strategy, retention and succession planning.

Woolworths Limited Group is one of Australia's largest employers, with more than 180 000 employees working in stores, support offices and distribution centres across Australia and New Zealand.

The group's retailing expertise stretches across food and grocery, liquor, hotels, petrol, general merchandise and consumer electronics. Its vision is to continue to drive its retail business, bringing to customers greater convenience, quality, lower prices and better value, range, freshness and service. Its corporate objective is to continue driving future growth.

Woolworths has an achievement and performance-oriented culture which is driven and supported by the performance management system. Once the organisation's business plans have been set and senior executive key performance indicators (KPIs) developed, these are then incorporated into the performance criteria of employees. This practice ensures all employees are working towards the same broad corporate goals. This approach is in keeping with contemporary trends in performance management which no longer rely on position descriptions to drive performance. Through formalising the relationship between setting objectives and linking these to organisational strategy, Woolworths uses the performance management system as a powerful way to effectively direct organisational efforts.

Woolworths uses the review process to set specific goals and objectives for each employee for the coming year, review the previous year's performance and identify a development plan for the employee. All salaried employees undertake half-yearly or annual performance reviews with their manager. The outcome of the review is reflected in the employee's annual remuneration review and share purchase scheme.

Woolworths takes a holistic approach to performance improvement and has implemented strategies and incentive programs designed to embed a culture of performance, align organisational goals to personal goals, improve employee performance and retain valuable employees. The following strategies both drive and support Woolworths' performance management system.

1. Remuneration and rewards

Remuneration comprises fixed remuneration and a variable, performance-based component. This strategy enables managers to align individual objectives to company- and business-specific objectives and provide rewards based on achieving performance targets. Woolworths also has a limited share purchase plan that acts as a reward for meeting performance objectives. Of Woolworths' 365 000 shareholders, approximately 40 000 are employee shareholders, giving the organisation one of the largest levels of employee ownership for corporations in Australia.

2. Recognition

Woolworths recognises the positive effect of recognition on performance improvement. A range of individual, team and store award programs that recognise outstanding accomplishments for community work, customer service excellence and business performance are offered throughout all divisions, including an annual awards program that specifically recognises the development of young people within Woolworths.

3. Training and development opportunities

Training and development opportunities, including skill-based training, job relief assignments, secondments and formal academic training, are important components of the performance management system at Woolworths; in 2007–08 their total training investment increased by more than 25% to $63 million. Woolworths recognises the importance of having motivated and well-skilled managers and strives to develop leaders who can create high-performing and engaged workplaces. Its framework

'REAL LIFE' CASE STUDY CONTINUED

for leadership development includes external assessment and feedback processes, and graduate and international programs that focus on self-development, self-awareness and business acumen.

4. Mentoring

Woolworths actively encourages employees and managers to take responsibility for their own development. Woolworths has found mentoring an effective strategy for employees to use the experience of more senior team members, including executives, in their own development and to support their career growth. Another successful initiative has been network forums. These include the CEO Network Forum, which provides young leaders with a forum to discuss and debate key business and community issues in an informal setting with the CEO, and breakfast network sessions which build on knowledge and business networks.

With a workforce where 47% are in the 15–24 age bracket and 20% in the 15–34 age bracket, succession planning is high on Woolworths' agenda, and the company attempts to retain valuable employees via growth opportunities through the performance management system. A significant proportion of Woolworths' management team have been with the company for many years and membership of Woolworths' prestigious '25 Year Club' now exceeds 3000 people. Indeed, CEO Michael Luscombe, on approaching his 30th anniversary with Woolworths, commented that one of the great things about Woolworths was the opportunity to have 'many careers at one company'. Results such as these suggest that Woolworths' integrated and holistic approach to performance management is a considerable factor in developing and retaining an engaged and productive workforce.

References

Reuters 2009. 'Woolworths Limited implements workforce optimization software from Verint Witness Actionable Solutions to support first-class customer service.' <www.reuters.com/article/pressRelease/idUS117982+24-Mar-2009+BW20090324>, 24 March 2009.

Woolworths Limited n.d. *Human Resources*, <www.wowcareers.com.au/wowcareers/corporate/yourcareer/supportservices/human+resources.htm>

Woolworths Limited 2008. *Corporate Responsibility Report 2008:*
- 'About Woolworths', <http://crreport08.woolworthslimited.com.au/about_woolworths.php>
- 'Recruitment and retention', <http://crreport08.woolworthslimited.com.au/recruitment.php>
- 'Remuneration, performance and recognition', <http://crreport08.woolworthslimited.com.au/remuneration.php>
- 'Training and development', <http://crreport08.woolworthslimited.com.au/training.php>

Woolworths Limited 2008. *Woolworths Limited Annual Report 2008*, <http://library.corporate-ir.net/library/14/144/144044/items/312267/FinalAnnualReport08.pdf>

QUESTIONS

1 The case study highlights strategies implemented by Woolworths to improve performance. Select three strategies and briefly describe how you might modify the strategy to suit your current or previous workplace. Make note of any shortcomings or reasons why such a strategy might not be appropriate or might be difficult to achieve in your workplace.

2 Based on your current or previous role, identify and briefly describe a specific performance problem with which you are familiar. Identify and describe three strategies other than those described in the case study that might be used in a performance management plan.

JOB AIDS

A performance improvement model

Step 1

Identify performance gaps/
opportunities

Identify performance
improvements needed for
future performance

Step 2

Identify specific causes of performance gaps

Identify specific skills and knowledge

Step 3

Categorise the needs—
both developmental and
non-developmental

Non-development needs

Step 4

Link needs to specific outputs

Development needs

- Performance results
  in punishment?
- Poor performance
  rewarded?
- Is performance
  meaningful?
- Are there barriers to
  performance?
- Does person have
  potential?

Step 5

Prioritise needs

Step 6

Select strategies to meet needs

Step 7

Identify resources required
to meet needs

Step 8

Develop performance
improvement plan

- Aim of the plan
- Development objectives
- Strategies
- Resources
- Responsibilities
- Action plans
- Monitoring progress

Step 9

Implement plan

Step 10

Monitor progress

✓ CHECKLISTS

- ❏ **Step 1—Identify gaps and needs**
  - ❏ Performance gaps
  - ❏ Areas for performance
  - ❏ Expected benefits of improved performance
  - ❏ Specific outcomes of improved performance
  - ❏ Improvements required to meet future performance
  - ❏ New challenges for work unit
- ❏ **Step 2—Record the specific causes of performance gaps and the specific skills and knowledge required for future performance**
  - ❏ All evidence reviewed
  - ❏ Specific causes of performance gaps
  - ❏ Specific improvement opportunities
  - ❏ New skills and knowledge
  - ❏ New resources required
  - ❏ Problem space framed
- ❏ **Step 3—Categorise the needs**
  - ❏ Development needs
  - ❏ Non-development needs
- ❏ **Step 4—Link specific needs to outputs**
  - ❏ Outputs linked to development needs
  - ❏ Outputs linked to non-development needs
- ❏ **Step 5—Prioritise needs**
  - ❏ Cost solutions
  - ❏ Development needs—greatest opportunity for improvement
  - ❏ Non-development needs—greatest opportunity for improvement
- ❏ **Step 6—Select strategies**
  - ❏ Strategies for development needs
  - ❏ On-the-job
  - ❏ Off-the-job
  - ❏ Strategies for non-development needs
  - ❏ Discussion with other managers
  - ❏ Feedback required
- ❏ **Step 7—Identify resources required to meet needs**
  - ❏ Money
  - ❏ Time
  - ❏ People
  - ❏ Materials or physical resources
- ❏ **Step 8—Develop performance improvement plan**
  - ❏ Aim of the plan
  - ❏ Development objectives
  - ❏ Strategies
  - ❏ Resources

CHECKLISTS CONTINUED

❑ Responsibilities
❑ Action plans
❑ Monitoring progress

❑ **Step 9—Implement the plan**
  ❑ Specific milestones
  ❑ Expected completion dates diarised
  ❑ Copies for staff member and manager
  ❑ Copy to Human Resources management
  ❑ Immediate commencement

❑ **Step 10—Monitor progress**
  ❑ Monitor in conjunction with performance objectives
  ❑ Design evidence collection process

References

1   Squires, A. & Adler, S. 1998. 'Linking appraisals to individual development and training.' In J.W. Smither (ed.), *Performance Appraisal: State of the Art in Practice*. Jossey Bass: San Francisco, pp. 445–495; Rudman, R. 1995. *Performance Planning and Review*. Pitman: Melbourne, p. 139.

2   Rummler, G. & Brache, A. 1995. *Improving Performance: How to Manage the White Space on the Organization Chart*. Jossey-Bass: San Francisco, p. 64.

3   Rummler & Brache, op. cit., 1995, p. 73.

4   Deming, W. E. 1982. *Quality, Productivity, and Competitive Position*. Centre for Advanced Engineering Study, Massachusetts Institute of Technology: Cambridge, MA.

5   Squires & Adler, op. cit., 1998; Rummler & Brache, op. cit., 1995; Rudman, op. cit., 1995.

6   Billett, S.R. 1994. 'Authenticity in workplace learning settings.' In J. Stevenson (ed.), *Cognition at Work: The Development of Expertise*. National Centre for Vocational Education Research: Adelaide, pp. 35–36; Tovey, M.D. 1999. *Mentoring in the Workplace*. Prentice Hall: Sydney; Tovey, M.D. & Lawlor, D.R. 2008, 3rd edn. *Training in Australia*. Pearson Australia: Frenchs Forest, Sydney.

7   See Tovey & Lawlor, op. cit., 2008, Ch. 6; Tovey, op. cit., 1999, pp. 27–36.

8   Tovey & Lawlor, op. cit., Ch 6; Tovey, op. cit., 1999, pp. 27–36.

CHAPTER ELEVEN

Unsatisfactory performance

Learning outcomes

After reading this chapter you should be able to:

* identify two reasons why managers may not manage unsatisfactory performance well
* explain the process of managing unsatisfactory performance
* state the main areas of legislation that pertain to the management of unsatisfactory performance
* explain why managing unsatisfactory performance should be tackled by managers immediately it is known to them
* state the possible consequences of wrongfully dismissing an employee
* state the conditions under which an employee may not be dismissed
* explain the stages of managing unsatisfactory performance from the first intervention to termination
* explain the term 'counselling discussion'
* explain the difference between a performance discussion and a counselling discussion
* state the benefits of analysing an unsatisfactory performance incident for the manager
* state the components of a counselling discussion
* explain the steps involved in the discussion component of the counselling discussion
* state the outputs required of a counselling discussion
* state the legal implications and remedies of unfair dismissal.

INTRODUCTION

Despite the focus of performance management systems on developing people, there are some people who for various reasons do not perform. Even after an appraisal has identified issues supported with evidence, and agreement is reached on a development plan, managers may be disappointed to note that performance has not improved in accordance with agreed targets. Until now this book has focused on how to motivate people to improve through a high level of participation, the use of evidence and its systematic analysis and appraisal, and development support. Undoubtedly, there will be times in a manager's career when the performance of a particular individual or team does not improve and appropriate action must be taken.

Unsatisfactory performance is an umbrella term covering both underperformance and non-performance. Signs of unsatisfactory performance may include absenteeism (for example, multiple instances of unauthorised leave, higher absenteeism rate than other employees, long coffee breaks); attendance and punctuality (for example, arriving late and leaving early); poor concentration (for example, continually forgetting instructions or taking a longer-than-appropriate time to finish a task); lower standards of work (for example, missed deadlines, mistakes, wasting resources and falling productivity); poor relationships with colleagues and customers (for example, mood swings, avoiding manager or colleagues); and failure to observe the organisation's policies and procedures.[1]

Unsatisfactory performance may result from a single incident or there may be a steady decline in satisfactory performance over a period of time. Unsatisfactory performance may need to be managed as part of the formal appraisal or outside the formal appraisal process. Either way, both situations are part of the performance management system.

There are many explanations for unsatisfactory performance, which will be explored later in this chapter. Performance and productivity depend on many factors including the ability of the employee, working conditions, rewards, expectations, motivation, and alignment between personal and organisational values. Causes of unsatisfactory performance may also include lack of role clarity, lack of feedback on performance, personal problems and interpersonal problems.[2]

The process of managing poor performance

The process of managing unsatisfactory performance is based on the same principles of fairness and equity as the management of people performance. Where a manager is compelled to deal with performance that is unsatisfactory, and possibly to invoke a termination process, it does not mean that this course of action cannot be managed as skilfully as other parts of the performance management system. This is not to suggest that the only outcome of unsatisfactory performance is termination. The aim of managing unsatisfactory performance is to improve it. Termination is a final option. Managing unsatisfactory performance through a well-structured performance improvement plan can reignite enthusiasm and motivation and contribute to a person's self-esteem, to say nothing of productivity improvement. Even though managers may not handle these matters with any regularity, provided the basic interpersonal skills are present, and the concept of collecting evidence and focusing on development is used, managers need only apply the processes already learned in this book. The components of managing unsatisfactory performance are:

- Collect evidence
- Analyse the evidence
- Appraise the evidence
- Plan improvement.

When an individual fails to improve, you call on a further process that repeats the steps already described, with the additional possible consequence of termination. Thus, the thought of termination for unsatisfactory performance should not be of concern to managers. It is regrettable, but not unfair or harsh, if appropriate processes have been used to offer the individual every opportunity to improve performance. Termination is a final option, but not so final that managers should be afraid to use it. It is the logical consequence of an employee's continued lack of improvement. Continued tolerance of unsatisfactory performance will result in more expense than the trouble it takes to invoke a termination process. Costs in such circumstances may involve wastage of funds, low productivity, low morale, higher stress levels in staff and managers, and safety hazards. Objectivity and proper process should be the focus of an effective manager.

The process of managing unsatisfactory performance is complex, but the principles that underpin all the legislative requirements (discussed below) are consistent, which facilitates a systematic management of poor performance. There is anecdotal evidence that managers are reluctant to manage poor performance because the process is complex and requires considerable effort and time. No more effort is required than the vigour that has been applied to all the other components of managing performance described in this book. Failure to act on poor performance—and failing to do so immediately it is recognisable—can make the process lengthier, more painful for all parties and more complex than it needs to be. The time needed to manage unsatisfactory performance to new levels of satisfactory performance, or to invoke a termination process, can be as little as a few days or as long as several months, depending on the circumstances of the unsatisfactory performance, the quality of the evidence and the particular policies of your organisation.

However, managers also need strong interpersonal skills, the absence of which may reduce their confidence in adopting an active approach to managing unsatisfactory performance. Chapter 12 provides guidance in the use of interpersonal skills in relation to managing performance.

Legal framework

Managing unsatisfactory performance is influenced by a large number of variables. These include awards and regulations, and specific industrial relations legislation on termination contained in state and federal laws. Other legislation such as equal employment opportunity, anti-discrimination, workplace health and safety, and workers' compensation also provides specific directions for the management and termination of non-performing individuals. Further, workplace agreements and specific employment contracts have clauses that deal with the management of unsatisfactory performance. Finally, the determinations of tribunals, commissions and industrial courts have added to the interpretation of legislation, awards, regulations, agreements and contracts, which may qualify or extend the meaning of the original documents.

On 1 April 2009 new industrial relations laws came into came into effect in Australia via the *Fair Work Act 2009* (Cth), which replaced the *Workplace Relations Act 1996* (Cth) and WorkChoices. The WorkChoices legislation was introduced by the Coalition Government in 2006, ostensibly to simplify the industrial relations framework which contained over 130 different pieces of industrial relations legislation and over 4000 awards, making agreement and administration complex and confusing. The *Fair Work Act* is, at time of writing, the main legislation that covers employment in Australia.[3]

The role of legislation

The termination of employees from organisations is the subject of legislation because the issue is essentially one of industrial relations. It is part of the employee–employer relationship, involving management interests and employee/union interests. Management is concerned to minimise the loss of productivity that a poorly performing worker can cause the organisation. Employees and unions are concerned with making sure that people are not unfairly dealt with when performing poorly or when termination occurs. Consequently, there are penalties for wrongfully dismissing a worker—for example, having to reinstate the worker to the original job or paying compensation to the worker to make up for lost wages. Wrongfully dismissing an employee may also demand a lot of management time in defending the action, high legal costs and union conflict, which may all result in poor morale for the remaining employees, especially where a drawn-out action results in media coverage and perhaps strikes.

Managers need to be familiar with the appropriate legislation for their enterprise, industry, awards and state. If in doubt, or when looking for a starting point, seek assistance from your Human Resource department, unit, branch or section.

Unfair dismissal

The legal framework presented in the *Fair Work Act 2009* (Cth) defines when an employee cannot be dismissed:

- where a person may be temporarily absent from work for illness or injury
- where a person is absent due to pregnancy or parental leave
- where a person chooses to join (or not to join) a union
- where a person may become a union representative
- where a person has been discriminated against because their race, colour, sex, sexual preference, age, physical or mental disability, marital status, family or carer's responsibilities, pregnancy, religion, political opinion, national extraction or social origin
- where it may be held that dismissal was unjust or harsh in the circumstances.

What is an unfair dismissal? A person has been unfairly dismissed if Fair Work Australia is satisfied that all of the following four actions occurred:

- the person has been dismissed
- the dismissal was harsh, unjust or unreasonable
- the dismissal was not consistent with the Small Business Fair Dismissal Code
- the dismissal was not a case of genuine redundancy.[4]

The second point relates mostly to circumstances of poor performance or redundancy. Where dismissal may be seen to be unjust or harsh, a commission or court will look at the process employers used to make a decision. If the dismissal is found not to be based on specific evidence, or not dealt with in accordance with principles of due process, and for valid reasons, it may be held to have been wrongful. Once a prima facie case is established, the employer must prove that the dismissal was not unlawful.

Decisions about performance that may lead to dismissal must be based on sound evidence and systematically analysed. Processes preceding the dismissal must offer employees opportunities to:

- improve
- be given specific warnings
- facilitate a right of reply
- ensure they are treated no differently from any other employee during the process as a result of any action taken to improve performance.

CHECK YOUR UNDERSTANDING

1 On what principles is the management of unsatisfactory performance based?
2 What must the processes of managing unsatisfactory performance offer employees?
3 What are the four main components of managing unsatisfactory performance?
4 From a legal perspective, why is the process of managing unsatisfactory performance so important?
5 Why might managers be reluctant to actively manage unsatisfactory performance?
6 What are the main areas of legislation that relate to employee termination?
7 What are the circumstances under which an employee may not be dismissed?

SKILL AND KNOWLEDGE APPLICATION

Update Health Products Pty Ltd is a major supplier of surgical instruments and diagnostic tests to the medical profession. The company has been operating for 21 years and is now in a major period of expansion and growth in the domestic and overseas markets. Throughout this current evolutionary process the company has been changing and restructuring as the need has arisen. One of these changes has involved the introduction of a performance management system. The Managing Director has insisted that those who cannot demonstrate their contribution to the results of the company should not be working, and their jobs should be abolished.

André Daniels is the Sales Manager for diagnostic products. He is aware that Khai Lee, one of the sales representatives, is not meeting her monthly sales targets. André has noticed that the target is being missed by less than $15 000 per month and he does not think it is a very big issue, given that Khai Lee is pregnant with her first child. The unsatisfactory performance has been tracked for four months now.

Craig Menslink, the Managing Director, bursts into André's office and says, 'I just saw Khai Lee at a customer's premises and I nearly had a fit. She looks like a bloated toadfish! What is her performance like?'

You tell him that she is just missing the targets.

He says, 'Good! Sack her this afternoon! She is not the look we want to portray to our customers'. He leaves the office.

TASK
- What are the issues you must deal with as André, Khai Lee's manager?
- What does the *Fair Work Act 2009* (Cth) say about such an incident?
- What do you think the chances are of defending a charge of wrongful dismissal raised by Khai Lee?
- What other Act or Acts would be relevant to this incident?

Managing poor performance

The first sign of unsatisfactory performance is likely to come in specific incidents that occur in the workplace; these become the basis for intervention by the manager to redirect performance in accordance with agreed standards or objectives. Often, feedback by the manager is all that is required to redirect the employee. This situation has been discussed in earlier chapters under the topic of 'intervention'. If poor performance is repeated, a counselling discussion may be required to reinforce the seriousness of the situation to the employee and to draw up a plan for improved performance (see Chapter 10).

If performance does not improve as a result of a counselling discussion and/or there is a failure to achieve the agreed performance improvement as documented in the performance improvement plan, you will have to recognise that there is continued poor performance and you must now manage it formally. Figure 11.1 illustrates the broad stages from feedback, through counselling, to written warnings and then termination if necessary.

Using the flowchart

Where a one-off incident occurs it can usually be remedied with feedback and a brief discussion. This process tends to be informal, and should take a constructive approach that presents a problem and the consequences, and asks for solutions. Nevertheless, the incident must be documented, including enough detail to be a reliable record of the event. Here is what should be recorded:

- date and time
- people involved
- summary of the situation/circumstances
- what was said during the discussion (in dot-point format)
- what was agreed during the discussion
- the follow-up that was agreed.

The incident itself probably constitutes evidence of performance for the purposes of your data collection for the performance appraisal process. If the incident recurs, or other incidents of unsatisfactory performance are evident, you will need to conduct a number of performance counselling discussions with the individual or team.

Figure 11.1 presents a stepped process from an informal approach to managing one-off incidents, through the more formal approach of counselling discussions combined with written warnings about the unsatisfactory performance, to termination. The figure will guide you in the use of these tools.

Counselling discussions

Counselling discussions follow the principles of data collection examined in Chapter 6 on monitoring performance. Even though this process lies outside the performance appraisal procedure, it does not lie outside the performance management system. The difference between a performance discussion and a counselling discussion is specific and clear.

Performance discussions are concerned with the total performance of an individual or team for a given period of time and cover the range of performance standards agreed for the job. *Counselling discussions* are usually about one incident or a number of incidents involving the same performance issue. Figure 11.2 demonstrates this difference.

FIGURE 11.1 Unsatisfactory performance management flowchart

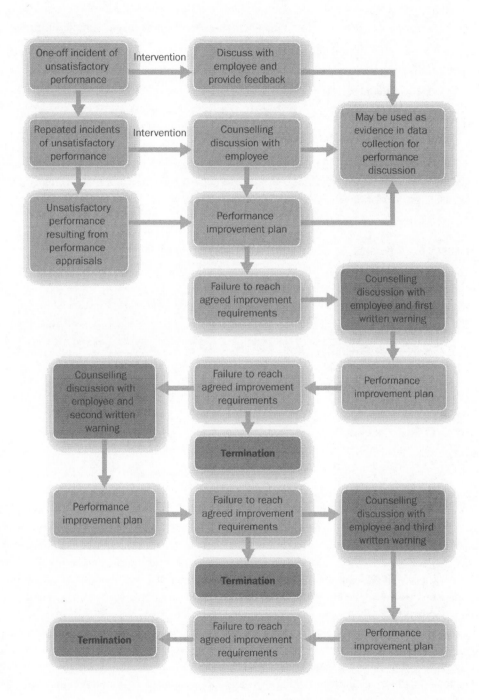

Before deciding to hold a discussion, ensure that you have adequate evidence of the performance problem. You may not have as much evidence as you would collect as part of the appraisal procedure, but you should obtain as much evidence as possible about the incident(s) of unsatisfactory performance. Evidence for counselling discussions may take a number of forms:

- an account of the unsatisfactory performance
- observers' accounts
- results of the unsatisfactory performance on others, the work unit and the organisation
- management information reports, if suitable, or samples of unsatisfactory reports.

Because a counselling discussion takes place immediately after or very close to the incident(s), it does not absolve you from obtaining appropriate evidence to support your case. Remember, you may be required to rely on the evidence in litigation, so it must be accurate and clearly demonstrate unsatisfactory performance.

FIGURE 11.2 Difference between performance and counselling discussions

Performance discussion	Counselling discussion
Multiple examples of performance for all performance standards across a range of situations and daily work activities, demonstrating all aspects of performance, both good and bad	Single example, or group of specific examples, of one issue of unsatisfactory performance relating to one performance standard in one situation and/or work activity

Analysis

Once the evidence is collected, you need to analyse it (see Chapter 7). Analysis ensures that you determine the actual performance problem, realistically understand its importance, and determine the context of the unsatisfactory performance. Analysis also ensures that you explore all the possible causes of unsatisfactory performance. A lack of analysis may place you in a difficult position should you not understand factors that may have contributed to unsatisfactory performance, especially where you proceed to a formal unsatisfactory performance process. From time to time there will be legitimate mitigating circumstances that will require you to be tolerant, or circumstances where the precipitation of the unsatisfactory performance is beyond the control of the individual.

Analysis also gives the manager an opportunity to cool off, particularly where the unsatisfactory performance triggers emotional reactions. It is more appropriate to speak to a staff member after all emotions have been released. This avoids 'emotional claptrap', that is, a discussion that is devoid of tangible, specific things that the parties can do something about. A counselling discussion based on emotional claptrap will not achieve any outcomes.

Appraisal

After you have analysed the collected evidence, you need to appraise it to determine possible solutions to the problem. Appraisal will require you to make decisions about the performance and thus take possible action to remedy it. It is unwise to conclude that the only solution to an unsatisfactory performance problem is termination. There are many alternatives to termination, including demotion, formal reprimand, reduction of certain benefits, and closer monitoring. Public sector legislation specifically provides for these options, although there is no reason why some of them cannot be adopted in the private sector, where appropriate. An assumption of termination at this stage will prejudice your actions, and if they are transparent will render an assumption indefensible in litigation.

Nor should you reach an immutable decision at this stage until you have heard the staff member's side of the story. You must allow due process to occur, and that means you must give staff an opportunity to present their case. It may not be as well prepared as yours, but you must take account of their point of view and seek to understand any evidence they present. As discussed in Chapters 8 and 9, there may be points that you have not uncovered in your analysis and appraisal; the evidence a staff member presents may be quite valid and provide a perspective you have not considered.

Even at this stage, unsatisfactory performance should not be considered a precursor to termination. Unsatisfactory performance should be seen as an opportunity to help a staff member develop and improve and to refocus their efforts. Remember, too, that most performance problems are to do with issues of context rather than individual shortcomings. Thus it is vital to get the input of the individual whose performance is in question so that genuine problem solving can occur with the focus on improving performance. This may result in the identification of contextual factors that demand attention by the manager or management group. This must be a priority for management, as contextual factors affecting one individual's performance are likely to have an impact on others' performance. Consequently, departmental and organisational key performance indicators will be affected and organisational performance limited. For further information on appraisal, see Chapters 8 and 9.

While Chapters 6, 7, 8 and 9—dealing with monitoring, analysis and appraisal—are quite detailed, you can still use the principles to deal quickly with specific incident(s) of unsatisfactory performance that require your attention. Use the checklists in each of these chapters as a guide. Figure 11.3 illustrates a framework for the counselling discussion.

CHECK YOUR UNDERSTANDING

8 Where is a manager likely to see the first signs of unsatisfactory performance?

9 How much evidence do you need to conduct a counselling discussion?

10 What is the difference between a performance discussion and a counselling discussion?

11 What does analysis of an unsatisfactory performance incident specifically offer a manager?

12 Why is it important for employees to have an opportunity to discuss the performance when their performance is seen as unsatisfactory?

FIGURE 11.3 Counselling discussion framework

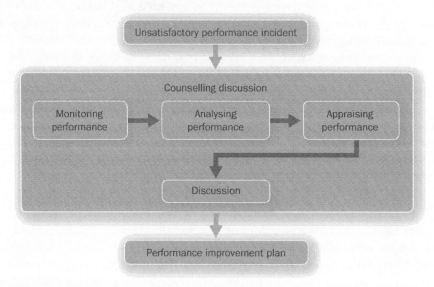

Outputs of the discussion model

The counselling discussion varies from the performance discussion model included in Chapter 9 because it is confined to specific incident(s) and does not require the detailed processes included in that model. You will need to:

- review the evidence
- analyse
- appraise
- discuss the evidence
- draw up a performance improvement plan with the individual.

As the process deals with only one aspect of performance, it is likely to be reasonably quick and straightforward. It becomes more complicated when performance does not improve after a performance improvement plan has been implemented. Further counselling is then required, with the addition of a written warning. This is only appropriate when non-performance can be clearly tied to individual issues and the contextual issues have either been addressed or no longer apply. Rossett claims that there are only four possible reasons for poor performance in individuals or teams.[5] These are:

1   *the absence of skill or knowledge*—where the individual is unable to perform the task because he/she does not know how to do it.

2   *the absence of incentive, or of improper incentive*—where there is no suitable reward for performing satisfactorily, or where non-performance may be rewarded in some way, whether intentionally or non-intentionally.

3   *the absence of environmental support*—where there is insufficient equipment, tools, forms, work space, materials or access to information for individuals to do their job.

4 *the absence of motivation.* Two factors influence motivation: efficacy and value. Where individuals do not see any worth in investing time and effort in learning how to perform the job well, they are not likely to be motivated to learn or perform. Whether or not individuals see any value in the job, or in the duties of a job— such as the systems that need to be used, the forms that need to be completed or the technology that has to be used—will determine their motivation towards the job.

Performance problems may have a single cause or a number of causes, and the manager should explore all possibilities before discussing the poor performance with the staff member. During the discussion, the manager should canvass the possible causes of the poor performance with the staff member. A model for use in counselling discussions is shown in Figure 11.4. This model has three components: set-up, the discussion, and documentation.

In Figure 11.4 the principles are the same as those described in Chapter 9, but the steps are fewer and focused on specific incident(s). The set-up of the discussion remains the same as described in Chapter 9. The discussion requires you to get the staff member talking. The aim of the discussion is to problem-solve together to find a way forward. Asking suitable questions to engage staff members is a more useful way of problem solving than presenting your opinion, offering evidence to support it and asking staff what they are going to do about it. The outputs you want from a counselling discussion are:

- acknowledgment by the staff member that there is a problem
- identification of causes of the problem
- solutions to the problem
- agreement on the implementation of a solution
- development of a performance improvement plan.

FIGURE 11.4 The counselling discussion model

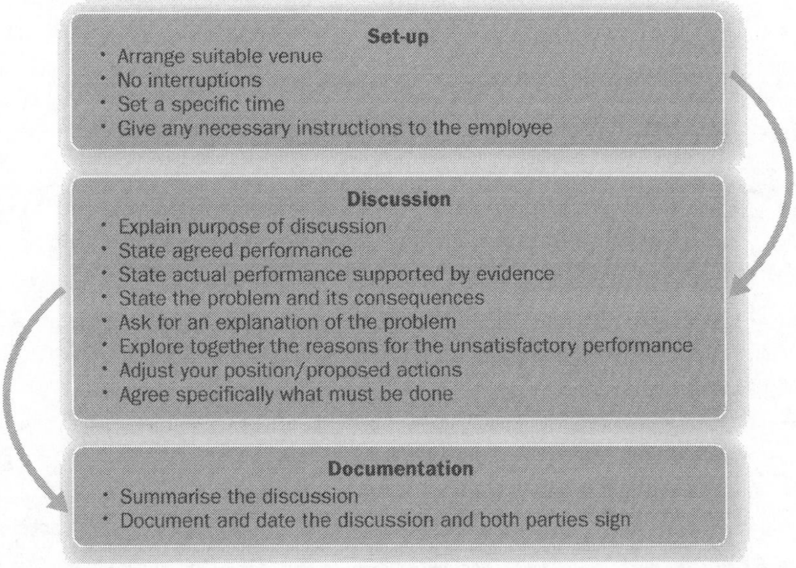

Set-up
- Arrange suitable venue
- No interruptions
- Set a specific time
- Give any necessary instructions to the employee

Discussion
- Explain purpose of discussion
- State agreed performance
- State actual performance supported by evidence
- State the problem and its consequences
- Ask for an explanation of the problem
- Explore together the reasons for the unsatisfactory performance
- Adjust your position/proposed actions
- Agree specifically what must be done

Documentation
- Summarise the discussion
- Document and date the discussion and both parties sign

The outcome you require from a counselling discussion is for the unsatisfactory performance to cease. The manager's role is to facilitate this through the discussion. It is not a communication through which managers blame or chastise staff but a further opportunity to help develop staff. Where performance improves after a counselling discussion, no further action is required. You may discover during the discussion that there are legitimate reasons for the level of performance. Illness, personal problems or difficulties such as a partner out of work or a family death may be examples of acceptable reasons for temporary poor performance. In such cases you may agree to allow further time for the individual to improve performance, offer assistance and support, and note this in a performance improvement plan. Several strategies might be implemented in such circumstances:

- Another member of staff may be designated to assist the individual for a number of hours each day or week.

- Certain duties or specific tasks may be reassigned by negotiation to other staff for a defined period of time.

- You may need to have discussions with other work areas to ensure that adequate levels of work flow are maintained.

- Team building may be needed to elicit appropriate cooperation among staff.

- Process and procedures may need to be redesigned or at least reviewed.

- Work flows may need to be reviewed to relieve bottlenecks or double handling, or to reduce turnaround times.

- Appropriate mentoring, coaching and skills development support should be provided for the staff member if required.

Regardless of the reasons for the poor performance, it has occurred and must therefore be documented. A mistake that managers often make is to let the incident pass without discussion or documentation. Managers must manage human performance. Ignoring or letting poor performance pass because there are 'reasons' for it is not acceptable. If performance deteriorates further you will have to start the documentation from scratch when you take action. While there may well be valid reasons for poor performance, it must be dealt with and documented, even where no further action will be taken. However, where performance continues to be a problem you will need to follow the unsatisfactory performance process outlined in Figure 11.1.

SKILL AND KNOWLEDGE APPLICATION

Kylie is a commercial manager in the coal division of a large, privately owned resource company. She is a well-liked and personable manager who takes the financial responsibilities of her role seriously. Kylie is concerned about Luke, a trainee accountant, who has been with the company for two years. Luke seems competent in the majority of his tasks, but seems to pay little attention to detail, which is integral to his role as an accountant.

In several senior management meetings Luke's performance has been raised with Kylie, with several incidents used as evidence of performance problems with Luke's work. Kylie places a lot of importance on being liked by her subordinates, but undertakes to discuss the problems with Luke at his performance appraisal next week. However, after the discussion, she feels bad and gives Luke a very high performance rating, regardless of the evidence.

SKILL AND KNOWLEDGE APPLICATION CONTINUED

TASK
- Identify the possible implications of Kylie's performance rating of Luke.
- If you were Kylie's manager, how would you respond to the high rating given to Luke in his performance appraisal, and what would your response to the situation be?

Continuing unsatisfactory performance

Where performance continues to be unsatisfactory after a performance improvement plan has been agreed on and implemented, you will need to manage the non-performance in a very formal way. From Figure 11.1 you will see that this involves another counselling discussion and the first of three formal warnings in writing. Your organisation is also likely to have specific procedures for managing unsatisfactory performance, and these should be melded into the procedure illustrated in Figure 11.1.

Using the skills of Human Resources

Before moving into an unsatisfactory performance procedure, it would be wise to seek the advice of the Human Resources department to ensure that you go about the process in accordance with all relevant procedures and principles of natural justice. Because you must be particular and meet the requirements of a number of procedures, legislation and awards, it is better to make sure that you are on solid ground. Human Resources is there to help line managers do their job by providing advice, guidance and assistance. Their experience in the more complex matters of managing people can make your task a lot easier, especially in times of great stress, which is often the case when possible termination must be considered.

Managers should not hesitate to involve staff in the unsatisfactory performance procedure if circumstances indicate the need to do so. The commencement of such a procedure does not mean that you will terminate a staff member. Indeed, it is hoped that no further action will be required. There are a number of reasons why it is important to invoke an unsatisfactory perform-ance procedure:

1   If managers do not make it clear to staff members that non-performance is serious, staff are unlikely to take it seriously. If a manager tolerates poor performance by doing nothing about it, staff will receive the message that it is acceptable. Attempts to improve performance will not be taken seriously as staff soon learn that nothing happens if performance is poor. If you do encounter continued poor performance, the formal warning usually conveys the message: staff usually improve their performance, and no further action is required.

2   If individuals are not pulling their weight in the work unit, others are probably doing more than their fair share. While staff may choose to do this for a short while, especially where a colleague is experiencing difficulties, it will soon lower morale if allowed to continue. This can create performance problems with other staff and will affect the productivity and outputs of the work unit.

3   If the situation becomes so bad that termination must be seriously considered, the organisa-tion will be unable to terminate the staff member if appropriate processes have not been

followed. For example, if a manager has been dealing with continued poor performance for eight months and decides that it is now time to dispense with the staff member's services, the manager must then provide the required number of warnings, development opportunities and discussions before termination can take place. Consequently, a considerable amount of time elapses before the staff member is terminated. If managers are doing their job, and performance is documented and dealt with appropriately, the process of termination can be quite swift.

4   If a staff member is prone to poor performance from time to time, and erratic in the quality of performance overall, a manager may wish to build a case for termination. Unless there is evidence on record that the staff member was subject to an unsatisfactory performance process, say five times in the past 12 months, it will not be possible to build a case that is considered fair and equitable.

The written warning

Combined with counselling, written warnings are the basis of any termination process. For termination to occur as a result of unsatisfactory performance, the law generally requires that the employee be warned of the unsatisfactory performance and given an opportunity to improve performance. As a result of all the legislation and awards that HR has had to deal with over the past decades, it has become convention to give up to three written warnings to staff who are not performing satisfactorily. However, it is not a legal requirement to give more than one written warning. Good HR practice dictates that appropriate processes are used, and it will depend on the nature of the unsatisfactory performance, the specific circumstances and the individuals involved how many written warnings you choose to give. Written warnings ensure that there is adequate documentation of the specific lack of performance, the steps taken to improve it and whether the steps were followed. Written evidence is required if a situation escalates to the Industrial Relations Commission, where you might need irrefutable evidence of your actions. The written warning can be powerful, as people attribute more weight to a written communication and it appears to be more official than a verbal communication. A written warning also has a certain amount of shock value that may not be achievable through verbal communication. Staff members who have not previously acknowledged that a problem exists often do so after receiving a written warning.

Warnings become stronger with each one issued. To be effective they must be clearly written, the original must be given to the staff member, and it is wise to get a signature from the staff member to confirm receipt. Written warnings do not replace discussion. Nor should warnings be sent to a staff member: they should be delivered by hand during a counselling discussion in which you discuss the poor performance and find ways of solving the problem. The first counselling discussion in which you hand over a written warning ought to achieve the same outputs as those described above, with the additional output of developing a shared understanding of the serious- ness of the problem.

Written warnings must include those items listed in Figure 11.5. The warning must be as precise as possible by clearly stating the agreed performance, the current level of performance and the performance gap. It must also refer to any previous discussions and performance improvement plans and, where appropriate, any previous written warnings. The warning must also state what the consequences of further unsatisfactory performance will be. You must be accurate about the consequences if you wish to rely on the written warning in litigation.

After the third written warning has been delivered and performance does not improve in accordance with the agreed improvement plan, termination may take place with no further discussion, provided the appropriate amount of time has elapsed as indicated in the improvement plan.

FIGURE 11.5 Contents of a written warning

Written warning

- Set out formally, in either letter or memo format
- Address to employee by name, position and employee number if possible
- Date the correspondence as the same day as the discussion
- Include a subject line: 'Unsatisfactory performance: First/Second/Third warning'

- State the performance required
- State the previously agreed performance improvement plan
- Describe the problem
- State that performance is unsatisfactory
- State what was agreed at the last counselling discussion and include a copy of the documentation
- Direct attention to the new performance improvement plan
- State what will happen if performance does not improve
- Sign the correspondence
- Have the staff member sign a copy certifying that they have the original correspondence

The process of three written warnings and accompanying counselling discussions may seem cumbersome and somewhat longwinded. The actual time taken will depend on the specific unsatisfactory performance. If the poor performance is something like consistently arriving late for work, the period of time required for improvement may be only a few days or a week. If the poor performance continues, it is likely that termination will occur in as little as three weeks. For more complex matters, which may require time to develop skills or to meet the performance requirements, it can take considerably longer to reach the termination stage.

Legal cases presented later in this chapter highlight that, in certain situations, termination can be immediate and without notice, show that a lack of capacity can lead to termination, and outline what remedies are available under law for termination issues.

CHECK YOUR UNDERSTANDING

13 What is the outcome required of a counselling discussion?
14 What outputs should a counselling discussion produce?
15 What are the benefits of proactively managing unsatisfactory performance?
16 What should be included in a written warning?
17 After which warning can you terminate an employee for unsatisfactory performance?

Termination of employment

Repairing human resources

It is desirable to try to 'repair' a human resource, because the cost of replacing one is high. A little time and effort invested in regular maintenance and servicing, with attention to the faults that occur from time to time, will keep the resource in tip-top shape. Unlike any other resource the manager manages, humans are able to think for themselves and act independently. Consequently, managers need a wide range of skills to manage this resource well so that the organisation, the manager and the staff member or team benefit from the experience. Termination is a costly decision, which may balloon if it is handled badly. A fair termination is one in which the individual is not treated in a way that could be considered to be harsh or unjust. This is an easy concept to grasp. Simply put yourself in the shoes of the staff member who is not performing. Wouldn't you want to be treated in a fair and equitable way?

A decision to terminate

A decision to terminate is one that will gradually become clear as unsatisfactory performance continues. The exception is where staff members engage in serious misconduct, which may endanger their own or others' lives, or commit a serious crime. (Courts have held that some crimes—such as assault on a supervisor—may not be adequate in themselves to justify termination, especially if the assault was provoked and the harm caused was minor.) In such circumstances you should consult your Human Resources department or, if you do not have such a section, the most senior management in the organisation. You may even need to seek legal advice on the matter. Managers should understand that it is better to delay action for a few hours or even a day if necessary, to ensure that they know and understand the processes they must use to move on such complex matters. If you act without the appropriate advice, using inappropriate processes, the situation can become costly, embarrassing and messy to deal with should things go wrong. As termination is an area most managers do not deal with on a regular basis, they would be expected to seek assistance and advice on the matter.

The most difficult aspect of managing unsatisfactory performance is the fact that managers are often slow to take appropriate action. By the time they realise there is a serious problem, it has become so complex and difficult to handle that very often nothing is done about it. In such cases it is managers who should be better managed, because they have clearly not managed performance effectively. They must also accept the consequences of their failure to manage performance. Managing unsatisfactory performance is an inextricable part of managing the overall performance system. Thus, where unsatisfactory performance is not managed well, the manager's ability must be called into question.

Constructive dismissal

Managers must be aware of the concept of *constructive dismissal*. While there is no formal definition of this term in industrial relations legislation, enough precedent is now established within the industrial commissions and courts to develop a solid understanding of the term. In certain circumstances, where an employee has left the employment, it may be determined by the industrial commissions or courts that a constructive dismissal has taken place and that therefore a termination by the employer has occurred. Where such a finding is held, the employee may seek remedies under appropriate unfair dismissal legislation if, in the circumstances, the dismissal is found to be harsh or unjust. Essentially, constructive dismissal means that the employer has been found to have constructed, created or made up the dismissal. For example, where an employee may not have been performing satisfactorily, rather than manage the unsatisfactory performance a manager may choose to 'find' situations that either singly or combined seem to make a case for dismissal. In such cases it is likely that the employer will be held to have constructed the dismissal.

Four criteria can be identified where it has been held that constructive dismissal has occurred:

1 *Where an employee has been forced to resign.* This might occur when an employee is given an ultimatum to resign or be fired over one or a number of alleged activities or misconduct. Where there has been no investigation or no right of reply given to the employee, it has sometimes been held that the employee has been constructively dismissed.

2 *Where an employer makes a fundamental, unilateral variation to the terms and conditions of an employee's employment.* If this happens to such an extent that a repudiation of the original contract occurs, the employee has a choice to accept or reject the repudiation. Where an employee accepts the repudiation, this is sometimes held to constitute a constructive dismissal and therefore a termination by the employer.

3 *Where a significant breach of the employment contract has occurred that goes to the root or essence of the contract.* A case of constructive dismissal may be found where the employer breaches an essential term of the contract that strikes at the very root of the contract or demonstrates that the employer does not intend to continue to be bound by one or more of the essential terms of the contract.

4 *Where an employer makes working conditions so unbearable that an employee is forced or appears to be left with no alternative but to resign.* This may give rise to a finding of constructive dismissal, which may take the form of unreasonable pressure, bluff, bullying, or unreasonable workloads. As there is an implied duty by an employer to employees not to damage or destroy their relationship of trust and confidence, making things difficult for the employee may be seen to be damaging or destroying the employment relationship.

Where dismissal is found to have been constructed by an employer, it will be held that the employer has terminated the employment of the employee and it will thus have occurred at the initiative of the employer. Penalties can be awarded against an employer where it is found that the termination was harsh, unjust and unreasonable. Orders may be made to reinstate the employee and make payment for lost wages. Consequently, managers should ensure that where they must invoke termination, it is based on specific evidence and for specific reasons. If in doubt, consult your Human Resources department.

Terminating employment

Even where managers do have appropriate skills and manage unsatisfactory performance well, some situations will become terminal. Once it is clear that the employee's services are to be terminated, the process must be handled with dignity and sensitivity. It goes without saying that the processes you use must be correct. When you have reached the stage of giving the third written warning and performance still does not improve, you will need to terminate the service of the employee. Before acting, discuss acceptable options with Human Resources. These might include offering the employee the opportunity to resign rather than be sacked, providing outplacement services and counselling and/or support, or even agreeing on what will be said in a written reference. While a termination discussion is never easy because the employee often becomes emotional, by trying to make the separation harmonious you will maintain the goodwill of the employee for your organisation in the long term. There will also be cases where it is not possible to make the transition from work to unemployment easy for the employee because of the nature of the unsatisfactory performance. In such cases be guided by the advice of Human Resources.

It is critical to maintain the dignity and esteem of people, even in the worst termination situations. People are entitled to common courtesy, respect and fairness no matter what the situation. This is the case even when staff do not demonstrate this respect for you. Remember that you are terminating the services of the employee, not because the employee is a bad person but because the employee has not performed in accordance with the agreed standards which the organisation needs. The employee may very well be successful at something else, in another organisation. You should concentrate on the specific reasons for the termination, and not become engaged in emotional discussions about the reasons why or the apparent heartlessness of the organisation in bringing about the termination. Also, the time for discussion of the circumstances that brought about the termination has passed, and you should not go over ground you have already covered. In the termination discussion, focus on the termination and the specific reasons for it, keeping it short and to the point.

Performance management and the law

This chapter deals with some legal aspects of the employment relationship because over the past few decades the courts have noticed that some employers have acted in an unsatisfactory manner when terminating employees. Legislation and the courts have combined to ensure that employees are given a fair and equitable chance when dealing with the matter of their employment. Thus the issue of termination is fraught with possible litigation if it is not handled skilfully. The law also influences every aspect of a performance management system. Over time, industrial commissions and courts have developed conventions that can be seen in their decisions across a wide range of cases.

Some recent decisions in Australian courts on unfair dismissal have highlighted the application of law to employment contracts and the performance of duties specified in contracts . Here we examine more closely the application of that law in several illustrative cases, covering summary termination, three warnings, and justifying termination on performance grounds.

Summary termination

Summary termination or dismissal is where an employee is terminated immediately, with no notice given. For summary termination to be justified there must be a serious breach of the employment contract or conduct that is repugnant to the employer–employee relationship.

The NSW Supreme Court found that a CEO who failed to inform his employer of performance problems at an overseas branch was appropriately terminated for breach of duty as a director. This termination was with no notice or payment in lieu. How could the courts rule this way? The former CEO's contract contained a specific clause allowing termination without notice in the event of an act of dishonesty, fraud, wilful disobedience, misbehaviour or breach of duty. The CEO was found to have breached his duty and misbehaved in his actions. Breach of duty came under the *Corporations Act 2001* (Cth), requiring a director to act with 'reasonable care and diligence' and 'in good faith'.

The facts that determined this case of summary termination focused on the express terms in employment contracts; the idea that CEOs are held to a higher standard; and the principle that conduct that has destroyed confidence and an ongoing relationship warrants termination.[5]

Three warnings rule

Under the *Fair Work Act 2009* (Cth) an employee may bring an application for reinstatement if the dismissal is considered to be harsh, unjust or unreasonable. The Act sets out the elements of fairness for termination.

Under the legal concept of procedural fairness, written warnings stating the specific performance issues and a time frame for review of those issues should be provided to, and discussed with, the employee. There is, however, no statutory or award requirement detailing that three written warnings and counselling must be given before termination can occur. One of the most important aspects in termination is to ensure that employees have been given an opportunity to respond to the allegations against them and have had sufficient time to show an improvement in their performance. The process used must be considered to be fair, in the circumstances, by a 'reasonable person'—the objective test. The court will decide what is fair on the specific facts of each individual case.

The Industrial Relations Commission of NSW found that a large employer who terminated an employee due to poor performance, giving the employee three written warnings, had to reinstate the employee and pay him for the entire period that he was off work. The Commission noted the employee's poor work history, but in the absence of hard evidence that the employee was not sick on the last occasion in question, the employer had no grounds to terminate his employment.[7]

Justifying termination on performance grounds

The Full Court of the Federal Court has held that a dismissal may still be considered fair if the employee has performed to the best of his/her ability even though the dismissal was procedurally deficient, in that three warnings were not given and the employee was not given an opportunity to respond.

The case facts were that a company advertised for a sales representative to source and develop new business opportunities through new and existing customers. The employee chosen for the position was given a letter of offer, stating that the main focus of the job was to generate new business. After six months the employee was terminated for generating only minimal new business. It was not that the employee was lazy; he was thought of as hardworking and experienced. The Australian Industrial Relations Commission (AIRC) found the employer to have a valid reason for dismissal, in that the employee did not have the capacity to perform the job successfully. The AIRC found the dismissal fair, despite the procedural deficiencies of not giving the employee any warnings or reason for dismissal and no opportunity to rectify the performance issue.[8]

Remedies for unfair dismissal

The remedies available to employees under the *Fair Work Act 2009* (Cth) for unfair dismissal are significant for employees (compared to remedies under a breach of employment contract). Under these statutory remedies an employee may be reinstated to the former position or awarded compensation, which can extend beyond any notice period given.

The first remedy considered by the courts is reinstatement, if the situation allows and the employment relationship can be successfully re-established. The Commission will decide whether reinstatement is an option. An alternative is compensation, which is most often the form of remedy in unfair dismissal cases. The Commission has developed assessment criteria for compensation with consideration given to distress caused by the dismissal. A cap has been set on compensation to limit the amount that can be paid out by employers.

These statutory remedies now available to those seeking unfair dismissal compensation against their employer are of major benefit to employees with access to them. The *Fair Work Act 2009* (Cth) endeavours to go beyond the employee–employer relationship to stimulate improvement in employment practices for both.

The application and outcomes of statutory remedies in relation to employment law are constantly evolving. Organisations needing to pursue this area of law are advised to seek the advice of experts in the field to ensure they are accessing and applying current laws and legislation in relation to employment issues and, more particularly, termination issues.

Guidelines for implementing and maintaining a performance management system

Generally speaking, the following points must be taken into account by managers engaged in implementing and maintaining a performance management system:

- People must be trained in the performance management system:
  — Managers must be trained in the right skills to manage people.
  — Managers must be trained in how to use the system.
  — Staff must be trained in how to use the system.
  — Staff must be trained in the skills to participate in the system.

- Performance standards and objectives must be agreed on soon after a new employee joins the organisation if the employer intends to rely on these as the basis for performance evaluation.

- There must be agreement between the employee and the employer on performance standards and objectives.

- The management of performance is clearly a management responsibility.

- Managers must become familiar with the organisation's HR policies and practices, especially in relation to unsatisfactory performance.

Adhering to these simple guidelines will result in more sustained performance, better relationships with staff and a focus on results. Additionally, and most importantly, following these guidelines will reduce the likelihood of unsatisfactory performance by employees. Managers must possess core skills in dealing with and managing people, otherwise the procedures, processes and policies that support any performance management system will not be enough to sustain the required results. Many systems fail—not because the system itself is faulty, or the forms are too cumbersome, or there is not enough time, but because managers do not possess or do not use the appropriate core soft skills on which any performance management system must be based. Chapter 12 identifies the core and supporting skills required by managers if they are to manage performance successfully. Remember, staff don't sabotage performance management systems—managers do.

CONCLUSION

Managing unsatisfactory performance is critical to managing the performance of an organisation. Unsatisfactory performance, including underperformance and non-performance, has the potential to inflict much damage on an organisation, not just in monetary terms but also by decreased productivity, low morale, conflict and dysfunctional teams. To minimise the effects of unsatisfactory performance, managers must deal with it immediately it is noticed. Because an individual who may not be performing satisfactorily may also be poorly managed, or even discriminated against, legislation exists to protect staff and ensure they are fairly and equitably treated while managers and supervisors work with them to improve performance. Similarly, legislation combined with the legal infrastructure acts to ensure that people are not dismissed in situations that may be considered harsh or unjust.

The model of managing unsatisfactory performance presented in this chapter is designed to guide managers through a process that uses the skills and knowledge from other chapters in the book and that serves the interests of both manager and staff member. Most incidents of unsatisfactory performance can be managed with appropriate feedback near the time of the specific incident. This is preferable to termination, which is a costly solution to unsatisfactory performance. Repeated unsatisfactory performance may require a counselling discussion, and more serious transgressions will necessitate a written warning of unsatisfactory performance. If managers do not manage unsatisfactory performance in the appropriate manner from the outset, dealing with the unsatisfactory performance later becomes very difficult; it is untenable to take termination action until the appropriate processes have been implemented.

'REAL LIFE' CASE STUDY

The case study highlights the effect that corporate culture has on the development of a performance appraisal system that is inappropriate and out of touch with contemporary thinking on managing unsatisfactory performance. It also highlights the possibility that a flawed performance management system can result in damaging litigation.

Telstra currently employs approximately 46 649 full-time equivalent employees, agency and contractor staff, including staff employed directly by Telstra Corporation, domestic-controlled entities and offshore-controlled entities.

In 2007, the Telstra management culture was exposed on the ABC's *Four Corners* program. The program centred on the suicides of two Telstra workers—a technician and a call centre worker. The program highlighted the claim that medical evidence suggested work pressures, particularly in relation to the performance management system then in place at Telstra, may have largely contributed to the suicides.

Under former chief Sol Trujillo the culture of Telstra was radically reformed. The move from public to private hands, and efforts to lift productivity and competitiveness in a crowded market and hyper-competitive global economy, saw Telstra move from a customer service to sales culture. Telstra's call centre employees were increasingly expected to not only service customers but actively contribute to the bottom line through sales of products and related services. Call centre success is often reliant on the setting of ever-increasing performance targets, and rigorous monitoring of time and movements of individual employees.

In Telstra, management used sophisticated tracking technology to closely monitor how much product or service each employee sold, what was said to the customer, waiting times, response times, the quality of the activity, how long it took and how soon they moved on to the next call. Even standard breaks including toilet breaks were measured and recorded as 'unproductive time'. Similarly, technicians in the field were increasingly rated on the number of repair jobs they attended rather than whether the work had been satisfactorily completed.

John Buchanan, from the Workplace Research Centre at Sydney University, noted this is typical of a process known as 'work intensification' and places employees working under these conditions under enormous pressure to perform.

In the *Four Corners* program, several alleged quotes of the leadership team were nothing short of alarming. Greg Winn, at the time Telstra's Chief Operations Officer, responded to a question concerning the excessive monitoring, unrealistic targets and how Telstra dealt with underperforming employees with:

We're not running a democracy. We don't manage by consensus. We're criticised for it but the fact of the matter is we run an absolute dictatorship and that's what's going to drive this transformation and deliver results.

And later he stated:

It's a cultural issue. If you can't get the people to go there, and you try once and you try twice, which is sometimes hard for me but I do believe in a second chance, then you just shoot 'em and get them out of the way, you know, and put people in that you can teach the new business process to and drive on.

Telstra is not the only large Australian company to have attempted to reform its workplace culture and practices in order to better compete in the world economy. However, most do not end up the subject of a *Four Corners* exposé and allegations that its culture and treatment of employees directly contributed to the suicide of two employees.

Indeed, in 2009 the Telstra staff performance management system was criticised by the Australian Industrial Relations Commission as a tool that could be used to intimidate and bully workers. The Commission criticised the management culture under Sol Trujillo that led to the implementation of human resources policies such as the Points Productivity Measure and Performance Improvement and Conduct Management. In its ruling, the Commission observed that such systems can be used improperly to 'bully employees'.

Nonetheless, the company's 2008 *Corporate Social Responsibility Report* suggests that Telstra is aware of the effects of stress caused from work. Indeed, the report claims that Telstra takes a proactive and holistic approach to support the health and wellbeing of its employees, as demonstrated by the establishment of ongoing support to employees through a range of mental health and resilience programs. The report, citing recognition in 2008 by the Mental Health Council of Australia for Telstra's leadership in mental health issues in the workplace, is welcome evidence of a changed culture and the organisation's greater regard for its human capital.

'REAL LIFE' CASE STUDY CONTINUED

References

ABC TV 2007. *Four Corners—18/06/2007: Program Transcript*. Episode: 'Tough Calls', <www.abc.net.
au/4corners/content/2007/s1954636.htm>

ABC TV 2007. *Four Corners—18/06/2007: Tough Calls*, <www.abc.net.au/4corners/content/2007/
s1952054.htm>

Telstra n.d. *About Telstra: Engagement*, <www.telstra.com.au/abouttelstra/csr/employees/engagement.
cfm>

Telstra 2008. *Corporate Responsibility Report 2008*, <www.telstra.com.au/abouttelstra/csr/reporting_
performance/reports/2008/employees/talent.cfm>

Weaselwords.com.au 2007. *Help us to Understand Telstra: 'Dragons, submarines and savages'*, <www.
weaselwords.com.au/downloads/Telstra.pdf>

Workers Health Centre 2005. *Fact Sheet: Bullying at Work*, <www.workershealth.com.au/facts027.
html>

QUESTIONS

1 Identify three strategies Telstra could implement to improve the effectiveness of the performance
   management system and reduce the possibility of improper use resulting in bullying.
2 As an HR officer, you have been asked to assist in the development of an anti-bullying policy, and
   procedure and a code of practice for acceptable behaviour at work. List what should be included in the
   policy and code of practice.

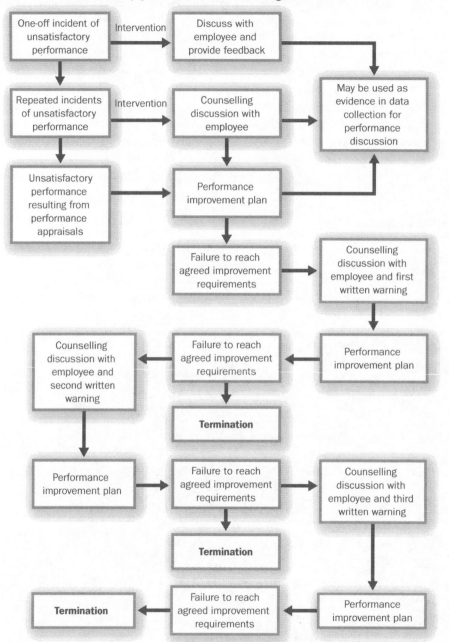

Unsatisfactory performance management flowchart

One-off incident of unsatisfactory performance → *Intervention* → Discuss with employee and provide feedback

Repeated incidents of unsatisfactory performance → *Intervention* → Counselling discussion with employee

May be used as evidence in data collection for performance discussion

Unsatisfactory performance resulting from performance appraisals → Performance improvement plan

Failure to reach agreed improvement requirements → Counselling discussion with employee and first written warning

Performance improvement plan

Failure to reach agreed improvement requirements → Counselling discussion with employee and second written warning

Termination

Performance improvement plan → Failure to reach agreed improvement requirements → Counselling discussion with employee and third written warning

Termination

Termination ← Failure to reach agreed improvement requirements ← Performance improvement plan

✓ CHECKLISTS

Managing unsatisfactory performance

Check:

- ❏ Relevant organisation policies
- ❏ Relevant industrial legislation
- ❏ Relevant awards and agreements
- ❏ Anti-discrimination legislation
- ❏ Equal opportunity legislation
- ❏ Health and safety legislation
- ❏ Workers' compensation legislation
- ❏ Is your approach structured on the principles of fairness and equity?
- ❏ Your first discussion should be informal:
  - ❏ Provide specific feedback.
  - ❏ Support with evidence.
  - ❏ Evidence should be analysed and appraised.
  - ❏ Document the discussion.
- ❏ Your second discussion should be more formal:
  - ❏ Use counselling discussion model in Figure 11.4.
  - ❏ Provide specific feedback.
  - ❏ Support with evidence.
  - ❏ Evidence should be analysed and appraised.
  - ❏ Document the discussion.
  - ❏ Develop a performance improvement/development plan.
- ❏ Your third discussion combines the counselling discussion with a written warning:
  - ❏ Use counselling discussion model in Figure 11.4.
  - ❏ Prepare the written warning in accordance with Figure 11.5.
  - ❏ Seek input from Human Resources.
  - ❏ Refer to the previous development plan.
  - ❏ Provide specific feedback.
  - ❏ Support with evidence.
  - ❏ Evidence should be analysed and appraised.
  - ❏ Document the discussion.
  - ❏ Explain the consequences of continued unsatisfactory performance.
  - ❏ Develop a new performance improvement/development plan.
- ❏ Your fourth discussion combines the counselling discussion with a second written warning (if necessary).

  Remember, you may use one, two or three written warnings depending on your particular needs:
  - ❏ Use counselling discussion model in Figure 11.4.
  - ❏ Prepare second written warning in accordance with Figure 11.5.
  - ❏ Seek input from Human Resources.
  - ❏ Refer to the previous development plan.
  - ❏ Provide specific feedback.
  - ❏ Support with evidence.
  - ❏ Evidence should be analysed and appraised.

✔ CHECKLISTS CONTINUED

- ❏ Document the discussion.
- ❏ Explain the consequences of continued unsatisfactory performance.
- ❏ Develop a new performance improvement/development plan.
- ❏ Your fifth discussion combines the counselling discussion with a third written warning (if this is necessary):
  - ❏ Use counselling discussion model in Figure 11.4.
  - ❏ Prepare third written warning in accordance with Figure 11.5.
  - ❏ Seek input from Human Resources.
  - ❏ Refer to the previous development plan.
  - ❏ Provide specific feedback.
  - ❏ Support with evidence.
  - ❏ Evidence should be analysed and appraised.
  - ❏ Document the discussion.
  - ❏ Explain clearly that termination is the next step.
  - ❏ Develop a new performance improvement/development plan.
- ❏ Your sixth discussion terminates the employment of the individual. This discussion occurs much earlier if you choose not to use three written warnings:
  - ❏ Seek input from Human Resources.
  - ❏ Prepare all required written documentation.
  - ❏ Conduct discussion with employee and notify of termination.
  - ❏ Provide specific reasons for termination.

References

1   Cole, K. 2005, 3rd edn. *Management Theory and Practice*. Pearson Australia: Frenchs Forest, Sydney, p. 398.

2   Jones, R. 2010, 2nd edn. *Managing Human Resource Systems*. Pearson Australia: Frenchs Forest, Sydney, p. 138.

3   For more information on current industrial relations legislation, and the difference between WorkChoices and the *Fair Work Act*, see Jones, R. 2010, 3rd edn. *Managing Human Resource Systems*. Pearson Australia: Frenchs Forest, Sydney, Ch 6 (Implementing performance management systems) and Ch 23 (Developing industrial relations policy and strategies).

4   *Fair Work Act 2009* (Cth), section 351 (Discrimination) and section 385 (What is an unfair dismissal), <www.fwa.gov.au>, accessed 23 October 2009.

5   Rossett, A. 1987. *Training Needs Assessment*. Educational Technology Publications: Englewood Cliffs, NJ, pp. 31–43.

6   Kemmis, L. & Bastick, M. 2004. *Executives Must Uphold Duties or Face Summary Termination*, <www.findlaw.com.au/article/12576.htm> accessed 23 October 2009.

7   Hilley, V. 2005. *Three Strikes and You're Out!*, <www.findlaw.com.au/article/13652.htm> accessed 23 October 2009.

8   Jhinku, S. 2001. *What's Your Capacity? Justifying Termination on Performance Grounds*, <www.findlaw.com.au/article/2112.htm> accessed 23 October 2009.

CHAPTER TWELVE

Skills for managing performance

Learning outcomes

After reading this chapter you should be able to:

* outline five different types of questions
* explain why questions should be planned
* list the barriers to effective listening
* explain the reasons for having a purpose when listening
* describe the term 'active listening'
* explain why feedback should be specific
* state the reasons why feedback must be a two-way process
* outline how to give feedback
* define the term 'coaching'
* describe the relationship between coaching and learning

* explain how to coach
* explain the difference between dumping and delegation
* outline how to delegate
* list the benefits of conflict
* explain the causes of conflict
* explain how to manage conflict
* explain how to negotiate
* state the need for diversity management
* explain the term 'discrimination'
* explain the value of diversity management
* list the four main interventions in developing diversity management
* understand ethical contexts.

INTRODUCTION

This chapter does not follow the formula used in the rest of the book. Instead, it outlines the essential skills you need to use to be successful in managing performance improvement. These skills are sometimes known as interpersonal skills or people skills. They were identified earlier in the book as 'soft' skills—in comparison with purely technical skills, referred to as 'hard' skills. For example, soft skills include the ability to listen effectively, manage conflict or negotiate, while hard skills include the ability to drive a tractor, use a complex software program or apply accounting principles.

Soft skills are required in managing performance improvement because many of the interactions you have when managing performance are with people. Thus, your ability to manage these interactions effectively will affect their performance and that will, in turn, affect your own performance as a manager. While one chapter cannot hope to provide you with the opportunity to master the skills, it presents a number of easy-to-use steps that should give you a conceptual understanding of the skill set and provide a framework through which you can practise the skills and become more proficient. Additionally, references for further reading, practice and skill building are provided, giving you a more in-depth understanding of the skills.

Core communication skills

There are three core communication skills that underpin the management of performance in the workplace. These are important and necessary skills in managing people generally, but are critical in managing performance. The critical core communication skills are questioning, listening and feedback. Each of these is now discussed.

Questioning

Anyone can ask a question, but it takes skill to ask the right question at the right time to obtain the specific information you require. Questioning is a form of two-way communication that is often not used as skilfully as it could be. It is a two-way communication method because it requires the full participation of at least two individuals in order to gain useful information. People use questions every day, mainly to obtain information or as a means of starting a conversation. Thus, questioning is an important skill and thought must be applied to constructing a question that will elicit the information you want. Having a specific purpose in mind when formulating a question, and being clear on what the outcomes are to be, will help you to construct a question that is effective. Asking questions can be a powerful tool in learning and in the building of new knowledge that comes from working through problems.

Purposes of questioning

The reasons for asking a question are many and varied, but may be grouped into the following broad categories:

- to develop an active environment in which to work and learn
- to focus attention
- to maintain interest and motivation
- to stimulate staff to accept more responsibility for their own learning and development

- to clarify

- to assess knowledge, understanding, experience and attitudes

- to facilitate learning and development

- to identify learning needs

- to facilitate feedback

- to allow staff to express feelings, thoughts and opinions

- to facilitate recognition, acceptance and creativity.

Types of question

Most people are familiar with two types of questions—open and closed. Open questions encourage a variety of answers, while closed questions limit responses significantly. Each has its role to play in communicating in the workplace and in managing workplace performance. Open questions facilitate discussion by encouraging the other person to talk. They are used for obtaining general information or details and in developing rapport with individuals. Closed questions are not necessarily those that elicit an answer of 'yes' or 'no'.[1] Closed questions can also be those to which there is a defined or limited answer, such as 'Do you travel by train or plane when you go interstate?' or 'In which month did you finish that project?' or 'Who was Winston Churchill?'. These questions are designed to elicit very specific information.

The two types of question form the basis of the development of other types of question. In the discussion below, the question types listed are not exhaustive. If you require further information on other question types, consult the Further reading section in this chapter.

Neutral questions

Neutral questions do not try to indicate the 'correct' answer to the receiver, nor do they exhibit any bias or preferred direction. For example, 'What do you think is the cause of the problem?' or 'How did you feel about that?' are neutral questions. These are based on open questions and are designed to elicit a person's opinion.

Leading questions

'Of course, I doubt that you would have included the unions in that process, would you?' is clearly a leading question that indicates the expected answer. This could be unfair, depending on the circumstances that gave rise to the question. 'Oh, you are certified to run SAP operations on our mainframe, aren't you?' is also a leading question that directs the listener to the issue and thus verifies assumptions you have made or facts you wish to check.

Leading questions may also be used in supporting situations where you may need to deliberately direct the person but not want to issue an order. To calm a person who may have had a fright by a near involvement in an accident, you may want to get them away from a group of people to a quieter place where they can compose themselves. You might ask the question: 'It might be best if you had some quiet time for a little while, don't you think, Sybil?'

Loaded questions

Loaded questions are similar to leading questions but are more forceful. They are usually emotive in nature and generally elicit emotive responses, which do not help to obtain information. For example, 'I expect you have moved beyond stupid to simply incompetent by now?' is a loaded question. You will see that no matter which way the person answers this question, it is damning.

Mirror questions

Mirror questions are similar to the reflecting process described in listening. The question is a reflection of the respondent's original statement, with the intent of drawing out further information from them. For example, if the following was said: 'Well, I just don't know what to do. It seems as if I am being kept in the dark deliberately', you might respond with the question, 'Being kept in the dark deliberately?' The response to that may be, 'Yes. I haven't been included on the usual circulations, and a number of meetings have taken place without me'. You might then respond with a further mirroring question: 'Without you?' A mirror question invites a person to continue.

Probing questions

Probing questions tend to follow up on points made by the speaker. They are usually unplanned questions, as they are triggered by information received in answer to other questions on which you may want further detail. For example, after the response: 'I thought I had all the information I needed and I made the decision', you might wish to probe: 'How did you decide that you had all the information?' This type of question is especially useful when analysing performance and in the performance discussion.

Using questions

Questions are used in many strategies, including personnel interviewing, performance management, general conversation and any formal interviews. They are the platform on which much communication is based. Questions may be used at any time but the more deliberate, planned, targeted and structured they are, the faster you will gather information. Skilful, positive use of questioning will also develop good working relationships with your staff, and generate confidence and trust. Poorly structured questions will prevent you from realising the full potential of the information gathering you must do.

Questions must also be appropriate to the person you are addressing. For example, a question framed in complex language would be unsuitable for a person who did not have great fluency in language or had received little education. The use of jargon would be inappropriate for a person who would be unlikely to know it. Question structure can be critical where you are appraising performance and need to uncover all the relevant facts. Being aware of what it is you need to know and planning appropriate questions is an invaluable tool for managers. Take care when planning questions that you do not ask two questions in one. This can be very confusing to the respondent, who may not reply satisfactorily to either question.

Listening

Listening is one of the most critical subsets of communication skills. Managers need to be able to listen effectively in order to obtain maximum information on which to base sound decisions. Listening often reveals things that you are unable to obtain from any other source. Yet research shows that humans tend to be poor listeners, despite the large amount of listening we do every day of our lives.[2] People are only about 25% effective at listening.[3] Part of the reason for this is that we can process information at the rate of 400 words a minute, while we speak at about

200 words a minute.[4] This leaves a gap of at least 200 words that are not spoken but the receiver has the capacity to listen to. Consequently, our minds can wander or we can be thinking of other things while a person is speaking.[5] Listening can also be rendered ineffective when the listener is emotional, when information is distorted from being passed on from one person to another, or where listeners are focused only on meeting their own needs. When listeners are emotional, prejudiced or judgmental, it becomes impossible for them to listen effectively. Their ability to think and be rational is reduced because they are focused on their own emotions. So when you become angry, hurt or distressed, you are unable to listen to the speaker, to hold a useful conversation or to problem solve. When focused on your own needs, there is a greater tendency for you to interrupt the speaker, be selective in what you hear, jump to conclusions or blame the messenger.

These barriers are illustrated in Figure 12.1. Managers can miss significant information if they do not master the art of listening effectively.

FIGURE 12.1 Barriers to effective listening

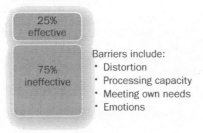

Purpose

To be a more effective listener you need to have a specific purpose in listening. For example, when conducting a performance discussion, you want to get to the issues that are constraining performance so that you can work with the individual to improve performance. As you ask questions and problem-solve with the individual, you will focus on listening to what is being said to see if you can discover the causes of constrained performance. This will secure information that allows you to develop appropriate strategies with the individual. However, if you have decided that the person is guilty of not caring and you are satisfied that this explains a poorer-than-expected performance, you are unlikely to discover critical information that you could gain. The person will sense your attitude and be too defensive to give the information, or you will not hear or interpret correctly what is being said.

Dwyer suggests there are two broad purposes in listening:[6]

1 As the sender of a message, you want to know how your message has been interpreted. This is revealed by listening to the answer from the receiver.

2 As a receiver of a message, you want to be able to understand what is being said to you.

If you do not have a clear purpose in listening, you will find that you do not hear everything that is said. Figure 12.2 demonstrates how a purpose in listening can spear through the barriers to make listening more effective.

FIGURE 12.2 Purposeful listening

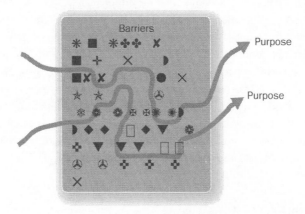

Active listening

A process called *active listening* has been designed to improve listening skills. This involves a number of principles to focus the listener's attention on what is being said:[7]

- Have a purpose for listening.
- Pay attention to the non-verbals of your speaker.
- Respond to the speaker by paraphrasing.
- Demonstrate that you understand the speaker.
- Encourage the speaker.
- When you are listening, do not be working out what you will say next.
- Be sensitive to the disposition of the speaker.
- Listen to the whole message. Let the speaker finish.
- Try to put the speaker at ease.
- Don't shoot the messenger; respond to the message, not the individual.

Listening actively means focusing and concentrating on what the speaker is saying, and blocking out all the potential barriers to listening. You can also use the following techniques to facilitate focus:

- *Reflecting*—repeat the feelings conveyed in the message you are hearing.
- *Paraphrasing*—restate, in your own words, the main ideas contained in the message you are hearing.
- *Clarifying*—ask suitable questions to clarify your understanding, or say what it is that you think has been said in the message you are hearing.
- *Summarising*—bring together the main points of the message you have heard.

These techniques help you concentrate on what is being said and ensure that you have a solid understanding of the communication. In this way you will glean more information from the interaction.

How to listen effectively

1   Listen for total meaning.

2   Respond to the feelings the speaker conveys.

3   Note all the cues the speaker gives you, both verbal and non-verbal.

4   Concentrate on what the speaker is saying:
    - Understand what is being said.
    - Focus on the message being sent.
    - Review the points made.
    - Ask questions about the message.
    - Don't interrupt the speaker.

Listening is an important communication skill and is vital in developing solid working relationships with staff. It is a crucial skill in giving and receiving feedback, and essential to the successful management of performance improvement.

Feedback

Giving feedback is an important management tool and a critical skill in effective communication.[8] It is a participative process that requires the involvement of both parties for the communication to be successful. Effective feedback may be described as a communication that results in identified behaviour being changed or continued by agreement between the participating parties to the communication. To be effective, feedback must be framed in such a manner that the receiver of the feedback can actually use it. Staff require feedback, and if it is not given they will devise informal ways of obtaining it, in which case it may not be correct or provide appropriate perspectives.[9]

Feedback must be specific and focused

Feedback that is vague is of little use because the receiver can do nothing about it. For example, if you were told 'You are very threatening', you would find it difficult to do anything about it because there is nothing substantial in the communication to help you focus on the behaviour that might be threatening. This has one of two effects. You may become defensive because the statement is generalised and unfavourable, or you may ask for evidence or examples. Unfortunately, it is usually the former of the two options that most people choose.

Feedback focused on a particular behaviour—for example, 'When you had finished your presentation, it might have helped to ask for questions or the audience's feelings about the proposal; that is usually more helpful'—provides some specific information that the individual can do something about. Also, it does not precipitate emotional reactions by appearing to be judgmental. The statement 'You were too airy-fairy' is likely to get the immediate response 'No, I wasn't', whereas the statement 'I think it would have helped to have a concrete example after the second point to aid understanding' is specific and focused on behaviours or actions that the receiver can do something about.

Feedback must be a two-way communication

It should never be the intention of people providing feedback to 'get something off their chest' or merely to chastise another individual. Such feedback does not meet the needs of receivers to obtain clear, focused information about their behaviours and how they might improve their performance. In improving performance, the receiver will also be meeting the needs of the provider of the feedback. Receivers may need to seek further information and ask for examples if the feedback is not specific enough for them. They should feel comfortable about doing this so that the feedback becomes a two-way, fully participative interaction that has as its purpose a change in behaviour (or a continuation of behaviour) that will result in improved performance. This must be the purpose of managers in providing feedback to their staff.

Feedback must be timely and appropriate

The timing of the feedback should be as close to the behaviour as possible. It is of little help if a manager saves up feedback until a scheduled formal discussion on the matter. Feedback should occur as close to the event as possible to ensure that the receiver of the feedback does not forget it. Delayed feedback may occur too late for the receiver to do anything with it, in which case the feedback is useless. It is also important that feedback be appropriate to the situation. For example, providing elaborate comments on a document's layout when you have been asked for feedback on the content of an early draft of a document is not useful to the receiver.

A useful approach to giving feedback

Communication is often destructive rather than supportive, validating and strengthening.[10] Carlopio, Andrewartha and Armstrong provide a useful guide to how to engage in *descriptive communication* rather than evaluative communication; this is the essence of providing effective feedback.[11] The three steps in descriptive communication are illustrated in Figure 12.3. You will note that this process is reflected in the approach to managing performance contained in this book.

FIGURE 12.3 Descriptive communication[12]

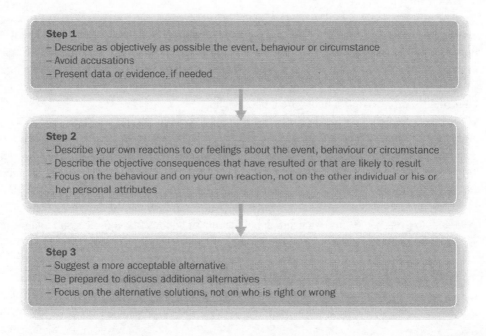

Step 1
– Describe as objectively as possible the event, behaviour or circumstance
– Avoid accusations
– Present data or evidence, if needed

Step 2
– Describe your own reactions to or feelings about the event, behaviour or circumstance
– Describe the objective consequences that have resulted or that are likely to result
– Focus on the behaviour and on your own reaction, not on the other individual or his or her personal attributes

Step 3
– Suggest a more acceptable alternative
– Be prepared to discuss additional alternatives
– Focus on the alternative solutions, not on who is right or wrong

How to give feedback

1 *Frame feedback so it is specific.*
   - Feedback needs to focus on specific issues or behaviours for it to be useful to the receiver.
   - General or vague feedback is unhelpful and precipitates emotional reactions in receivers.
   - Specific feedback supported by specific examples reduces defensiveness and focuses discussion on the real matter. For example, 'I reviewed that report you gave me and found mistakes on pages 3, 6, 12, 14, 17 and 18. I noticed that they all related to calculations from the spreadsheet you used to generate graphs'.

2 *Focus feedback on behaviours that the receiver can do something about.*
   - In combination with point 1, focusing on behaviours that the receiver can do something about helps to improve performance and reduce emotional reactions to feedback. For example, a comment like 'What a huge mess this is!' refers to a specific situation but it does not help the receiver to do anything about the mess.
   - Feedback that is specific and focused on what the receiver can do is more helpful: 'This is a mess. It seems that the termination proceeded without approval from the Industrial Relations Manager, and during the discussion with the person the usual guidelines were not followed'.
   - Such a focus identifies the areas that can be improved, areas that both parties can concentrate on, and highlights specific things the receiver can do something about.

3 *The needs of both giver and receiver of feedback must be taken into account.*
   - Givers of feedback may very well need to clear the air about something that is annoying them or is wrong or needs improvement or change.
   - Feedback must never be given in anger, however.
   - These needs must be balanced against the need for the receiver to be able to use the feedback.
   - Staff receiving feedback need to learn and to develop, thereby improving their performance.
   - Feedback presented in anger renders the feedback unusable because it creates negativity in the receiver, thus worsening the emotional reaction and making rational thought impossible.

4 *Feedback must be two-way.*
   - Contrary to popular belief, feedback is not just one person communicating with another.
   - For feedback to be really useful and to trigger improved performance, the receiver of the feedback needs to ask questions, clarify, seek examples, identify incidents, understand implications and realise what needs to be done.
   - Receivers denied two-way feedback are not likely to improve performance.

5 *Feedback should be appropriate to the situation.*
   - If asked to give feedback, or if you are providing feedback to improve performance, it is not useful to the receiver if you describe what your old boss from 20 years ago said or did.

- It is appropriate if you tell the person what you have learned from your experience with the particular equipment or software or situation.
- Likewise, it is inappropriate if you launch into what is wrong with the younger generation in the workplace these days if you are giving feedback about a mistake that a new graduate has made.
- It is appropriate to draw attention to what most people do in this particular circumstance and what the better performers do in the same situation.
- Feedback that all members of a team can participate in and learn from is appropriately done in front of the team.
- Feedback that is personal in nature and applies to the individual is not appropriately done in front of the team.

6 *Feedback should be timely.*
- Give feedback as close to the occurrence of the behaviour, task or incident as possible.
- Delaying feedback lessens its effectiveness and allows unsatisfactory performance to continue, which makes it harder to bring into line at a later stage (see Chapter 11). The culprits may think they are doing a good job.

Feedback that is based in descriptive communication and follows the six points above should enable you to provide focused and useful information that will be empowering to staff in your organisation. This applies to both positive and negative feedback. It should be remembered that negative feedback has a greater impact on performance improvement than positive feedback.[13] Negative feedback that is specific in nature, focused on what the receiver can do, sensitive to the receiver's needs, two-way, appropriate to the situation and timely provides clear pathways to improvement rather than humiliating, angering and frustrating those who are criticised. However, this does not suggest that positive feedback should not be given. Positive feedback is essential, an important reward, and necessary in maintaining motivation.

Other critical skills

If the core communication skills form the platform on which performance management is based, the critical skills facilitate the application of the platform to the day-to-day activities in the workplace. The six skills are coaching, mentoring, delegation, managing conflict, negotiation, and managing diversity. It is through these skills that the three core skills of questioning, listening and feedback are applied.

1 *Coaching*—Performance improvement relies on the ability of the manager to provide support if and when a staff member requires it. Thus, the ability to coach in order to develop skills and knowledge in individuals is a basic requirement for managers who want to help staff improve performance.

2 *Mentoring*—Mentoring is a useful management tool that can be incorporated in a performance management system. It can be utilised to help high-potential employees achieve their goals or to help employees achieve their full potential. If those involved in the mentoring process are aware of the benefits it provides to mentor, protégé and thus organisation, it can be an invaluable performance management tool.

3 *Delegation*—This is an important tool for management, as it can be used as a training and development activity, and as a way of developing responsibility in staff. It also affords staff

opportunities to expand their experience and to use skills that they have but do not use in their normal job activities, and enables managers to achieve more through the efficient deployment of staff.

4   *Managing conflict*—Within the organisation, this is a task that is constantly required of managers. Organisations need conflict to be healthy, but it must be managed and channelled into useful outcomes. Environments in which conflict is not appropriately channelled are likely to be underperforming.

5   *Negotiation*—This is a daily activity that occurs as part of the normal course of human interaction. Without this skill, managers may find they are unable to focus staff activity effectively to achieve specified results. It is no longer acceptable, or possible, simply to give orders and expect them to be obeyed.

6   *Managing diversity*—This is an integral part of management today. As the nature of the workforce changes, managers must be able to manage the diverse individuals that form the organisational community. The different perspectives that individuals of different cultures, disciplines, educational levels and experience bring to the table are a rich source of market intelligence, management processes and strategies, which can give an organisation a real competitive edge in the marketplace.

Coaching

Coaching is an on-the-job training technique. It can be used in a variety of situations to help people develop new knowledge, skills and attributes. It can be used for specific tasks, such as word processing or operating a boiler in a sugar mill; or for processes such as those within a performance management system; or for logging harassment or discrimination complaints. It can also be used for specific knowledge or skill building, such as learning about the termination sections of a piece of industrial legislation, or batting in the game of cricket.

Coaching is an age-old process used for the development of performance. It can occur between two individuals or between one individual and a whole team. The latter is instantly recognisable as a method that sporting teams use, but is not so easily recognised (although it is equally valid) within organisations. It is especially valid in the current organisational climate, where more and more staff and managers find themselves working as part of a team. Coaching is useful for specific, individual training needs within a work unit, where training can be provided as needed at exactly the right time.[14]

What is coaching?

Kinlaw defines successful coaching as 'a mutual conversation that follows a predictable process and leads to superior performance, commitment to sustained improvement, and positive relationships'.[15] This definition suggests there are four parts to understanding coaching:

1   It is a process, and like any other process it must be applied in a logical, systematic way to achieve results.

2   Its aim is to improve performance to an agreed level or as high as it can possibly go.

3   Coaching is concerned with securing long-term continuous performance improvement on top of existing performance.

4   It is focused on the development of positive and ongoing relationships between people.

Through this process, coaching develops confidence, trust and cooperation between staff and management, and results in better commitment and performance by all.

Coaching is a guiding process, during which the coach may provide hints, clues, feedback, cues, reminders, practice, problem solving, exposure to models and demonstrations while the learner is developing the knowledge, skills or attributes required.[16] Coaching will become more detailed as time goes on and the learner practises and becomes more expert at the task. For the process of coaching to work, coaches need base communication skills, interpersonal skills, and training and development skills, as well as technical and subject expertise. Kinlaw suggests that at least two common attributes are shared by all coaching interactions:[17]

1 They are discussions of personal discovery.

2 They focus on performance or performance-related topics.

These attributes reinforce the performance emphasis and the individual nature of coaching. The process of coaching is illustrated in Figure 12.4.

FIGURE 12.4 The process of coaching

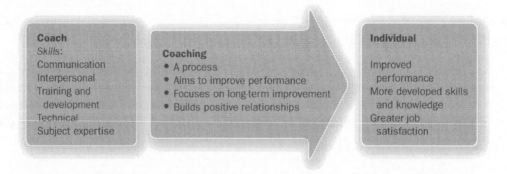

Successful coaching

To be successful, Kinlaw suggests that seven criteria need to be met in coaching:[18]

1 It must result in positive performance change and new or renewed commitment to:
   - self-sufficiency
   - the organisation's goals and values
   - continuous learning
   - continuous improved achievement.

2 It must result in achievement or maintenance of positive work relationships.

3 It is a mutual interaction.

4 It communicates respect.

5 It is problem-focused.

6 It is change-oriented.

7 It follows an identifiable sequence or flow and requires the use of specific communication skills.

Coaching must be a planned activity that has specific objectives or it will fail. It also requires an investment of time and effort by both manager and staff member. Managers will reap from coaching only what they are prepared to put into the process in terms of effort, as with any successful management endeavour.

Learning and coaching

We learn a great deal from experience—informal learning that takes place outside learning institutions or training courses. The majority of our learning takes place in these informal environments. Much of our early childhood learning occurs through observing our parents and siblings. Current learning theory suggests that learning is a dynamic process, unique to each individual, and develops through experience over the course of our lives.[19]

Performance may also be seen in this light. As we have opportunities to perform in different environments, using different skill mixes, in different situations, our knowledge grows and develops, facilitating more expert performance. Consequently, how individuals create knowledge and how it is organised in memory are critical components of expert performance.[20] It is possible to define work performance as a function of an individual's ability to problem-solve, and to construct and then use different types of knowledge. Workplace learning therefore offers great opportunities for learning and enhancing performance through participation in everyday problems, which strengthens existing knowledge, and through unusual problems, during which new knowledge is constructed. New knowledge facilitates higher levels of performance. Figure 12.5 illustrates this point.

Coaching maximises workplace opportunities for learning and developing better performance by guiding individuals as they perform tasks, duties and jobs. Coaching provides practically focused, individual assistance to people when it is needed, thus maximising learning opportunities. Communication skills are the foundations on which coaching depends. Coaches are of no help to an individual if they cannot communicate effectively.

How to coach

1 Determine what the performance issues are.
2 Identify the knowledge and skills required.
3 State the goals of the coaching program.
4 Discuss the expectations of both parties.
5 Set the learning objectives for the program.
6 Consider suitable learning strategies.
7 Map out a development plan.
8 Implement the development plan.
9 Review progress.
10 Evaluate the program.

Mentoring

Mentoring is not just for high-potential employees or senior managers; it is also about ensuring that all employees are afforded the opportunity to achieve their goals within the organisational structure. Mentoring can be utilised at all levels within an organisation. It can be used at the workshop level by the senior foreman mentoring an apprentice, in the office by an office manager mentoring an administrative trainee, or at the senior management level, where a CEO might mentor a newly appointed general manager.

FIGURE 12.5 How individuals learn[21]

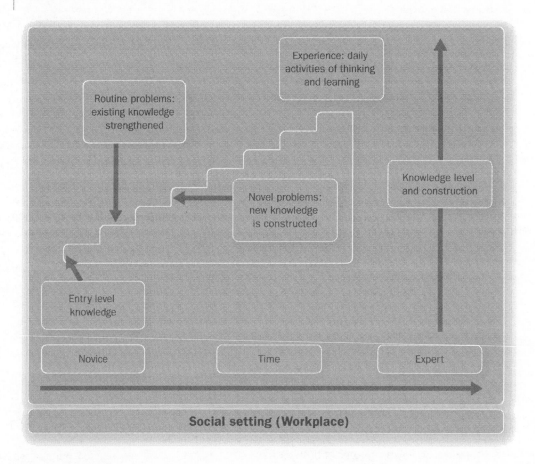

What is mentoring?

Mentoring is a relationship formed between a senior employee and a junior employee that is based on support and sponsorship. The junior employee is often referred to as a protégé. Through the process of mentoring, the mentor will use three main techniques to develop the protégé: coaching, counselling and sponsorship.

1 *Coaching*—as covered earlier in this chapter, is an on-the-job training technique used to help people develop new knowledge, skills and attributes.

2 *Counselling*—relates to the discussions, advice and feedback given to the protégé to build self-confidence.

3 *Sponsorship*—is shown where the mentor stands up for the protégé in a political arena or for a promotional opportunity. The sponsor vouches for and espouses the virtues of the protégé in an endeavour to secure the protégé's career progression.[22]

Choosing a mentor

Not every senior employee is capable of becoming a mentor. Mentors need to be chosen carefully to ensure the protégé is offered the best opportunity for success. Attributes to be considered when choosing a mentor are:

- good communication skills
- empathy—the ability to put themselves in the shoes of the other person
- skill at providing clear directions
- ability and willingness to share their experiences
- suitability as a role model.

These attributes are similar to those required of a good manager.

Benefits of mentoring

There are benefits to mentoring for the mentor, the protégé and the organisation:[23]

- The relationship in a mentoring program can provide the mentor with the immense satisfaction of being responsible for protégés achieving to their full potential; mentors also gain respect for their judgment and are able to share their knowledge and experience.

- The mentoring system allows the mentor access to the grapevine at the lower levels of an organisation, which could avoid potential problems before they arise.

- Protégés are more likely to be promoted, have higher pay raises and show more loyalty to an organisation than those who have not been mentored.

The most effective utilisation of the mentoring relationship is outside the direct reporting relationship, as this removes the anguish associated with the mentor being a boss and the person who conducts the performance appraisal.

The traditional views are slowly changing to allow the mentoring role to be seen as a strength rather than a weakness or an indication that the protégés are unable to survive on their own.

Delegation

Delegation is one of the most powerful on-the-job training techniques available to managers, and it is intrinsically connected with the job of managing. Managing requires that managers achieve things through others. The assignment of work to others is part of the process of delegation which, in turn, is part of management. Effective delegation of work to staff can enhance participation, confidence and trust in staff, and form a basic building block in team development. Primarily, delegation is a way in which managers are able to accomplish more work than they could do on their own. It also results in more planning time and less fire-fighting for managers who are able to delegate effectively, while increasing the challenge and satisfaction of work for staff.

Despite the benefits of delegation, it is often performed so poorly that staff have the opposite reactions to those identified above. Bad delegation can demotivate and cause resentment in staff. No delegation at all will mean you become overstressed and poorly organised; your staff will be confused and lacking direction to the extent that you will not be managing, but doing. Ineffective managers are characterised by their failure to delegate, mistakenly believing that keeping control means doing all the work themselves.

A definition

Delegation is the process through which managers transfer responsibility for a task, activity or duty to a subordinate with the appropriate authority to carry it out. Managers retain the account-ability for the task, activity or duty because one cannot delegate accountability. For example, a manager can delegate the task of preparing the monthly progress report and the responsibility and authority to get the task done. The manager is still answerable for the completion of the report on time and for its accuracy. Delegation therefore is not simply a process of giving a job to someone else. Figure 12.6 illustrates the delegation of tasks to other people, also the delegation of a task to the manager from the next level up.

FIGURE 12.6 Delegation

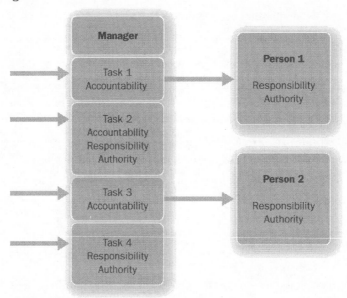

Delegation, not dumping

Managers often simply 'dump' things with their staff and call it delegation. These same managers will complain in despair that every time they delegate, they end up doing the job themselves, so they don't bother in the first place. Delegation is not a process of giving jobs to others to do and leaving them alone. It carries with it great responsibilities and an expectation that the person to whom a job has been delegated will achieve the results required. To do this, there are specific requirements of both manager and staff member.

To be able to delegate effectively, the delegator needs to accept five essential tenets about delegation:

1 Everyone makes mistakes.

2 A delegated job may not be done in the same way as the delegator would do it.

3 The completed job may not look exactly the way it would look if the delegator did it.

4 Managers are not paid to 'pretty' things up or edit the work of others so that it more closely fits the manager's (delegator's) perception of how it should be. Managers are paid to get results through others.

5   Skilfully setting objectives that focus on results or outcomes will provide the best framework for effective delegation.

A staff member must be willing to take on the delegation. If you suspect that a staff member will not want the delegation or, no matter what you do, will resent it, you should not delegate until you have discussed the situation with that person. Staff must also have the appropriate skills and knowledge to perform the delegation. If they don't have the required training, you will need to help them and monitor more closely and/or provide training to enable them to take on the delegation.

Why managers should delegate

There are four very good reasons why managers should delegate. The overall reason is that it makes managers more effective. Managers become more effective when they:

1   *utilise available skills.* Staff may have particular experience or expertise in specific areas where you do not. Use these skills.

2   *utilise time.* You may not have enough time to do a task to the standard you would like, or as soon as you would wish, because of other, more important, matters.

3   *utilise costs.* A manager is a more costly resource than staff. Where it is possible that staff can perform a task, delegate it to them. You can still schedule time to check that it is correct.

4   *utilise training.* Delegating is a method of training. It facilitates growth in staff and prepares them for more responsibility through a wider range of experiences.

How to delegate

1   *Decide to whom to delegate.* When choosing a person for delegation, there are a number of options: you may select someone who is already able to perform the task or a person who is not yet able, or you may wish to delegate to a team of people. Obviously, the choice will depend on a number of factors, including whether you have the time available for basic training, how much time is available to complete the job, and whether the person is likely to be interested in doing the job. This last point is important. Don't choose a person who is not interested in the job or fails to see the importance of doing it. They may well see the job as 'dumping' by a manager, regardless of how effectively you carry out the delegation. People may need to be rewarded for taking on delegated duties. This does not necessarily mean higher pay; the reward may be as simple as public recognition.

2   *Explain the importance of the job.* This is a critical step in effective delegation. Unless the person understands the reason for doing the job, they are unlikely to appreciate its true value. A person must understand where the job fits into the bigger picture of the organisation and how important it is, especially how it affects tasks or jobs that may depend on the delegated job being done correctly. It is worth taking a few extra minutes to explain the nature, scope and importance of the job, so that the right attitude will be developed about doing the job and doing it right. Remember, you will transfer responsibility and authority for the job, but you will retain accountability for it.

3   *Describe the results required.* This can be seen as a mini setting-of-performance-standards exercise. While it may not be as formal as the process discussed in Chapter 5, the principles

of that chapter apply here. Describe the expected results and include appropriate standards and measures. Also describe any appropriate behaviour that may need to be demonstrated in going about the job. For example, there may be a need for confidentiality.

4 *Define the authority the individual has.* There is no point in giving people a job if they don't have the authority to carry it out: this will set them, and you, up for failure. What authority people will need will depend on the circumstances. For example, you may have to give them authority to set deadlines for receipt of reports, to direct other staff, to take certain priority over other work, or to call meetings. Whatever authority is needed, you must let all staff know so there is no confusion.

5 *Define the resources the individual can use.* The provision of appropriate resources is also critical if the delegation is to be effective. Delegating a job without access to the appropriate resources to complete it will result in resentment by the person once it is realised that the job cannot be completed. For example, delegating the task of preparing some financial information may require access to restricted parts of the financial software. While you cannot grant access to the delegatee, you can provide an authorised person for two hours to collect data and run appropriate reports.

6 *Agree on a deadline for completion.* You will recall from Chapter 5 that a time frame is required on all performance standards and objectives. When delegating, it is critical that people know exactly how much time they have to complete the job. While this should be open to negotiation once they discover exactly what must be done, ensure that you build in adequate time to check the accuracy of the work and to do what you must do with the result. Stress the importance of the deadline and encourage them to come forward at the first sign of a problem so that you can work on it together to ensure it does not run overtime.

7 *Ask for feedback (does the delegatee understand?).* Once the person begins work on the job, time will be of the essence. You cannot afford misunderstandings that may affect the result you are expecting. Ask the person to tell you what must be done, as they understand it. This is your opportunity to make sure the directions and standards you have set have been understood before the work begins. Ask for clarification if you are not convinced of a shared understanding between the two of you. Ensure that you are fully satisfied that the person knows what must be achieved, for you will only have yourself to blame from this point on.

8 *Agree on monitoring process.* After confirming the understanding of the delegatee, you do not cast them aside to complete the job. As you still have accountability for the job, you will need to monitor the progress of the job, as described in Chapter 6. Set up appropriate checkpoints. These may require you to get together with the person for only five minutes, but this will facilitate effective monitoring controls over the job and ensure that you identify problems before they become major.

These eight steps do not necessarily take a large amount of time—it depends on the job or task to be delegated. Usually they will take only a few minutes. Delegation is a process, and, like any process, if it is not applied correctly it is unlikely to work. You may find the process cumbersome at first, but you will find that with very little practice you can become an effective delegator.

Managing conflict

Conflict is a natural and ever-present part of everyday life. It can take the form of a simple disagreement between two workers, a heated argument between two division directors on the use of a particular resource, or a disagreement on policy and direction. Conflict nearly always accompanies change, and change management plans need to include suitable strategies to manage conflict in the workplace. Note the phrase 'managing conflict'. Conflict is inevitable. It cannot be eradicated, even though many people would probably prefer that it way. While too much conflict is dysfunctional, too little conflict is also dysfunctional.[24] Some conflict is needed to challenge existing ideas and to precipitate change and development, or organisations and people would stagnate and decline. Research shows that organisations in which there is little or no conflict usually fail in competitive markets.[25] Conflict must be managed for the good of all.

The pros and cons of conflict

The benefits of conflict are many, including:

- reduction of petty annoyances
- breaking of boredom
- facilitation of quality communication
- increased understanding of others
- improved motivation
- improved decision making and better quality decisions
- triggering change
- prompting creativity
- stimulating innovation
- increased development and growth.

Conflict can cause significant problems for individuals and organisations if it is not managed. It can:

- drain energy from the organisation and the people within it
- decrease morale
- lower productivity
- heighten personal and organisational stress
- render work dysfunctional
- damage relationships
- foster pettiness
- disrupt operations.

If conflict is managed appropriately, everyone can gain from the benefits it provides, and the negative and sometimes destructive aspects of conflict can be minimised.

Causes of conflict

The meeting of two different wants or needs causes conflict; because they are coming from two different directions, the initial impact of the meeting causes conflict. It is because of the convictions of the two people who have the different needs or wants that there is conflict. At first it is likely they will both try to get their own way by forcing their point of view. This can generate more forceful actions by the other individual, and major conflict suddenly erupts in the work group. Managers need to find ways of managing conflict so that everybody wins. The potentially destructive nature of unmanaged conflict is illustrated in Figure 12.7.

FIGURE 12.7 The destructive nature of unmanaged conflict

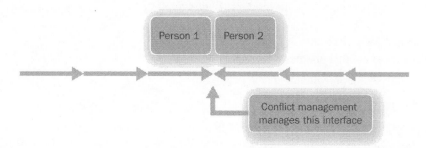

Carlopio, Andrewartha and Armstrong suggest a model that outlines the four main causes of conflict:[26]

1 *Personal differences.* These relate to the different personalities, opinions, beliefs, education, upbringing, religion, desires, values, culture, sensitivities, needs and habits that people have. Because of a lack of understanding of things that are different to our frame of reference, conflict can occur. Managing diversity is about how these differences can be managed effectively.

2 *Information processes.* These relate mainly to communication. When communication fails it precipitates conflict. Poor communication triggers misunderstandings, rumours, distorted information, contradictions and falsehoods. The speed of communications today intensifies the effects of poor communication; this underscores the need to have clear and effective communications in organisations.

3 *Role incompatibility.* This refers to the inherent conflict that is structured into organisations. Conflict occurs between functions, as in the case of production/sales, inventory control/distribution, accounting/service departments and staff positions/line management. It also occurs in specific roles that people have in teams or particular specialties, such as the Equal Employment Opportunity Manager, and in areas of an organisation that may find compliance with EEO principles a nuisance or even disrupting. Managers need to manage these structural conflicts. Recent organisational approaches aimed at eradicating this structural conflict include a restructuring based on project teams, which have members from all functions of the organisation.

4 *Environmental stress.* This covers a multitude of things that may affect the working environment and cause stress to employees. Examples range from a telephone technician wanting access to a busy telephone in a call centre, to major renovations in the workplace.

Cost-cutting environments, scarce resources, significant change and lack of information can also precipitate conflict. Uncertainty, which usually stems from change, is a major cause of conflict as people become confused, have confidence and trust destroyed, and jockey for positions and access to information. High levels of noise, vibrating machinery, poor interpersonal skills and faulty equipment can also generate conflict in the workplace. Managers need to manage environmental stress in ways that suit the situation.

Managers must manage conflict, but research suggests that they do not. Further, those people who are identified as being associated with conflict are often isolated from work groups, even where it is proven that the quality of the work of the group was superior because of the conflict generated by the individual.[27]

It has been suggested that conflict progresses through five stages, beginning with discomfort and ending in crisis[28] (see Figure 12.8). Managers should be able to intervene in conflict at all stages. The earlier a manager is able to intervene, the better. The higher the level of conflict becomes, the greater the chance of permanent damage to the workplace and the relationships within it.

Conflict management

There are five documented ways of managing conflict, categorised by the style and approach used to manage the conflict:

1 *Competing*—one party wins and the other party loses: can generate aggression and uncooperativeness through competition.

2 *Accommodating*—one party wins and the other loses: the opposite of competing, where one party puts the needs of the other before their own.

3 *Avoiding*—both parties lose; the conflict is ignored.

4 *Collaborating*—both parties win: cooperative in nature, both parties explore options that will satisfy the needs of both.

5 *Compromising*—both parties win some, no party is fully satisfied: an agreement is reached where both compromise.

There are situations in which it may be legitimate to use any one of these methods. However, it is desirable to work towards the use and adoption of the collaborative style, because this supports the satisfaction of both parties' needs. To do this:

1 Discuss the situation.

2 Gather information from the other person.

3 Give information to the other person.

4 Use a problem-solving approach.

5 Generate solutions.

6 Agree on a solution.

7 Implement the solution.

8 Follow up with each other.

FIGURE 12.8 Stages of conflict

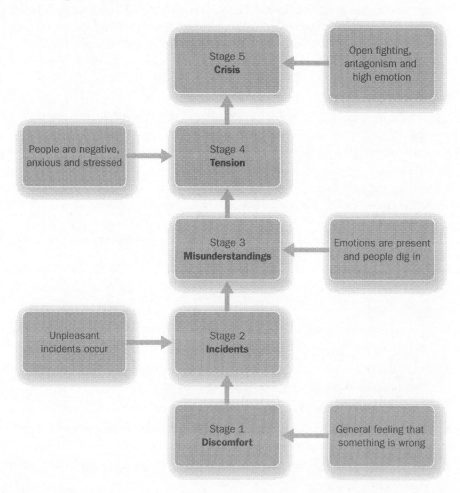

Negotiation

As individuals in a society, we negotiate every day in one form or another—whether it's with your spouse over who will take the boys to football, or where you will have lunch with colleagues, or when you will have a report ready for your boss, or whether you will watch one TV program in preference to another. Negotiation is another form of communicating, except that there are generally specific goals at which negotiation is directed. It is an important process of workplaces as people negotiate for limited resources, workloads, sales opportunities and even salaries. Some basic skills and processes can make the task of negotiating easier for all concerned.

Strategies

Most writers on the subject use the five conflict management styles of competing, accommodating, avoiding, collaborating, and compromising as strategies for negotiation. The styles are a useful way to frame an approach to negotiation. They can be divided into two types: *distributive negotiation* is concerned with how much a fixed pie of things can be divided up; *integrative negotiation* is based on collaborative ways of expanding the pie. Distributive negotiation is of necessity an adversarial approach that is confrontational in nature. By contrast, integrative negotiation is based on combined efforts to problem-solve and arrive at a suitable solution. Of the five conflict management styles, only collaboration is integrative.[29]

Carlopio, Andrewartha and Armstrong suggest six specific strategies:[30]

1 Establish shared goals.

2 Separate the people from the problem.

3 Focus on interests, not positions.

4 Invent options for mutual gains.

5 Use objective criteria.

6 Define success in terms of gains, not losses.

How to negotiate

Dwyer suggests there are five steps involved in negotiation. You will notice some similarity to the six strategies above:[31]

1 *Plan the negotiation.* Develop objectives, gather appropriate information and consider other points of view.

2 *Discuss.* Develop rapport; set an appropriate climate; table objectives, feelings and issues; and summarise.

3 *Propose.* State what it is you wish to resolve. Don't generalise, link to the other party's interests, and focus on interests instead of positions.

4 *Negotiate the issue.* Focus on issues, not people. Ask for what you want and summarise regularly to aid understanding.

5 *Confirm.* When agreement has been reached, confirm that all parties will commit to it.

Negotiation is assisted by the common courtesies of good communication, respect and trust. Where these are poor or non-existent, negotiation will be difficult and is likely to revert to the distributive type, which usually generates a great deal of unnecessary conflict.

Managing diversity

The nature of the workplace in the global economy is such that managers can expect their workforce to be composed of many different individuals from diverse cultural backgrounds. Remember that when we refer to diversity, we are referring to any group that identifies itself as a minority including migrants; refugees; gay or lesbian, aged or socially disadvantaged Australians; people with disabilities.

An understanding of these differences and how they can add value to the work group and the organisation is essential if managers are to manage effectively. The global marketplace has precipitated major challenges for the manager of an organisation. These include managing in a foreign country, managing a larger range of people from many backgrounds, market demographic changes that have precipitated changes in demand and consumer preferences, and changes in the demographics of staff that have led to different demands for pay and conditions.

There is increasing pressure on managers to manage skilfully and master the skills outlined in this chapter. The added factor of greater diversity in the workforce dictates the issue, as managers must manage all people equally, counteracting decades of discrimination and managing the interface between cultures, beliefs and values. From the perspective of managing performance, managers need to consider the effect of culture on an employee's attitudes to, and beliefs about, personal accountability and responsibility, cooperation with others, perceptions of management, motivation to achieve a task or outcome, and orientation to the workplace versus other commitments (such as family). It also means being aware of communication nuances, such as the use of silence in performance reviews, and understanding how a cultural background in which disclosure or self-criticism is not customary, which is common in some cultures, affects how decisions are made and conflicts resolved.

While equal employment opportunity legislation around the world has deliberately striven to repair the unequal position of disadvantaged groups of individuals, the more recent concept of *diversity management* focuses more on providing all people with equal developmental opportunities that are linked to corporate business strategy.[32]

Discrimination

In most liberal democracies, it is illegal to discriminate against people when making decisions about employment, education, accommodation, and the provision of goods and services. When dealing with employment-related issues, only those factors that pertain to the requirements of the job are valid and legal foundations on which to base decisions. Managers must also treat all people according to their merits, not according to the characteristics of the groups in society that they may belong to or are associated with. The aim of diversity management is to include and respect everyone. Legislation makes it unlawful to discriminate in acts or behaviour towards people on the basis of race, sex, marital status, impairment, pregnancy, sexuality or sexual preference, religious or political beliefs, age, medical or criminal record, or trade union activity.[33]

Such legislation has forced managers and organisations to develop and use policies that reduce and eradicate discrimination. This has also facilitated new and different ways of managing the organisation. While writers in the field find it difficult to gather substantive evidence to claim success,[34] there is general agreement that there has been an impact by equal employment opportunity (EEO) legislation and the associated policies and procedures implemented by organisations to effect protection from prosecution. Complaints of harassment of any sort, including sexual harassment, must be managed by organisations or the tribunals or commissions around the country that deal with these issues. Unless an organisation embraces the principles of EEO and embeds them in the strategic and operational processes of the organisation, there is little likelihood that EEO will be any more than an addition to the value system. If this is the case, those who have the responsibility to police it must continually reinforce EEO.[35] Where EEO is integrated in the plans and processes of the organisation, it becomes part of the value system of the organisation and is intrinsic rather than imposed.

Valuing diversity

Where diversity is embraced as a strategic issue, and an essential element for survival in the marketplace, it becomes an aspect of organisational culture that filters through policies, processes, procedures, plans and accountabilities.[36] Thus, it is more than an add-on value. By learning to value the different perspectives, experiences, interests, skill levels and knowledge of their staff that bring about greater creativity, more innovation and better decision making, organisations can maintain a competitive edge. A particular challenge for management has been the consequences of flatter organisation structures left behind in the wake of the significant restructuring of the 1980s and 1990s. These new structures left gaping holes in the career paths of people who viewed success as moving through progressively higher levels of management. In recent years there has been increased emphasis on balanced approaches to life, which acknowledge the multiple responsibilities of workers—for example, as partners, parents, and carers. Job satisfaction, which may once have been tied exclusively to promotional prospects, may now be gained in other ways that facilitate an acceptable level of participation in the out-of-work activities of child rearing, sporting interests, lifestyle choices and other options. Further management challenges are presented in the form of increased understanding of the needs of many groups within our society—Indigenous Australians, migrants, homosexuals, single parents, people with disabilities and other minority groups. With increased understanding comes greater participation and interaction.

Valuing diversity means understanding the great potential benefit that may be gained from the variety of talent, flexibility, self-actualisation, confidence, trust, openness, team participation, and new perspectives and understandings that can result from valuing worker individuality. A highly diverse workforce where individuals are valued for who they are can contribute to greater productivity, satisfaction and results.

Developing diversity management

Cultural diversity management is a relatively new field of management theory and practice and refers to management efforts at both the organisational and personal levels. Wilson holds that the majority of interventions into organisations to develop diversity management will fall into one of four groups:[37]

1   a general change of values and culture, which reaches out to individual attitudes
2   individual career development for all employees
3   special support, which empowers disadvantaged groups and individuals but is not targeted solely at them
4   managerial skills for a diverse workforce.

Senior management, line management and staff all have a role to play in these interventions. The management skills required to manage a diverse workforce are the same as those needed for any management position: the skills to manage people. Using only one style or set of tools for managing is not appropriate considering the diverse individuals who make up the workforce in the new century. Flexible work arrangements that allow people to arrange their working hours to suit their needs, to maximise their skills and talents, and to contribute their unique set of experiences facilitate greater morale and job satisfaction, which evidences itself in better results for the organisation. However, managers need to be able to manage performance in this flexible environment and to master the appropriate soft skills to ensure quality communication and interpersonal relationships. The management of diversity demands no less than equal opportunity for every worker, and respect for each one as an individual. Management's skills in managing people are critical in the maintenance of any diversity strategy.

Jamieson and O'Mara, cited in Wilson, have identified four tasks that need to be completed to manage diversity successfully:[38]

1   attracting and retaining competent employees within a slower growing labour force
2   motivating all employees

3   rewarding employees

4   supporting employees in ways that recognise their individuality.

The skills required for managing diversity successfully are the skills covered in this chapter. Now and in the future, organisations will demand that managers match their technical expertise with equal expertise in the management of people. Without that, organisations will find it difficult to maintain a competitive edge in the world marketplace.

Ethics and performance management

The eighth characteristic of an ideal manager, identified by the Karpin Report and covered in Part A of this text, is that of ethical/high personal standards. For managers to compete in world markets they must possess the skills to deal ethically with the performance management of their employees, wherever this may be in the global environment. In applying the previous material in this chapter on valuing diversity and developing diversity management, managers should understand that what is considered an ethical decision in China or Indonesia may not be an ethical decision in Australia, due to the cultural differences between these countries. Managers may take into account cultural norms and ethics when making decisions to ensure that the organisations entering into business arrangements share values and ethics that are compatible in a business environment.

Ethics is important not only in a global environmental perspective but also in the performance management system of an organisation. As it is a manager's role to achieve through their employees, a manager may overinflate the performance of these employees in order to look good.

How can a manager's ethical behaviour affect the performance of others? This question has many answers. The pressure placed on today's managers to meet the goals and objectives set by their organisations can lead them to break rules, cut corners or cut back on quality to meet expectations. If a manager exhibits this behaviour it can influence the people who report to that manager. These types of deviant behaviour may detrimentally shape the attitudes of a manager's subordinates towards the organisation and their role in it.

Ethics relate to the moral values of individuals, which will differ for each employee. It is part of the manager's role to create an ethically healthy context for their employees—one where the manager can lead by example and espouse the code of conduct adhered to by those in the organisation.

CONCLUSION

To manage performance effectively, managers need to master those skills that will help them manage people and personal interactions. At each step along the way of managing performance, managers require strong skills in handling people, from communicating listening to managing conflicts and negotiating. No amount of job aids, checklists or processes will substitute for a lack of interpersonal skills in managers. Without them, a manager cannot manage performance.

The use of appropriate communication techniques and skills will enhance the performance of both manager and staff. While managers have a responsibility to ensure that they develop the appropriate soft skills to manage performance, they also have a responsibility to develop those same skills in their staff to facilitate improved performance in the workplace and to do so in an ethically healthy context.

Further reading

Boulton, R. 1987. *People Skills*. Simon & Schuster: Sydney.

Carlopio, J., Andrewartha, G. & Armstrong, H. 1997. *Developing Management Skills*. Longman: Melbourne, Chs 5, 8, 9.

Cole, K. 2010, 4th edn. *Management: Theory and Practice*. Pearson Australia: Frenchs Forest, Sydney, Chs 5, 10, 11, 15, 16.

Dessler, G., Griffiths, J. & Lloyd-Walker, B. 2007, 3rd edn. *Human Resource Management*. Pearson Australia: Frenchs Forest, Sydney.

Dwyer, J. 2009, 8th edn. *The Business Communication Handbook*. Pearson Australia: Frenchs Forest, Sydney, Chs 1, 4, 5.

Fields, M. 2009. *Managing Diversity—Pocket Mentor*. Boston: Harvard Business Press.

Hogan, M. 2007. *Four Skills of Cultural Diversity Competence: A Process for Understanding and Practice*. Belmont, CA: Thomson Brooks/Cole.

Khurana, S. 2009. *Diversity Quotes*, <http://quotations.about.com/od/moretypes/a/diversityquotes.htm>.

Kinlaw, D. 1999, 2nd edn. *Coaching for Commitment*. Jossey-Bass Pfeiffer: San Francisco.

Nutting, J. & White, G. 1990, 2nd edn. *The Business of Communicating*. McGraw-Hill: Sydney, Ch 8.

Robbins, S., Bergman, R., Stagg, I. & Coulter, M. 2009, 5th edn. *Management*. Pearson Australia: Frenchs Forest, Sydney.

Robbins, S. & Hunsaker, P. 2006, 4th edn. *Training in Interpersonal Skills: Tips for Managing People at Work*. Prentice Hall: New York.

Thomas, D. & Inkson, K. 2003. *Cultural Intelligence*. Berrett-Koehler: San Francisco.

Ting-Toomey, S. and Chung, L.C. 2005. *Understanding Intercultural Communication*. Roxbury Publishing Co: Los Angeles.

Tovey, M.D. 1999. *Mentoring in the Workplace*. Prentice Hall: Sydney.

Tovey, M.D. & Lawlor, D.R., 2008, 2nd edn. *Training in Australia*. Pearson Australia: Frenchs Forest, Sydney (helpful when planning delegation as a training exercise).

References

1   Carlopio, J., Andrewartha, G. & Armstrong, H. 1997. *Developing Management Skills*. Longman: Melbourne, pp. 592–593.

2   Huseman, R., Lahiff, J. & Hatfield, J. 1976. *Interpersonal Communication in Organizations*. Holbrook Press: Boston.

3   Huseman, R., Galvin, M. & Prescott, D. 1988, 3rd edn. *Business Communication Strategies and Skills*. Harcourt Brace Jovanovich: Sydney, pp. 232–233.

4   Huseman et al., op. cit., 1988, p. 237.

5   Carlopio et al., op. cit., 1997, p. 237.

6   Dwyer, J. 2009, 8th edn. *The Business Communication Handbook*. Pearson Australia: Frenchs Forest, Sydney, p. 14.

7   Nutting, J. & White, G. 1990, 2nd edn. *The Business of Communicating*. McGraw-Hill: Sydney.

8   Carlopio et al., op. cit., 1997, pp. 213–257.

9   Leap, T. & Crino, M. 1990. *Personnel/Human Resource Management*. Macmillan: New York, p. 322.

10 Barnlund, D.C. 1968. 'Interpersonal communication: Survey and studies.' Cited in Carlopio et al, op. cit., p. 230.

11 Carlopio et al., op. cit., 1997, p. 228.

12 Carlopio et al., op. cit.,1997, pp. 592–593. Used with permission.

13 Podsakoff, P.M. 1989. 'Effects of feedback sign and credibility on goal setting and task performance.' *Organizational Behavior and Human Decision Processes*, 44(1), pp. 45–67.

14 Laird, D. 1985, 2nd edn. *Approaches to Training and Development*. Addison-Wesley: Reading, MA, pp. 69–70.

15 Kinlaw, D. 1999, 2nd edn. *Coaching for Commitment*. Jossey-Bass Pfeiffer: San Francisco, p. 31.

16 Tovey, M.D. 1999. *Mentoring in the Workplace*. Prentice Hall: Sydney, pp. 31–32.

17 Kinlaw, op. cit., 1999, p. 23.

18 Kinlaw, op. cit., 1999, pp. 24–25.

19   Tovey, op. cit., 1999, pp. 6–8.

20   Tovey, op. cit., 1999, p. 6.

21   Source: Tovey, op.cit., 1999, p. 8. Reproduced with permission.

22   Robbins, S.P., Millett, B., Waters-Marsh, T., 4th edn. *Organisational Behaviour*, p. 375.

23   Robbins et al., op. cit., 2004.

24   Carlopio et al., op. cit., 1997, pp. 360–361.

25   Carlopio et al., op. cit., 1997, p. 360.

26   Carlopio et al., op. cit., 1997, pp. 362–364.

27   Carlopio et al., op. cit., 1997, pp. 361–362.

28   Conflict Resolution Network. 1997, Sydney.

29   Carlopio et al., op. cit., 1997, pp. 369–370.

30   Carlopio et al., op. cit., 1997, pp. 370–371.

31   Dwyer, op. cit., 2009, pp. 160–161.

32   Wilson, E. 1996. 'Managing diversity and HRD.' In J. Stewart & J. McGoldrick, *Human Resources Development: Perspectives, Strategies and Practice*. Pitman: London, p. 159.

33   Gardner, M. & Palmer, G. 1997, 2nd edn. *Employment Relations: Industrial Relations and Human Resource Management in Australia*. Macmillan Education Australia: Melbourne, p. 458.

34   Wilson, op. cit., 1996, pp. 158–179; Gardner & Palmer, op. cit., 1997, pp. 452–484.

35   Wilson, op. cit., 1996, p. 159.

36   Wilson, op. cit., 1996, p. 163.

37   Wilson, op. cit., 1996, p. 166.

38   Jamieson, D. & O'Mara, J. 1991. 'Managing workforce 2000: Gaining the diversity advantage.' Cited in Wilson, op. cit., 1996, p. 165.

Active listening To listen for full meaning without making a premature interpretation or judgment.

Anti-discrimination legislation Legislation designed to stop specific groups and individual members of those groups from being treated unfairly and to ensure that they are treated solely on the basis of their skills and abilities.

Appraisal interview Part of the performance management process. In an appraisal interview the manager and employee review the appraisal and make plans to reinforce and develop strengths, and to remedy deficiencies or problems.

Attitudes Evaluative statements, either positive or negative, concerning people, object or events.

Attitude surveys Surveys that ask employees how they feel about their work, jobs, team, managers and the organisation. Sometimes also called climate surveys.

Attribution theory A theory that explains how people judge others differently depending on the meaning and importance we attribute to a given behaviour.

Balanced scorecard method A measurement-based management system or tool that translates organisational vision and strategy into action. It is based on the premise that a range of variables, in addition to financial performance, contribute to organisational performance, and as such should also be measured. Typically the tool looks at four areas—financial, customer, internal processes, and people/innovation/growth assets.

Behaviour anchored rating scale (BARS) A performance appraisal method that appraises an employee using a rating scale on examples of actual job behaviour that demonstrate good or poor performance.

Behavioural observation scale (BOS) A technique that identifies the key tasks for a job and specifies what an employee 'must do' to implement an organisation's vision, strategy and values effectively.

Bias The tendency to allow individual differences such as nationality, ethnicity, age or sex to affect a performance appraisal rating.

Career development A series of activities that contribute to an employee's career exploration, establishment, success and fulfilment.

Central tendency The tendency to rate all employees at the middle of the rating scale, which is usually an average rating.

Coaching An on-the-job training or development approach that can be used to develop new knowledge, skills, behaviours or attributes in order to improve work performance. It has a strong focus on the development of positive and ongoing relationships between people.

Code of ethics A formal statement of an organisation's primary values, and the ethical behaviours and rules it expects its employees to follow.

Communication The interchange of messages, verbal or non-verbal, between people, which require a sender, a message and a receiver.

Competency The state of being competent to perform particular activities at a particular standard in the workplace; a skill, knowledge or attribute needed to carry out a task successfully; observable behaviours that enable a person to perform an activity to the standard expected.

Competency-based job description   A job description that states the competencies required by the job holder.

Competency-based training (CBT)   Training that focuses on the skills and knowledge the learner has and what the learner can do after completing the training.

Competency standard   A description of actual job performance, which is usually derived from analysing people considered competent in performing a particular job. Defines what is to be done, to what standard, and under what condition; often includes knowledge (cognitive), manual (psychomotor) and attitudinal (affective) skills.

Constructive dismissal   Where the employer has constructed, created or made up the dismissal. It also includes behaviours by management that may include forcing an employee to resign, not providing an employee with an opportunity to improve performance, changing the terms and conditions of employment, breaching the terms and conditions of employment, and making conditions so unbearable an employee feels compelled to resign.

Consultation   A management approach that seeks the opinions of employees before reaching decisions.

Core competencies   Activities or practices that have been identified by an organisation as critical to its long-term success and growth.

Counselling discussion   A discussion between a manager and a subordinate about one incident or several incidents involving the same performance issue.

Critical incident method   A method of performance appraisal that involves an employee or manager recording examples of an employee's effective or ineffective work-related behaviour relevant to matters that are crucial to the success of the job.

Critical success factor (CSF)   A factor that is vital to an organisation's current operating activities to ensure its success.

Cultural competence   In its broadest context, refers to being able to effectively provide services cross-culturally. At an individual level it refers to five skills: awareness and acceptance of difference; self-awareness; awareness of the dynamics of difference; knowledge of other cultures; and being able to adapt your skills.

Culture   The pattern of values, beliefs and expectations that shapes the behaviour of individuals and teams in an organisation.

Customer   The person/group/organisation who benefits from the employee's efforts. Can be internal or external to the organisation.

Data   Raw, unanalysed facts.

Demotion   Reassignment to a job of lower rank and usually lower pay.

Development needs   Those things the individual or team need to develop as individuals; generally, knowledge or skills.

Direct discrimination   Occurs when a person with specific attributes is treated differently to a person without those attributes.

Discrimination   Unequal treatment before, during or after employment on the basis of sex, age, national origin, religion, criminal record, sexual preference, trade union activities, political opinion, physical or intellectual disability, marital status, medical record, parental status or social origin; a distinction, exclusion or preference on the basis of any of the above which impairs equality of opportunity.

Diverse workforce   A workforce that is made up of people with different cultural values, beliefs and identities.

Diversity   The state of having a mixture of people with different cultural identities within the same social system.

Emotional intelligence   The ability to notice and manage emotional cues and information.

Employee development   The process of providing employees with the knowledge, skills and attitudes they will need to perform jobs they aspire to in the future.

Employee productivity Refers to the ratio of output against a unit of input. For example, in a bank this might be the number of completed transactions the employee makes per hour. In a manufacturing environment it might be completed products per machine hour. In a service organisation it might be the number of completed projects per staffing hour.

Ethics A set of guidelines that describe acceptable conduct directed towards resolving conflict or interests, so as to enhance the wellbeing of a society; rules and principles that define right and wrong conduct and behaviours.

Feedback The degree to which completing work activities and tasks required by a job results in an employee receiving clear and direct information about his or her performance effectiveness.

Feedback analysis A technique to analyse and improve performance of an employee. Outcomes of work are compared to expected outcomes to highlight where improved or new skills, behaviours and attitudes are required.

Flexible work hours A system of scheduling that enables employees to work a certain number of hours each week but allows them to vary the hours of work within certain limits.

Forced distribution method A method of performance appraisal in which predetermined percentages of rates are placed in various performance categories, similar to grading on a curve.

Goal Desired outcomes for an individual, a team or group, or an entire organisation. A goal needs to be specific, challenging, time limited and decided participatively, and to include feedback provisions.

Graphic rating scale A method of performance appraisal that lists a number of traits with a performance range for each.

Halo effect Occurs when a manager or supervisor rating of an employee on one trait biases the rating of all other traits and results in a general impression based on a single positive characteristic.

Horns effect Results from the overall rating of an employee on a single negative characteristic.

Indirect discrimination Occurs where a person seeks to impose a condition with which someone with one of the specified attributes cannot possibly comply, while others can.

Instant dismissal Termination of employment without notice or pay in lieu of notice for a serious offence such as theft.

Job Generally defined as a set of closely related activities, usually carried out for pay.

Job analysis An assessment that defines a job, and the behaviours and skills required to perform the job.

Job description A document that outlines the key objectives, duties, tasks, activities, responsibilities and relationships of a job and any special conditions of the job (such as educational requirements, working away from home etc.). Also referred to as a position description.

Job satisfaction An employee's general attitude towards their job.

Job sharing The practice of having more than one person splitting a full-time job.

Job specification Describes the type of person that would be best suited to the job, and the knowledge, skills, attitudes and other characteristics, experience and qualifications that are needed to perform the job.

Key focus area Used in organisations to refer to key performance indicators (KPIs).

Key performance indicator (KPI) Directly related to results of great importance to the organisation, also known as key result areas (KRAs). They are the measurable aspect of an organisation's strategic objectives and focus on the results or outcomes to be achieved. They are the measures of success in reaching targets and goals. See also *measures of success*.

Key result area (KRA)   Describes the main areas of responsibility and accountability in a job. They are not individual tasks and they are not goals. Rather, they group together tasks that help achieve results in a specific area.

Learning organisation   An organisation that has developed the capacity to continuously learn, adapt to and change their internal and external environments.

Management   The process of coordinating and overseeing the work activities of others so that their activities are completed efficiently and contribute to organisational objectives.

Management by objectives (MBO)   A system of performance management where employees and management agree on specific performance objectives and targets, aligned with corporate goals, to be accomplished within a given period of time. These goals are used to evaluate employee performance.

Management development   The process of providing managers, or those aspiring to management roles in the future, with the necessary knowledge, skills and attitudes to successfully perform the management role.

Measures of success   Also called measures of performance, key performance indicators, objectives and targets. These are ways to quantify and measure important aspects of a job or task to track how well it is being performed. See also *performance measure*.

Mentor   A person (often older, or more senior and experienced) who takes an interest in someone's career and provides positive help, support, advice and encouragement.

Mentoring   A relationship formed between a senior and junior employee that is based on support and sponsorship to assist in personal growth and development.

Mission   A statement that describes the purpose of an organisation. It answers the questions, 'What business are we in?' and 'How can we achieve our vision?'

Motivation   The process by which an employee's efforts are energised, directed and sustained towards attaining an organisational goal; how willing an employee is to expend energy and effort in doing a job.

Motivators   Those factors that increase an employee's job satisfaction and motivation.

National culture   Those values and attitudes shared by groups of individuals from a specific country that shape their behaviour and beliefs about what is important and right.

Non-development needs   Those things that are not in the control of employees or which they cannot act on by themselves. They may include redesigning a job, changing work flow, removing barriers to performance, re-engineering systems and procedures, making resources available, curbing influence of context where appropriate etc.

Non-verbal communication   Communication transmitted without words, including symbols, facial expressions, body language, voice and silence.

Objective   A clear, specific measuring post indicating progress towards achieving a goal.

Open systems   Systems that dynamically interact and engage with their environment.

Operational plan   Operational plans (often referred to as business plans) are usually written in advance for a 12-month period (though they can stretch to several years). Operational planning is generally predictable, systemised and specific. The plans specify the details of how the overall goals of an organisation are to be achieved.

Organisation   A deliberate arrangement of people to accomplish some specific purpose.

Organisational culture   The shared values, traditions, principles and ways of doing things that influence the way an organisation's members behave.

Organisational performance   The accumulated end results of all the organisation's work activities.

Performance   The end result of an activity.

Performance analysis   The process of comparing actual performance with agreed performance standards and looking at the possible reasons why the actual performance is the same as, or different from, the agreed performance. This process uses the evidence collected over the period of the performance management cycle.

Performance appraisal   The process that identifies, evaluates and develops employee performance to meet employee and organisational goals, involving formal documentation and feedback. A formalised, systematic assessment and discussion of an employee's performance, and their potential and desire for development and training.

The process requires making decisions about performance, determining possible solutions to any problems and taking action to remedy a solution.

Performance counselling   The process of discussing an employee's performance with a view to improving it so that performance expectations are met.

Performance development objective
A record of what is to be achieved by an employee or team. The formula: Performance objective = Result + Measure + Conditions + Time limit make it specific and measurable.

Performance discussion   A discussion concerned with the total performance of an individual or team for a specific period and covering the range of performance standards agreed for the job.

Performance gap   The difference between expected performance and actual performance. Ideally a performance gap can be measured.

Performance improvement plan   Designed to facilitate constructive discussion between an employee and supervisor/manager to clarify the work performance to be improved. The plan includes setting goals, establishing measures, conducting review sessions and charting progress. If no improvement is made, a performance improvement plan may be used in the termination process.

Performance indicator   A measure of some part of the organisation's performance. Performance indicators play an important role in focusing staff on outcomes that need to be reached, and specify the type of evidence the organisation requires to demonstrate the achievement of desired results.

Performance management   A process that consolidates goal setting, performance appraisal and development into a single system to support an organisation's strategic goals. Performance management links each employee's and each manager's responsibilities with those of the team and the overall organisation, providing the organisation with a snapshot of progress towards strategic plans.

Performance management is also the process of setting and monitoring measures and objectives of employees. It is a closed loop process where objectives are constantly reviewed and diaries are maintained by the employee and manager, detailing ongoing successes and challenge.
Source: <http://www.pmia.org.au/events/index.htm>.

Performance management system
A system of establishing performance standards that are used to evaluate employee performance.

Performance measure   A clear, quantifiable standard of performance. See also *measures of success.*

Performance standard   A measure by which performance is evaluated. It refers to the work performance expected from an employee in terms of quantity and quality. These standards form the basis of most performance review systems. A performance standard is made up of two components: performance (the output or result) and standard (measure of the performance).

Planning   A management function that involves defining goals, establishing strategies for achieving these goals, and developing plans to integrate and coordinate activities.

Plans   Documents that outline how goals are going to be met; typically describe how resources are to be allocated, and schedules and actions to accomplish goals.

Position description   See *job description*.

Problem   A discrepancy between an existing and desired state of affairs.

Procedure   A series of interrelated sequential steps that can be used by a manager to respond to structural problems.

Productivity   The overall output of goods or services produced divided by the inputs needed to generate that output.

Public sector   Organisations directly or indirectly involved in the business of governing the country.

Quality   The ability of a product or service to reliably do what it is supposed to do and satisfy customer expectations.

Quantitative approach   The use of quantitative techniques and data to improve decision making.

Range of variation   The acceptable parameters of variance between actual performance and standard.

Reliability   In tests, reliability refers to the consistency of scores obtained by the same person when retested. The ability of a selection device or tool to measure the same thing twice.

Responsibility   The obligation that an employee has to his or her manager to do a job that has been assigned.

Retention   Refers to the desire of an employer to retain key employees in order to achieve their organisation's business objectives. The role of HR is to redesign activities to provide increased job satisfaction, improve employee commitment and reduce turnover of employees.

Role   Behaviour patterns expected of someone occupying a given position.

Role clarification   A process to ensure that each member of a team is clear about what is expected of them in their job role (task) and behaviours (process).

Specific plan   A plan that is clearly defined and leaves no room for misinterpretation.

Staff turnover   The unplanned loss of employees who voluntarily leave the organisation and who it would have been desirable for the organisation to retain.

Stereotyping   Judging a person on the basis of one's perceptions of a group to which the person belongs.

Strategic plan   A plan that applies to the entire organisation, establishes its overall goals, and seeks to position the organisation effectively in terms of its environment; focuses on time frames of three to five years into the future. Strategic planning is ambiguous, complex, non-routine, and usually involves significant change.

Succession planning and management   Involves identifying and developing high-potential and talented employees so that the organisation will have the people necessary to succeed in a rapidly changing business environment.

Target   A specific, measurable and trackable indicator of performance or measure of success.

Termination of employment   A permanent separation from the organisation, usually a result of poor job performance or a serious offence by the employee.

360-degree feedback   A performance management appraisal method that utilises feedback from managers, employees and co-workers.

Traditional goal setting   An approach to setting goals in which goals are set at the top level of the organisation and then cascade down into subgoals for each level of the organisation.

Training The process of providing employees with the knowledge, skills and attitudes they need to successfully perform their current role.

Training needs analysis Gathering information to identify gaps between required job performance or competency and what a person or group actually achieves.

Training plan An important part of managing performance improvement. A document that describes how an employee or group of employees will be developed, in what areas, with what objectives and by when.

Trust The belief in the integrity, character and ability of a manager or leader.

Turnover The voluntary and involuntary permanent withdrawal from an organisation.

Unclear performance standards Standards that are not precise, measurable or time-framed. Unclear performance standards lead to misinterpretation of what they mean and how they will be measured. They can lead to disputes about whether the performance has been achieved to the standard required.

Unfair dismissal Termination of employment without providing notice, warning about unsatisfactory behaviour or performance, or giving the employee an opportunity to respond or improve performance.

Unlawful dismissal Termination of employment for reasons of age, pregnancy, sexuality, ethic or cultural background, marital status etc.

Validity The proven relationship that exists between a selection device or tool and specific job criteria.

Values Basic convictions about what is right or wrong. What a person or an organisation believes is important and worthwhile; operating principles that guide actions and behaviours.

Vision A statement that describes the cultures, operating philosophy and beliefs an organisation aspires to. It answers the questions, 'Who are we?' and 'How do we operate?'

Weaknesses Activities the organisation does not do well, or resources it needs but does not possess.

Work–life balance The commitment of an organisation to provide flexible working arrangements that assist employees to balance their personal and work commitments.

Workforce planning A continual process of arranging the workforce to ensure that the organisation has the right types and numbers of people at the right place at the right time, and that they are able to deliver current and future organisational objectives.

Workplace diversity Describes a workplace made up of people with different cultural values and beliefs and who identify themselves as a minority or different from the prevailing, dominant identity. Typically, they include migrants, immigrants, refugees and asylum seekers, but might also include Indigenous, rural, gay or lesbian, aged and socially disadvantaged people, and people with disabilities.

Numbers in *italics* indicate figures